D1027739

Get the eBooks FREE!

(PDF, ePub, Kindle, and liveBook all included)

We believe that once you buy a book from us, you should be able to read it in any format we have available. To get electronic versions of this book at no additional cost to you, purchase and then register this book at the Manning website.

Go to https://www.manning.com/freebook and follow the instructions to complete your pBook registration.

That's it!
Thanks from Manning!

The Tao of Microservices

RICHARD RODGER

MANNING
Shelter Island

For online information and ordering of this and other Manning books, please visit
www.manning.com. The publisher offers discounts on this book when ordered in quantity.
For more information, please contact

Special Sales Department
Manning Publications Co.
20 Baldwin Road
PO Box 761
Shelter Island, NY 11964
Email: orders@manning.com

Manning Publications Co.   Acquisitions editor: Mike Stephens
20 Baldwin Road   Developmental editor: Christina Taylor
PO Box 761   Review editor: Aleksandar Dragosavljevic
Shelter Island, NY 11964   Senior technical development editor: Francesco Bianchi
                         Technical development editor: Andrew Siemer
                              Technical proofreader: Karsten Strobaek
                                     Project editor: David Novak
                                       Copyeditor: Tiffany Taylor
                                       Proofreader: Katie Tennant
                                        Typesetter: Gordan Salinovic
                                    Cover designer: Leslie Haimes

ISBN 9781617293146
Printed and bound by CPI Group (UK) Ltd, Croydon, CR0 4YY
   2 3 4 5 6 7 8 9 10 – CPI – 22 21 20 19

To Lochlann, Ruadhán, Lola,
Saorla, and Orla

brief contents

v

contents

vii

preface

When I visit a city, if I have time, I like to wander around by myself, exploring, without looking at a map. It's a privilege to work in an industry where I get to experience this feeling—the impulse to discover, to chart new territory, is irresistible.

Exploration isn't limited to physical spaces. It's also a privilege to work as a software developer and explore mental spaces. Isn't it fascinating that we can define simple rules that create immense spaces for us to explore? Often, we end up in trouble—we're lost. But at other times, we discover a trail of conceptual breadcrumbs and use them to construct a map. It's ridiculous how much fun this is!

When we find and explore something interesting, like microservices, we should draw a map so others can follow and explore further. This book is the map of my journey over the last six years—all the mistakes, revisions, theories, and victories of building microservice systems for production. It isn't a chronological journal. Instead, I've organized my discoveries and distilled them into rules of thumb that others can use. Building a map is hard work, and there are probably better ways to do it, but I've found the conceptual structures in this book useful in my own work, and I hope you will, too.

But concepts are useless without practice. You can't understand how to build software in a new way, without building software in a new way. This book uses case studies to help you gain intuitive knowledge quickly. There's such as thing as knowledge that you have but don't "know." The neural network of your brain is better at learning by example than by study; and the craft of software development, like all crafts, is best learned this way. The discrete knowledge in this book—the abstract concepts, the classifications and definitions—is a pale shadow of the skills you'll eventually master. Taking inspiration from Taoist philosophy, this book can only show you the way: you must walk it yourself to truly learn. And although the map isn't the territory, having it is definitely better than being lost.

Microservices are hyped, but they aren't hype. I see them as a natural evolution of the quest for software components that actually work. Good empirical, psychological, and mathematical arguments can be made to support the view that microservices are a better way to build large software systems with large teams. Many people are exploring the idea of microservices, which is wonderful. This area will take many years to map fully. We should do so enthusiastically while remembering that this is just another small step on the road to better software. The topic shouldn't be dismissed because there are pitfalls or insufficient tools, or because the fundamental ideas are old. Nor should we be afraid to call out the failures of older approaches. I don't hold back in my criticism of the monolithic architecture, though I'll never build a monolith again. But I also don't think microservices are free of failings. They certainly have them, and those issues bring real trade-offs and downsides that you must consider carefully. I've also highlighted these in the text.

Enjoy this book, and enjoy building microservices. They've renewed my faith in our collective ability to get things done and to make a better work/life balance possible. Delivering software shouldn't be about weekend heroics; the process should be calm and deliberate, yet fast and effective, and finished at 6 p.m. on Friday.

acknowledgments

This is my second book. After the first, I promised myself that I'd never write another. It was too difficult—especially for pretty much everybody around me. Somehow, I find myself with another completed manuscript, and this time the process has been a little easier. I'm deeply grateful to everyone who helped make this book possible—I owe them all a debt I can't repay. Any remaining faults are entirely my own.

First, I thank the team at Manning. Christina Taylor, my editor, was a joy to work with, and patient with my glacial writing speed. Christina, thanks for keeping the faith! Thank you also Erin Twohey, Michael Stephens, Marjan Bace, Jeff Bleiel, Rebecca Rinehart, Aleksandar Dragosavljevic, Maureen Spencer, Lynn Beighley, Ana Romac, Candace Gillhoolley, Janet Vail, Tiffany Taylor, Katie Tennant, and everyone else at Manning. It's a pleasure to work with such a professional team.

I'm also grateful to my reviewers: Alexander Myltsev, Anto Aravinth, Brian Cole, Bruno Figueiredo, Cindy Turpin, Doug Sparling, Humberto A. Sanchez, Jared Duncan, Joshua White, Lukasz Sowa, Manash Chakraborty, Marcin Grzejszczak, Norbert Kuchenmeister, Peter Perlepes, Quintin Smith, Scott M. Gardner, Sujith S. Pillai, Unnikrishnan Kumar, and Victor Tatai. This book is much better thanks to their feedback and comments. They forced me to tighten things up, called me out on intellectual laziness, and made sure I didn't forget anything important. And they encouraged me and gave me the energy to finish!

Orla, my wonderful wife, life partner, and best friend: you made this book possible. Your sacrifice and hard work gave me the time to write. As a fellow writer, you were able to commiserate on the awfulness that is writing and get me through to the end. I only hope I can help you as much.

Lochlann, Ruadhán, Lola, and Saorla, you're the best fun and the best distraction. I know you missed me when I was writing. Thank you for your unconditional love and support.

To my sister Lauren (and Jack): you believe in me even when I don't—thank you. To my parents, Hamish and Noreen, and to Orla's parents, Noel and Kay: you made this book possible, along with so much else for us. We wouldn't survive without you. To all of my family, and especially to my aunt Carol, who taught me to code; my Aunt Betty, who cared for me as her own; my Grandfather Lex, who inspired me with his own writing; and my Grandmother Rose, with her iron will to survive: thank you for your kindness and many acts of support and encouragement over the years.

Alaister and Conor, you tell it to me straight, and you've known me too long to take anything I say seriously. Thank you.

This book, and all the things I've been able to learn, wouldn't be possible without the wonderful people who work at nearForm. I had great fun working with you through thick and thin. You were more than patient with my mistakes as a founder, and you taught me more than you can imagine. To my cofounders, Cian, Peter, Paul: it was a privilege to work with you. We built something great together, and I know nearForm is in good hands.

To my new team at voxgig—we get to build a startup using microservices from day one. It's going to be awesome! Thank you all for your confidence in me as a founder.

Thank you, Fred and Godfrey, for my first real programming job. It's still the best job I ever had. Thank you, Ralph and Thomas, for giving a crazy Irish kid a chance.

To Emer and Flash at BoxWorks: I only finished this book because of the beautiful, inspiring workspace you've created. Finally, some peace to think!

My journey to microservices began when I heard Fred George speak at a meetup. The topic blew my mind and changed the way I built software. Thank you, George— you're an inspiration. Never stop coding!

Finally, thank you, everybody in the community. To all the developers who've used Seneca and helped me build it: I'm deeply humbled by your support and feel utterly unworthy of your confidence. To the microservice and Node.js communities: your friendliness and openness are deep, valuable virtues. And we're only getting started!

about this book

This book teaches you how to build microservice systems. If you're in a startup, you can focus on part 1, which covers engineering the microservice architecture. If you're in a bigger company (or once your startup grows), you'll also need part 2, which covers organization of microservice projects.

If you're excited by the idea of microservices—if they make sense to you, but you're unclear about the details—this book is for you. If your organization is moving to microservices or performing a serious evaluation, but you want to learn from the experience of others to avoid mistakes and accelerate your execution, this book is for you. If you're a skeptic and need to understand the opposition so you can tear them down—well, this book is also for you! Microservices can help you deliver software faster, but they come with trade-offs. I hope you find this book most useful when it makes these trade-offs clear, so you can make the best decisions for your situation.

If you decide to use microservices, how do you design and build them? How do you decide which services go where? How many should you have? How should they communicate? This book takes the position, learned from experience on real enterprise projects, that the best place to start is with the messages between services. Using a messages-first perspective—using messages as a design language—you can develop a structured approach to engineering microservice systems. The value of this book lies in teaching you the skills to do that.

What will that skill set give you? The ability to deliver software that makes a real difference to your business, and the ability to deliver it more quickly, with less stress, fewer late nights, and a lower risk of failure. There's a real effect here—I've built a consulting business on the back of it—that's more than the usual hype cycle new technologies experience. This is a step forward, and we're only just figuring out how to regain our balance. By introducing microservices to your organization, you'll be part of that story.

Who should read this book

This book is written for senior developers, software architects, and technical project and product managers. If you're a junior developer, you'll still find much of the material helpful in years to come, but you may need to do some background reading to fully appreciate the arguments; start with Frederick P. Brook's *The Mythical Man-Month* (Addison-Wesley, 1975).

This book is also for anybody who cares about building software more efficiently and more humanely. As an industry, we're far too quick to use brute force and long hours as our first problem-solving tactic. This drives a lot of people out of the industry, which nobody wants. Let's try to work a little smarter and go home a little earlier.

Roadmap

This book teaches you the art and craft of designing microservice systems. In addition to mathematics and engineering, it also requires the application of a great degree of professional judgment and experience. There are no obvious right answers.

The content of the chapters, the concepts they introduce, and the case studies that demonstrate the ideas build on each other, so you should read the chapters in sequence. Many skills can be developed properly only by repeated exposure to examples and by refining general principles into practical knowledge of exceptions and trade-offs. You don't need to grasp every single detail; that would be inefficient, in any case, because you need to put the ideas to work on real systems in the real world to really develop understanding.

Some of the chapters contain reference sections that are essentially reference material—chapters 5 and 6, in particular. You should feel free to skim these sections on a first pass.

Part 1 of the book focuses on the engineering principles that make microservices work. These principles are applicable to any language platform and any hosting environment. Part 1 also introduces a diagramming convention for visualizing microservice architectures that's used throughout the book and that you should also find useful for whiteboarding:

- Chapter 1 introduces microservices using a Twitter clone case study and asks whether technical debt can be avoided with the right choice of component model.
- Chapter 2 explores this question: "Given these badly specified business requirements, what services shall we build?" The advantages of microservices over monoliths are examined in detail.

- Chapter 3 shifts the discussion to the most important element of the microservice architecture: messages. The chapter advocates for a messages-first approach to system design.
- Chapter 4 shows you how microservices can work with persistent data, why not all data is the same, and why microservices reduce the technical debt that creeps into database schemas.
- Chapter 5 addresses the biggest problem with microservices: how to manage and control the risk of failure when you have so many moving parts in production.

Part 2 focuses on the less-tangible factors you'll have to deal with when building microservices. You don't write commercial software in a vacuum: what you write has a commercial purpose, and you do so with other developers. When there are more than two humans in a room, you have politics, and you need to negotiate, persuade, and lead to make things happen. Unfortunately for you, as the agent of change bringing microservices to the table, this game won't be easy. This part of the book helps you deal with this aspect of delivering microservices professionally:

- Chapter 6 teaches ways of measuring microservice systems, and messages in particular, in order to get a true gauge of the health of your system.
- Chapter 7 guides you iteration by iteration through the process of moving from a hard-to-change legacy monolith to a vibrant set of microservices that can easily adapt to new feature requirements.
- Chapter 8 is an honest, direct discussion of the corporate politics that will stand in your way and the tactics you can use to overcome your biggest roadblock.
- Chapter 9 shows you the code. A full system is built from the ground up, using all the principles introduced in earlier chapters.

About the code

This book is more about thinking than coding, but two of the cases studies are fully developed in code. I use Node.js as the platform: that's what I use commercially, and the language is JavaScript, which is widely understood, so you should be able to follow along even if your day-to-day language is something else. The nice thing about microservices is that they dramatically reduce the occurrence of Node.js annoyances such as callback hell, because each microservice is small and simple.

The source code for the example systems is available at www.manning.com/books/the-tao-of-microservices, http://ramanujan.io, and http://nodezoo.com. The source code is also available as a http://github.com repository, linked from those sites. Everything is open source and under the commercially friendly MIT license, so feel free to use it in your own projects and work.

The code examples in the text of this book are abridged to save space. Comments, error handling, and functionality that isn't relevant to the discussion have been removed. But you can review the full source on GitHub, and it's worth doing so to understand the extra work needed to get your microservices closer to production.

Some simple conventions are used in the text. The names of microservices and messages are shown in italics, for example: *article-page*. The property patterns used to route messages are shown in fixed-width font: `store:save`, `kind:entry`. Fixed-width font is also used for code inlined in the text: `if (err) return`.

Other online resources

The microservice community is large and diverse, and there are microservice frameworks and implementations for most language platforms. My own writings about microservices can be found on my blog, http://richardrodger.com, where I talk about microservices in general and in the context of building a startup. I use (and am the maintainer of) the Seneca Node.js microservices framework: http://senecajs.org.

For an overview of the major microservice patterns and links to many other great resources, you can't do much better than Chris Richardson's http://microservices.io site. Subscribe to https://microserviceweekly.com to keep up to date with all the latest news. For the seminal article on the subject, Martin Fowler is a must-read: https://martinfowler.com/microservices. Finally, watch all of Fred George's videos: http://mng.bz/0Ttf.

about the author

Richard Rodger started coding on the Sinclair ZX Spectrum in 1986 and hasn't stopped since. He's a difficult employee and, left with no other options, has been forced to cofound software companies; the most recent is voxgig, a social network for the conference industry, where he's absolutely using microservices to pay the mortgage. He also cofounded nearForm, one of the first (and best!) Node.js and microservice consultancies. Before that, he was CTO of FeedHenry, a SaaS platform for mobile apps, since acquired by Red Hat.

Richard studied mathematics and philosophy at Trinity College Dublin, Ireland, and computer science at the Waterford Institute of Technology, Ireland. He's a terrible mathematician and a worse philosopher, and he can't code in C++; hence, the obsession with JavaScript.

Richard is the author of *Mobile Application Development in the Cloud* (Wiley, 2011), which, obviously, you should also read. He's the maintainer of the Seneca microservice framework, which you should definitely use. He speaks at the occasional technology conference and blogs at http://richardrodger.com.

about the cover illustration

The image on the cover of *The Tao of Microservices* is a reproduction of a seventeenth-century woodblock print depicting Emperor Reigen of Japan, whose reign spanned 23 years, from 1663 through 1687. He was the 112th emperor of Japan, according to the traditional order of succession of the Chrysanthemum Throne. The role of the emperor of Japan has historically alternated between a largely ceremonial one and that of an actual imperial ruler. Since the establishment of the first shogunate in 1192, the Emperors of Japan have rarely taken on the role of supreme battlefield commander, unlike many Western monarchs. Japanese emperors have nearly always been controlled by external political forces, to varying degrees. In fact, between 1192 and 1867, the shoguns or military dictators were the de facto rulers of Japan, although they were appointed by the emperor. After the Meiji Restoration in 1867, the emperor once again became the embodiment of all sovereign power in the realm, as enshrined in the Meiji Constitution of 1889. The emperor's current status as a figurehead dates from the 1947 Constitution.

At a time when it's hard to tell one computer book from another, Manning celebrates the inventiveness and initiative of the computer business with book covers based on the rich diversity of historical figures and costumes of the past, brought back to life with illustrations such as this one.

Part 1

Building microservices

Microservices aren't a silver bullet that can solve all of your software development problems overnight. But microservices are a better way to design and engineer software, and that does help. Better engineering comes from the painful lessons of hard experience and careful analytical thinking about the problem space, and it takes inspiration from other sciences. This part of the book lays out the fine details needed to engineer microservices for the best chance of success and grounds those details in a practical conceptual framework that can guide your decision making:

- Chapter 1 starts with a concrete case study—a Twitter clone—and introduces you to microservices directly and immediately. With this background, you'll begin to see how microservices can reduce technical debt and understand the consequences of choosing the microservice architecture.

- Chapter 2 introduces a new case study—an online newspaper—and shows you how to decide what services to build and how services can communicate with each other. We'll examine the differences between microservices and monoliths.

- Chapter 3 advocates for a messages-first approach. By representing your business requirements as messages, you can derive the services you need to build. This chapter carefully examines how messages work and the essential properties and behavior they should have.

- Chapter 4 challenges the dogmas of enterprise data and shows how microservices make it possible to store and handle different kinds of data in naturally appropriate ways. Data operations are represented as messages between microservices, and this opens up many new strategies for system design.

- Chapter 5 helps you come to grips with the hardest part of the microservice architecture: running many microservices in production. We'll take a risk-management approach, driven by business goals rather than technical perfectionism. This chapter covers the many deployment patterns that microservices make practical.

When you finish this part of the book, you'll be prepared to design and build a microservice system on your own. Although you'll be able to build a minimum viable product, you won't yet be ready to use microservices to help scale your system, work better with other people, or change your organization. Those are all topics for part 2.

Brave new world 1

Software development is an art. It isn't predictable enough to be engineering. It isn't rigorous enough to be science. We're artists—and that's *not* a good thing. We find it hard to work in teams, we find it hard to deliver on deadlines, and we find it hard to focus on practical results. Anyone can claim to be a software developer; opening a text editor is no more difficult than picking up a paint brush. A small number of painters are 10 times better than others. A small number of coders also are 10 times better than others. But most of us are working on bad instincts.

Unlike art, software has to work. It has business problems to solve, users to serve, and content to deliver. We have a thousand opinions among ourselves about how to do things correctly, yet many software projects are delivered late and over budget. Much software, especially that produced by large companies, offers users a terrible experience. We have a self-important belief in our work, as artists, that isn't connected to the reality of our systematic failure. We need to admit we have a problem, understand the nature of that problem, and use science and engineering to solve the problem.

1.1 The technical debt crisis

The problem is that we can't write software fast enough. We can't write software that meets business needs and that is sufficiently accurate and reliable, within the time constraints set by the markets in which our companies operate. When requirements change in the middle of a project, it damages our architecture so badly that we spiral into a death march of hacks and kludges to force our data structures, concepts, and entity relationships into compliance. We try to refactor or rewrite, and that delays things even further.

3

You might be tempted to blame the business itself for this state of affairs. Requirements are always underspecified, and they keep changing. Deadlines are imposed without regard to the complexity of the problem. Bad management wastes time and eats up development schedules. It's easy to become cynical and blame these issues on the stupidity of others.

Such cynicism is self-defeating and naïve. The world of business is harsh, and markets are unforgiving. Our nontechnical colleagues have complex challenges of their own. It's time to grow up and accept that we have a problem: we can't write software fast enough.

But *why?*

Be careful. If there were a silver bullet, we'd already be using it. Take methodologies: we fight over them because there are no clear winners. Some methodologies certainly are better than others, in the same way that a sword is a better weapon than a dagger, but neither is of much use in the gun fight that is enterprise software development. Or take a best practice like unit testing, which feels like it's valuable. Just because something feels good doesn't mean it *is* good. Intuitions can be misleading. We have a natural tendency toward superstition, forcing development practices into Procrustean beds.[1] Few of our best practices have any measure of scientific validation.

The problem is that we don't know how to pay down technical debt. No matter how beautifully we crystallize our initial designs, they fracture against the changing nature of reality. We try to make our software perfect: perfectly correct and able to perfectly meet requirements. We have all sorts of perfection-seeking behavior, from coding standards, to type systems, to strict languages, to hard integration boundaries, to canonical data models. And yet we still end up with a legacy mess to support.

We're not stupid. We know that we have to cope with change. We use flexible data structures, with scope for growth (in the right places, if we're lucky). We have this thing called *refactoring*, which is the technical term for getting caught making bad guesses. At least we have a professional-sounding term for the time we waste rewriting code so that we can start moving forward again.

We have *components*, which are the machine guns of software architecture: force multipliers that let you build big things out of small things. You only have to solve each problem once. At heart, object-oriented languages are trying to be component systems, and so are web services.[2] So was structured programming (a fancy name for

---

[1] Procrustes was a son of the Greek god Poseidon. He took great pleasure in fitting his house guests into an iron bed. To make the guest fit, he would either amputate their feet or stretch them on a rack. A *Procrustean bed* is a behavior that doesn't serve its intended purpose; it only perpetuates a superstition. Insistence on high levels of unit-test coverage is the prime example in our industry. The coverage target and the effort to achieve it are seldom adjusted to match the value generated by the code in production.

[2] We even have fancy component systems that were designed from the ground up, like OSGi and CORBA. They haven't delivered composability. The Node.js module system is a relatively strong approach and makes good use of semantic versioning, but it's restricted to one platform and exposes all the nuts and bolts of the JavaScript language. UNIX pipes are about as good as it gets, if you're looking for something that's widely used.

dropping the GOTO statement). We have all these technical best practices, and we're still too slow. Components, in particular, should make us faster. Why don't they?

We haven't been thinking about components in the right way for a long time in mainstream enterprise programming.[3] We can just about build library components to talk to databases, perform HTTP requests, and package up sorting algorithms. But these components are technical infrastructure. We're not so good at writing reusable components that deliver *business logic*. Components like that would speed up development. We've focused on making our components so comprehensive in functionality that it's difficult to compose them together; we have to write lots of glue code. By trying to cover too many cases, we make the simple ones too complex.

> **What is business logic?**
>
> In this book, *business logic* is the part of the functionality that's directly specific to the business goal at hand. User-profile management is business logic. A caching layer isn't.
>
> Business logic is your representation of the processes of your business using the structures of your programming language. What is business logic in one system many not be in another. It can change within the same system over time. The term is suggestive, not prescriptive.

The thing that makes components work is *composition*: making big things out of small things. The component models that reduce your workload, such as UNIX pipes and functional programming, have this feature. You combine parts to create something new.

Composition is powerful. It works because it only does one thing: adds components together. You don't modify components; instead, you write new ones to handle special cases. You can code faster because you never have to modify old code. That's the promise of components.

Consider the state of the software nation. The problem is that we can't code fast enough. We have this problem because we can't cope with technical debt. We don't work with an engineering mindset. We haven't used scientific methods to validate our beliefs. As a solution, components should be working, but they aren't. We need to go back to basics and create a component model that delivers practical composition. Microservices,[4] built the right way, can help do that.

---

[3] This isn't universally true. The functional language communities in particular treat composability as a first-class citizen. But consider that, whereas you can compose pretty much anything on the UNIX command line using pipes, functions aren't generically composable without extra work to make their inputs and outputs play nicely together.

[4] If you're looking for a definition of the term *microservice*, you're not going to find it in this book. We're discussing an approach to software architecture that has its own benefits and trade-offs. Substance counts more than sound bites.

1.2   *Case study: A microblogging startup*

We'll use case studies throughout this book to illustrate practical applications of the microservice approach. We'll use this first one to introduce some of the core principles of the architecture before we analyze them more deeply. The case studies will keep you connected to the practical side of the discussion and allow you to make a critical assessment of the ideas presented—would you build things the same way?

In this case study, you're building the *minimum viable product* (MVP)[5] for a new startup. The startup has come up with a crazy new idea called *microblogging*. Each blog entry can be only a few paragraphs long, with a maximum of 1,729 characters. This somewhat arbitrary limit was chosen by the founders as the most uninteresting number they could think of. The startup is called ramanujan.io.[6] It may seem strange to use a startup as a case study when our primary concern is enterprise software development. But isn't the goal to be as nimble as a startup?

We'll follow the startup through a series of iterations as it gets the MVP up and running. It's sometimes said that microservices create too much overhead at the start of a project. That misses the primary benefit of microservices—the ability to add functionality quickly!

1.2.1   *Iteration 0: Posting entries*

This is the first iteration. We'll use iterations to follow the story of the startup.

A microblogging system lets users post *entries*: short pieces of text. There's a page where users can view their own entries. This set of activities seems like a good place to start.

What activities happen in the system?

- Posting an entry
- Listing previous entries

There are all sorts of other things, like having a user account and logging in, that we'll ignore for the sake of keeping the case study focused. These activities are amenable to the same style of analysis.

The activities can be represented by messages. No need to overthink the structure of these messages, because you can always change the mapping from message to microservice later. To post an entry, let's have a message that tells you which user is posting the entry, and the text of the entry. You'll also need to classify the message in some way so that you know what sort of message it is. The property-value pair `post:entry` does this job—a little namespacing is always a good idea. Let's use JSON as the data format.

---

[5] The MVP is a product-development strategy developed by Eric Ries, a founder of the IMVU chat service (founded 2004): build only the minimum set of features that lets you validate your assumptions about a market, and then iterate on those features and assumptions until you find a product that fits the market.

[6] You can find the full source code and a workshop at www.manning.com/books/the-tao-of-microservices and http://ramanujan.io.

Listing 1.1 Posting an entry

```
{
  post: 'entry',
  user: 'alice',
  text: 'Curiouser and curiouser!'
}
```

Any interested microservices can recognize this message by looking for the pattern post:entry in the message's top-level properties. For now, you'll assume that messages can make their way to the right microservice without worrying too much about how that happens. (Chapter 2 has much more to say about message routing.)

You also need a message for listing entries. Standing back for a moment, you can assume that the system may include other kinds of data down the road. There are certainly common operations that you'll perform on data entities, such as *loading*, *saving*, and *listing*. Let's add a store property to the message to create a namespace for messages concerned with persistent data. In this case, you want to list things from the data store, so the property-value pair store:list seems natural. You'll use kind:entry to identify the data entity as an *entry*, assuming you'll have other kinds of data entities later.

Listing 1.2 Listing entries for the user *alice*

```
{
  store: 'list',
  kind: 'entry',
  user: 'alice'
}
```

Time to put on your architecture hat. There's a family of data-operation messages here, with a corresponding set of patterns:

- store:list,kind:entry—Lists entries, perhaps with a query constraint on the result list
- store:load,kind:entry—Loads a single entry, perhaps using an id property in the message
- store:save,kind:entry—Saves an entry, creating a new database row if necessary
- store:remove,kind:entry—Removes an entry from the database, using the id property to select it

This is an initial outline of the possible data-operation message patterns. This set of properties feels workable, but is it correct? It doesn't matter. You can always change the patterns later. Also, you don't need to implement messages you aren't using yet.

Now that you have some initial messages, you can think about their interactions. Let's assume you have a web server handling inbound HTTP requests on the external side and generating microservice messages on the internal side:

- When the user posts a new entry, the web server sends a `post:entry` message, which triggers a `store:save,kind:entry` message.
- When the user lists their previous entries, the web server sends a `store:list, kind:entry` message to get this list.

Here's another thing to think about: are these messages *synchronous* or *asynchronous*? In more-concrete terms, does the sender of the message expect to get a response (synchronous), or does the sender not care about a response (asynchronous)?

- `post:entry` is *synchronous*, because it's nice for the user to get confirmation that their entry has been posted.
- `store:save,kind:entry` is also *synchronous*, because it has to provide confirmation of the *save* operation and probably returns the generated unique identifier of the new data record.
- `store:list,kind:entry` is necessarily *synchronous*, because its purpose is to return a result list.

Are there any asynchronous messages in this simple first iteration? As a rule of thumb, microservice systems often benefit from announcement messages. That is, you should let the world know that something happened, and the world can decide if it cares. This suggests another kind of message:

- `info:entry` is *asynchronous* and announces that a new entry has been posted. No reply is expected. There may be a microservice out there that cares, or maybe nobody cares.

These architectural musings lead you to tabulate for your two activities the message flows shown in table 1.1.

Table 1.1 Business activities and their associated message flows

Activity	Message flow
Post entry	1 `post:entry` 2 `store:save,kind:entry` 3 `info:entry`
List entry	4 `store:list,kind:entry`

You haven't even thought about microservices yet. By thinking about messages *first*, you've avoided falling into the trap of working on the implementation before understanding what you need to build.

At this point, you have enough to go on, and you can group messages into sensible divisions, suggesting the appropriate microservices to build in this iteration. Here are the microservices:

- *front*—The web server that handles HTTP requests. It sits behind a traditional load balancer.
- *entry-store*—Handles persistence of entry data.
- *post*—Handles the message flow for posting an entry.

Each microservice sends and receives specific messages, which you can tabulate as shown in table 1.2. The diagram in figure 1.1 shows how this all fits together.

Table 1.2   Messages that each microservice sends and receives

Microservice	Sends	Receives
front	`post:entry` `store:list,kind:entry`	
entry-store		`store:list,kind:entry` `store:save,kind:entry`
post	`store:save,kind:entry` `info:entry`	`post:entry`

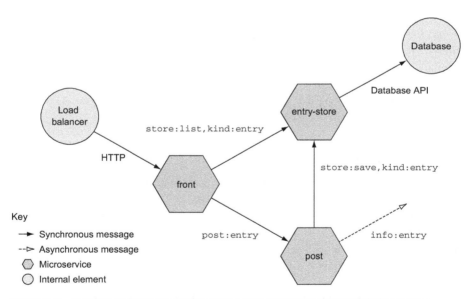

Figure 1.1   Iteration 0: Messages and services that support posting and listing entries

Here are the architectural decisions you've made:

- There's a traditional load balancer in front of everything.
- The web server is also a microservice (*front*) and participates in the message flows. It doesn't accept messages from external clients, only proxied HTTP requests from the load balancer.

- The *front* service should be considered the boundary of the system. It translates HTTP requests into internal messages.
- The *entry-store* microservice exposes a data store, but only via messages. No other microservice can access the underlying database.
- The *post* service orchestrates the message flow that implements posting an entry. First it performs the synchronous `store:save,kind:entry`; once it has a confirmed save, it emits an asynchronous `info:entry`.

This little microblogging system allows users to post entries and see a list of their previous entries. For now, assume deployment is fully automated; chapter 5 covers deployment of microservices. It's Friday, you've pushed code, and you can go home.

1.2.2 *Iteration 1: A search index*

In the last iteration, you used a method of system design that works very well for microservice architectures. First, you informally described the *activities* in the system. Then, you represented those activities as *messages*. Finally, you derived *services* from the messages. Messages, it turns out, are more important than services.

The task in this iteration is to introduce a search index so that users can search through entries to find wonderful gems of microblogging wit and insight amid a sea of sentiment. Much like a database, the system will use a search engine running inside the network to provide the search functionality. This suggests a microservice to expose the search engine, similar to the way the entry database is exposed by the *entry-store* microservice.

But we're getting ahead of ourselves. First, what are the messages? Users can add entries to the search engine, and they can query the search engine. That's enough for now. This gives you the following message patterns:

- `search:insert`—Inserts an entry
- `search:query`—Performs a query, returning a list of results

The *front* microservice can issue `search:query` messages to get search results. That seems OK. The *post* microservice can orchestrate a `search:insert` message into its entry-posting workflow. That doesn't seem OK. Didn't you introduce an `info:entry` asynchronous message for exactly the purpose of acting on new entries? The search engine microservice— let's call it *index*—should listen for `info:entry` and then insert the new entry into its search index. That keeps the *post* and *index* microservices decoupled (almost).

Something still isn't right. The problem is that the *index* microservice is concerned only with activities related to search—why should it know anything about posting microblogging entries? Why should *index* know that it has to listen for `info:entry` messages? How can you avoid this semantic coupling?

The answer is *translation*. The business logic of the *index* microservice shouldn't know about microblogging entries, but it's fine if the runtime configuration of the *index* microservice does.

The runtime configuration of *index* can listen for `info:entry` messages and translate them into `search:insert` messages locally. Loose coupling is preserved. The ability to perform this type of integration, without creating the tight coupling that accumulates technical debt, is the payoff you're seeking from microservices. The business logic implementing a microservice can have multiple runtime configurations, meaning it can participate in the system in many ways, without requiring changes to the business-logic code.

Table 1.3 shows the new list of services and their message allocations.

Table 1.3   Messages that each microservice sends and receives

Microservice	Sends	Receives

front	`post:entry`
	`store:list,kind:entry`
	`search:list`	

entry-store		`store:list,kind:entry` `store:save,kind:entry`
post	`store:save,kind:entry` `info:entry`	`post:entry`

index		`search:query`
		`search:insert`
		`info:entry`

Now, you'll also apply the principle of *additivity*. To your live system, running in production, you'll deploy the new *index* microservice. It starts listening for `info:entry` messages and adding entries to the search index. This has no effect on the rest of the system. You review your monitoring system and find that clients still experience good performance and nothing has broken. Your only action has been to add a new microservice, leaving the others running. There's been no downtime, and the risk of breakage was low.

You still need to support the search functionality, which requires making changes to an existing microservice. The *front* service needs to expose a search endpoint and display a search page. This is a riskier change. How do you roll back if you break something? In a traditional monolithic[7] architecture, teams often use a *blue-green configuration,* where two copies (blue and green) of the entire system are kept running at the same time. Only one is live; the other is used for deployments. Once validated, the systems are switched. If there's a glitch, you can roll back by switching the systems again. This is a lot of overhead to set up and maintain.

Consider the microservice case, where you can use the property of additivity. You deploy a new version of the *front* microservice—one that can handle searches—by starting one or more instances of the new version of *front* alongside running instances of the old version of *front.* You now have multiple versions in production, but you haven't broken anything, because the new version of *front* can handle entry posting

---

[7]   The term *monolith* stands for enterprise systems with large volumes of code that run as one process.

and listing just as well as the old version. The load balancer splits traffic evenly between the new and old versions of *front*. You have the option to adjust this if you want to be extra careful and use the load balancer to send only a small amount of traffic to the new version of *front*. You get this capability without having to build it into the system; it's part of the deployment configuration.

Again, you monitor, and after a little while, if all is well, you shut down the running instances of the old version of *front*. Your system has gained a new feature by means of you adding and removing services, not via global modification and restart. Yes, you did "modify" the *front* service, but you could treat the new version as an entirely new microservice and stage its introduction into the live system. This is very different from updating the entire system and hoping there are no unforeseen effects in production. The new system is shown in figure 1.2.

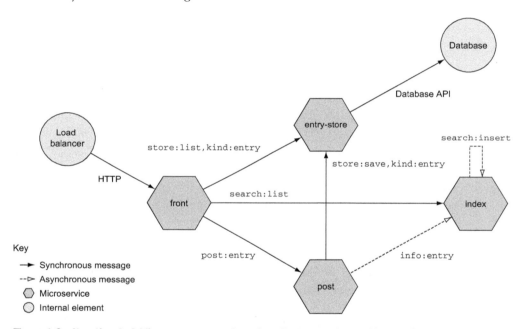

Figure 1.2   Iteration 1: Adding messages and services that support searching entries

Consider table 1.4, which lists the series of small, safe deployment steps that got you here from the iteration 0 system. Another successful week! It's Friday, and you can go home.

Table 1.4   A sequence of small deployment steps

Step	Microservice/Version	Action
0	*index/1.0*	Add
1	*front/2.0*	Add
2	*front/1.0*	Remove

1.2.3 Iteration 2: Simple composition

Microservices are supposed to be components, and a good component model enables composition of components. Let's see how this works in a microservice context. The *entry-store* microservice loads data from an underlying database. This operation has a relatively high latency—it takes time to talk to the database. One way to improve perceived performance is to decrease latency, and one way to do that is to use a cache. When a request comes in to load a given entry, you check the cache first, before performing a database query.

In a traditional system, you'd use an abstraction layer within the code base to hide the caching interactions. In particularly bad code bases, you may have to refactor first to even introduce an abstraction layer. As a practical matter, you have to make significant changes to the logic of the code and then deploy a new version of the entire system.

In the little microservice architecture, you can take a different road: you can introduce an *entry-cache* microservice that captures all the messages that match the pattern `store:*,kind:entry`. This pattern matches all the data-storage messages for entries, such as `store:list,kind:entry` and `store:load,kind:entry`. The new microservice provides caching functionality: if entry data is cached, return the cached data; if not, send a message to the *entry-store* service to retrieve it. The new *entry-cache* microservice captures messages intended for the existing *entry-store*.

There's a practical question here: how does message capture work? There's no single solution, because it depends on the underlying message transportation and routing.

One way to do message capture is to introduce an extra property into the `store:*` messages—say, `cache:true`. You tag the message with a property that you'll use for routing. Then, you deploy a new version (2.0) of the *entry-store* service that can also listen for this pattern. By "new version," I mean only that the runtime message-routing configuration has changed. Then, you deploy the *entry-cache* service, which listens for `store:*` as well, but sends `store:*,cache:true` when it needs original data:

- *entry-store*—Listens for `store:*` and `store:*,cache:true`
- *entry-cache*—Listens for `store:*`, and sends `store:*,cache:true`

The other services then load-balance `store:*` messages between these two services[8] and receive the same responses as before, with no knowledge that 50% of messages are now passing through a cache.

Finally, you deploy another new version (3.0) of *entry-store* that only listens for `store:*,cache:true`. Now, 100% of `store:*` messages pass through the cache:

- *entry-store*—Listens for `store:*,cache:true` only
- *entry-cache*—Listens for `store:*`, and sends `store:*,cache:true`

You added new functionality to the system by adding a new microservice. You did *not* change the functionality of any existing service.

---

[8] Let's assume this "just works" for now. The example code at www.manning.com/books/the-tao-of-microservices and http://ramanujan.io has all the details, of course.

Table 1.5 shows the deployment history.

Table 1.5   **Modifications to the behavior of *entry-store* over time**

Step	Microservice/Version	Action	Message patterns
0	*entry-store/2.0*	Add	`store:*` and `store:*,cache:true`
1	*entry-store/1.0*	Remove	`store:*`
2	*entry-cache/1.0*	Add	`store:*`
3	*entry-store/3.0*	Add	`store:*,cache:true`
4	*entry-store/2.0*	Remove	`store:*` and `store:*,cache:true`

You can see that the ability to perform deployments as a series of add and remove actions gives you fine-grained control over your microservice system. In production, this ability is an important way to manage risk, because you can validate the system after each add or remove action to make sure you haven't broken anything. Figure 1.3 shows the updated system.

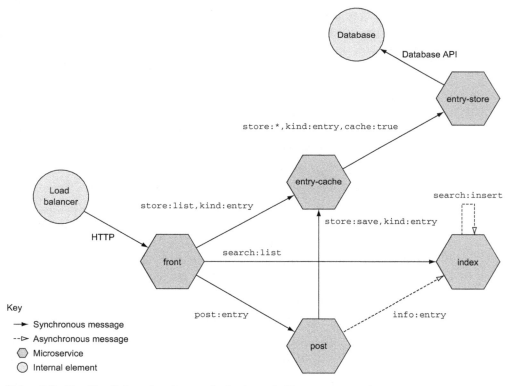

Figure 1.3   Iteration 2: An entry store cache implemented by message capture

The message-tagging approach assumes you have a transport system where each microservice can inspect every message to see whether the message is something it can handle. For a developer, this is a wonderfully useful fiction. But in practice, this isn't something you want to do, because the volume of network traffic, and the work on each service, would be too high. Just because you can assume universal access to all messages as a microservice developer doesn't mean you have to run your production system this way. In the message-routing layer, you can cheat, because you already know which messages which microservice cares about—you specified them!

You've *composed* together the caching functionality of *entry-cache* and the data-storage functionality of *entry-store*. The rest of the world has no idea that the `store:*`, `kind:entry` messages are implemented by an interaction of two microservices. The important thing is that you were able to do this without exposing internal implementation details, and the microservices interact only via their public messages.

This is powerful. You don't have to stop at caching. You can add data validation, message-size throttling, auditing, permissions, and all sorts of other functionality. And you can deliver this functionality by composing microservices together at the component level. The ability to do fine-grained deployment is often cited as the primary benefit of microservices, but it isn't. The primary benefit is composition under a practical component model.

Another successful week.

1.2.4 Iteration 3: Timelines

The core feature of a microblogging framework is the ability to follow other users and read their entries. Let's implement a Follow button on the search result list, so that if a user sees somebody interesting, they can follow that person. You'll also need a home page for each user, where they can see a timeline of entries from all the other users they follow. What are the messages?

- `follow:user`—Follows somebody
- `follow:list,kind:followers|following`—Lists a user's followers, or who they're following
- `timeline:insert`—Inserts an entry into a user's timeline
- `timeline:list`—Lists the entries in a user's timeline

This set of messages suggests two services: *follow*, which keeps track of the social graph (who is following who), and *timeline*, which maintains a list of entries for each user, based on who they follow.

You aren't going to extend the functionality of any existing services. To add new features, you'll add new microservices. This avoids technical debt by moving complexity into the message-routing configuration and out of conditional code and intricate data structures.

Using pattern matching to route messages can handle this complexity more effectively than programming language structures because it's a *homogeneous* representation of the business activities you're modelling. The representation consists *only* of pattern matching on messages and using these patterns to assign them to microservices. Nothing more than simple pattern matching is needed. You understand the system by organizing the message patterns into a hierarchy, which is much easier to comprehend than an object-relationship graph.

At this point, you face an implementation question: should timelines be constructed in advance or on demand? To construct a timeline for a user on demand, you'd have to get the list of users that the user follows—the user's "following" list. Then, for each user followed, you'd need to get a list of their entries and merge the entries into a single timeline. This list would be hard to cache, because the timeline changes continuously as users post new entries. This doesn't feel right.

On the other hand, if you listen for `info:entry` messages, you can construct each timeline in advance. When a user posts an entry, you can get the list of their followers; then, for each follower, you can insert the entry into the follower's timeline. This may be more expensive, because you'll need extra hardware to store duplicate data, but it feels much more workable and scalable.[9] Hardware is cheap.

Building the timelines in advance requires reacting to an `info:entry` message with an orchestration of the `follow:list,kind:followers` and `timeline:insert` messages. A good way to do orchestration is to put it into a microservice built for exactly that purpose. This keeps intelligence at the edges of the network, which is a good way to manage complexity. Instead of complex routing and workflow rules for everything, you understand the system in terms of the inbound and outbound message patterns for each service. In this case, let's introduce a *fanout* service that handles timeline updates. This *fanout* service listens for `info:entry` messages and then updates the appropriate timelines. The updated system with the interactions of the new *fanout, follow,* and *timeline* services is shown in figure 1.4.

Both the *follow* and *timeline* services store persistent data, the social graph, and the timelines, respectively. Where do they store this data? Is it in the same database that the *entry-store* microservice uses? In a traditional system, you end up putting most of your data in one big, central database, because that's the path of least resistance at the code level. With microservices, you're freed from this constraint. In the little microblogging system, there are four separate databases:

- The entry store, which is probably a relational database
- The search engine, which is definitely a specialist full-text search solution
- The social graph, which might be best handled by a graph database
- The user timelines, which can be handled by a key-value store

None of these database decisions are absolute, and you could certainly implement the underlying databases using different approaches. The microservices aren't affected by each other's choice of data store, and this makes changes easier. Later in the project,

---

[9] Timeline insertion is how the real Twitter works, apparently. A little bird told me.

Figure 1.4   Iteration 3: Adding social timelines

if you find that you need to migrate to a different database, then the impact of that change will be minimized.

At this point, you have a relatively complete microblogging service. Another good Friday for the team!

1.2.5   *Iteration 4: Scaling*

This is the last iteration before the big pitch for a series A venture capital round. You're seeing so much traction that you're definitely going to get funded. The trouble is, your system keeps falling over. Your microservices are scaling fine, because you can keep adding more instances, but the underlying databases can't handle the data volumes. In particular, the timeline data is becoming too large for one database, and you need to split the data into multiple databases to keep growing.

This problem can be solved with database *sharding*. Sharding works by assigning each item of data to a separate database, based on key values in the data. Here's a simplistic example: to shard an address book into 26 databases, you could shard on the first letter of a person's name. To shard data, you'd typically rely on the specific sharding capabilities of a database driver component, or the sharding feature of the underlying database. Neither of these approaches is appealing in a microservice context (although they will work), because you lose flexibility.

You can use microservices to do the sharding by adding a `shard` property to the `timeline:*` messages. Run new instances of the *timeline* service, one group for each shard, that react only to messages containing the `shard` property. At this point, you have the old *timeline* service running against the old database, and a set of new sharding *timeline* services. The implementation of both types of *timeline* is the same; you're just changing the deployment configuration and pointing some instances at new databases.

Now, you migrate over to the sharding configuration by using microservice composition. Introduce a new version of the *timeline* microservice, which responds to the old `timeline:*` messages that don't have a `shard` property. It then determines the shard based on the user, adds a `shard` property, and sends the messages onward to the sharded *timeline* microservices. This is the same structure as the relationship between *entry-cache* and *entry-store*.

There are complications. You'll be in a transitional state for a while, and during this period you'll have to batch-transfer the old data from the original database into the new database shards. Your new *timeline* microservice will need logic to look for data in the old database if it can't find it in the new shard. You'll want to move carefully, leaving the old database active and still receiving data until you're sure the sharding is working properly. You should probably test the whole thing against a subset of users first. This isn't an easy transition, but microservices make it less risky. Far more of the work occurs as careful, small steps—simple configuration changes to message routing that can be easily rolled back. It's a tough iteration, but not something that brings everything else to a halt and requires months of validation and testing.[10] The new sharding system is shown in figure 1.5.

Now, let's assume that everything goes according to plan, and you get funded and scale up to hundreds of millions of users. Although you've solved your technology problems, you still haven't figured out how to monetize all those users. You take your leave as you roll out yet another advertising play—at least it's quick to implement using microservices!

---

[10] Sharding using microservices is by no means the "best" way. That depends on your own judgment as an architect for your own system. But it's possible, using only message routing, and it's a good example of the flexibility that microservices give you.

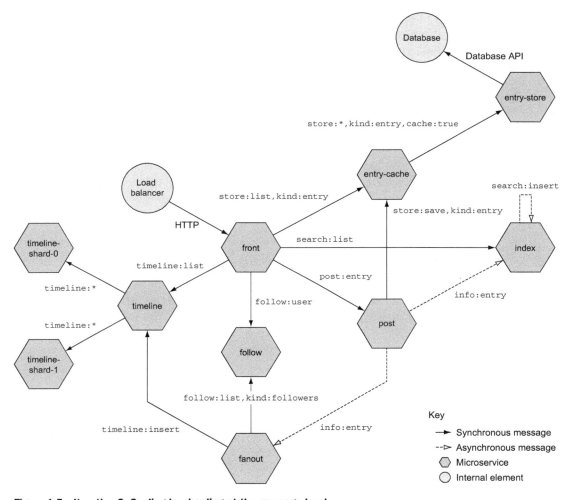

Figure 1.5   Iteration 3: Scaling by sharding at the message level

Wouldn't it be great if enterprise software development worked like this? The vast majority of software developers don't have the freedom that startup software development brings, not because of organizational issues, but because they're drowning in technical debt. That's a hard truth to accept, because it requires honest reflection on our effectiveness as builders of software.

The microservice architecture offers a solution to this problem based on sound engineering principles, not on the latest project management or technology platform fashions. Yes, there are trade-offs, and yes, it does require you to think in a new way. In particular, the criticism that complexity is being moved around, not reduced, must be addressed. It isn't so. Message flows (being one kind of thing) are more understandable than the internals of a monolith (being many kinds of things). Microservices interact only by means of messages and are completely defined by these interactions. The internal programming structures of monoliths interact in all sorts of weird and wonderful ways, and offer only weak protection against interference with each other.

A microservice system can be fully understood at an architectural level by doing the following:

1   Listing the messages. These define a language that maps back to business activities.

2   Listing the services and the messages they send and receive.

On a practical level, yes, you do need to define and automate your deployment configuration. That is a best practice and not hard to do with modern tools. And you need to monitor your system—but at the level of messages and their expected flows. This is far more useful than monitoring the health of individual microservice instances.

The case study is concluded. Let's review some of the concepts that underlie the microservice approach.

1.3   *How the monolith betrays the promise of components*

When I talk about *monoliths* in this book, I mean large, object-oriented systems[11] developed within, and used by, large organizations. These systems are long-lived, under constant modification to meet ongoing business requirements, and essential to the health of the business. They're layered, with business logic in all the layers, from the frontend down to the database. They have wide and deep class hierarchies that no longer represent business reality accurately. Complex dependencies between classes and objects have arisen in response. Data structures not only suffer from legacy artifacts but must be twisted to meet new models of the world and are translated between representations with varying degrees of fidelity. New features must touch many parts of the system and inevitably cause regressions (new versions break previously working features).

The components of the system have lost encapsulation. The boundaries between components are shot full of holes. The internal implementation of components has become exposed. Too many components know about too many other components, and dependency management has become difficult. What went wrong? First, object-oriented languages offer too many ways to interfere with other objects. Second, every developer has access to the entire code base and can create dependencies faster than the poor architects can shoot them down. Third, even when it's clear that encapsulation is suffering, there's often no time for the refactoring necessary to preserve it. And the need for constant refactoring compounds the problem. This is a recipe for ballooning technical debt.

---

[11] The essential characteristic of a monolith isn't that a large body of code executes inside a single process. It's that the monolith makes full use of its language platform to connect separate functional elements, thereby mortally wounding the composability of those elements as components. The object-oriented nature of these systems and the fact that they form the majority of enterprise software are mostly due to historical accident. There are other kinds of monoliths, but the object-oriented architecture has been such a pretender to the crown of software excellence, particularly in its broken promise to deliver reusable components, that it's the primary target of this book's ire.

The components don't deliver on reusability. As a consequence of losing encapsulation, they're deeply connected to other components and difficult to extract and use again. Some level of reuse can be achieved at the infrastructure level (database layers, utility code, and the like). The real win would be to reuse business logic, but this is rarely achieved. Each new project writes business logic anew, with new bugs and new technical debt.

The components don't have well-defined interfaces. Certainly, they may have strict interfaces with a great deal of type safety, but the interfaces are too intricate to be well defined. There's a combinatorial explosion of possibilities when you consider the many ways in which you can interact with an object: construction dependencies, method calls, property access, and inheritance; and that's not even counting the extra frills that any given language platform might give you. And to use the object properly, you need to build a mental model of its state, and the transitions of that state, giving the entire interface an additional temporal dimension.

Components don't compose, betraying the very thing for which they were named. In general, it's hard to take two objects and combine them to create enhanced functionality. There are special cases, such as inheritance and mixins,[12] but these are limited and now considered harmful. Modern object-oriented best practice is explicit: favor composition over inheritance. Keep an internal instance of what would have been your superclass, and call its methods directly. This is better, but you still need too much knowledge of the internal instance.

The problem with the object-oriented model is that universal composition is difficult to do well as an afterthought of language design. It's much better to design it in from the start so that it always works the same way and has a small, consistent, predictable, stateless, easily understood implementation model. A compositional model has hit the bull's-eye when it can be defined in a fully declarative manner, completely independent of the internal state of any given component.

Why is composition so important? First, it's one of the most effective conceptual mechanisms we have for managing complexity. The problem isn't in the machine; the problem is in our heads. Composition imposes a strict containment of complexity. The elements of the composition are hidden by the result of the composition and aren't accessible. There's no way to create interconnected spaghetti code, because composition can only build strict hierarchies. Second, there's significantly less shared state. By definition, composed components communicate with each other via a stateless model, which reduces complexity. Peer communication between components is still subject to all the nastiness of traditional object communication. But a little discipline in reducing the communication mechanisms, perhaps by limiting them to message passing, can work wonders. Reducing the impact of state management means the

---

[12] Inheritance was to be the primary mechanism of composition for object-oriented programming. It fails because the coupling between superclass and subclass is too tight, and it's tricky to subclass from more than one superclass. Multiple inheritance (alternatively, mixins) as a solution introduces more combinatorial complexity.

temporal axis of complexity is much less of a concern. Third, composition is additive.[13] You create new functionality by combining existing functionality. You don't modify existing components. This means technical debt inside a component doesn't grow. Certainly, there's technical debt in the details of the composition, and it grows over time. But it's necessarily less than the technical debt of a traditional monolith, which has the debt of compositional kludges, the debt of feature creep within components, and the debt of increasing interconnectedness.

What is complexity?

You might say that the fraction 111/222 is somehow more complex that the fraction 1/2.[14] You can make that statement rigorous by using the *Kolmogorov complexity measure*. First, express the complex thing as a binary string by choosing a suitable encoding. (I realize I'm leaving entire industries, like recorded music, as an exercise for you to solve, but bear with me!) The length of the shortest program that can output that binary string is a numeric measure of the complexity of the thing. Before you start, choose some implementation of a universal Turing machine so the idea of a "program" is consistent and sensible.

Here are the two programs, in (unoptimized!) colloquial C. One prints the value of 111/222:

```
printf("%f", 111.0/222.0);
```

And the other print the value of 1/2:

```
printf("%f", 1.0/2.0);
```

Feel free to compile and compress them any way you like. It will always take more bits to express the values 111 and 222 than it will to express 1 and 2 (sorry, compiler optimizations don't count). Thus, 111/222 is more complex than 1/2. This also satisfies our intuition that fractions can be reduced to their simplest terms and that this is a less complex representation of the fraction.

A software system that combines elements in a small number of ways (additive composition) compared to a system that can combine elements in many ways (object orientation) grows in complexity far more slowly as the number of elements increases. If you use complexity as a proxy measure of technical debt, you can see that object-oriented monoliths are more vulnerable to technical debt.

---

[13] A system is *additive* when it allows you to provide additional implementations of functionality without requiring changes in those that depend on you. For a technical description, see Harold Abelson, Gerald Sussman, and Julie Sussman, *Structure and Interpretation of Computer Programs* (MIT Press, 1996), section 2.4.

[14] Mandelbrot Set fractal is a good example of low complexity. It can be generated from a simple recurrence formula on complex numbers: http://mathworld.wolfram.com/MandelbrotSet.html. For details on Kolmogorov complexity, start here: https://en.wikipedia.org/wiki/Kolmogorov_complexity

> **(continued)**
> How much more vulnerable? Very much more! The total possible interactions between elements grows exponentially with the number of elements and the number of ways of connecting them.[15]

1.4 The microservice idea

Large-scale software systems are best built using a component architecture that makes composition both possible and easy. The term *microservice* captures two important aspects of this idea. The prefix *micro* indicates that the components are small, avoiding accumulation of technical debt. In any substantial system, there will be many small components, rather than fewer large ones. The root *service* indicates that the components shouldn't be constrained by the limitations of a single process or machine and should be free to form a large network. Components—that is, microservices—can communicate with each other freely. As a practical matter, communication via messages, rather than shared state, is essential to scaling the network.

That said, the heart of the microservice idea is bigger than these two facets. It's the more general idea that composable components are the units of software construction, and that composition works well only when the means of communication between components is sufficiently uniform to make composition practical. It isn't the choice of the mechanism of communication that matters. What matters is the simplicity of the mechanism.

The core axioms of the microservice architecture are as follows:

- No components are privileged (*no privilege*).
- All components communicate in the same simple, homogeneous way (*uniform communication*).
- Components can be composed from other components (*composition*).

From these axioms proceed the more concrete features of the microservice architecture. Microservices in practice are small, because the smaller a service is, the easier it is to compose. And if it's small, its implementation language matters less. In fact, a service may be disposable, because rewriting its functionality doesn't require much work. And pushing even further, does the quality of its code really matter? We'll explore these heresies in chapter 8.

Microservices communicate over the network using messages. In this way, they share a surface feature with service-oriented architectures. Don't be fooled by the similarity; it's immaterial to the microservice architecture what data format the messages use or the protocols by which they're transported. Microservices are entirely defined by the messages they accept and the messages they emit. From the perspective of an individual microservice instance, and from the perspective of the developer writing

---

[15] For the mathematically inclined, $k^{\wedge}(n(n-1)/2)$, where k is the number of ways to connect elements and n is the number of elements. This model is a worst case, because the graph of object dependencies isn't quite as dense, but it's still pretty bad.

that microservice, there are only messages arriving and messages to send. In deployment, a microservice instance may be participating in a request/response configuration, a publish/subscribe configuration, or any number of variants. The way in which messages are distributed isn't a defining characteristic of the microservice architecture. All distribution strategies are welcome without prejudice.[16]

The messages themselves need not be strictly controlled. It's up to the individual microservice to decide whether an arriving message is acceptable. Thus, there's no need for schemas or even validation. If you're tempted to establish contracts between microservices, think again. All that does is create a single large service with two separate, tightly coupled parts. This is no different from traditional monolithic architectures, except that now you have the network to deal with as well.[17] Flexibility in the structure of messages makes composition much easier to achieve and makes development faster, because you can solve the simple, general cases first and then specialize with more microservices later. This is the power of additivity: technical debt is contained, and changing business requirements can be met by adding new microservices, not modifying (and breaking) old ones.

A network of microservices is dynamic. It consists of large numbers of independent processes running in parallel. You're free to add and remove services at will. This makes scaling, fault tolerance, and continuous delivery practical and low risk. Naturally, you'll need some automation to control the large network of services. This is a good thing: it gives you control over your production system and immunizes you against human error. Your default operational action is to add or remove a single microservice instance and then to verify that the system is still healthy. This is a low-risk procedure, compared to big-bang monolith deployments.

1.4.1   *The core technical principles*

A microservice network can deliver on the axioms by meeting a small set of technical capabilities. These are *transport independence* and *pattern matching*, which together give you *additivity*.

TRANSPORT INDEPENDENCE

Transport independence is the ability to move messages from one microservice to another without requiring microservices to know about each other or how to send messages. If one microservice needs to know about another microservice and its message protocol in order to send it a message, this is a fatal flaw. It breaks the *no privilege* axiom, because the receiver is privileged from the perspective of the sender. You're no longer able to compose other microservices over the receiver without also changing the sender.

There are degrees of transport independence. Just as all programming languages are executed ultimately as machine code, all message-transport layers must ultimately resolve senders and receivers to exact network locations. The important factor is how

---

[16] Many criticisms of the microservice architecture use the straw man argument that managing and understanding hordes of web server instances exposing HTTP REST APIs hurts too much. Well, if it hurts, stop doing it!

[17] The appropriate pejorative is "Distributed monolith!"

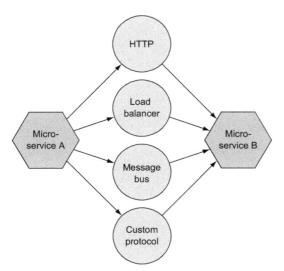

Figure 1.6 The underlying infrastructure that moves messages shouldn't be known to microservices.

much information is exposed to the internal business logic of the microservice to allow it to send a message. Different message transports (shown in figure 1.6) have different levels of coupling.

For example, requiring a microservice to look up another service using a service registry is asking for trouble, because doing so creates a dangerous coupling. But service discovery need not be so blatant. You can hide services behind load balancers. The load balancers must know where the services are located, so you haven't solved the problem; but you've made services easier to write, because they only need to find the load balancer, and they've become more transport independent. Another approach is to use message queues. Your service must still know the correct topics for messages, and topics are a weak form of network address. The extreme degree, where microservices know nothing of each other, is the goal, because that gives you the full benefits of the architecture.

PATTERN MATCHING

Pattern matching is the ability to route messages based on the data inside the messages.[18] This capability lets you dynamically define the network. It allows you to add and remove, on the fly, microservices that handle special cases, and to do so without affecting existing messages or microservices. For example, suppose the initial version of your enterprise system has generic users; but later, new requirements mean you have different kinds of users, with different associated functionalities. Instead of rewriting or extending the generic *user-profile* service (which still does the job perfectly well for generic users), you can create a new *user-profile* service for each kind of user.

---

[18] Message routing is free to use any available contextual information to route messages and isn't necessarily limited to data within the messages. For example, microservices under high load can use back-pressure alerts to force traffic onto microservices with less load.

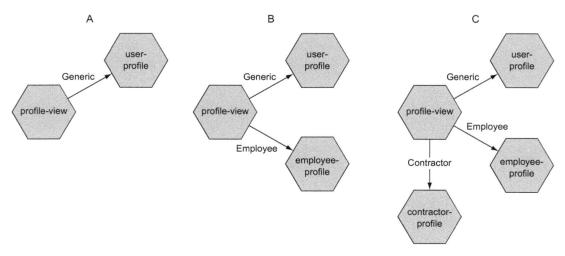

Figure 1.7   Introducing support for new user profiles

Then, you can use pattern matching to route user profile request messages to the appropriate service. The power of this approach to reduce technical debt is evident from the fact that no knowledge or dependency exists between different user profile services—they all think that only their kind of user exists. Figure 1.7 shows how the user profile functionality is extended by new microservices.

Pattern matching is also subject to degrees of application. The allocation of separate URL endpoints to separate microservices via a load balancer matching against HTTP request paths is an example of a simple case. A full-scale enterprise service bus with myriad complex rules is the extreme end case. Unlike transport independence, the goal isn't to reach an extreme. Rather, you must seek to balance effectiveness with simplicity. You need pattern matching that's deep enough to express business requirements yet simple enough to make composition workable. There's no right answer, and the *uniform communication* axiom's exhortation to keep things simple and homogeneous reflects that. This book proposes that URL matching isn't powerful enough and provides examples of slightly more powerful techniques. There are many ways to shoot yourself in the foot, and it's easy to end up with systems that are impossible to reason about. Err on the side of simplicity, and preserve composability!

ADDITIVITY

Additivity is the ability to change a system by adding new parts (see figure 1.8). The essential constraint is that other parts of the system must not change. Systems with this characteristic can deliver very complex functionality and be very complex themselves, and yet maintain low levels of technical debt.[19] Technical debt is a measure of how

---

[19] The venerable Emacs editor is an example of such a system. It's incredibly easy to extend, despite being a relic of the 1970s. LISP supports additivity.

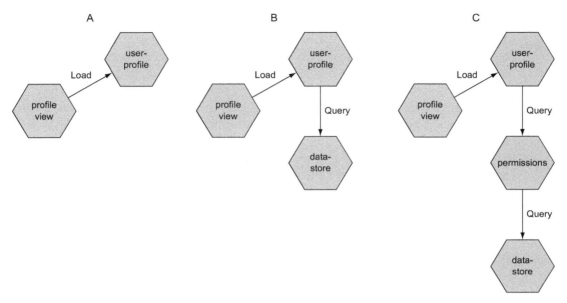

Figure 1.8 Additivity allows a system to change in discrete, observable steps.

hard it is to add new functionality to a system. The more technical debt, the more effort it takes to add functionality. A system that supports additivity is one that can support ongoing, unpredictable changes to business requirements. A messaging layer based on pattern matching and transport independence makes additivity much easier to achieve because it lets you reorganize services dynamically in production.

There are degrees of additivity. A microservice architecture that relies on the business logic of microservices to determine the destination of messages will require changes in both the sender and receiver when you add new functionality. A service registry won't help you, because you'll still need to write the code that looks up the new service. Additivity is stronger if you use intelligent load balancers, pattern matching, and dynamic registration of new upstream receivers to shield senders from changes to the set of receivers. Message bus architectures give you the same flexibility, although you'll have to manage the topic namespace carefully. You can achieve near-perfect additivity using peer-to-peer service discovery.[20] By supporting the addition of new microservices and allowing them to wrap, extend, and alter messages that are inbound or outbound to other services, you can satisfy the *composition* axiom.

---

[20] The SWIM algorithm, which provides efficient dissemination of group membership over a distributed network, is an example of the work emerging in this space. See Abhinandan Das, Indranil Gupta, and Ashish Motivala, "SWIM: Scalable Weakly-consistent Infection-style Process Group Membership Protocol," *Proceedings of the International Conference on Dependable Systems and Networks* (2002), www.cs.cornell.edu/~asdas/research/dsn02-swim.pdf.

1.5   *Practical implications*

The practice of enterprise development is riven with *doublethink*.[21] The accumulation of technical debt is the most politically expedient short-term success strategy. The organization simultaneously demands perfect software while imposing constraints that can't be satisfied. Everybody understands the consequences yet participates in what might be called "quality theater," because to do otherwise is a career-limiting move. The expectation of perfection, without understanding its true cost, is the root cause of most software development headaches.[22] Both developers, chasing intellectual highs by building castles in the sky, and the business, lacking an engineering mindset to make trade-offs, are guilty.

Sometimes, this problem can be solved with an edict from on high. Facebook's infamous mantra to "move fast and break things" implicitly acknowledges that perfection is too expensive to justify. Enterprise software developers don't often have the option to use this approach. The more usual business solution is to externalize the problem by converting it into high-stress software development death marches.

The microservice architecture is both a technical and a political strategy. It takes a cannon to intellectual castles and demands honesty from the business. The payoff includes regular work hours and accelerated delivery of business goals. From a technical standpoint, it removes many opportunities for technical debt to accumulate and makes large, distributed teams easier to manage. From a business standpoint, it forces acceptance of system failures and defects. A more honest discussion of the acceptable levels of failure can then begin, and business leaders can make accurate decisions about return on investment in the face of quantified risks. This is something they're good at, given the chance.

1.5.1   *Specification*

Given that microservices are different from traditional architectures, how do you specify such systems? The first thing to realize is that microservices aren't a radical or revolutionary approach. The architecture emphasizes a component-oriented mindset. As developers, this allows us to ignore language frills. If class hierarchies, object relationships, and data schemas were so effective, we wouldn't be firing blanks all the time, would we?

Microservice system design is very direct. You take the informal business requirements,[23] determine the behaviors of the system, and map the behaviors to messages. This is a messages-first approach. Ironically, designing a microservice system doesn't start by

---

[21] A fabulously useful concept from George Orwell's *1984*: "The power of holding two contradictory beliefs in one's mind simultaneously, and accepting both of them."

[22] The cost of the space shuttle software system, one of the most defect-free code bases ever written, has been estimated to be at least $1,000 per line of code. See Charles Fishman, "They Write the Right Stuff," *Fast Company*, December 31, 1996, www.fastcompany.com/28121/they-write-right-stuff. The doublethink of enterprise software development is that space shuttle quality is possible without space shuttle spending.

[23] Business requirements aren't made formal by accumulating detail. Better to avoid overspecification and stay focused on the desired business outcomes.

asking what services to build; it starts by asking what messages the services will exchange. Once you have the messages, natural groupings will suggest the services to build.

Why do things this way? You have a direct route from business requirements to implementation. This route is traceable and even measurable, because message behavior in production represents desired business outcomes. Your design is independent of implementation, deployment, and data structures. This flexibility allows you to keep up with changing business requirements. Finally, you get a *domain language*—the list of messages is a language that describes the system. From this language, you can derive shared understanding, quality expectations, and performance constraints, and validate correctness in production. All of this is much easier than traditional systems, because messages are homogeneous: they're always the same kind of thing.[24]

The practice of microservice specification is guided by a single key principle: *move from the general to the specific*. First, you solve the simplest general problem you can. Then, you add more microservices to handle special cases. This approach preserves additivity and delivers the core benefit of microservices: lower technical debt. Let's say you're building an internal employee-management system for a global organization. You can start with the simple case of local employees and local regulations. Then, you add microservices for regional community rules, such as those for the United States or the EU. Finally, you handle each country as a special case. As the project progresses, you can deliver more and more value and handle larger and larger subsets of the employee base. Compare this approach to the more common attempt to design sufficiently complex and flexible data structures to handle the entire employee base. Inevitable exceptions will disrupt the integrity of the initial design, ricocheting off false assumptions to cause the collateral damage of technical debt.

1.5.2 Deployment

The systems-management needs of microservices are presented as a weakness of the architecture. It's true that managing the deployment of many hundreds or thousands of individual services in production isn't a trivial task; but this is a strength, not a weakness, because you're forced to automate the management of your system in production. Monoliths are amenable to manual deployment, and it's just about possible to get by. But manual deployment is extremely risky and the cause of a great deal of stress for project teams.[25] The need to automate the deployment of your microservices, and the

---

[24] *Non sunt multiplicanda entia sine necessitate*, otherwise known as *Occam's razor*, is the philosophical position that entities must not be multiplied beyond necessity. It puts the onus on those adding complexity to justify doing so. Object-oriented systems provide lots of ways for objects to interact, without much justification.

[25] On the morning of Wednesday, August 1, 2012, Knight Capital, a financial services firm on the New York Stock Exchange, lost $460 million in 45 minutes. The firm used a manual deployment process for its automated trading system and had erroneously updated only seven or eight production servers. The resulting operation of the new and old versions of the system, with mismatched configuration files, triggered a trading test sequence to execute in the real market. Automate your production systems! For a detailed technical analysis, see "In the Matter of Knight Capital Americas LLC," Securities Exchange Act Release No. 34-70694, October 16, 2013, www.sec.gov/litigation/admin/2013/34-70694.pdf.

need to face this requirement early, raises the professionalism of the entire project, because another hiding place for sloppy practices is shot down.

The volume of microservices in production also makes scaling much easier. By design, you're already running multiple instances of many services, and you can scale by increasing the number of running instances. This scaling ability is more powerful than it first appears, because you can scale at the level of system capabilities. Unlike with monoliths, where scaling is all or nothing, you can easily have variable numbers of different microservices running, applying scaling only where needed. This is far more efficient. There's no excuse for not doing this, and it isn't a criticism of the microservice architecture to say that it's difficult to achieve—this is a baseline feature of any reasonable deployment tool or cloud platform.

The fault tolerance of your overall system also increases. No individual microservice instance is that important to the functioning of the system as a whole. Taking this to an extreme, let's say you have a high-load microservice that suffers from a memory leak. Any individual instance of this microservice has a useful lifetime of only 15 minutes before it exhausts its memory allocation. In the world of monoliths, this is a catastrophic failure mode. In the world of microservices, you have so many instances that it's easy to keep your system running without any downtime or service degradation, and you have time to debug the problem in a calm, stress-free manner.[26]

The monitoring of microservice systems is different from that of monoliths, because the usual measurements of low-level health, such as CPU load and memory usage, are far less significant. From a system perspective, what matters is the flow of messages. By monitoring the way messages flow through the system, you can verify that the business requirements and rules are being met, because there's a direct mapping from behavior to messages. We'll explore this in detail in chapter 6.

Monitoring message-flow rates is akin to the measurements that doctors use. Blood pressure and heart rate tell a physician much more about a patient that the ion-channel performance of any given cell. Monitoring at this higher level reduces deployment risk. You only ever change the system one microservice instance at a time. Each time, you can verify production health by confirming expected flow rates. With microservices, continuous deployment is the default way to deploy. The irony is that this mode of deployment, despite being far more frequent and subject to less testing, is far less risky than big-bang monolithic deployments, because its impact is so much smaller.

1.5.3   Security

It's important to step away from the notion that microservices are nothing more than small REST web services. Microservices are independent of transport mechanism, and fixation on the security best practices of any one transport in itself creates exposure. As a guiding principle, external entry points to the system shouldn't be presented in the same way as internally generated messages.

---

[26] This benefit is best expressed by Adrian Cockcroft, a former director of engineering at Netflix: "You want cattle, not pets."

Microservices that serve external clients should do so explicitly, using the desired communication mechanism of the client directly. The requests of external clients shouldn't be translated into messages and then presented to the microservice. There's considerable temptation to do this, because it's more convenient. A microservice that delivers HTTP content or serves an API endpoint should do so explicitly. Such a microservice may receive and emit internal messages in its interactions with other microservices, but at no time should there be any question of conflation. The microservice's purpose is to expose an externally facing communication mechanism, which falls outside the communication model between microservices.

It shouldn't be possible to tell from the outside that a system uses the microservice architecture. Security best practices for microservice systems are no different than for monoliths. The implementation of a hard and secure system boundary is always necessary and is independent of the internal network topology.

The microservice architecture must also deal with the additional exposure created by the fact that there are large numbers of network actors sending and receiving messages. Just because the boundary of the network is secure doesn't mean communication between microservices doesn't need to be secured.

Securing messages between services is best handled by a messaging layer that can provide the desired level of security. The messaging layer should handle certificate verification, shared secrets, access control, and other mechanisms of message validation. The need for security at this level casts a harsh light on naïve approaches to microservice communication. Using HTTP utility libraries directly within your microservices means you have to get the security configuration right every time, in each microservice.

Getting the security aspect right is tricky because you'll have to work against a strict checklist from your enterprise security group. No such group is known for its compromising spirit. This is another advantage of the message abstraction layer—it gives you a place to put all the security implementation details, keeping them away from business logic. It also gives you a way to validate your security infrastructure independently of other layers of the system.

1.5.4 People

The software development process isn't independent of the architecture under development. If you look closely, you'll observe that the monolithic architecture drives many behaviors we've come to accept as necessary. For example, why are daily stand-ups so important to the agile process? Perhaps it's because monolithic code bases are highly sensitive to unintended consequences. It's easy for one developer's work over here to break another's over there. Careful branching rituals exist for the same reason. Open source projects that rely heavily on plugin architectures don't seem to need stand-ups in the same way—perhaps because they use a component model.

The ceremonial demands of software development methodologies are dreamed up with the best of intentions. They're all attempts to tame complexity and keep technical debt under control. Some methodologies focus on psychology, some on estimation, and others on a rigorous process. They may improve matters, but if any of them had a significant beneficial effect, we'd all adopt that practice without further discussion.[27] The counterargument is that most projects aren't doing it right, and if only they would be disciplined in their approach, then they would be successful. One response is to observe that a methodology so fragile that most teams can't execute it correctly is not fit for the purpose.

Unit testing stands out as a practice that has seen wide adoption because it has clear benefits. This is even more of an indictment of other practices in the traditional methodologies of software development. Unfortunately, because it's so effective, the unit-testing tail often wags the development dog. Projects impose global unit-testing requirements on all code—you must reach such and such a level of coverage, every method must have a test, you must create complex mock objects, and so forth. Stand back and ask these questions: Does all code need the same coverage? Is all code subject to the same production constraints? Some features deliver orders of magnitude more business value than others—shouldn't you spend more time testing them and less time testing obscure features? The microservice architecture gives you a useful unit of division for quality. Different microservices can have different quality levels as a matter of deliberate choice. This is a more efficient way to allocate resources.

The microservice is also a unit of labor and thus a unit of estimation. Microservices are small, and it's easier to estimate the amount of work required to build small things. This means more-accurate project estimates, especially if you can follow the strategy of moving from general to specific services over time. The older, more general services don't change, so your estimation remains accurate in the later stages of the project, unlike more-traditional code bases where estimation accuracy deteriorates over time as internal coupling increases.

Finally, microservices are disposable. This is perhaps one of the greatest benefits of the architecture from a people perspective. Software developers are known for their large, fragile egos. There's an economic explanation for this: it takes a great deal of effort to build a working monolith and a great deal of further investment to maintain it. This is accidental (rather than essential) knowledge, and it remains valuable only as long as the code base remains in production. From the perspective of a rational economic actor, there's every incentive to keep old spaghetti code alive. Microservices don't suffer from the same effect. They're easy to understand by inspection—there isn't much code. And they get replaced all the time; you write so many of them that individual ones aren't that important. The microservice architecture cleans itself.

1.6   *What you get for your money*

Microservices can plausibly address the needs of custom enterprise software. By aligning the software architecture of the system more closely with the real intent of the business, software projects can have far more successful outcomes. Real business value

---

[27] To use an example from another domain, the adoption of wheeled luggage by airline passengers was astonishing in the speed of its universal adoption.

is delivered more quickly. Microservice systems approach MVP status faster and thus can be put into production sooner. Once in production, they make it easier to keep up with changing requirements.

Waste and rework, also known as *refactoring*, are reduced because complexity within each microservice can't grow to dangerous levels. It's more efficient and easier to write new microservices to handle business change than it is to modify old ones. As a software developer, you can make a bigger professional impact with the evolutionary approach to systems building offered by microservices. It lets you be successful by making the best use of your time. It also frees you from the collective delusion that the building of intricate monolithic code can be accurately estimated. Instead, your value is clear from day one, and discussions with the business are of healthier variety, focused on how you can add value, not on gaming indirect measures of code volume.

In the next chapter, we'll start to explore the technical foundations of the microservice architecture, starting with the nature of the services.

1.7 Summary

- The easy accumulation of technical debt is the principle failure of the monolithic architecture.
- Technical debt is caused by language platforms and architectures that make a high degree of coupling possible. Components know too much about each other.
- The most effective way to hide components from each other is to compose them together. Composition allows you to make new components from existing ones, without accelerating the growth of complexity.
- The microservice architecture provides a component model that provides a strong composition mechanism. This enables additivity, the ability to add functionality by adding new parts rather than modifying old ones.
- The practical implications of the microservice architecture demand that you let go of some dearly held beliefs, like uniform code quality, and force acceptance of certain best practices, like deployment automation. These are all good things, because you end up with more efficient resource allocation.

Services

This chapter covers

- Refining the concept of microservices
- Exploring principle variants of the microservice architecture
- Comparing monoliths versus microservices
- Using a concrete study to explore microservices
- Thinking of microservices as software components

To understand the implications and trade-offs of moving to a new architecture, you need to understand how it differs from the old way of doing things, and how the new way will solve old problems. What are the essential differences between monolithic and microservice architectures? What are the new ways of thinking? And how do microservices solve the problems of enterprise software development?

A *microservice* is a unit of software development. The microservice architecture provides a mental model that simplifies the world at a useful level. The proposition of this book is that microservices are the closest thing yet to ideal software components. They're perfectly sized artifacts for fine-grained deployment into production. They're easily measured to ensure correct operation. The microservice attitude is the belief that these three aspects of the architecture deliver a fast, practical, efficient way to create business value with software. Let's dig into the details to see how this works in practice.

2.1   *Defining microservices*

The term *microservice* is inherently fuzzy, as a social effect of the increasing popularity of the architecture. When we use the term, we should be specific in our meaning. Much of the writing on microservices shares the same attitude toward software development but uses differing definitions of the key term. Enthusiasm for weak definitions, in turn, limits our thinking and provides an easy target for criticism from vested interests. Let's examine a sample of the proposed definitions:

- *Microservices are self-contained software components that are no more than 100 lines of code.* This definition captures the desire to keep microservices small and maintainable by one developer, rather than a team. It's an appeal to the idea that extreme simplicity has extreme benefits: 100 lines of code can be quickly and confidently reviewed for errors.[1] The small body of code is also inherently disposable in that it can easily be rewritten if necessary. These are desirable qualities for microservices, but not exhaustive. For example, the questions of deployment and interservice communication aren't addressed. The fundamental weakness in this definition is the use of an arbitrary numerical constraint that falls apart if we change programming languages. As we consider other definitions, let's retain the desire for code small enough to verify easily and to throw away if need be.

- *Microservices are independently deployable processes communicating asynchronously using lightweight mechanisms focused on specific business capabilities running in an automated but platform- and language-independent environment,* or words to that effect. On the opposite end of the spectrum are catchall general definitions. These definitions contain a laundry list of desired attributes. Are the attributes ordered by importance? Are they exhaustive? Are they well defined? General definitions give you a feeling that you're in the right galaxy, but they don't provide directions to get to a microservice system. They invite endless semantic debate over the definitions of the attributes. What, for example, is a *truly* lightweight communication mechanism?[2] What we can take from these definitions is a working set of ideas that can be used in practice but that don't by themselves provide much clarity.

---

[1]   C. A. R. Hoare, the inventor of the *quicksort* algorithm, in his 1980 Turing Award Lecture, famously said, "There are two ways of constructing a software design: One way is to make it so simple that there are *obviously* no deficiencies and the other way is to make it so complicated that there are no *obvious* deficiencies."

[2]   It's impossible to win a war of definitions. As soon as you provide a conclusive counter-example, your opponent denies that the counter-example is actually an example of the subject under discussion. The British philosopher Antony Flew provides the canonical example of this tactic, which can be paraphrased as follows: *Robert*: "All Scotsmen wear kilts!"; *Hamish*: "My uncle Duncan wears trousers."; *Robert*: "Yes, but no *true* Scotsman does."

- *Microservices are mini web servers offering a small REST-based HTTP API that accepts and returns JSON documents.* This is certainly a common implementation. And these are microservices. But how big are they? And how does it address all the other concerns, such as independent deployability? This definition is both too prescriptive on some questions and not prescriptive enough on others. It's definition by archetype. Few would disagree that these are microservices. And yet it excludes most of the interesting microservice architectural patterns, particularly those that take advantage of asynchronous messages. This definition is not only weak but dangerous. Empirical evidence from the field suggests it often leads to tightly coupled services that need to be deployed together.[3] The takeaway from this failed definition is that limiting ourselves to thinking only in terms of web-service APIs prevents us from appreciating the radical possibilities that a wider concept can bring. A definition should provide power to our thinking, not constrain it.

- *A microservice is an independent software component that takes no more than one iteration to build and deploy.* In this definition, the focus is on the human side of the architecture. The phrase *independent software component* is suggestive and wide ranging, so this definition also attempts to be inclusive of implementation strategies. Microservices are software components, using the common understanding of the term.[4] This definition expresses the desire for microservices to indeed be "micro" by limiting the resources available to write them: one iteration is all you get. It also gives a nod to continuous delivery—you have to be able to deploy within an iteration. The definition is careful to avoid mention of operating system processes, networking, distributed computing, and message protocols; none of these are essential properties.[5]

We must accept that we aren't school children, but professional software developers, and we live in the messy world of grownups. There's no tidy definition of microservices, and any definition we choose restricts our thinking. Rather than seek a definition that's dependent on numerical parameters, or attempts to be exhaustive, or is too narrow, we should aim to develop a conceptual framework that's *generative*. The concepts within the framework generate an accurate understanding of the inherent trade-offs of the microservice architecture. We then apply these concepts to the context at hand to deliver working software.[6]

---

[3] In my previous life as a consultant, I directed my poor teams to build many large systems this way, and we tied ourselves in the most wonderful Gordian knots.

[4] *Software components* are self-contained, extensible, well-defined, reusable building blocks.

[5] Erlang processes are most certainly microservices or, perhaps more correctly, nanoservices! You're strongly advised to read Joe Armstrong's Ph.D. thesis for the full details: "Making Reliable Distributed Systems in the Presence of Software Errors," Royal Institute of Technology, 2003, http://erlang.org/download/armstrong_thesis_2003.pdf.

[6] Microservices are a subject worthy of an entire book, not a trite summary definition. But then, I *would* say that.

2.2　*Case study: The digital edition of a newspaper*

Most chapters in this book use a case study to provide practical examples of the concepts under discussion. The studies are software systems that need to deliver a range of functionalities; in each chapter, we'll explore how the microservice architecture can deliver those functionalities. For each system, we'll focus on a subset of the functionality that's relevant to the topic of the chapter. Chapter 9 is a full case study, including code, that gives you a practical example of a microservice system using the architectural techniques developed in this book.

Our study in this chapter is the digital edition of a newspaper.[7] Let's break down this system, starting from the business goals. These generate requirements that we'll specify informally. Over the course of the chapter, we'll look at some partial implementations of these informal requirements, using microservices.

2.2.1　*The business goals*

The newspaper offers both free and paywalled content. To view the paywalled content, users need to subscribe. Revenue is driven by both subscriptions and advertising. The advertising is content- and user-targeted to increase relevance. To increase advertising revenue, user time on the site should be maximized.

The newspaper staff using the site should be able to publish content on a continuous basis using a content management system. They should be able to review analytics pertaining to the content they've written so that they can get feedback on their effectiveness.

The newspaper is delivered via website, tablet, and mobile app versions to maximize readership access. Article content, including paywalled content, should be search engine optimized to gain the widest potential readership.

2.2.2　*The informal requirements*

Using these goals, you can outline a list of informal requirements. These requirements will drive your implementation decisions:

- The content consists of articles, each of which has its own separate page.
- There are also special article-listing pages, such as the front page, and special-interest sections.
- The website, tablet, and app versions should all use a common REST API, provided by the server side of the system.
- The website should deliver static versions of primary content for search engines to index, but it can load secondary content dynamically.
- The system needs to have a concept of *users* that includes both readers and authors, with appropriate rights for different levels of access.

---

[7] As a mental model, think *The New York Times*. It isn't averse to a microservice or two.

- Content on pages needs to be targeted to the current user by matching content to the user's profile using business rules or optimization algorithms.
- The site is under continuous development, because online newspapers are in fierce competition, so new features need to be added quickly. These include special short-term mini apps, such as special interactive content for elections.

2.2.3   *A functional breakdown*

From a purely functional perspective, and without reference to any architecture choice, these requirements already allow you to think about how to implement the newspaper system. Here are some of the things the system should do:

- Handle article data and have the expected read, write, and query operations
- Construct content pages and provide a cache for scaling
- Handle user accounts: login, logout, profiles, and so on
- Deliver targeted content and map user identities to appropriate articles

These functions suggest some software components you should build. Let's pretend they're object-oriented classes for now:

- *ArticleHandler*—Provides article data operations
- *PageBuilder*—Generates pages
- *PageCache*—Caches pages
- *UserManager*—Manages users
- *ContentMapper*—Decides how to target content

You can even draw the possible dependencies between these components, as shown in figure 2.1.

Are these the right components? Are these the right dependencies? It's too soon to tell. Are these microservices? Perhaps. The microservice architecture must provide an analytical process for deciding what microservices to build. Somehow, you have to get from the informal requirements to the specific set of services in production. To start developing this process, let's take a closer look at the properties of microservice architectures and the options for constructing them.

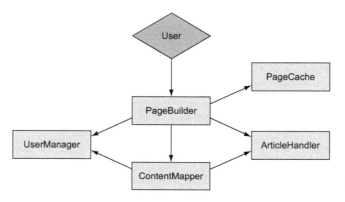

Figure 2.1   A possible component architecture for the newspaper system

[handwritten: Event driven arch: event happens send message]

2.3 Microservice architectures

If we accept that microservices should communicate with each other using messages, and we want them to be independent, that implies that microservices must have a well-defined communication interface. Discrete messages are the most natural mechanism for defining this interface.[8]

Understanding that interservice communication can be specified in terms of messages leads to a more powerful way to understand the dynamic nature of microservices. At one level, you need to understand which services talk to which other services. In practice, this understanding is less useful than you may think. As the number of services grows, the number of connections does too, and it becomes difficult to visualize the full set of interactions. One way to mitigate this complexity is to take a message-focused approach to describing the system. Consider that services and messages are two aspects of the same structure. It's often more useful to think about a microservice system in terms of the messages that pass through the system, rather than the services that respond to them. Taking this perspective, you can analyze the patterns of message interactions, find common patterns, and generate microservice architecture designs.

2.3.1 The mini web servers architecture

In the mini web servers architecture, microservices are nothing more than web servers that offer small REST interfaces. Messages are HTTP requests and responses. Message content is JSON or XML documents, or simple queries. This is a synchronous architecture. HTTP requests require a response. We'll take this as a starting point and then consider how to make these mini web servers more like software components.

Each microservice needs to know the location of other services that it wants to call. This is an important characteristic, and weakness, of mini web servers. When there are just a few services, you can configure each service with the network locations of the other services, but this quickly becomes unmanageable as the number of services grows. The standard solution is a service-discovery mechanism.

To provide service discovery, you need to run a service in your system that keeps a list of all microservices and their locations on the network. Each microservice must query the discovery service to find the services it wants to talk to. Sadly, this solution has lots of hidden complexity. First, keeping the discovery service consistent with the real state of the world is non-trivial—writing a good discovery implementation is difficult.[9] Second, microservices need to maintain the knowledge of other services that they've obtained from the discovery service, and deal with staleness and correctness issues in this knowledge. Third, discovery invites tight coupling between services. Why? Consider

---

[8] This doesn't exclude other communication mechanisms such as streaming data, but these are generally special cases or used as a transport layer for embedded messages.

[9] Some relatively robust service discovery implementations are available: ZooKeeper (https://zookeeper.apache.org), Consul (https://consul.io), etcd (https://github.com/coreos/etcd), and others. None of them deliver fully on the fault-tolerance and data-consistency claims they make, although all are suitable for production. Check out Kyle Kingsbury's "Jepsen" series of articles at https://aphyr.com/tags/jepsen for detailed analysis.

that inside monolithic code, you need a reference to an object to call a method. Now you're just doing it over the network—you need a network location and a URL endpoint. If you do use service discovery, you introduce the need to provide infrastructure code and modules for your services to interact with the discovery mechanism.

In its simplest configuration, this architecture is point-to-point. Microservices communicate directly with each other. You can extend this architecture with more-flexible message patterns by using intelligent load balancing. To scale a given microservice, place an HTTP load balancer[10] in front of a set of microservice instances. You'll need to do this for each microservice you want to scale. This increases your deployment complexity, because you'll need to manage the load balancer configurations as well as your microservices.

If you make your load balancer intelligent, you can start to get some of the deeper benefits of microservices. Nothing says all the microservices behind a given load balancer need to be the same version of the same microservice. You can partially deploy and test new versions of a microservice in production by introducing it into the balance set. This is an easy way to run multiple versions of the same microservice at the same time.

You can place different microservices behind the same load balancer and then use the load balancer to pattern-match on the properties of inbound messages to assign them to the correct type of microservice.[11] Consider the power this gives you—you can extend the functionality of your system by adding a new microservice and updating the load balancer rules. No need to change, update, redeploy, or otherwise touch other running services. The ability to make these kinds of small, low-impact, low-risk production changes is a large part of the attraction of the microservice architecture. It makes continuous delivery of code to production much more feasible.

> **Client-side load balancers**
>
> The load balancer doesn't have to be a separate process in front of the listening microservices. You can use a client-side library, embedded in the client microservice, to perform the intelligent load balancing. The advantage is that you don't have to worry about deploying and configuring lots of load balancers in your network. And the client-side load balancer can use service discovery to determine where to send balanced messages.

2.4   *Diagrams for microservices*

Let's draw some of these configurations so that they're easier to visualize. Traditional networking diagrams are less useful for microservices, because there are many more components; and, in any case, we're far more concerned with the details of the message

---

[10] Suitable load balancers are NGINX (http://nginx.org), HAProxy (www.haproxy.org), and Eureka (https://github.com/Netflix/eureka).

[11] One way to do this is to use extension modules for servers such as NGINX. It's also perfectly workable to roll your own, using a platform such as Node.js (https://nodejs.org).

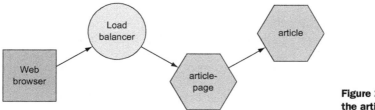

Figure 2.2 Building the article page

flows than their mere existence. Figure 2.2 shows a simple point-to-point system: part of the newspaper website. Later, we'll build a full structure, but let's focus first on the microservice interactions that build an article page.

The *article* service stores article data. The *article-page* service constructs the HTML for an article. Articles each have their own unique page URL. An intelligent load balancer routes article URL requests from web browser clients to the *article-page* service.

Let's take for granted that these are the services to build. You can see that they're different from the more traditional object-oriented components originally suggested (*PageBuilder, ArticleHandler*). In due course, you'll derive these services from the messages that define the system. Right now, let's see how diagrammatic conventions can help demonstrate the design of the system.

In figure 2.2, the solid lines represent synchronous messages. That means the client service expects an immediate response from the listening service; it can't proceed in its work without this response. The arrows are directed toward the listening service from the client service. The arrows are solid, meaning the listening service consumes the message. No one else sees that message.

Microservices are represented by hexagons. Entities external to the system (such as the web browser) are represented as rectangles, and entities internal to the system (the load balancer) are represented as circles. In the case of microservices, a hexagon doesn't represent a single microservice but means one or more running instances of the same kind of microservice. This is important to remember. In production, you almost never run just a single instance of a microservice.

2.5 *The microservice dependency tree*

Microservices are dependent on each other by design, because each performs only a small part of the work for any given HTTP request or other task in the system. In the point-to-point synchronous architecture, which we might call *entry-level microservices,* the dependency tree can become difficult to manage as it grows.

In particular, the primary danger is *service coupling,* where one or more microservices become codependent and new versions must be deployed at the same time. This can happen easily if you use object-serialization libraries that insist on fully matching all the properties they find in JSON or XML messages. Add a field to an entity in one microservice, and you have to add it to all microservices that use that entity. You end up with a distributed monolith—the worst of both worlds.

The trap of the distributed monolith

A *distributed monolith* is a nasty trap awaiting first-time microservice builders who naïvely use traditional object-oriented patterns in a microservice context. In mainstream object-oriented languages, you must provide exact method and object type signatures. You get a compilation error if your types don't match. (Whether this is a true benefit to software productivity is a debate for another day.)

In a microservice architecture, type mismatches aren't compilation errors, they're runtime errors—runtime errors that bring down your system. Using strict types means you're building a distributed monolith, where method calls run over the network.

It's much easier to build a traditional monolith! To obtain the benefits of the microservices architecture, you need to leave behind some of the best practices of the monolithic world.

Let's return to the case study. Viewing a newspaper article involves more activities than retrieving the article data and formatting it. Some of these activities are shown in figure 2.3. You probably have an active logged-in user; you need to display the user's status in a box at the top of the page, where the user can log out or choose to manage their account. That suggests a microservice with responsibility for users. You'll have an advertising service, because that's part of the business model for the newspaper.

The *article-page* service pulls in content from the *adverts*, *user*, and *article* services. It makes no sense to make these network requests in series, waiting for each one, in turn, to complete successfully. Instead, you need to send out all the requests at the same time and combine the responses once they come in. Writing code to do this isn't rocket science but does make your

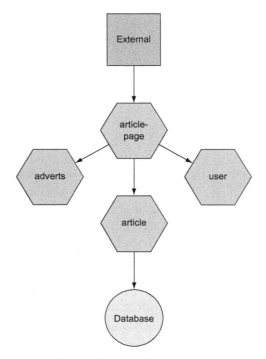

Figure 2.3   Building the full article page

code base messier. You need to develop some abstractions around message sending and receiving so that you can make the transportation of messages between services uniform.

In the figure, you can see how the database is fronted by the *article* service. Never expose your underlying implementation choices to other services! This is almost a golden rule. One of the big benefits you're supposed to get as a trade-off for the extra complexity of managing microservices in production is the ability to change almost anything in your system independently of everything else. You should be able to change the database without even rebooting the *article-page* service.

You could count the number of times an article is read from the *article-page* service, but this isn't a good responsibility for *article-page* to have. There may be other things you want to do when an article is read (such as training a recommendation engine), performed by other services. One way to decouple these functions from *article-page* is to use an *asynchronous* message, indicated by the dotted line in figure 2.4. The *article-page* service emits a message that announces the event that an article has been read, but *article-page* doesn't care how many people receive it or need a response.

In this case, the *analytics* and *recommend* services don't *consume* messages sent to them. These messages are instead *observed*, as indicated by the open arrowheads. To achieve this, you might use a message queue to duplicate the messages.[12] It's

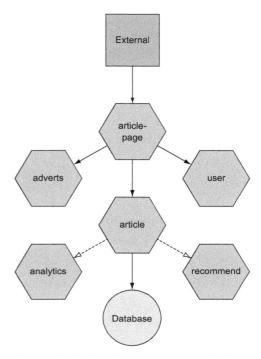

Figure 2.4 Letting other services know that an article has been read

important to think at the right architectural level. What matters is that the messages are asynchronous and observed, not how you implement that style of message interaction.

"Don't repeat yourself" isn't a golden rule

Microservices allow you to violate the DRY (don't repeat yourself) principle safely. Traditional software design recommends that you generalize repetitive code so that you don't end up maintaining many copies of slightly different code. Microservice design is exactly the opposite: each microservice is allowed to go its own way. It's an anti-pattern to seek out common business logic (infrastructure, as always, is a special case) and try to write general modules for multiple microservices to use. Why? Because general code is complex, must deal with edge cases, and is a primary cause of incremental technical debt.

General business rules and domain models always become "hairy" over time, because the general case isn't sufficient to handle the complexities of the real world. Better to keep everything separate, in simpler case-specific rules and small models on a per-microservice basis. This keeps your microservices independent and allows developers to work in parallel on simpler code bases.

---

[12] The publish/subscribe feature of Redis is just one of many ways to do this: https://redis.io/commands/pubsub.

As your system grows over time, the dependency tree of services also grows, both in breadth and depth. Fortunately, experience in the field suggests[13] that breadth grows more quickly than depth. As the tree eventually grows deeper, you'll run into latency issues. Here's the heart of the problem: response times over a network follow a skewed distribution where most responses return quickly, but some take much longer than average. This why we use percentiles[14] to set performance targets, because the average isn't informative. When multiple elements communicate in series, the response times for the worst cases grow much faster than average, and what was slow performance in a small number of cases becomes, in effect, downtime, as timeouts are hit.

How do you deal with this issue? One way is to merge services[15] so that there's less need for network traffic. This is a valid performance optimization, especially in mature systems. It's made much less painful by making sure your infrastructure code is in good shape and abstracting away the networking and service-discovery work from your main microservice business logic.

2.5.1 *The asynchronous message architecture*

As a complete alternative to the point-to-point approach, why not transport all of your messages via a message queue? In this architecture, you have one or more message queues that handle all your messages. Your client services publish messages onto the queue, and your listening services retrieve them.

Using a message queue gives you a lot more flexibility, at the price of increased system complexity. A message queue is another point of failure and requires the same care and attention as your database in production. Moreover, in order to scale, message queues need to be distributed, just like databases.

You'll need to decide how to route your messages. With a queue, at least your services don't need to know each others' network locations. They still need to know how to find the queue. You have to use message topics to route messages, and your services need to know about those, too. Let's develop your understanding of this approach by looking at a common strategy: *scatter/gather*.

Most kinds of content are useful even when they aren't complete or entirely correct. In the newspaper example, showing a stale version of an article page from a cache is far preferable, from a business perspective, to showing a page error if the *article* service is misbehaving. The leaders of most organizations prefer to keep their

---

[13] It's a valuable investment in your understanding of the microservice architecture to view the many conference talk videos that are available online, where issues like this are discussed from a practical, production viewpoint.

[14] A *percentile* tells you what percentage of responses came in under the given time. For example, a 500 ms response time at the 90th percentile means 90% of responses took less than or equal to 500 ms.

[15] Merging services is a perfectly acceptable performance optimization—but it's a performance optimization, nonetheless. You lose many of the benefits of the microservice architecture. The guideline that a microservice should take at most an iteration to rewrite is also just that: a guideline. You get paid to exercise your professional judgment on these matters.

businesses open even when they can't offer full service.[16] This is just plain business common sense. Businesses want to be available to their customers, even if their products aren't consistent. Moreover, customers tend to have this preference too—a ham-and-cheese sandwich from hotel room service when your flight got in at 2:00 a.m. is better than no food at all!

Let's consider an asynchronous approach to building the article page. This page consists of multiple elements: user status, advertising, article text, article metadata, mini author profile, related content links, and so on. The page is still useful even if most of these elements fail to appear. That suggests *scattering* a message to the microservices responsible for generating this content and then *gathering* the responses, asynchronously, under a timeout. Everybody gets, say, 200 ms to respond. If they don't make it back in time, their content element isn't displayed, but at least the user gets something. This technique also has the advantage that your site feels much faster, because page delivery isn't slowed down by slow services.

In figure 2.5, the *article-page* service emits an asynchronous message. The *article*, *adverts*, and *user* services observe but don't consume this message. They do some work and generate responses. The responses are also asynchronous. The *article-page* service consumes these responses, indicated by the solid arrowhead, which is offset from the *article-page* hexagon to indicate that *article-page* is the originator of this message flow. This pattern is common, so the diagram abbreviates the scatter and gather messages into one dotted line. Again, remember that these aren't individual instances of the services, but rather multiple instances.[17]

A message queue makes the scatter/gather pattern easy to implement and is much more suited to asynchronous patterns in general. In practical terms, you create an announcement topic for the article page to post content requests and a fulfillment topic for the content-providing services to post responses. You also need to identify and tag the messages so they'll be ignored by services that aren't interested in them. But be warned: the failure modes of message queues are many, varied, and colorful. We'll examine message patterns and their failure modes in more detail in chapter 3.

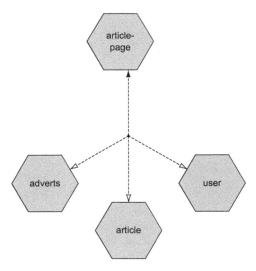

Figure 2.5 The scatter/gather pattern

---

[16] Do banks refuse to process payments when they can't perform ACID transactions? Did you ever exceed your overdraft limit? Banks solve that problem with a business rule (penalty fees), not with computer science that would damage their business.

[17] Netflix, a major proponent of microservices, normally deploys in units of an Amazon Web Services Auto Scaling group. It doesn't think in terms of individual machines or containers.

What do people use in production when choosing between synchronous and asynchronous strategies? Almost universally, production systems are hybrids. Asynchronous message queues allow you to be more fault tolerant and let you distribute work more easily. Adding new services is easy, and you don't have to worry too much about service discovery. On the other hand, synchronous point-to-point is an absolute must when you need low latency. Also, in the early days of a project, it's much quicker to get started using point-to-point.

2.6   *Monolithic projects vs. microservice projects*

The monolithic software architecture creates negative consequences, which many have assumed are fundamental challenges that apply to all software development. On closer examination, with critical questioning, this assumption can be turned on its head. Many of the challenges, and many of the supposed solutions to these challenges, arise directly from the engineering effects of monolithic architecture and become moot when you take a different engineering approach.

There are three consequences of the monolith. First, all members of the software development team must carefully coordinate their activities so as not to block each other. There's one code base. If a single developer breaks the build, then all developers are blocked. The code naturally tends toward deep, multidimensional dependency. This is a consequence of perceived best practices. Refactoring common code into shared libraries creates deep dependency trees. The amount of rework needed when changing the code structure is exponentially proportional to the depth of that structure in the dependency tree. Teams often make the rational choice to wrap complexity in ever more layers, in an attempt to hide and contain it. Monoliths make the cost of parallel work much higher and thus slow development.

The second consequence of monoliths is that they gather technical debt rapidly. There's no natural limiting force. A well-structured, properly decoupled, clean, object-oriented initial design is too weak to resist the immediate needs of an entire team working against the clock to deliver today's features. There are too many ways that one piece of code can invade other pieces of code—too many ways to create dependencies.

A primary example is data-structure corrosion. Given an initial requirements definition, the senior developers and architects design appropriate data structures to describe the problem domain. These are shared data structures and must accommodate all known requirements and anticipate future requirements, so they tend toward the complex. Deeply nested cross-referencing is a tell-tale sign of attempted future proofing. Unfortunately, the world often outwits our meager intelligence, and the data structures can't accommodate real business needs as they emerge. The team is forced to introduce kludges, implicit conventions, and ad hoc extension points.[18]

---

[18] Declarative structures are usually the best option for representing the world, because they can be manipulated in repeatable, consistent, deliberately limited ways. If you introduce ways to embed executable code to handle special cases as a "get out of jail free card," things can get complicated fast, and you end up in technical debtors' prison anyway.

Later, new developers and junior developers, lacking understanding of the forces on the data structure, may introduce subtle and devious bugs, costing the team vastly disproportionate time in fixes and performance-tuning workarounds.[19] Eventually, the team must engage in extensive refactoring efforts to regain some measure of development velocity. Globally shared data structures and models are just as bad as global variables and have no natural defenses against technical debt.

Finally, the third consequence of monoliths is that they are all-or-nothing deployments. You have an old version of a monolith running in production, and you have a new version on staging. To upgrade production without impacting the business, you have a very stressful weekend ahead of you.

Perhaps you're more sophisticated and use blue-green deployments to mitigate risk.[20] You still have to expend energy building the blue-green infrastructure, and it's still not much help if you have database schema migrations, because those aren't easily reversible.

The basic problem is that any change to production requires a full redeployment of the entire code base. This creates high-risk exposure to failures at all levels of the system. No amount of unit testing, acceptance testing, integration testing, manual testing, and trialing can give you a true measure of the probability of failed deployment, because the failure conditions are often direct consequences of production conditions that you can't simulate. Production data (which you may not even have access to, due to client confidentiality rules) only needs one unforeseen aspect to cause critical failures. It's difficult to verify performance using test data—production can be orders of magnitude larger. Users can behave in unanticipated ways, especially with new features, that break the system because the team wasn't able to imagine those use cases. The deployment risk associated with monoliths causes slow, infrequent releases of new features, holding back fast delivery.

These engineering challenges, for that's precisely what they are, can't be solved with any given project management approach. They're in a different problem domain. And yet, almost universally and exclusively, businesses try to solve them with software development methodologies and project management techniques. Rather than stepping back and searching for the real reason projects are delivered late and over budget, software development stakeholders blame themselves for poor execution. No amount of good execution will let you build skyscrapers with bullshit.[21] The solution lies elsewhere.

---

[19] An example from a former client is instructive: The client added a database column for XML content so that they could store small amounts of unstructured data. The schema for that XML included several elements that could be repeated, to store lists. These lists were unbounded. In the problem domain, a small number of users generated very long lists, leading to massive XML content, leading to strange and wonderful garbage collection issues that were long separated from the root cause.

[20] The *blue-green deployment strategy* means you have two versions of the system in production at all times: the blue version and the green version. Only one of them is live. To deploy, you upgrade the offline version and swap.

[21] Wattle-and-daub construction has been used since Neolithic times and is an excellent construction technique that can get you to three or four small stories, given a sufficiently large herd of cattle to generate excrement. It won't help you build the Empire State Building.

The microservices architecture, as an engineering approach, allows us, as software developers, to revisit all of our cherished best practices and ask whether they really make delivery faster and more predictable. Or are they merely poor mitigations of the fundamental problems of monolithic development? Frederick P. Brooks, in his seminal 1975 book *The Mythical Man-Month*, explains in graphic detail the challenges of monolith development.[22] He then suggests a set of techniques and practices, not to solve the problem, but to contain and mitigate it. This is the core message of the phrase "no silver bullet": no project management techniques can overcome the engineering deficits of the monolithic architecture.

2.6.1 *How microservices change project management*

The engineering features of the microservice architecture have a direct impact on the amount of project management effort needed to ensure successful delivery. There's less need for detailed task management and for much of the useless ceremony of explicit methodologies.[23] Project management of microservice projects can use a light touch. Let's work through the implications.

2.6.2 *Uniformity makes estimation easier*

Microservices are small, and a good practice is to limit them to at most one iteration's worth of work from one developer. Microservice estimation is thus a much easier task than general software-effort estimation, because you force yourself to chunk features into iteration-sized bites. This is an important observation. Traditional monolithic systems are composed of heterogeneous components of various sizes and complexity. Accurate estimation is extremely difficult, because each component is a special case and has a multifaceted set of interactions with other components via method calls, shared objects and data structures, and shared database schemas. The result is a project task list that bends to the demands of the system architecture.[24]

With microservices, the one-iteration complexity limit forces uniformity on components that increases estimation accuracy. In practice, even more accuracy can be achieved by classifying microservices into, say, three complexity levels, also classifying developers into three experience levels, and matching microservices to developers. For example, a level-1 microservice can be completed by a level-1 developer in one iteration, whereas a level-3 microservice needs a level-3 developer to be completed in one iteration. This approach gives far more accuracy than generic agile story point estimates that ignore variations in developer ability. A microservice project can be

---

[22] Brooks was the manager for the IBM System/360 mainframe project and the first to make the written observation that adding more developers to an already-late project just makes it even later.

[23] To spare embarrassment, no methodologies will be named. But you know who you are. If there were a project management approach to software development that could consistently deliver, over many kinds of teams, we'd already be narrowing down toward the solution. But we see no signs of significant progress.

[24] Somewhat ironically, Fibonacci estimation (where agile story point estimates must be Fibonacci numbers: 1, 2, 3, 5, 8, 13, …) is proof enough that a local maximum has been reached in the estimation accuracy of monolithic systems.

accurately planned using a sensible, meaningful mapping from microservices to iterations. We'll explore this idea in more detail in part 2 of this book.

> ### Why is software estimation difficult?
>
> Why is it so difficult to estimate the complexity of components of a larger system? The tight coupling that invariably occurs in monolithic architectures means development in the later stages of a project is exponentially slower, making the initial estimates of late-stage components highly skewed toward the overoptimistic. The exponential slowness arises from the mathematical fact (known as *Metcalfe's law*) that the number of possible connections between nodes in a network increases proportionally to the square of the number of nodes.
>
> And there's another factor: human psychology suffers from many cognitive biases—we're not good at working with probabilities, for instance. Many of these come into play to sabotage accurate project estimation. Just one example: *anchoring* is the bias for staying close to the first number you hear. The complexity and thus completion time for software components follow a power law: most take a short amount of time, but some take much longer.[25]
>
> The largest and most difficult components are underestimated, because the bulk of the estimation work concerns small components. The old joke that the last 10% of the schedule takes 90% of the time expresses much truth.

2.6.3   *Disposable code makes for friendlier teams*

Microservice code is disposable. It's literally throw-away. Any given microservice is one iteration's worth of work, for one developer. If the microservice was badly written, is underperformant in the chosen language, or isn't needed anymore because requirements have changed, then it can be decommissioned without much soul searching. This realization has a healthy effect on team dynamics: nobody becomes emotionally attached to their code, nor do they feel possessive of it.

Suppose Alice thinks microservice A, written by Bob several iterations back in Java, will be twice as performant if written in C++. She should go for it! It's an extra iteration invested either way, and if the attempt is a failure, the team is no worse off, because they still have Bob's Java code.

The knowledge that each microservice must live or die on its own merits is a natural limiting function for complexity. Complexity makes you weak. Better to write a new, special-case microservice than extend an existing one. If you reserve, say, 20% of iterations for rewrites and unforeseen special cases, you can have more confidence that this is real contingency, rather than a political tactic in the effort-negotiation game.[26]

---

[25] Power laws describe many phenomena where small causes can have outsize effects: earthquake durations, executive salaries, and letter frequencies in text, for example.

[26] Software project estimation often deteriorates into a political game. Software developers give optimistic estimates to get gold stars. Business stakeholders, burned before by failed projects, forcefully demand all features on an arbitrary schedule. The final schedule is determined by horse-trading rather than engineering. Both sides have legitimate needs but end up in a lose-lose situation because it isn't politically safe to communicate these needs.

2.6.4 *Homogeneous components allow for heterogeneous configuration*

You can group microservices into different classes with differing business constraints. Some are mission critical and high load—for example, the checkout microservice on an e-commerce website. Others are core features, but not mission critical. Still others are nice-to-haves, where failure has no immediate impact. Questions: Is it necessary for all of these different kinds of microservices to have the same quality level? Do they all need the same level of unit-test coverage? Does it make sense to expend the same quality control effort uniformly on all microservices? No. There's no justifiable business case for those views.

You should expend effort where it counts. You should have different levels of unit-test coverage for different classes of microservice. Similarly, there are different performance, data-safety, security, and scaling requirements. Monolithic code bases have to meet the highest levels across the board, as a matter of engineering fact. Microservices allow a finer-grained focus on applying limited developer resources where they count.[27]

Microservices make successful failures successful. The typical software system must often pass user-acceptance testing. In practice, this means the entity with the checkbook won't sign until a set of features has been ticked off. Step back for a minute, and ask yourself whether this is a good way to ensure that the delivered software will meet the business goals for which it was originally commissioned. How can anyone be sure that a given feature delivers actual value until it's measured in production? Perhaps certain features will never be used or are overly complex. Perhaps you're missing critical features nobody thought of. And yet user-acceptance testing treats all features as having the same value. In practice, what happens is that the team delivers a mostly complete system with a mostly random subset of the originally desired features. After much grumbling, this is accepted, because the business needs the system to go into production.

A microservice approach doesn't change the reality that developer resources are limited and ultimately there may not be enough time to build everything. It does let you take a breadth-first approach. Most projects take a depth-first approach: user stories are assigned to iterations, and the team burns down the requirements. At the end of the original schedule, this leaves you with, say, 80% of the features completed and 20% untouched. In a breadth-first approach, you deliver incomplete versions of all features. At the end of the project, you have 100% of features mostly complete, but a substantial number of edge cases aren't finished. Which of these is the better position to be in for go-live? With the breadth-first approach, you cover all the cases the business people thought of, at some level. You haven't wasted effort fully completing features that will turn out to have no value. And you've given the business the opportunity during the project to redirect effort without giving up on entire features—a much easier discussion to have with stakeholders. Microservices make allocation of finite development resources more efficient and friendly.

---

[27] Chapter 6 discusses a way to quantify these fine-grained measurements.

2.6.5 *There are different types of code*

Microservices allow you to separate business-logic code from infrastructure code. Business-logic code is driven directly from business requirements. It's determined by the best guesses of the business stakeholders, given incomplete and inadequate business information. It's naturally subject to rapid change, hidden depths, and obsolescence. Corralling this business-logic code into microservice units is a practical engineering approach to managing rapid change.

There's another type of code in the system: infrastructure code. This is where system integration, algorithms, data-structure manipulation, parsing, and utility code happen. This code is less subject to the vagaries of the business world. There's often a relatively complete technical specification, an API to work against, or specifically limited requirements. This code can safely be kept separate from the business-logic code, so it neither slows down business code nor is negatively impacted by incidental business logic.

The problem with most monolithic architectures is that these two types of code—business-logic and infrastructure—end up mixed together, with predictably negative effects on team velocity and levels of technical debt. Business logic belongs in microservices; infrastructure belongs in software libraries. The ability to allocate coding effort correctly in this way makes estimating the level of effort required for each more accurate, and increases the predictability of the project schedule.

2.7 *The unit of software*

The preceding discussion makes the case that microservices are incredibly useful as structural units of software. Can they be considered fundamental units, much like objects, functions, or processes? Yes, because they give us a powerful conceptual model for thinking about system design.

The essence of the problem we're trying to solve is one of multidimensional scaling: scaling software systems in production, scaling the complexity of the software that makes up those systems, and scaling the teams of developers that build them. The power of the microservices concept comes from the fact that it offers a unified solution to many different scaling problems.

Scaling problems are difficult because they're exponential in nature. There are no 12-foot-tall humans, because doubling height means you increase body volume 8-fold, and the materials of our bodies, and our body architecture, can't handle the increased weight.[28] Scaling problems have this characteristic. Increasing one input parameter linearly causes disproportionate accelerated change in other aspects of the system.

If you double the size of a software team, you won't double the output speed. Beyond more than a few people, you'll move even slower as you add more people.[29] Double the complexity of a software system, and you won't double the number of bugs; you'll

---

[28] You also need to double width and depth, to maintain proportions; hence, 2^3.

[29] Amazon has a scientific rule for the size of a software team: it must be possible to feed the entire team with no more than two pizzas.

increase them by the square of the size of the code base. Double the number of clients you need to serve, and suddenly you need to manage a distributed system.

Scaling can be addressed in two principle dimensions:[30] the vertical and the horizontal. *Vertical scaling* means making what you have bigger, stronger, or faster. This works until the physical, mathematical, or functional aspects of the system reach their structural limits. Thus, you can't keep buying more-powerful machines. *Vertical scaling* tends to have exponential decay in effectiveness and exponential growth in cost, which gives it hard limits in practice. That said, don't be afraid to scale vertically when you can afford it—hardware is much cheaper than developers.

Horizontal scaling escapes hard limits. Instead of making each piece more powerful, just keep adding more pieces. This has no fundamental limits, as long as your system is designed to be linearly scalable. Most aren't, because they have inherent communication limits that require too many pieces to talk to too many other pieces.

Biological systems comprising billions of individual cells have overcome horizontal-scaling limits by making communication as local as possible. Cells only communicate with their close neighbors, and they do so asynchronously using pattern matching on undirected hormonal signals. We should learn a lesson from this architecture!

High-capacity scaling arises when the system is composed of large numbers of independent homogeneous units. Sound familiar? The principle qualities of microservices lend themselves powerfully to effective scaling—not just in terms of load, but also in terms of complexity.

2.8 *Requirements to messages to services*

Let's return to earth. How do you apply these ideas in practice? Let's take the newspaper system and perform some further analysis. You need to know what services to build—how do you get there?

Trying to guess the appropriate services isn't particularly effective, although your intuitions for what makes a good service will build over time. It's more useful to start with messages. Specifically, break down each requirement into a set of messages that describe the activities that constitute the requirement. Then organize the messages into services, taking care to maintain the small size of services. More-complex services may implement more messages, and these you should assign to stronger members of the team. It isn't necessary to fully implement all messages immediately, but you should still aim for breadth rather than depth, providing at least basic implementations within the first few iterations.

Let's do this for the newspaper site. Table 2.1 lists the requirements, with corresponding messages. This is the first cut, and you may change this set of messages over the course of the project. This is different from a traditional approach, where you'd think about what entities form the system. Instead, think in terms of activities—answer the question, "What happens?" You'll notice that this analysis refines the

---

[30] You can add dimensions and get scale cubes and scale hypercubes. This lets you refine your analysis, but two dimensions will do just fine for decision making.

earlier experiments with the *article* service, exploring variations of the possible message interactions. This is deliberate so that you can see the flexibility this approach provides. You'll modify the architecture again before you're finished.

Table 2.1   Mapping requirements to messages

Requirement	Messages
Article pages	*build-article, get-article, article-view*
Article list pages	*build-article-list, list-article*
REST API	*get-article, add-article, remove-article, list-article*
Static and dynamic content	*article-need, article-collect*
User management	*login, logout, register, get-profile*
Content targeting	*visitor-need, visitor-collect*
Special-purpose mini apps	App-specific

Some activities will share messages. This is to be expected. In large systems, you'd namespace the messages; but for our purposes here, this isn't necessary. You should also make the intent of your messages clear by describing the activities they're meant to represent:

- *build-article*—Constructs the article HTML page
- *get-article*—Gets article entity data
- *article-view*—Announces the viewing of an article
- *build-article-list*—Constructs a page that lists articles
- *list-article*—Queries the article store
- *add-article*—Adds an article to the store
- *remove-article*—Removes an article from the store
- *article-need*—Expresses a need for article page content
- *article-collect*—Collects some element of article page content
- *login*—Logs a user in
- *logout*—Logs a user out
- *register*—Registers a new user
- *get-profile*—Gets a user profile
- *visitor-need*—Expresses a need for targeted content for a site visitor
- *visitor-collect*—Collects some targeted content

These messages can then be organized into services. For each service, you need to define the inbound and outbound messages; see tables 2.2–2.9. You'll also need to decide whether a message is synchronous or asynchronous (asynchronous is indicated by "(A)" in the tables). Synchronous messages expect an immediate response—assume this is the default. And you'll need to decide whether a message is consumed or just observed by a service. Consumed messages can't be seen by other services—assume this is the default.

Table 2.2   *article-page*

In	*build-article, build-article-list, article-collect (A), visitor-collect (A)*
Out	*get-article, article-need (A), visitor-need (A)*
Notes	We make no assumptions about how the HTML is constructed. Perhaps the providing services sent HTML, or perhaps just metadata.

Table 2.3   *article-list-page*

In	*build-article-list, visitor-collect (A)*
Out	*list-article, visitor-need (A)*

Table 2.4   *article*

In	*get-article, add-article, remove-article, list-article*
Out	*add-cache-item (A), get-cache-item*
Notes	This service interacts with the cache to store articles.

Table 2.5   *cache*

In	*get-cache-item, add-cache-item (A)*
Out	None
Notes	Cache messages aren't derived from the requirements list. Instead, we use our experience as software architects to derive the need for caching in the system to ensure adequate performance. Messages such as these arise naturally from system analysis work.

Table 2.6   *api-gateway*

In	None
Out	*build-article, build-article-list, get-article, list-article, add-article, remove-article, login, logout, register, get-profile*
Notes	Inbound messages to this service are traditional HTTP REST calls, not microservice messages. This service translates them into internal microservice messages.

Table 2.7   *user*

In	*login, logout, register, get-profile, article-need*
Out	*article-collect*

Table 2.8 *adverts*

In	*article-need*
Out	*article-collect*

Table 2.9 *target-content*

In	*visitor-need*
Out	*visitor-collect*
Notes	This is a simple initial implementation that returns a Register Now! call to action for unknown users, and empty content for known, logged-in users. The intention is to extend this capability by adding more services.

The list of services from an initial analysis can be assessed in terms of complexity and adjusted so that the initial version of each service can be built within one iteration. Some services' features are added incrementally so that later versions also take an iteration to build. Be careful not to do this too frequently, because such services can grow in complexity and become essential, rather than disposable. When possible, it's better to add functionality by adding services.

Lists of requirements, messages, and services are one way to view the system. Let's look at the newspaper system architecture visually with a microservice diagram.

2.9 Microservice architecture diagrams

We diagrammed smaller parts of the system earlier in the chapter. Now, let's create a complete system architecture diagram: see figure 2.6.

> **NOTE** In most network diagramming, connections between elements are represented as plain lines, often without direction. The lines indicate network traffic, but not much else. Network elements are assumed to be individual instances. In a microservice system, it's better to make the default *one or more*, because that's the common case. I use this diagramming convention throughout this book to give immediate insight into the microservice case studies.

The full newspaper system includes and refines the article subsystem you saw earlier. The synchronous versus asynchronous message flows can be clearly seen and mapped back to the message and service specification. Use this diagram as a reference example for the visual conventions that follow.

In this diagram of the newspaper system, I use the following conventions for groups of network elements:

- Hexagons represent microservices.
- Circles represent internal systems.
- Rectangles represent external systems.

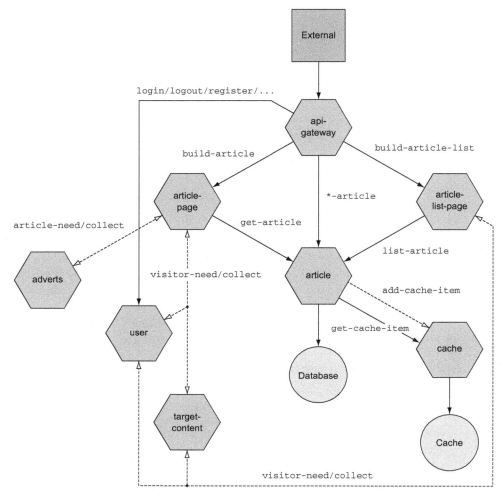

Figure 2.6   The full newspaper system

Internal systems are databases, caching engines, directory servers, and so on. They're the non-microservice infrastructure of the network. An internal system may consist of microservices, and the circle shape can be used to represent entire subsystems composed of microservices.

All communication is assumed to be in the form of messages. This applies to non-microservice elements as well, so that they can be connected via the same message-line conventions. Special cases, such as streaming data flow, must be annotated with callouts.

Such figures can contain further information, as shown in figure 2.7:

- *Solid boundary line*—One or more instances and versions of a given element
- *Dashed boundary line*—A family of related elements
- *Name*—Required; identifies the element or family

- *Cardinality*—The number of live instances (optional), above the name
- *Version tag*—The version number of these instances (optional) below the name

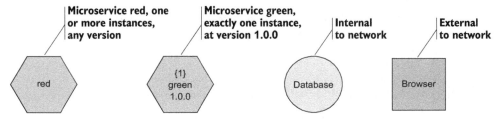

Figure 2.7   Service and network element deployment characteristics

The solid boundary line indicates a cardinality of one or more, which is the default. *Cardinality* means the number of running instances.[31] The full list of cardinalities is as follows:

- ?—Zero or one instances
- *—Zero or more instances
- +—One or more instances
- {n}—Exactly *n* instances
- {n:m}—Between *n* and *m* instances
- {n: }—At least *n* instances
- { :m}—At most *m* instances

Numeric cardinalities must always be inside braces to avoid suggesting that they're version numbers.

A dashed boundary line means the element is composed of a group of related services. In this case, cardinality applies to each member of the family, and finer-grained resolution requires you to break out individual members.

The version tag appears below the name and is optional. It follows the *semver* standard,[32] except that you may omit any of the internal numbers, which are then assumed to be 0. You can even omit all of them and use only a suffix tag. Use the version number when it's important to communicate that different versions of the same service participate in the network.

2.9.1   *Diagramming message flows*

Understanding the message flows in a system is vital. In particular, all messages have an originating client service and a listening service that receives the message. All message

---

[31] I use the cardinalities to disambiguate the deployment strategies discussed in chapter 5.
[32] Version identifiers follow the pattern *MAJOR.MINOR.PATCH.* You can omit *MINOR* and *PATCH* numbers. See "Semantic Versioning 2.0.0" (http://semver.org).

lines that connect elements must, therefore, be directed, with an arrowhead at the receiving end. You can convey this information using the following conventions:

- *Solid line*—Synchronous message that expects a response
- *Dashed line*—Asynchronous message that doesn't expect a response
- *Closed arrow*—Message is consumed by the receiver
- *Open arrow*—Message is observed by the receiver

Because message lines can be solid or dashed, and arrowheads can be closed or open, there are four possibilities (which will be discussed in greater detail in the next chapter):

- *Solid-closed—synchronous actor*—Only one of the receiving instances consumes the message and responds.
- *Solid-open—synchronous subscribers*—All of the receiving instances observe the message, and the originator accepts the first response.
- *Dashed-closed—asynchronous actor*—Only one of the receiving instances consumes the message.
- *Dashed-open—asynchronous subscriber*—All of the receiving instances observe the message.

Figure 2.8 shows you how to represent the four interactions.

Message lines can be bidirectional to reduce visual clutter. To indicate the originating service, offset the arrowhead so it doesn't contact the boundary line of the figure.

Messages may be intended for multiple recipients, and the same message can be indicated by separate arrows originating from the same service. To declutter, you can also split the arrow into multiple sub-arrows. The split point is indicated by a small dot.

In the synchronous case, when you have multiple recipients, each message is delivered to only one receiver according

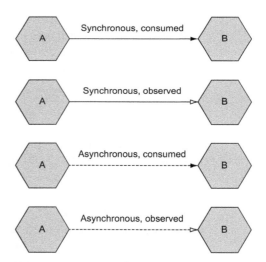

Figure 2.8   Message interactions

to some algorithm (which can be indicated by an annotation). The default algorithm is round-robin. In the asynchronous case, the message is delivered to all recipients. In both cases, whether the message is consumed or observed is a separate matter indicated by the arrowhead.

Message lines can be annotated with either the full message pattern (as you'll use later) or an abbreviated name for the pattern (as used in this study). Message lines can also be annotated with preceding sequence numbers. These have the format x.i.j.k... where x is a letter and i,j, and k are positive integers. Separate sequences are indicated by the letter, and no temporal ordering is implied. The positive integers indicate the temporal order of messages within a sequence. Only the first number is required, and separator dots indicate the ordering of subsequences.

Any part of the diagram can be annotated with callouts to disambiguate microservice interactions. To avoid confusion with external element rectangles, callouts consist of a line connecting the annotated figure with explanatory text adjacent to a single horizontal or vertical boundary line.

Microservice diagrams aren't intended to be formal specifications—they're for team communication. It's therefore acceptable to omit elements for the sake of brevity, even if this creates ambiguity. In particular, the diagrams aren't intended to show the transport mechanism chosen for messages, because transport independence is assumed. Use annotations if you wish to indicate specific transport mechanisms.

2.10 *Microservices are software components*

In this book, I claim that microservices make excellent—almost perfect—software components. It's worth examining this claim in more detail. Software components have relatively well-defined characteristics, and there's broad general agreement on the most important of them. Let's see how microservices stack up against this understanding.

2.10.1 *Encapsulated*

Software components are self contained. They encapsulate a set of semantically consistent activities and data. The outside world isn't privy to this internal representation and can't pollute it. Likewise, the component doesn't expose its internal implementation. The purpose of this characteristic is to make components interchangeable.

Microservices deliver on encapsulation in a very strong way—far stronger than language constructs such as modules and classes. Because each microservice must assume a physical separation from other microservices, it can only communicate with them via messages, and it has no backdoor access to the internals of other microservices. Creating such backdoor access requires more effort for developers, so encapsulation is strongly preserved throughout the lifetime of the system.

2.10.2 *Reusable*

Reusability is a holy grail of software development. A good component can be reused in many different systems over a long period of time. In practice, this is difficult to achieve, because each system has different needs. The component evolves over time and so has different versions. Reusability also implies extensibility: it should be easy to reuse the component in a new context without always needing to modify it. The purpose of this characteristic is to make components useful beyond a single project.

Microservices are inherently reusable, because they're network services that can be called by anyone. There's no need to worry about code integration or library linking. Microservices address the versioning and extensibility requirement not by enhancing the capabilities of the individual microservice,[33] but by allowing the system to add new special-case microservices and then using message routing to trigger the right service. We'll talk about this in detail in chapter 3.

2.10.3 *Well-defined interfaces*

The interface offered by a component is the full definition of its contract with the outside world. This interface should have sufficient detail (but no more!) to allow the component to be interchangeable with other implementations and with other systems. The purpose of this characteristic is to enable free choice of components.

Microservices use messages, and only messages, to communicate with the outside world. These messages can be explicitly listed and their contents constrained as needed.[34] Microservices have well-defined (but not necessarily strict) interfaces by design.

2.10.4 *Composable*

The real power of components to accelerate software development comes not from reusability, which is merely a linear accelerator, but from combining components to do far more interesting things than each component can do separately. Components can be composed together into more capable components that themselves can be composed into larger systems.[35] The purpose of this characteristic is to make software development predictable by declaring the behavior of the system rather than constructing it.

Microservices are easily composable because the network flow of messages can be manipulated as desired. For example, one microservice can wrap another by intercepting all of the latter's messages, modifying them in some way, and passing them on to the wrapped service.

2.10.5 *Microservices in practice as components*

An example of the utility of microservices as components is the *wrapping cache* message interaction. This demonstrates service composition in particular, which is a powerful technique for extending live systems. In this example, an entity service, such as the *article* service from the newspaper system, supports activity messages for the underlying article data entity. Most of these are data-access messages. There's one weakness with the design that we arrived at: the *article* service needs to know about the *cache* service! This is extra logic. The *article* service would be smaller, and a better microservice, if it knew nothing about caches. Be on the lookout for these types of dependencies.

---

[33] Traditionally, component systems rely on API hooks for extensibility. This is an inherently nonscalable approach because it isn't homogeneous—every component and API hook is different.

[34] Resist the temptation to use message schemas and to enforce contracts between services. Doing so may seem like a good idea at the time, until you find yourself painted into a corner by your perfect schema. Microservices are for messy business logic, where strict schemas die every day.

[35] The most successful component architecture is UNIX pipes. By constraining the integration interface to be streams of bytes, individual command-line utilities can be composed into complex data-processing pipelines. The compositional power of this architecture is a major reason for the success of the operating system.

I created one here for the purposes of deconstructing it, but it's easy to end up with unnecessary dependencies.

An alternative configuration is to introduce an *article-cache* service that intercepts all the messages for the *article* service. It forwards most of them, but *get-article*, *add-article*, and *remove-article* messages also cause *article-cache* to inject and remove articles from the cache. From the perspective of the rest of the system, article messages are handled the same way; nothing has changed. Yet we get caching of articles! We've composed the *article-cache* and *article* services together.

To get this to work in practice, you need to orchestrate message interactions. Typically, you'll want to make this type of change to a system running in production, without service interruption. One way to do this is to use an intelligent load balancer in front of the *article* service. To add *article-cache*, as shown in figure 2.9, update the configuration of the load balancer. You'll need a load balancer that can handle live configuration changes.[36]

Another way is to use a message queue.[37] You could introduce *article-cache* as another subscriber and then remove the *article* service from direct contact with the

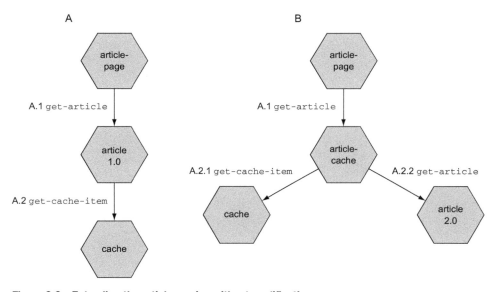

Figure 2.9 Extending the article service without modification

---

[36] Load balancers specifically built for microservices are the best choice here. Try Eureka (https://github.com/Netflix/eureka), Synapse (https://github.com/airbnb/synapse), and Baker Street (http://bakerstreet.io).

[37] Message queues are asynchronous by design, but that doesn't mean message flows over them are inherently asynchronous. Synchronous messages are those that require a response so that the client can continue working. They can be delivered via a message queue using request and response topics for each message type, or by embedding a return path network address as metadata in the request message.

message queue (as per the steps shown in figure 2.10). The *article-cache* and *article* services would then communicate point to point. Or you could use a separate message queue topic if you wanted to avoid the service discovery overhead.

A very important principle to note here is this: to enhance and modify the functionality of the system with respect to article caching, you don't extend existing services.[38] You don't make existing services more complex. The principle actions are to add and remove services, one at a time, to and from the live system, without service

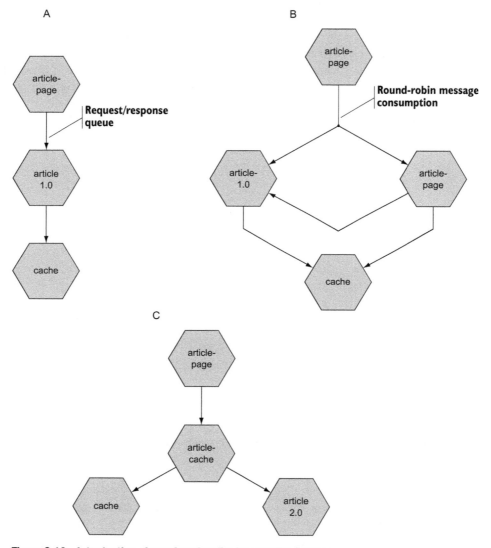

Figure 2.10   Introduction of new functionality into the live system

---

[38] In fact, you reduce the complexity of the *article* service.

interruption. At each step, you can verify the system by measuring its behavior and making sure nothing is broken. Then, at each step, if you did break something, you can easily roll back to a known good state. This is how microservices make deployments risk free.

2.11 *The internal structure of a microservice*

The primary purpose of a microservice is to implement business logic. You should be able to concentrate on this purpose. You shouldn't have to concern yourself with service discovery, logging, fault tolerance, and other standard behaviors; those are perfect candidates for framework or infrastructure code.

Microservices need a communications layer for messages. This should completely abstract the sending and receiving of messages, and the knowledge of where those messages need to go. As soon as one microservice knows about another, you have coupling, and you're on a slippery slope to a fragile system. Message delivery should be transport independent: messages can travel over any medium, whether it's HTTP, a message bus, raw TCP, web sockets, or anything else. This abstraction is the most important piece of infrastructure code.

In addition, microservices need a way to record behavior and errors. This means they need logging and a way to report their status. These are essentially the same, and a microservice shouldn't concern itself with the details of log files or event reporting. In particular, microservices need to be able to fail fast, and fail loudly, so that the system and the team can take action quickly. A logging and reporting abstraction is also essential.[39]

Microservices also need an executive function. They should let service registries know about their existence so they can be managed. They should be able to accept external commands from administration and control functions in the system. Although communications and logging layers can often be provided by standalone libraries that you link into your services, the executive function depends on more-complex interactions with your custom administration and control functions. These layers must also play nicely with your deployment strategy and tooling. We'll examine this in more detail in chapter 5.

2.12 *Summary*

- The homogeneous nature of microservices makes them highly suitable as a fundamental unit of software construction. They're practical units of functionality, planning, measuring, specification, and deployment. This characteristic arises from the fact that they're uniform in size and complexity and are restricted to using messages to communicate with the outside world.

- A strict definition of the term *microservice* is too limiting. Rather, you generate ideas and expand the space of potential solutions by taking a more holistic viewpoint from a position of deeper understanding.

---

[39] Using containers to deploy your microservices is a great way to get this type of tooling for free.

- Microservice architectures fall into two broad categories: synchronous (typically REST web services) and asynchronous (typically via a message queue). Neither is a full solution, and production systems are often hybrids.

- Monolithic architectures create three negative outcomes. They need more team coordination, causing management overhead; they suffer from higher levels of technical debt, causing development speed to stall; and they're high risk because deployments affect the entire system.

- The small size of microservices has positive outcomes. Estimation is more accurate, because microservices are mostly the same size; code is disposable, eliminating egocentric developer behaviors; and the system is dynamically configurable and so can more readily handle the unexpected.

- There are two types of code: business logic and infrastructure libraries. They have very different needs. Microservices are for business logic, because they can handle the fuzzy, ever-changing requirements.

- To design a microservice system, start with requirements, express them as messages, and then group the messages into services. Then think about how messages are handled by services: Synchronously or asynchronously? Observed or consumed?

- Microservices are natural software components. They are encapsulated and reusable, have well-defined interfaces, and, most important, can be composed together.

Messages

This chapter covers

- Using messages as the key to designing microservice architectures
- Deciding when to go synchronous, and when to go asynchronous
- Pattern matching and transport independence
- Examining patterns for microservice message interactions
- Understanding failure modes of microservice interactions

The term *microservices* invites you to think in terms of services. You'll naturally be drawn to ask, "What are the microservices in this system?" Resist that temptation. Microservice systems are powerful because they allow you to think in terms of messages. If you take a messages-first approach to your system design, you free yourself from premature implementation decisions. The intended behavior of the system can be described in terms of a language of messages, independent of the underlying microservices that generate and react to those messages.

3.1   *Messages are first-class citizens*

A messages-first approach is more useful than a services-first approach to system design. Messages are a direct expression of intent. Business requirements are expressed as the activities that should happen in the system. Strangely, we're traditionally taught to extract the nouns from business requirements, so that we can build objects. Are business requirements that obscure? Perhaps we should pay more attention to the activities they describe.

If break business requirements down into activities, this naturally suggests the messages within the system; see table 3.1. Messages represent actions, not things. Take, for example, a typical e-commerce website. You put some items in your shopping cart, and then you proceed to the checkout. On checkout, the system records the purchase, sends you an email confirmation, and sends the warehouse delivery instructions, among other things. Doesn't that naturally break down into some obvious activities?

Table 3.1   Messages representing activities

Activity description	Message name	Message data
Checking out	*checkout*	Cart items and prices
Recording the purchase	*record-purchase*	Cart items and prices; sales tax and total; customer details
Sending an email confirming the purchase	*checkout-email*	Recipient; cart summary; template identifier
Delivering the goods	*deliver-cart*	Cart items; customer address

How about this: checking out, recording the purchase, sending an email confirming the purchase, delivering the goods. You're one step away from the messages that contain the data that describe these activities. Write down the activities in a table, write down a code name for the activity (which gives you a name for the message), and write down the data contents of the message. By doing this, you can see that there's no need at this level of analysis to think about which services handle these messages.

Analytical thinking, using messages as a primitive element, can *scale*, in the sense that you can develop a good understanding of the system design at this level.[1] Designing the system using services as the primitive element doesn't scale in the same way. Although there are fewer kinds of services than messages, in practice it's hard not to think of them from the perspective of network architecture. You have to decide which services talk to which other services, which services handle which messages, and whether services observe or consume messages. You end up having to think about many more different kinds of things. Even worse, you lock yourself into architectural decisions. And your thinking is static from the start, rather than allowing you to adapt message behavior as requirements change and emerge.

---

[1]   The quality of *good* in this sense means your understanding generates "true" statements: that is, statements the business stakeholders agree with.

Messages are just one kind of thing. They're homogeneous entities. Thinking about them is easy. You can list them, and you can list the messages that each message generates, so you have a natural description of causality. You can group and regroup messages to organize them conceptually, which may suggest appropriate services to generate or handle those messages. Messages provide a conceptual level that bridges informal business requirements and formal, technical, system specifications. In particular, messages make services and their communication arrangements of less interest—these are implementation details.

The three-step analytical strategy discussed in this book (requirements to messages to services) is shown in figure 3.1.

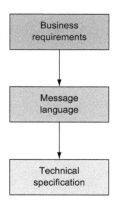

Figure 3.1 Conceptual levels of system design

3.1.1 Synchronous and asynchronous

Microservice messages fall into two broad types: synchronous and asynchronous. A synchronous message is composed of two parts: a request and a response. The request is the primary aspect of the message, and the response is secondary. Synchronous messages are often implemented as HTTP calls, because the HTTP protocol is such a neat fit to the request/response model. An asynchronous message doesn't have a directly associated response. It's emitted by a service and observed or consumed later by other services.

The essential difference between synchronous and asynchronous messages isn't in the nature of the message transfer protocol; it's in the intent of the originating microservice. The originator of a synchronous message needs an immediate response to continue its work and is blocked until it gets a response. The originator of an asynchronous message isn't blocked, is prepared to wait for results, and can handle scenarios where there are no results:[2]

- *Synchronous*—A *shopping-cart* service, when adding a product to a cart, needs the *sales-tax* service to calculate the updated sales tax before providing a new total to the user. The scenario is a natural fit for a synchronous message.
- *Asynchronous*—Alternatively, to display a list of recommended products below the current shopping cart, the *recommendation* service first issues a message asking for recommendations. Call this a *need* message. Multiple recommendation services, using different algorithms, may respond with messages containing recommendations. The *recommendation* service needs to collect all of these recommendations, so call these *collect* messages. The *recommendation* service can aggregate all the *collect* messages it receives to generate the list of recommendations. It may receive none, in which case it falls back to some default behavior (say, offering a random list of recommendations, after a timeout).

---

[2] Microservices don't need to wait on human time scales. The waiting period could be on the order of milliseconds.

Synchronous and asynchronous messages are convertible

Workflows that use synchronous messages can always be converted to workflows that use asynchronous messages. Any synchronous message can be broken into explicit request and response messages, which are asynchronous. Any asynchronous message that triggers messages in reaction can be aggregated into a single synchronous message that blocks, waiting for the first response.

Beware: Moving between these message workflows requires refactoring of your microservices. The decision to make a given message type synchronous or asynchronous is a core design decision and an expression of your intent as an architect.

3.1.2   *When to go synchronous*

The synchronous style is well suited to the command pattern, where messages are commands to do something. The response is an acknowledgment that the thing to be done, was done, with such-and-such results. Activities that fit this model include data-storage and data-manipulation operations, instructions to and from external services, serial workflows, control instructions, and, perhaps most commonly, instructions from user interfaces.

The user-interface question

Should user interfaces be built using the microservice architecture? At the time of this writing, this is an open question, because there are no viable examples in the wild, especially at scale. User interface implementations are monolithic in nature as a matter of practicality. This isn't to say that the flexibility of the microservice approach as an inspiration for a user interface component model isn't credible, nor does it preclude a message-oriented approach. Nonetheless, the microservice architecture is driven by a very different set of needs and requirements: those relating to building scalable systems at an accelerated pace of development.

This book takes an open-minded position on this question. As the philosopher Ludwig Wittgenstein said, "Whereof one cannot speak, thereof one must be silent."[3]

Synchronous messages are a naturalistic style and can often be the first design that comes to mind. In many cases, a serial workflow of synchronous messages can be unwound into a parallel set of asynchronous messages. For example, when building a complete content page of a website, each content unit is a mostly independent rectangular area. In a traditional monolith, such pages are often built with simple linear code that blocks, waiting for each item of content to be retrieved. It's more effort to put in place infrastructure code to parallelize the page construction. In a microservice context, a first cut of the page-construction service might work the same way by issuing

---

[3] From Ludwig Wittgenstein's *Tractatus Logico-Philosophicus* (1922), one of the most hard-line works of early twentieth century positivist philosophy. This is a dangerous quote, because it may be a fair assessment of this entire book!

content-retrieval messages in series, following the linear mental model of the monolith. But because the microservice context offers an asynchronous model as well, and because the page-construction service is isolated from the rest of the system, it's far less effort to rewrite the service to use a parallel approach.[4] Thus, it shouldn't be a matter of much anxiety if you find yourself designing a system that uses synchronous messages to a significant degree.

Business requirements that are expressed as explicit workflows tend to need synchronous messages as part of their implementation. You've already seen such a workflow in the example of the e-commerce checkout process. Such workflows contain gates that prevent further work unless specific operations have completed, and this maps well to the request/response mental model. Traditionally, heavyweight solutions are often used to define such workflows; but in the microservice world, the correct approach is to encode the workflow directly in a special-purpose orchestrating microservice. In practice, this orchestration typically involves both synchronous and asynchronous elements.

Synchronous messages do have drawbacks. They create stronger coupling between services. They can often be seen as remote procedure calls, and adopting this mindset leads to the distributed monolith anti-pattern. A bias toward synchronous messages can lead to deep service dependency trees, where an original inbound message triggers a cascade of multilevel synchronous submessages. This is inherently fragile. Finally, synchronous messages block code execution while waiting for a response. In thread-based language platforms,[5] this can lead to complete failure if all message-handling threads become blocked. In event-based platforms,[6] the problem is less severe but is still a waste of compute resources.

3.1.3 *When to go asynchronous*

The asynchronous style takes a little getting used to. You have to stop thinking in terms of the programming model of function calls that return results, and start thinking in a more event-driven style. The payoff is much greater flexibility. It's easier to add new microservices to an asynchronous interaction. The trade-off is that interactions are no longer linear chains of causality.

The asynchronous approach is particularly strong when you need to extend the system to handle new business requirements. By announcing key pieces of information, you allow other microservices to react appropriately without needing any knowledge of those services. Returning to the earlier example, a shopping cart service can announce the fact that a checkout has occurred by publishing a *checkout* message. Microservices that store a record of the purchase, send out confirmation emails, and perform delivery can each listen for this message independently. There's no need for specific command messages to trigger these activities, nor is there a need for the *shopping-cart* service to know about these

---

[4] This is a good example of the ease of refactoring when you use microservices; a similar refactoring inside a monolith would involve much code munging (to use the technical term). In the microservice case, refactoring is mostly reconfiguration of message interactions.

[5] Such as the Java JVM or .NET CLR.

[6] Node.js is the prime example.

other services. This makes it easier to add new activities, such as a microservice to add loy-alty points, because no changes are required to existing production services.

As a general principle, even when you're using synchronous messages, you should consider also publishing asynchronous information messages. Such messages announce a new fact about the world that others can choose to act on. This gives you an extremely decoupled, extensible architecture.

The drawback of this approach is the implicit nature of the system's behavior. As the number of messages and microservices grows, understanding of all the system interactions will be lost. The system will begin to exhibit emergent behavior and may develop unde-sired modes of behavior. These risks can be mitigated by a strictly incremental approach to system change twinned with meaningful measurement of system behavior. Microser-vices can't evaporate inherent complexity, but at least they make it more observable.

3.1.4 *Thinking distributed from day one*

Microservice systems are distributed systems. Distributed systems present difficult prob-lems that are often intractable. When faced with such challenges, there's a psychological tendency to pretend they don't exist and to hope that they'll just go away by themselves. This style of thinking is the reason many distributed computing frameworks try to make remote and local appear the same: remote procedures and remote objects are pre-sented behind facades that make them look local.[7] This approach trades temporary relief for ongoing insanity. Hiding inherent complexity and the fundamental properties of a system makes the architecture fragile and subject to catastrophic failure modes.

> ### Fallacies of distributed computing
> The following fallacies are a warning to programmers everywhere to tread carefully when you take your first steps into the world of distributed computing. They were first outlined informally by David Deutsch (a Sun Microsystems engineer) in 1994:
>
> - The network is reliable.
> - Latency is zero.
> - Bandwidth is infinite.
> - The network is secure.
> - Topology doesn't change.
> - There's one administrator.
> - Transport cost is zero.
> - The network is homogeneous.
>
> Microservices don't allow you to escape from these fallacies. It's a feature of the microservice world view that we embrace the warnings of the fallacies rather than try to solve them.[8]

---

[7] This is a feature of approaches such as Java RMI and CORBA.

[8] For a wonderfully sardonic discussion of the fallacies, you won't do better than Arnon Rotem-Gal-Oz's paper "Fallacies of Distributed Computing Explained," www.rgoarchitects.com/Files/fallacies.pdf.

No matter how good your code is, distributed computing will always be difficult. This is because there are fundamental logical limits on the ability of distributed systems to communicate consistently. A good illustration is the problem of the Byzantine Generals.[9]

Let's start with two generals of the Byzantine Empire: one is the leader, and the other is a follower. Each general commands an army of 1,000 soldiers on opposite sides of an enemy army of 1,500. If they both attack at the same time, their combined force of 2,000 will be victorious. To attack alone will ensure certain defeat. The leader must choose the time of the attack. To communicate, the generals can send messengers who sneak through enemy lines. Some of these messengers will be captured, but the messages are secured with an unbreakable secret code.

The problem is this: what pattern of messages can be used to guarantee that the two generals attack at the same time? A simple protocol suggests itself immediately: require an acknowledgment of each message. But the acknowledgment requires a messenger, who could be captured. And even if the acknowledgment does arrive, the sender doesn't know this.

Place yourself in the position of the follower. You receive this message: "Attack at dawn!" You acknowledge the message by sending back a messenger of your own. Dawn arrives—do you attack?

What if your acknowledgment messenger was captured? You have no way of knowing if they arrived safely. And your leader has no way of knowing what you know. You'll both reach the logical conclusion not to attack, even though all messages have been successfully delivered! More acknowledgments won't help. The last general to send a message can never be sure of its delivery.

For more fun and games, you can increase the number of generals, question the trustworthiness and sanity of both generals and messengers, allow the enemy to subvert or invent messages, and so on. The general case of the Byzantine Generals problem isn't so far from the reality of running a large-scale microservices deployment!

Pragmatically, this problem is solved by accepting that certainty isn't possible and then asking how many messages, of what kind, subject to limits such as timeouts, with what meta-information such as sequence numbers, can be used to establish an acceptable level of probability that agreement has been reached. The TCP/IP protocol is a fine example of such a solution.[10]

The key point is that you must accept the unreliable nature of message transmission between microservices. Your design thinking can never be based on an assumption that messages will be delivered as you intend them to be delivered. This assumption isn't safe. Messages aren't like method calls in a monolithic application,

---

[9] Leslie Lamport, Robert Shostak, and Marshall Pease, "The Byzantine Generals Problem," *ACM Transactions on Programming Languages and Systems* 4, no. 3 (July 1982), www.cs.cornell.edu/courses/cs614/2004sp/papers/lsp82.pdf. This seminal paper explains the basis of distributed consensus.

[10] Transmission Control Protocol/Internet Protocol (TCP/IP) uses algorithms such as slow start (increasing data volume until maximum capacity is found) and exponential backoff (waiting longer and longer when retrying sends) to achieve an acceptable level of transmission reliability.

where the metaphor of objects exchanging messages is just that: a metaphor. In a distributed system, message delivery can't be made reliable.

What you *can* do is make message delivery—and, indirectly, system behavior—predictable to within acceptable tolerances. You can limit failure by spending money and time. It's your job, and your responsibility as an engineer, to deliver systems to agreed tolerances.

3.1.5 *Tactics to limit failure*

Just because failure is inevitable doesn't mean you can't do anything about it. As an ethical engineer, you should know and apply reasonable mitigating tactics:

- *Message delivery will be unreliable.* Accept that this is a reality and will happen. You can get closer to 100% reliability by spending ever-larger sums of money, but you'll suffer from diminishing marginal returns, and you'll never get to 100%. Always ask, "What happens if this message is lost?" Timeouts, duplication, logging, and other mitigations can help, but not if you aren't asking that question.
- *Latency and throughput are trade-offs.* Latency tells you how quickly messages are acted on (most commonly, by measuring the response time of synchronous messages). Low latency is a legitimate goal. Throughput tells you how many messages you can handle. High throughput is also a legitimate goal. To a first approximation, these goals are inversely related. Designing a system for high throughput means you need to put in place scalability housekeeping (such as proxy servers) that increases latency, because there are extra network hops. Conversely, designing for low latency means high throughput, although possible, will be much more expensive (for example, you might be using more-powerful machines).
- *Bandwidth matters.* The networked nature of microservice systems means they're vulnerable to bandwidth limitations. Even if you start out with a plentiful supply, you must adopt a mentality of scarcity. Misbehaving microservices can easily cause an internally generated denial-of-service attack. Keep your messages small and lean. Don't use them to send much data; send references to bulk data storage, instead.[11] Bandwidth as a resource is becoming cheaper and more plentiful, but we aren't yet in a post-scarcity world.
- *Security doesn't stop at the firewall.* You may be tempted to engage in security theater, such as encrypting all interservice messages. Or you might be forced into it by your clients. In some ways, this is mostly harmless, although it does drain resources. It's more effective to adopt the stance, within each microservice, that inbound messages are potentially malign and may come from malicious actors. Semantic attacks[12] are your primary concern. Microservices are naturally more resistant to syntactic attacks because they offer a significantly reduced attack

---

[11] To send an image between services, don't send the image binary data, send a URL pointing to the image.

[12] Explained in detail by Bruce Schneier, a respected security expert, on his blog: "Semantic Attacks: The Third Wave of Network Attacks," *Schneier on Security*, October 15, 2000, http://mng.bz/Ai4Q.

surface—you can only get in via messages. Semantic attacks, in the form of malicious messages generated by improper external interactions, are the principle attack vector. Message schema validation won't help here, because the dangerous messages are exactly those that work and are, by definition, syntactically correct.

- *Avoid local solutions to global problems.* Let's say you've decided to use a synchronous approach to microservices, with HTTP REST as the message transport. Every microservice needs to know the network location of every other microservice it wants to talk to, because it has to direct those HTTP requests somewhere. So what do you do? *Verschlimmbessern!*[13] Obviously, a distributed key store running some sort of distributed shared-state consensus algorithm will give you a service-discovery solution, and problem solved! It isn't that this is not a legitimate solution; the real question is whether the problem (service discovery) is one you should be solving in the first place.

- *Automate or die.* There's no such thing as a free lunch. For all the benefits of microservices, you can't escape the fact that you have to manage lots of little things spread over many servers. Traditional tools and approaches won't work, because they can't handle the ramp-up in complexity. You'll need to use automation that scales. More on this in chapter 5.

3.2 Case study: Sales tax rules

Our case study in this chapter focuses on one part of the work of building a general e-commerce solution: calculating sales tax. This may not seem very challenging, but a full solution has wonderful hidden depths.

To set the scene, imagine a successful company that has grown quickly and offers products in multiple categories and geographies. The company started out selling one type of good in one country; but then things took off, and the company quickly had to adapt to rapid growth. For the sake of argument, let's imagine this company began by selling books online and then branched into electronics, shoes, and online services.[14]

Here's the business problem when it comes to sales tax: you have to account for differences based on many variables. For example, determining the correct rate might involve the category of good, the country of the seller, the country of the buyer, the location in the country of either, local bylaws, the date and time of the purchase, and so on. You need a way to take in all of these variables and generate the right result.

3.2.1 The wider context

An e-commerce website is a good example of a common problem space for microservices. There's a user interface that must be low latency, and there's a backend that has

---

[13] One of those wonderful German loan words, perhaps even better than *schadenfreude*. To *verschlimmbessern* is to make something much worse by earnestly trying to make it better, all the while blissfully ignoring the real problem.

[14] Our example is deliberately implausible. Such a thing would never catch on.

a set of horizontal and vertical functionalities. *Horizontal functionalities*, such as user account management, transactional email workflows, and data storage, are mostly similar for many different kinds of applications. *Vertical functionalities* are particular to the business problem at hand; in the e-commerce case, these are functionalities such as the shopping cart, order fulfillment, and the product catalog.

Horizontal functionalities can often be implemented using a standard set of prebuilt microservices. Over time, you should invest in developing such a set of functionalities, because they can be used in many applications, thus kick-starting your development. While working on this project, you'll almost certainly extend, enhance, and obsolesce these starter microservices, because they won't be sufficient for full delivery. How to do this in a safe way, with pattern matching on messages, is one of the core techniques we'll explore in this chapter.

Vertical microservices start as greenfield implementations, which makes them even more vulnerable to obsolescence. You'll invariably make incorrect assumptions about the business domain. You'll also misunderstand the depth of the requirements. The requirements will change in any case, because business stakeholders develop a deeper understanding too. To deal with this, you can use the same strategic approach as with horizontals: pattern matching. And for verticals, it's a vital strategy to avoid running up technical debt.

3.3   *Pattern matching*

Pattern matching is one of the key strategies for building scalable microservice architectures—not just technically scalable, but also psychologically scalable, so that human software developers can understand the system. A large part of the complexity of microservice systems comes from the question of how to route messages. When a microservice emits a message, where should it go? And when you're designing the system, how should you specify these routes?

The traditional way to describe network relationships, by defining the dependencies and data flows between services, doesn't work well for microservices. There are too many services and too many messages. The solution is to turn the problem on its head. Start instead from the properties of the messages, and allow the network architecture to emerge dynamically from there.

In the e-commerce example, some messages will interact with the shopping cart. There's a subset of messages in the message language that the shopping cart would like to receive: say, *add-product*, *remove-product*, and *checkout*. Ultimately, all messages are collections of data. You can think of them as collections of key-value pairs. Imagine an all-seeing messaging deity that observes all messages and, by identifying the key-value pairs, sends the messages to the correct service.

Message routing can be reduced to the following simple steps:

1 Represent the message as key-value pairs (regardless of the actual message data).
2 Map key-value pairs to microservices, using the simplest algorithm you can think of.

The way you represent the message as key-value pairs isn't important. Key-value pairs are just the lowest-common-denominator data representation that has enough information to be useful. The algorithm isn't important; but as a practical matter, it should be easy enough for fallible humans to run in their heads.

This approach—routing based on message properties—has been used many ways; it isn't a new idea. Any form of intelligent proxying is an example. What's new is the explicit decision to use it as the common basis for message routing. This means you have a homogeneous solution to the problem and no special cases. Understanding the system reduces to reviewing the list of messages and the patterns used to route them; this can even be done in isolation from the services that will receive them!

The big benefit of this approach is that you no longer need metainformation to route a message; you don't need a service address. Service addresses come in many flavors—some not so obvious. A domain name is obviously an address, but so is a REST URL. The topic or channel name on a message bus and the location of the bus on the network are also addresses. The port number representing a remote service, exposed by an overlay network, is still an address! Microservices shouldn't know about other microservices.

To be clear, addressing information has to exist somewhere. It exists in the configuration of the abstraction layer that you use to send and receive messages. Although this requires work to configure, it isn't the same as having that information embedded in the service. From a microservice perspective, messages arrive and depart, and they can be any messages. If the service knows how to deal with a message, because it recognizes that message in some way, all to the good; but it's that microservice's business alone. The mapping from patterns to delivery routes is an implementation detail.

Let's explore the consequences of this approach. You'll see how it makes it much easier to focus on solving the business problem, rather than obsessing about accidental technical details.

3.3.1 Sales tax: starting simple

Let's start with the business requirement for handling sales tax. We'll focus narrowly on the requirement to recalculate sales tax after an item is added to the cart.

When a user adds a product to their shopping cart, they should see an updated cart listing all the products they previously added together with the new one. The cart should also have an entry for total sales tax due.[15] Let's use a synchronous *add-product* message that responds with an updated cart and a synchronous *calculate-sales-tax* message that responds with the gross price, to model this business requirement. We won't concern ourselves with the underlying services.

The list of messages has only two entries:

- *add-product*—Triggers *calculate-sales-tax*, and contains details of the product and cart
- *calculate-sales-tax*—Triggers nothing, and contains the net price and relevant details of the product

---

[15] For our purposes, consider value-added tax (VAT, as used in Europe) to be calculated in the same way.

Let's focus on the *calculate-sales-tax*—what properties might it have?

- Net price
- Product category
- Customer location
- Time of purchase
- Others you haven't thought of

The microservice architecture allows you to put this question to one side. You don't need to think about it much, because you're not trying to solve everything at once. The best practice is to build the simplest possible implementation you can think of: solve the simple, general case first.

Let's make some simplifying assumptions. You're selling one type of product in one country, and this fully defines the sales tax rate to apply. You can handle the *calculate-sales-tax* message by writing a *sales-tax* microservice that responds synchronously. It applies a fixed rate, hardcoded into the service, to the net price, to generate a gross price: `gross = net * rate`.

Let's also return to the useful fiction that every microservice sees every message. How does the *sales-tax* microservice recognize *calculate-sales-tax* messages? Which properties are relevant? In fact, there's nothing special about the properties listed previously. There isn't enough information to distinguish this message from others that also contain product details, such as *add-product* messages. The simple answer is to label the message. This isn't a trick question: labels are a valid ways to namespace the set of messages. Let's give *calculate-sales-tax* messages a label with the string value `"sales-tax"`.

The label allows you to perform pattern matching. All messages that match the pattern `label:sales-tax` go to the *sales-tax* microservice. You're careful not to say how that happens in terms of data flowing over the network; nor are you saying where that intelligence lies. You're only concerned with defining a pattern that can pick out messages you care about.

Here's an example message:

```
label: sales-tax
net: 1.00
```

The *sales-tax* service, with a hardcoded rate of, say, 10%, responds like this:

```
gross: 1.10
```

What is the pattern-matching algorithm? There's no best choice. The best practice is to keep it simple. In this example, you might say, "Match the value of the `label` property." As straightforward as that.

3.3.2 *Sales tax: handling categories*

Different categories of products can have different sales tax rates. Many countries have special, reduced sales tax rates that apply only to certain products or only in certain situations. Luckily, you include a category property in your messages. If you didn't, you'd have to add one anyway. In general, if you're missing information in your messages, you update the microservice generating those messages first, so that the new information is present even if nobody is using it. Of course, if you use strict message schemas, this is much more difficult. It's precisely this type of flexibility that microservices enable; by having a general rule that you ignore new properties you don't understand, the system can continue functioning.

To support different rates for different product categories, a simple approach is to modify the existing *sales-tax* microservice so that it has a lookup table for the different rates. You keep the pattern matching the same. Now you can deploy the new version of *sales-tax* in a systematic fashion, ensuring a smooth transition from the old rules to the new. Depending on your use case, you might tolerate some discrepancies during the transition, or you might use feature flags in your messages to trigger the new rules once everything is in place.

An alternative approach is to write a new *sales-tax* microservice for each category. This is a better approach in the long term. With the right automation and management in place, the marginal cost of adding new microservices is low. Initially, they'll be simple—effectively, just duplicates of the single-rate service with a different hardcoded rate.

You might feel uneasy about this suggestion. Surely these are now *nanoservices*; it feels like the granularity is too fine. Isn't a lookup table of categories and rates sufficient? But the lookup table is an open door to technical debt. It's a data structure that models the world and must be maintained. As new complexities arise, it will need to be extended and modified. The alternative—using separate microservices—keeps the code simple and linear.

The statement of the business problem was misleading. Yes, different product categories have different sales tax rates. But if you look at the details, every tax code of every country in the world contains a morass of subdivisions, special cases, and exclusions, and legislatures add more every day. It's impossible to know what business rules you'll need to apply using your lookup table data model. And after a few iterations, you'll be stuck with that model, because it will be internally complex.

Separating the product categories into separate microservices is a good move when faced with this type of business rule instability. At first, it seems like overkill, and you're definitely breaking the DRY principle, but it quickly pays dividends. The code in each microservice is more concrete, and the algorithmic complexity is lower.

With this approach, the next question is how to route messages to the new microservices. Pattern matching again comes into play. Let's use a better, but still simple, algorithm. Each sales-tax microservice examines inbound messages and responds to them if they have a `label:sales-tax` property and a category property whose value matches the category they can handle. For example, the message

```
label: sales-tax
net: 1.00
category: standard
```

is handled by the existing *sales-tax* microservice. But the message

```
label: sales-tax
net: 1.00
category: reduced
```

is handled by the *sales-tax-reduced* microservice. The mapping between patterns and services is listed table 3.2.

Table 3.2   Pattern to service mapping

Pattern	Microservice
`label:sales-tax`	*sales-tax*
`label:sales-tax,category:standard`	*sales-tax*
`label:sales-tax,category:reduced`	*sales-tax-reduced*

Notice that the general-case microservice, *sales-tax*, handles messages that have no category. The calculation may be incorrect, but you'll get something back, rather than failure. If you're going for availability rather than consistency, this is an acceptable trade-off.

It's the responsibility of the underlying microservice messaging implementation to adhere to these pattern-matching rules. Perhaps you'll hardcode them into a thin layer over a message queue API. Or maybe you'll use the patterns to construct message-queue topics. Or you can use a discovery service that responds with a URL to call for any given message. For now, the key idea is this: choose a simple pattern-matching algorithm, and use it to declaratively define which types of messages should be handled by which types of services. You're thus communicating your intent as architect of the microservice system.

The pattern-matching algorithm

You might ask, "Which pattern-matching algorithm should I use? How complex should it be?" The answer is, as simple as possible. You should be able to scan the list of pattern-to-microservice mappings and manually assign any given message to a microservice based on the content of the message. There's no magic pattern-matching algorithm that suits all cases. The Seneca framework[16] used for the case study in chapter 9 uses the following algorithm:

- Each pattern picks out a finite set of top-level properties by name.
- The value of each property is considered to be a character string.
- A message matches a pattern if all property values match under string equality.
- Patterns with more properties have precedence over patterns with fewer.
- Patterns with the same number of properties use alphabetical precedence.

---

[16] I'm the maintainer of this open source project. See http://senecajs.org.

(continued)

Given the following pattern-to-microservice mapping:

- a:0 maps to microservice *A*.
- b:1 maps to microservice *B*.
- a:0,b:1 maps to microservice *A*.
- a:0,c:2 maps to microservice *C*.

The following messages will be mapped as indicated:

- Message {a:0, x:9} goes to *A*.
- Matches pattern a:0, because property a in the message has value 0.
- Message {b:1, x:8} goes to *B*.
- Matches pattern b:1, because property b in the message has value 1.
- Message {a:0, b:1, x:7} goes to *A*.
- Matches pattern a:0,b:1 rather than a:0 or b:1, because a:0,b:1 has more properties.
- Message {a:1, b:1, x:6} goes to *B*.
- Matches pattern b:1, because property b in the message has value 1, and there's no pattern for a:1.
- Message {a:0, c:2, x:5} goes to *C*.
- Matches pattern a:0,c:2 by the values of properties a and c.
- Message {a:0, b:1, c:2, x:9} goes to *A*.
  - Matches pattern a:0,b:1 by the values of properties a and b but not c, because b is before c alphabetically.

In all of these cases, property x is data and isn't used for pattern matching. That said, there's nothing to prevent future patterns from using x, should it become necessary due to emerging requirements.

3.3.3 Sales tax: going global

The business grows, as businesses do. This creates the proverbial nice problem to have: the business wants to expand into international markets. The e-commerce system now needs to handle sales tax in a wide range of countries. How do you do this? It's a classic case of combinatorial explosion, in that you have to think in terms of per-country, per-category rules.

The traditional strategy is to refactor the data models and try to accommodate the complexity in the models. It's an empirical observation that this leads to technical debt; the traditional approach leads to traditional problems. Alternatively, if you follow the microservice approach, you end up with per-country, per-category microservices. Doesn't the number of microservices increase exponentially as you add parameters?

In reality, there's a natural limit on this combinatorial explosion: the natural complexity size of an individual microservice. We explored this in chapter 2 and agreed that it's about one week of developer effort, perhaps coarsely graded by skill level. This fact means you'll tend to build data models up to this level of complexity, but no further. And many of these data models can handle multiple combinations of messages.

Certain countries have similar systems with similar business rules. These can be handled by a microservice with that dreaded lookup table. But exceptions and special cases won't be handled by extending the model: instead, you'll write a special-case microservice.

Let's look at an example. Most European Union countries use the standard and reduced-rates structure. So, let's build an *eu-vat* microservice that uses a lookup table keyed by country and category. If this seems heretical, given the existing *sales-tax* and *sales-tax-reduced* microservices, you could be right—you may need to embrace the heresy, end-of-life those services, and use a different approach. This isn't a problem! You can run both models at the same time and use pattern matching to route messages appropriately.

3.3.4 *Business requirements change, by definition*

Any approach to software development that expects business requirements to remain constant over the course of a project is doomed to deliver weak results. Even projects that have strict, contract-defined specifications suffer from requirement drift. Words on paper are always subject to reinterpretation, so you can take for granted that the initial business requirements will change almost as soon as the ink is dry. They will also change during the project and after the project goes live.

The agile family of software project management methodologies attempts to deal with this reality by using a set of working practices, that encourages flexibility. The agile working practices—iterations, unit testing, pair programming, refactoring, and so on—are useful, but they can't overcome the weight of technical debt that accumulates in monolithic systems. Unit testing, in particular, is meant to enable refactoring, but in practice it doesn't achieve this effectively.

Why is refactoring a monolithic code base difficult? Because monolithic code bases enable the growth of complex data structures. The ease of access to internal representations of the data model means it's easy to extend and enhance. Even if the poor project architect initially defines strict API boundaries, there's no strong defense against sharing data and structures. In the heat of battle, rules are broken to overcome project deadlines.

The microservice architecture is far less vulnerable to this effect, because it's much harder for one microservice to reach inside another and interfere with its data structures. Messages naturally tend to be small. Large messages aren't efficient when transported over the network. A natural force makes messages concise, including only the data that's needed, and in the form of simpler data structures.

Combined, the small size of microservices, the smaller size of messages, and the resulting lower complexity of data structures internal to microservices result in an architecture that's easier to refactor. This ease derives from the engineering approach, rather than project management discipline, and so is robust in response to variances in team size, ability, and politics.

3.3.5   *Pattern matching lowers the cost of refactoring*

The pattern-matching tactic has a key role to play in making refactoring easier. When first building microservices, developers have a tendency to apply schema validation to the messages. This is an attempt to enforce a quality of correctness in the system, but it's misguided.

Consider the scenario where you want to upgrade a particular microservice. For scale, you might have multiple instances of the microservice running. Let's say this microservice is at version 1.0. You need to deploy version 2.0, which adds new functionality. The new functionality uses new fields in the messages that the microservice sends and receives.

Taking advantage of the deployment flexibility of microservices, you deploy a new instance of v2.0 while leaving the existing v1.0 instances running. This lets you monitor the system to see whether you've broken anything. Unfortunately, you have! The strict schema you're enforcing for v1.0 messages isn't compatible with the changes in v2.0, and you can't run both instances of the service at the same time. This negates one of the main reasons for using microservices in the first place.

Alternatively, you can use pattern matching. With pattern matching, as you've seen in the sales tax example, it's easy to modify the messages without breaking anything. Older microservices ignore new fields that they don't understand. Newer microservices can claim messages with new fields and operate on them correctly. It becomes much easier to refactor.

> **Postel's law**
>
> Jon Postel, who was instrumental in the design of the TCP/IP protocol (among others), espoused this principle: "Be conservative in what you do, be liberal in what you accept from others." This principle informed the design of TCP/IP. Formally, it's defined as being contravariant on input (that is, you accept supersets of the protocol specification) and covariant on output (you emit subsets of the protocol specification). This approach is a powerful way to ensure that many independent systems can continue to work well with one another. It's useful in the microservice world.

This style of refactoring has a natural safety feature. The production system is changed by adding and subtracting microservice instances, but it isn't changed by modifying code and redeploying. It's easier to control and measure possible side effects at the granularity level of the microservice—all changes occur at the same level, so every change can be monitored the same way. We'll discuss techniques for measuring microservice systems in chapter 6—in particular, how measurement can be used to lower deployment risk in a quantifiable way.

3.4   *Transport independence*

Microservices must communicate with each other, but this doesn't mean they need to *know* about each other. When a microservice knows about another microservice, this creates an explicit coupling. One of the strongest criticisms of the microservice architecture is that it's a more complex, less manageable version of traditional monolithic architectures. In this criticism, messages over the network are nothing more than elaborate remote procedure calls, and the system is a mess of dependencies—the so-called *distributed monolith*.

This problem arises if you consider the issue of identity to be essential. The naïve model of microservice communication is one where you need to know the identity of the microservice to which you want to send a message: you need the address of the receiving microservice. An architecture that uses direct HTTP calls for request/response messages suffers from this problem—you need a URL endpoint to construct your message-sending calls. Under this model, a message consists not only of the content of the message but also the identity of the recipient.

There's an alternative. Each microservice views the world as a universe from which it receives messages and to which it emits messages. But it has no knowledge of the senders or receivers. How is this possible? How do you ensure that messages go to the right place? This knowledge must exist somewhere. It does: in the configuration of the transport system for microservice messages. But ultimately, that's merely an implementation detail. The key idea is that microservices don't need to know about each other, how messages are transported from one microservice to another, or how many other microservices see the message. This is the idea of *transport independence*, and using it means your microservices can remain fully decoupled from each other.

3.4.1   *A useful fiction: the omnipotent observer*

Transport independence means you can defer consideration of practical networking questions. This is extremely powerful from the perspective of the microservice developer. It enables the false, but highly useful, assumption that any microservice can receive and send any message. This is useful because it allows you to separate the question of how messages are transported from the behavior of microservices.

With transport independence, you can map messages from the message language to microservices in a completely flexible way. You're free to create new microservices that group messages in new ways, without impacting the design or implementation of other microservices.

This is why you were able to work at the design level with the messages describing the e-commerce system, without first determining what services to build. Implicitly, you assumed that any service can see any messages, so you were free to assign messages to services at a late stage in the design process. You get even more confidence that you haven't painted yourself into a corner when you realize that this implicit assumption remains useful for production systems. Microservices are disposable, so reassigning messages to new services is low cost.

This magical routing of messages is enabled by dropping the idea that individual microservices have identities, and by using pattern matching to define the mapping from message to microservice. You can then fully describe the design of the system by listing the patterns that each microservice recognizes and emits. And as you've seen with the sales tax example, this is the place you want to be.

The implementation and physical transport of messages isn't something to neglect—it's a real engineering problem that any system, particularly large systems, must deal with. But microservices should be written *as if* transport is an independent consideration. This means you're free to use any transport mechanism, from HTTP to messages queues, and free to change the transport mechanism at any time.

You also get the freedom to change the way messages are distributed. Messages may be participants in request/response patterns, publish/subscribe patterns, actor patterns, or any other variant, without reference to the microservices. Microservices neither know nor care who else interacts with messages.

In the real world, at the deployment level, you must care. We'll discuss mechanisms for implementing transport independence in chapter 5.

3.5 Message patterns

The core principles of pattern matching and transport independence allow you to define a set of message patterns, somewhat akin to object-oriented design patterns. We'll use the conventions introduced in chapter 2 to describe these patterns.

As a reminder, we're focusing on two aspects of message interaction:

- *Synchronous/asynchronous (solid/dashed line)*—The message expects/doesn't expect a response.
- *Observe/consume (empty/full arrowhead)*—The message is either observed (others can see it too) or consumed (others can't see it).

We'll consider these interactions in the context of increasing numbers of services. A further reminder: in all cases, unless explicitly noted, we assume a scalable system where each microservice is run as multiple instances. We assume that the deployment infrastructure, or microservice framework, provides capabilities such as load balancing to make this possible.

To formalize the categorization of the patterns, you can think of them in terms of the number of message patterns and the number of microservices (not instances!). In the simplest case, there's a single message of a particular pattern between two microservices. This is a 1/2 pattern, using the form m/n, where m is the number of message patterns and n is the number of microservices.

3.5.1 Core patterns: one message/two services

In these patterns, you enumerate the four permutations of the synchronous/ asynchronous and observe/consume axes. In general, enumerating the permutations of message interactions, especially with higher numbers of microservices, is a great way to discover possibilities for microservice interaction patterns. But we'll start simple, with the big four.

1/2: REQUEST/RESPONSE

This pattern, illustrated in figure 3.2, describes the common HTTP message transport model. Messages are synchronous: the initiating microservice expects a response. The listening microservice consumes the message, and nobody else gets to see it. This mode of interaction covers traditional REST-style APIs and a great many first-generation microservice architectures. Considerable tooling is available to make this interaction highly robust.[17]

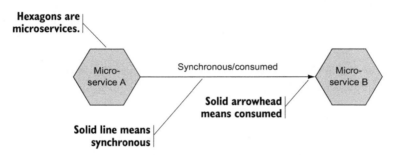

Figure 3.2   Request/response pattern: the calculation of sales tax, where microservice A **is the** *shopping-cart* **service, microservice** *B* **is the** *sales-tax* **service, and the message is** *calculate-sales-tax.* **The** *shopping-cart* **service expects an immediate answer so it can update the cart total.**

If the cardinality of the listening microservice is greater than a single instance, then you have an actor-style pattern. Each listener responds in turn, with a load balancer[18] distributing work according to some desired algorithm.

When you develop a microservice system locally, it's often convenient to run the system as a set of individual microservices, with a single instance of each type. Message transport is implemented by hardcoding routes as HTTP calls to specific port numbers, and most messages are of the request/response form. It can't be stressed forcefully enough that *the microservices must be sheltered from the details of this local configuration.* The benefit is that it's much easier to develop and verify message interactions in this simplified configuration.

1/2: SIDEWINDER

This pattern may at first seem rather strange (see figure 3.3). It's a synchronous message that isn't consumed. So who else observes the message? This is a good example of the level that this model operates at—you aren't concerned with the details of the network traffic. How others observe this message is a secondary consideration. This pattern communicates *intent.* The message is observable. Other microservices, such as an auditing service, may have an interest in the message, but there's still one microservice

---

[17] The open source toolset from Netflix is well worth exploring: https://netflix.github.io.

[18] The load balancer isn't necessarily a standalone server. Client-side load balancing has the advantage that it can be achieved with lightweight libraries and removes a server from the deployment configuration of your system.

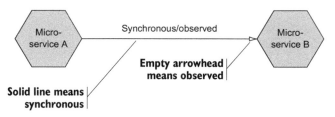

Figure 3.3 Sidewinder pattern: in the e-commerce system, the *shopping-cart* service may send a *checkout* message to the *delivery* service. A recommendation service can observe the *checkout* messages to understand the purchasing behavior of customers and generate recommendations for other products they might be interested in. But the existence of the recommendation service isn't known to the *shopping-cart* and *delivery* services, which believe they're participating in a simple request/response interaction.

that will supply the response. This is also a good example of the way a model generates new ways of looking at systems by enumerating the combinations of elements the model provides.

1/2: WINNER-TAKE-ALL

This is a classic distributed-systems pattern (see figure 3.4). Workers take tasks from a queue and operate on them in parallel. In this world view, asynchronous messages are sent out to instances of listening microservices; one of the services is the winner and acts on the message. The message is asynchronous, so no response is expected.

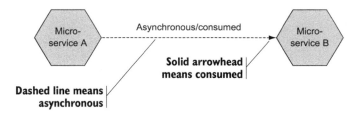

Figure 3.4 Winner-take-all pattern: in the e-commerce system, you can configure the *delivery* service to work in this mode. For redundancy and fault tolerance, you run multiple instances of the delivery service. It's important that the physical goods are delivered only once, so only one instance of the *delivery* service should act on any given *checkout* message. The message interaction is asynchronous in this configuration, because *shopping-cart* doesn't expect a response (ensuring delivery isn't its responsibility!). You could use a message bus that provides work queues to implement this mode of interaction.

In reality, a message queue is a good mechanism for implementing this behavior, but it isn't absolutely necessary—perhaps you're using a sharding approach and ignoring messages that don't belong to your shard. As an architect using this pattern, you're again providing intent, rather than focusing on the network configuration of the microservices.

1/2: FIRE-AND-FORGET

This is another classic distributed pattern: publish/subscribe (see figure 3.5). In this case, all the listening microservice instances observe the message and act on it in some way.

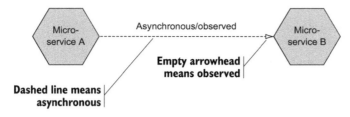

Figure 3.5   Fire-and-forget pattern: the general form of this interaction involves a set of different microservices observing an emitted message. The *shopping-cart* service emits a *checkout* message, and various other services react to it: *delivery*, *checkout-email*, and perhaps *audit*. This is a common pattern.

From a idealistic perspective, this is the purest form of microservice interaction. Messages are sent out into the world, and whoever cares may act on them. All the other patterns can be interpreted as constraints on this model.

Strictly speaking, figure 3.5 shows a special case: multiple instances of the *same* microservice will all receive the message. Diagrams of real systems typically include two or more listening services. This special case is sometimes useful because although it performs the same work more than once, you can use it to deliver guaranteed service levels. The catch is that the task must be idempotent.[19]

For example, the e-commerce website will display photos of products. These come in a standard large format, and you need to generate thumbnail images for search result listings. Resizing the large image to a thumbnail always generates the same output, so the operation is idempotent. If you have a catalog of millions of products (remember, your company is quite successful at this stage), then some resizing operations will fail due to disk failures or other random issues. If 2% of resizings fail on average, then performing the resizing twice using different microservice instances means only 0.04% (2% x 2%) of resizings will fail in production. Adding more microservice instances gives you even greater fault tolerance. Of course, you pay the price in redundant work. We'll examine this trade-off in chapter 5.

3.5.2   *Core patterns: two messages/two services*

These are the simplest message-interaction patterns; they capture causality between messages. These patterns describe how one type of message generates other types of messages. In one sense, this is an odd perspective: normally, you'd think in terms of the dependency relationships between microservices, rather than causality between messages.

From a messages-first perspective, it makes more sense. The causal relationships between messages are more stable than the relationships between the microservices that support the messages. It's easier to handle the messages with a different grouping of microservices than it is to change the message language.

---

[19] An *idempotent* task can be performed over and over again and always has the same output: for example, setting a data field to a specific value. No matter how many times the data record is updated, the data field always gets the same value, so the result is always the same.

2/2: REQUEST/REACT

This is a classic enterprise pattern (see figure 3.6).[20] The requesting microservice enables the listening microservice to respond asynchronously by accepting a separate message in reaction to the initial request message. The requesting microservice is responsible for correlating the outbound request message and its separate response message. This is a more manual version of traditional request/response.

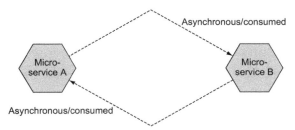

Figure 3.6   Request/react pattern

The advantage here is that you create temporal decoupling. Resources aren't consumed on the requesting side while you wait for a response from the listener. This is most effective when you expect the listener to take a nontrivial amount of time to complete the request. For example, generating a secure password hash necessarily requires expending significant CPU time. Doing so on the main line of microservices that respond to user requests would negatively impact response times. Offloading the work to a separate set of worker microservices solves the problem, but you must allow for the fact that the work is still too slow for a normal request/response pattern. In this case, request/react is a much better fit.

2/2: BATCH PROGRESS REPORTER

This a variant of the request/react pattern that gives you a way to bring batch processes into the fold of microservices (see figure 3.7). Batch processes, such as daily data uploads, consistency checks, and date-based business rules, are often written as programs that run separately from the main request-serving system. This arrangement is fragile, because those batch processes don't fall under the same control and monitoring mechanisms.

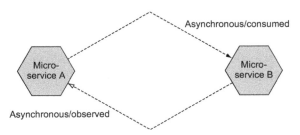

Figure 3.7   Batch progress reporter

---

[20] For more, see the excellent book *SOA Patterns* by Arnon Rotem-Gal-Oz, (Manning, 2012), https://www.manning.com/books/soa-patterns.

By turning batch processes into microservices, you can bring them under control in the same way. This is much more efficient from a systems management perspective. And it follows the underlying principle that you should think of your system in microservice terms: small services that respond to messages.

In this case, the message interaction is similar to request/react, but there's series of reaction messages announcing the state of the batch process. This allows the triggering microservice, and others, to monitor the state of the batch process. To enable this, reaction messages (in this case) are observed rather than consumed.

3.5.3 *Core patterns: one message/n services*

In these patterns, you begin to see some of the core benefits of using microservices: the ability to deploy code to production in a partial and staged way. In monolithic applications, you'd implement some of these patterns using feature flags or other custom code. That approach is difficult to measure and incurs technical debt. With microservices, you can achieve the same effect under the same simple model as all other deployments. This level of homogeneity makes it easier to manage and measure.

1/N: ORCHESTRA

In this pattern, an orchestrating service coordinates the activities of a set of supporting services (see figure 3.8, which shows that microservice *A* interacts with *B* first, then *C*, in the context of some workflow *a*). A criticism of the microservice architecture is that it's difficult to understand microservice interactions, and thus service orchestration must be an important infrastructural support. This function can be performed directly by orchestration microservices that coordinate workflows directly, removing the need for a specialist network component to perform this role. In most large production microservice systems, you'll find many microservices performing orchestration roles to varying degrees.

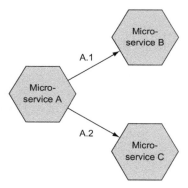

Figure 3.8   Orchestra

1/N: SCATTER/GATHER

This is one of the more important microservice patterns (see figure 3.9). Instead of a deterministic, serial procedure for generating and collecting results, you announce your need and collect results as they come in. Let's say you want to construct a product page for the e-commerce site. In the old world, you'd gather all the content from its providers and only return the page once everything was available. If one content provider failed, the whole page would fail, unless you'd written specific code to deal with this situation.

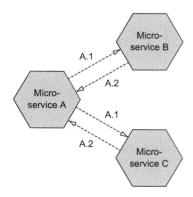

Figure 3.9   Scatter/gather

In the microservice world, individual microservices generate the content pieces and can't affect others if they fail. You must construct the result (the product page) asynchronously, because your content components arrive asynchronously, so you build in fault tolerance by default. The product page can still display if certain elements aren't ready—these can be injected as they become available. You get this flexibility as part of the basic architecture.

How do you coordinate responses and decide that your work is complete? There are a number of approaches. When you announce your need, you can set a time limit for responses; any response received after the time limit expires isn't included. This is the approach taken in the case study in chapter 9. You can also return once you get a minimum number of results.

For an extreme version, consider the sales tax use case. If you're willing to take availability over consistency, you can apply sales tax calculations and adapt to changes in rules in a flexible way. You announce that you need a sales tax calculation. *All* of the sales tax microservices respond, but you can rank the results in order of specificity. The more specific the result, the more likely it is to be the correct sales tax calculation, because it takes into account more information about the purchase. Perhaps this seems like a recipe for disaster and inaccurate billing. But consider that pricing and sales tax errors occur every minute of every day, and businesses deal with them by making compensating payments or absorbing the cost of errors. This is normal business practice. Why? Because companies prefer to stay open rather than close their doors—there's business to be done! We've allowed ourselves as software developers to believe that our systems must achieve perfect accuracy, but we should always ask whether the business wants to pay for it.

1/N: MULTIVERSION DEPLOYMENT

This is the scenario we discussed in the section on the sales tax microservices earlier (see figure 3.10). You want to be able to deploy updated versions of a given microservice as new instances while keeping the old instances running. To do this, you can use the actor-style patterns (winner-take-all, fire-and-forget); but instead of distributing messages to a set of instances, all of which are the same version, you distribute to instances of differing versions. The figure shows some interaction, *a*, where messages are sent to versions 1.0 and 2.0 of microservice *A*.

The facts that this deployment configuration is an extension of an existing pattern, and easy to achieve by changing the details of the deployment, show again the power of microservices. We've converted a feature from custom implementation in code to explicit declarative configuration.

This pattern becomes even more powerful when you combine it with the deployment and measurement

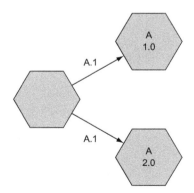

Figure 3.10   Multiversion deployment

techniques we'll discuss in chapters 5 and 6. To lower the risk of deploying a new version of a service, you don't need to serve production results back from that new version. Instead, you can duplicate traffic so that the old versions of a microservice, proven in production, keep everything working correctly as before. But now you have the output from the new microservice, and you can compare that to the output from the old microservice and see whether it's correct. Any new bugs or errors can be detected using production traffic, but without causing issues. You can iterate deployment of the new version in this traffic-duplication mode until you have a high degree of confidence, using production traffic, that it won't break things. This is a fantastic way to enable high-velocity continuous delivery.

1/N: MULTI-IMPLEMENTATION DEPLOYMENT

Expanding the possibilities offered by multiversion deployment, you can do multi-implementation deployment (see figure 3.11). This means you can try out different approaches to solve the same problem. In particular, and powerfully, you can do A/B testing. And you can do it without additional infrastructure. A/B testing becomes a capability of your system, without being something you need to build in or integrate. The figure shows microservices *A* and *B* both performing the same role in message interaction *a*.

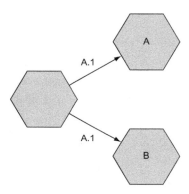

Figure 3.11   Multi-implementation deployment

You can take this further than user interface A/B testing: you can A/B-test all aspects of your system, trialing new algorithms or performance enhancements, without taking massive deployment risks.

3.5.4   *Core patterns: m messages/n services*

The possibilities offered by configuration of multiple services and multiple messages expand exponentially. That said, bear in mind that all message patterns can be decomposed into the four core 1/2 patterns. This is often a good way to understand a large microservice system. There are a few larger-scale patterns that are worth knowing, which we'll explore here.

3.5.5   *m/n: chain*

The chain represents a serial workflow. Although this is often implemented using an orchestrating microservice (discussed in section 3.5.3), it can also be implemented in the configuration shown in figure 3.12, where the messages of the *a* workflow are choreographed;[21] the serial nature of the workflow is an emergent property of the individual microservices following their local rules.

---

[21] Sam Newman, author of *Building Microservices* (O'Reilly, 2011), introduced the terms *orchestration* and *choreography* to describe microservice configurations.

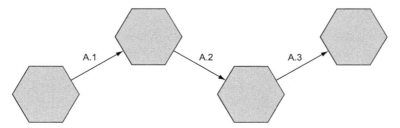

Figure 3.12 Chain

Generally, distributed systems that can perform work in parallel are always bounded by the work that can't be parallelized. There's always some work that must be done serially. In an enterprise software context, this is often the case where actions are gated: certain conditions must be met before work can proceed.

3.5.6 *m/n: Tree*

The tree represents a complex workflow with multiple parallel chains (see figure 3.13, which shows the message flow subsequences). It arises in contexts where triggering actions cause multiple independent workflows. For example, the checkout process of an e-commerce site requires multiple streams of work, from customer communication to fulfillment.

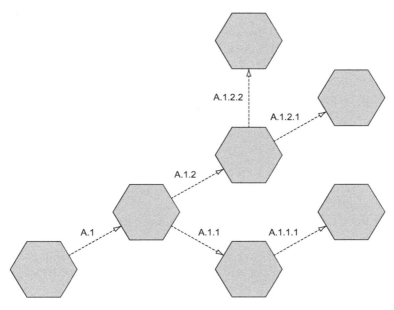

Figure 3.13 Tree

3.5.7   *Scaling messages*

There can be no question that the microservice architecture introduces additional load on the network and thus reduces performance overall. The foremost way to address this issue is to ask whether you have an actual problem. In many scenarios, the performance cost of microservices is more than offset by their wide-ranging benefits. You'll gain a deeper understanding of how this trade-off works, and how it can be adjusted, in chapters 5, 6, and 7.

To frame this discussion, it's important to be specific about terminology:

- *Latency*—The amount of time it takes for the system to complete an action. You could measure latency by measuring the average response time of inbound requests, but this isn't a good measure because it doesn't capture highly variant response times. It's better to measure latency using percentiles: a latency of 100 ms at the 90th percentile means 90% of requests responded within 100 ms. This approach captures behavior that spikes unacceptably. Low latency is the desired outcome.
- *Throughput*—The amount of load the system can sustain, given as a rate: the number of requests per second. By itself, the throughput rate isn't very useful. It's better to quote throughput and latency together: such a rate at such a percentile.

High throughput with low latency is the place you want to be, but it isn't something you can achieve often. Like so much else in systems engineering, you must sacrifice one for the other or spend exponentially large amounts of money to compensate.

Choosing the microservice architecture means making an explicit trade-off: higher throughput, but also higher latency. You get higher throughput because it's much easier to scale horizontally—just add more service instances. Because different microservices handle different levels of load, you can do this in a precise way, scaling up only those microservices that need to scale and allocating resources far more efficiently. But you also get higher latency, because you have more network traffic and more network hops. Messages need to travel between services, and this takes time.

LOWERING LATENCY

When you build a microservices system with a messages-first approach, you find that certain message interactions require lower latency than others: those that must respond to user input, those that must provide data in a timely fashion, and those that use resources under contention. These message interactions, if implemented asynchronously, will have higher latency. To reduce latency in these cases, you'll have to make another trade-off: increase the complexity of the system. You can do this by introducing synchronous messages, particularly of the request/response variety. You can also combine microservices into single processes that are larger than average, but that increase in size brings with it the associated downsides of monolithic architectures.

These are legitimate trade-offs. As with all performance optimizations, addressing them ahead of time, before you have a proper measurement, is usually wasted effort.

The microservice architecture makes your life easier by giving you the measurement aspect for a lower cost, because you monitor message flow rates in any case. Identifying performance bottlenecks is much easier.

It's worth noting that lower-level optimizations at the code level are almost useless in a microservices context. The latency introduced by network hops swamps everything else by several orders of magnitude.

INCREASING THROUGHPUT

Achieving higher message throughput is easier, because it requires fewer compromises and can be achieved by spending money. You can increase the number of service instances, or use message queues[22] with better performance characteristics, or run on bigger CPUs.

In addition to adding muscle at the system level, you can make your life easier at the architectural level. Messages should be small: resist the urge to use them for transferring large volumes of data or large amounts of binary data, such as images. Instead, messages should contain references to the original data. Microservices can then retrieve the original data directly from the data-storage layer of your system in the most efficient manner.

Be careful to separate CPU-bound activity into separate processes, so it doesn't impact throughout. This is a significant danger in event-based platforms such as a Node.js, where CPU activity blocks input/output activity. For thread-based platforms, it's less of an issue, but resources are still consumed and have limits. In the sales tax example, as the complexity of the rules grows, computation time increases; it's better to perform the calculation in a separate microservice. For highly CPU-intensive activities such as image resizing and password hashing, this is even more important.

3.6 *When messages go bad*

Microservice systems are complex. They don't even start out simple, because they require deployment automation from the beginning. There are lots of moving parts, in terms of both the types of messages and microservices and on-the-ground instances of them. Such systems demonstrate emergent behavior—their internal complexity is difficult to comprehend as a whole. Not only that, but with so many interacting parts, subtle feedback loops can develop, leading to behavior that's almost impossible to explain.

Such systems are discussed, in the general case, by Nassim Nicholas Taleb, author of the books *Black Swan* (Penguin, 2008) and *Antifragile* (Random House, 2014). His conceptual model is a useful framework for understanding microservice architectures. He classifies systems as fragile, robust, and antifragile:

---

[22] Kafka is fast, if that's what you need: http://kafka.apache.org.

- *Fragile* systems degrade when exposed to disorder and pressure. Most software falls into this category, failing to cope with the disorder generated by high loads.
- *Robust* systems can resist disorder, up to a point. They're designed to impose rigid discipline. The problem is that they suffer catastrophic failure modes—they work until they don't. Most large-scale software is of this variety: a significant investment is made in debugging, testing, and process control, and the system can withstand pressure until it hits a boundary condition, such as a schema change.
- *Antifragile* systems benefit from disorder and become stronger. The human immune system is an example. The microservice architecture is weakly antifragile by design and can be made more so by accepting the realities of communication over the network.

The key to antifragility is to accept lots of small failures, in order to avoid large failures. You want failures to be high in frequency but of low consequence. Traditional software quality and deployment practices, geared for the monolith, are biased toward low-frequency, high-consequence failures. It's much better for individual microservices to fail by design (rebooting themselves as needed) than for the entire system to fail.

The best strategy for microservices, when handling internal errors, is to fail fast and reset. Microservices are crash-first software. Instances are small and plentiful, so there's always somebody to take up the slack.

Dealing with external failure is more challenging. From the perspective of the individual microservice, external failures appear as misbehaving messages. When messages go bad, it's easy for them to consume resources and cause the system to degrade. It's therefore vital that the message-transportation infrastructure and the microservices adopt a stance that expects failure from external actors. No microservice should expect good behavior from the rest of the network. Luckily, many of the failure modes can be dealt with using a common set of strategies.

3.6.1 *The common failure scenarios, and what to do about them*

In this section, the failure modes are organized under the message interactions that are most susceptible to them. All failure modes can occur with any message interaction, but it's useful to organize your thinking. All message interactions ultimately break down into the four core 1/2 interactions, so I'll use the core interactions to catalog the failure modes.

For each failure mode, I'll present options for mitigation. No failure mode can be eliminated entirely, and the principle of antifragility teaches that this is a bad idea anyway. Instead, you should adopt mitigation strategies that keep the whole healthy, even if a part must be sacrificed.

> **NOTE** In the following scenarios, microservice *A* is the sending service, and microservice *B* is the listening service.

3.6.2 *Failures dominating the request/response interaction*

The request/response interaction is vulnerable to high latency, which can cause excessive resource consumption as you wait for responses.

SLOW DOWNSTREAM

Microservice *A* is generating work for microservice *B*. *A* might be an orchestrater, for example. *B* performs resource-intensive work. If *B* becomes slow for some reason, perhaps because one of its dependencies has become slow, then resources in *A* will be consumed waiting for responses from *B*. In an event-based platform, this will consume memory; but in a thread-based platform, it will consume threads. This is much worse, because eventually all threads will block waiting for *B*, meaning no new work can proceed.

Mitigation: use a circuit breaker. When *B* slows below a triggering level of throughput, consider *B* to be dead, and remove it from interactions with *A*. *B* either is irretrievably corrupt and will die anyway in due course and be replaced, or is overloaded and will recover once load is reduced. In either case, a healthy *B* will eventually result. The circuit breaker logic can operate either within *A* or in an intelligent load balancer in front of *B*. The net result is that throughput and latency remain healthy, if less performant than usual.

UPSTREAM OVERLOAD

Similar to the previous scenario, microservice *A* is generating work for microservice *B*. But in this scenario, *A* isn't well behaved and doesn't use a circuit breaker. *B* must fend for itself. As the load increases, *B* is placed under increasing strain, and performance suffers. Even if you assume that the system has implemented some form of automated scaling, load can increase faster than new instances of B can be deployed. And there are always cost limits to adding new instances of *B*. Simply blindly increasing the system size creates significant downside exposure to denial-of-service attacks.

Mitigation: *B* must selectively drop messages from *A* that push *B* beyond its performance limits. This is known as *load shedding*. Although it may seem aggressive, it's more important to keep the system up for as many users as possible. Under high-load scenarios, performance tends to degrade across the board for all users. With load shedding, some users will receive no service, but at least those that do will receive normal service levels.

If you allow your system to have supervisory microservices that control scaling in response to load, you can also use signaling from *B* to mitigate this failure mode. *B* should announce via asynchronous messages to the system in general that it's under too much load. The system can then reduce inbound requests further upstream from *A*. This is known as *applying backpressure*.

3.6.3 *Failures dominating the sidewinder interaction*

Failure in this interaction is insidious—you may not notice it for many days, leading to data corruption.

LOST ACTIONS

In this scenario, microservices *A* and *B* have the primary interaction, but *C* is also observing, performing its own actions. Any of these microservices can be upgraded independently of the others. If this introduces changes to message content or different message behavior, then either *B* or *C* may begin to fail. Because one of the key benefits of microservices is the ability to perform independent updates, and because this enables continuous delivery, this failure mode is almost to be expected. It's often used as a criticism of the microservice architecture, because the naïve mitigation is to attempt coordinated deployments. This is a losing strategy that's difficult to do reliably in practice.

Mitigation: measure the system. When *A* sends the message, it should be received by *B* and *C*. Thus, the outbound and inbound flow rates for this message must be in the ratio 1:2. Allowing for transient variations, this ratio can be used as a health indicator. In production systems, there are many instances of *A*, *B*, and *C*. Updates don't replace all of *A*, for example; rather, following microservice best practice, *A* is updated in stages, one instance at a time. This allows you to monitor the message-flow-rate ratio to see whether it maintains its expected value. If not, you can roll back and review. This is discussed more fully in chapter 6.

3.6.4   *Failures dominating the winner-take-all interaction*

These failures can bring your system down and keep it down. Simple restarts won't fix the problem, because the issue is in the messages themselves.

POISON MESSAGES

This is a common failure mode for actor-style distributed systems. Microservice *A* generates what it thinks is a perfectly acceptable message. But a bug in microservice *B* means B always crashes on the message. The message goes back onto the queue, and the next instance of *B* attempts to process it and fails. Eventually, all instances of *B* are stuck in a crash-reboot cycle, and no new messages are processed.

Mitigation: microservice *B* needs to keep track of recently received messages and drop duplicates on the floor. This requires messages to have some sort of identifier or signature. To aid debugging, the duplicate should be consumed but not acted on. Instead, it should be sent to a dead-letter queue.[23] This mitigation should happen at the transport layer, because it's common to most message interactions.

GUARANTEED DELIVERY

Asynchronous messages are best delivered using a message queue. Some message-queue solutions claim to guarantee that messages will be delivered to listeners at most once, exactly once, or at least once. None of these guarantees can be given in practice, because it's fundamentally impossible to make them. Message delivery, in general, suffers from the Byzantine Generals problem: it's impossible to know for sure whether your message has been delivered.

---

[23] The *dead-letter queue* is the place you send copies of broken messages for later analysis. It can be as simple as a microservice that takes no actions but logs every message sent to it.

Mitigation: skew delivery to prefer at-least-once behavior. Then, you have to deal with the problem of duplicate messages. Making behavior idempotent as much as possible reduces the effect of duplicates, because they then have no effect. As explained earlier in the chapter, idempotency refers to the property of a system where it can safely perform the same action multiple times and end up in the same state: for example, the sales tax calculation is naturally idempotent because it always returns the same result for the same inputs.

3.6.5 Failures dominating the fire-and-forget interaction

These failure modes are a reminder that the gods will always find our mortal plans amusing. They gave us brains just powerful enough to build machines that we can never fully comprehend.

EMERGENT BEHAVIOR

As your system grows, with many microservices interacting, emergent behavior will occur. This may take the form of messages appearing that shouldn't appear, microservices taking unexpected actions, or unexplained surges in message volume.

Mitigation: a microservice system isn't a neural network, however appealing the analogy. It's still a system designed to operate in a specific fashion, with defined interactions. Emergent behavior is difficult to diagnose and resolve, because it arises from the interplay of microservice behavior rather than from one microservice misbehaving. Thus, you must debug each case individually. To make this possible, use correlation identifiers. Each message should contain metadata to identify the message, because it moves between microservices; this allows you to trace the flow of messages. You should also include the identifiers of originating messages, because this will let you trace causality—see which messages generated further messages.

CATASTROPHIC COLLAPSE

Sometimes, emergent behavior suffers from a feedback loop. In this case, the system enters a death spiral caused by ever-increasing numbers of unwanted messages triggering even more messages. Rolling back recent microservice deployments—the standard safety valve—doesn't work in this scenario, because the system has entered a chaotic state. The triggering microservice may not even be a participant in the problematic behavior.

Mitigation: the last resort is to bring the system down completely and boot it up again, one set of services at a time. This is a disaster scenario, but it can be mitigated. It may be sufficient to shut down some parts of the system and leave others running. This may be enough to cut the feedback loop. All of your microservices should include kill switches that allow you to shut down arbitrary subsets of the system. They can be used in an emergency to progressively bring down functionality until nominal behavior is restored.

3.7   Summary

- One of the most important strategies for avoiding the curse of the distributed monolith is to put messages at the core your microservices thinking. With a messages-first approach, the microservice architecture becomes much easier to specify, design, run, and reason about.
- It's better to think about your business requirements in terms of the messages that represent them. This is an action-oriented stance rather than a data-oriented one. It's powerful because it gives you the freedom to define a language of messages without predetermining the microservices that will handle them.
- The synchronous/asynchronous dichotomy is fundamental to the way messages interact. It's important to understand the constraints that each of these message-interaction models imposes, as well as the possibilities the models offer.
- Pattern matching is the principle mechanism for deciding which microservice will act on which message. Using pattern matching, instead of service discovery and addressing, gives you a flexible and understandable model for defining message behavior.
- Transport independence is the principle mechanism for keeping services fully decoupled from the concrete topology of the network. Microservices can be written in complete isolation, seeing the world only in terms of inbound and outbound messages. Message transport and routing become an implementation and configuration concern.
- Message interactions can be understood along two axes: synchronous/asynchronous and observed/consumed. This model generates four core message-interaction patterns, which can be used to define interactions between many messages and microservices.
- The failure modes of message interactions can also be cataloged and understood in the context of this model.

Data

This chapter covers

- Accepting that data isn't sacrosanct and can be inaccurate
- Building alternative storage solutions with microservice messages
- Representing data operations as microservices messages
- Exploring alternatives to traditional data-management strategies
- Storing different types of data

Using a central relational database is common practice for most software projects. Almost all data is stored there, and the system accesses the data in the database directly. The data schema is represented in the programming language used to build the system.

The advantage of a central database is that almost all of your data is in one place under one schema. You have to manage and administer only one kind of database. Scaling issues can usually be solved by throwing money at the problem. You're building on the knowledge and practice of generations of software developers.

The disadvantage of a central database is that it provides a fertile breeding ground for technical debt. Your schema and stored procedures will become complex, and you'll use the database as a communication layer between different parts of your system. You'll have to accept that all of your data, regardless of business value, gets the same treatment.

The microservice architecture makes it possible to break out of this way of thinking. The decision to use a central relational database is just that: a decision. Microservices make it possible to use a wider variety of data-persistence strategies and fine-tune them depending on the kind of data you store. We'll use the digital newspaper case study from chapter 2 to help you understand the new possibilities.

4.1   *Data doesn't mean what you think it means*

To understand how to adopt this approach at a practical level, it's necessary to reset your understanding of what data is. The abstract models used to describe data in a classical system are only a drop in the ocean of models that can describe data. Let's question the implicit assumptions by making some assertions about data in practice.

4.1.1   *Data is heterogeneous, not homogeneous*

Some data in your system is mission critical. In the context of the newspaper example, consider payment records for reader subscriptions. You need to get these right. Other data is useful, but you can live without it (for example, what the most-read article on the site was yesterday). If you impose the same constraints on all of your data by using the same database for everything, you can't adjust your data-persistence strategies to reflect the value of the data they're handling.

The constraints on each data entity in your system are different. Awareness of this fact is a useful step toward making the right decisions regarding data storage. Consider some examples relevant to the newspaper:

- *User subscriptions*—Details of what the user has paid for and which articles they can read. This data needs to have high accuracy, because it has a high impact on customer satisfaction. Modifications to this data need high levels of consistency and should probably use transactions. All services should use the same database, to achieve these desired data behaviors. A good, old-fashioned relational database is needed here.[1]

- *User preferences*—Font size for articles; news categories to show on the home page; whether to hide article comments. These features improve the user's experience with the newspaper but aren't critical. Incorrect data doesn't prevent the user from reading articles. It's a good business decision to keep the cost of operating on this data as low as possible; and to do that, trading off some accuracy makes sense. If the font size is different than the reader's preferred

---

[1]   MySQL, Postgres, SQL Server, Oracle, and so on.

setting, it's annoying but not fatal. A document store that isn't too strict about schemas is helpful in this case.[2]

- *Article read counts*—Used as input to an analytics system, to get insight into the content that appeals to readers. The aggregate data matters here, along with the relationships between data—not exact numbers. In any case, you're only guessing at user behavior: just because a user opens an article page doesn't mean they'll read it. High throughput that doesn't cause latency anywhere else is what you want in this case. A simple key-value store will do.[3]

The microservice architecture makes it much easier to apply these observations about your data in practice. Different microservices can deal with data in different ways and use different data-storage solutions. Over time, if data constraints change, you can also migrate data to more-appropriate storage solutions; when you do, you'll only need to change individual microservices.

Figure 4.1 shows the proposed persistence strategy, diagramming only the relevant services. The *user-profile*, *subs*, and *tracker* services are new introductions. They look after user preferences, subscription payments, and tracking article views, respectively.

The advantage of the microservice architecture is not so much that you can decide in advance to use all of these different databases. In the early days of a project, it's most useful to use a schema-free document store for everything, because doing so gives you maximum flexibility. Rather, the advantage is that later, in production, you can migrate to using multiple fit-for-purpose databases *if you need to*.

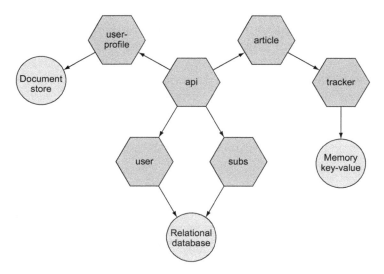

Figure 4.1 Using different databases for different microservices

---

[2]   MongoDB, CouchDB, and so on.
[3]   Redis, LevelDB, and so on.

4.1.2   *Data can be private*

The purpose of a relational database is to make data access easier. In practice, this means application code usually has access to all database tables. As the application expands and changes, more code accesses more of the database, and technical debt increases as this swamp of dependencies grows.

A nasty anti-pattern can easily develop. The database comes to be used as a communication mechanism between software components: different components read and write data to a shared set of tables. This implicit communication channel exists in many monolithic code bases. It's an anti-pattern because communication happens outside of the expected channels, without well-defined semantics, and often without any explicit design. There are no control mechanisms to reign in the growth of complexity, so technical debt soon manifests.

To prevent this, it's better to restrict access to data entities so that only business logic concerned with a given kind of entity modifies the storage table for that entity. This strategy is much easier to implement with microservices. Related data entities can be associated with limited groups of microservices. These microservices mediate access to the data entities, ensuring consistent application of business rules. No other microservices can access the data directly. Data access can even be completely hidden behind business-logic operations. Other times, the microservice may offer more-traditional read/write operations for individual entity instances. But in all cases, access to the data entity is represented by messages, rather than a data schema. These messages are no different from others in the microservice system, and thus data operations can be manipulated the same way as other messages.

In the context of the newspaper example, the *User* data entity is private to the *user* service, and the *UserProfile* data entity is private to the *user-profile* service. This is appropriate, because sensitive information such as usernames, password hashes, and recovery email addresses needs to be kept separate from user-preference settings such as font sizes and favorited articles. Even if these entities are stored in the same database in the initial versions of the system, you can enforce this separation by insisting that all access be via the responsible microservice. The correspondence between microservices and data entities isn't necessarily one to one; and simplistic rules of thumb, such as one microservice per entity, shouldn't be adopted as general principles.

Data entities

The term *data entity* is used in this chapter to refer to a single coherent data type, from the perspective of a given system domain.[4] Data entities are typically represented by relational tables, document types, or a specific set of key-value pairs. They represent a set of records that have a common internal structure: a set of data fields of various types.

---

[4] Large systems may have multiple *domains*. Each domain is an internally consistent view of the world. Communication between domains necessarily involves some form of entity translation. Explicitly setting things up this way is known as *domain-driven design* (DDD). The microservice architecture can make DDD easier to achieve but should be considered at a lower level of abstraction than DDD. For more, read *Domain-Driven Design* by Eric Evans (Addison-Wesley, 2003).

(continued)
These fields may be subject to constraints imposed by the database; they may also be subject to additional semantic interpretation (for example, they could be country codes). The term *data entity* is used only in an informal manner to indicate families of data.

4.1.3 Data can be local

A traditional database architecture uses a shared database as the only persistent store. Caching may be used for transient results, but data isn't generally stored outside of the database. In the microservice architecture, you have more freedom to store data in separate locations. You can make data local to a microservice by restricting access to a database table, assigning a database exclusively to a microservice, or storing the data locally with the microservice.

Microservice instances can have local storage capabilities, perhaps using an embedded database engine such as SQLite or LevelDB. Data can persist for the duration of the microservice's lifetime, which could be hours, days, or weeks. Data can also persist separately on virtual data volumes that are reconnected to running microservice instances.

Consider the user profile data. To scale to millions of users, you can use a set of user profile services and distribute user profiles evenly over them. You can achieve this even distribution by sharding the key space of users and using message translation to hide the sharding from the rest of the system.[5] Each user profile service stores user profile data locally. For fault tolerance, you run multiple instances of each shard service. When you need to read user profile data, the sharding service picks one of the shard instances to get the data, as shown in figure 4.2. When you need to write user profile data, you publish a message to all instances for the relevant shard. To populate a new shard instance, let it look for missing data on older, sibling shards. You can do this on demand or as a batch job. Because adding new shard instances is easy, any given shard instance is disposable; so if you detect data corruption in a shard, you can throw the shard away.

This persistence strategy is vulnerable to loss of data accuracy. If a given update message is published and doesn't reach all shard instances, then the user profile data will be inconsistent. How bad is this? It depends on your business goals. It may be perfectly acceptable to have a consistency level of 99%.[6] So what if the font size is wrong! Just set it again, and it will probably be saved this time. In the early stages of a project, before you have large numbers of users, this trade-off allows you to focus effort on other, more valuable features.

---

[5] This ability to scale is a great example of the flexibility of microservices. You can start with just one service and not worry *at all* about how you'll scale. You know that you'll be able to use message manipulation to migrate to a different data-persistence solution if you have to.

[6] Here, *consistency level* is defined as the percentage of reads that match the most recent write.

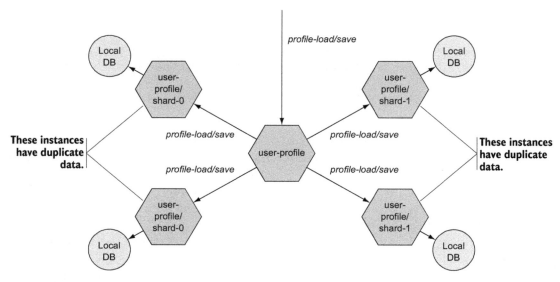

Figure 4.2   Local user profile data stored only on shard instances

But the day will come when you need to solve this problem. One angry user per week is materially different from 100, even if both numbers represent only 1% of users.

The solution is to delocalize the data in one of the following ways: use a single traditional database that all microservices access, use a versioned caching strategy, use a distributed data store with a conflict resolution algorithm, move to a cloud database that provides what you need, or separate reads from writes.[7]

All of these solutions are *more complex* than storing everything locally and slow you down if you use them from the start.

Microservices make the quick-and-dirty local storage approach safer because you can migrate away from it only when you need to. This migration is easier than you may think—the new database is just another sibling shard instance. We'll discuss this kind of shard migration later in this chapter. For a practical example of the local data strategy, see chapter 9.

4.1.4   *Data can be disposable*

A useful consequence of local data is that it's disposable. Local databases can always be reconstructed from each other or from the system of record (SOR).[8] Although this observation may seem manifestly true for in-memory caches, it now becomes true for

---

[7] The fancy name for this approach is Command Query Responsibility Segregation (CQRS), a family of asynchronous data-flow patterns, described by Martin Fowler at https://martinfowler.com/bliki/CQRS.html. The pattern-matching and transport-independence principles make CQRS more a matter of message-routing configuration rather than fundamental architecture, so don't be afraid to try it with your own microservices.

[8] None of the microservice data strategies preclude you from building a SOR, which is the ultimate authority on your data. They do make it much easier to protect the SOR from load and from performance issues.

more persistent data. When many instances of data-exposing microservices are running, each storing a subset of the full dataset, the individual instances aren't critical to the correct functioning of the system.

Compare this to a more traditional sharding scenario, where there are many shards. Each shard must be managed properly and treated as a full database in its own right: maintained, upgraded, patched, and backed up. Microservice instances, on the other hand, aren't as fragile, in aggregate. Any individual data store is disposable. It doesn't need the same level of management.

For local data, backups aren't needed, because the multiplicity of instances takes that responsibility. The operational complexity of backing up hundreds of microservice database instances isn't necessary. To do so would be an architectural smell. Maintenance isn't required: you upgrade the database by deploying new instances, not modifying old ones. Patching is also unnecessary; you can apply the same tactic. Configuration changes go the same way.

This approach is particularly useful in the world of containers. Containers are designed to be transient, and the abstraction leaks when you have persistent data. You have to answer the question, "How do I connect my long-lived storage to database engines running in containers that come and go?" A common solution is to not do so at all and instead retain the monolithic model of a sacred, separate, database cluster. Another solution is to punt and use a cloud database. With local data, you have another option: the data is stored in the container and dies when the container dies. Local data fits within the container abstraction.

As always with system architecture, you must be aware of the downsides. When you're running lots of local-data microservices and refreshing from the well of the SOR, you can easily drown the SOR with too many requests. Remember the basic best practices: microservice systems should change only one instance at a time. You need to control the rate of entry of new microservices to prevent flooding the SOR. Microservices aren't practical without automation.

4.1.5 Data doesn't have to be accurate

There's an implicit assumption in most enterprise software development that data must be 100% accurate at all times. The unquestioning acceptance of this assumption drives the feature sets and cost implications of enterprise database solutions. One of the most useful consequences of using the microservice architecture is that it forces you to question this assumption. As an architect, and as a developer, you must take a closer look at your data. You don't get to avoid making a decision about the cost implications of your chosen storage solution. Microservices are distributed, which allows them to scale. The trade-off is that you can't assume a simplistic relational model that looks after accuracy for you.

How do you handle inaccurate data? Start by asking the business what level of accuracy is actually needed. What are the business goals? How are they impacted by data accuracy? Are you comparing the cost of high accuracy with the benefits? The answers to these questions are requirements that drive your technical approach. The answers don't need to cover the entire dataset—different data has different constraints. Nor do the answers have to remain constant—they can change over time. The fine-grained nature of the microservice architecture makes this possible.

4.2 Data strategies for microservices

The microservice architecture gives you a greater degree of choice when it comes to data persistence. That presents a strategic problem: you need to choose the most effective strategies for handling data in the microservice context. This section provides a framework for decision making.

4.2.1 Using messages to expose data

A fundamental principle of the microservice architecture is that you limit communication between services to messages. This limitation preserves a desirable characteristic of the architecture: that services are independent of each other. This principle breaks down if you use the database for communication. You can easily end up doing this: if you have one service write data to a table, and you have another service read data from the same table, that's a communication channel.

The problem is that you're creating coupling between your services—exactly the coupling that generates technical debt. To avoid this, you need to keep data entities behind microservices. This doesn't mean that there's a one-to-one mapping between microservices and data entities, or that each table has its own microservice, or that one microservice handles all operations for a given database. These may all be true, but they're not fundamental attributes of the architecture.

Keeping data entities behind microservices means exposing them only through messages. This follows the *messages-first* principle discussed in chapter 3. To perform a data operation, you send a message. If it's synchronous, you expect a result. If it's asynchronous, you don't. The data operations can be traditional create/read/update/delete operations, or they may be higher-level operations defined by your business logic.

The data-operation messages give a unified interface to your data but don't impose a requirement that your data be stored or managed in only one place. This gives you considerable freedom regarding the approach you take to data persistence and allows you to match persistence solutions to your performance and accuracy needs.

You have the freedom to use different databases for different kinds of data entities. In the online newspaper example, articles are suitable for a document-oriented database, user profiles are suitable for local storage, and payment records are suitable for a relational database with transaction support. In all cases, you can expose the data via messages, and the business-logic microservices have no knowledge of the underlying data stores.

You're also free to switch databases. All you need is a microservice that translates between a given database solution and your data-operation messages. This isn't the weak flexibility of limiting yourself to a common subset of SQL. Theoretically, that gives you the ability to at least change relational databases;[9] it certainly doesn't let you move to NoSQL databases, because you'll inevitably develop a reliance on the capabilities of the SQL language. The situation is different with messages. Because they're the only way to talk to the data store, you automatically define a simple, small set of interactions with the database. Implementing these operations for a new database requires a feasible, self-contained amount of work.

> **Allowing database schemas to emerge**
>
> The ability to easily change databases opens up a highly effective rapid-development strategy. Even in a project scenario where you must ultimately use a relational database due to external constraints (such as a policy decision above your pay grade), you can still use a NoSQL database in the earlier stages of the project, as a "development tool." The advantages of doing so are that you don't have to decide about the schema design too early, you avoid the need for schema migrations, and you won't be tempted to create dependencies between data entities (aka JOIN queries).
>
> Once you've completed a significant number of iterations, discovered and unraveled the client's deeper requirements, and gotten a clearer understanding of the business problem you're modeling, you can move to a relational database. You take the implicit schema that has emerged within the NoSQL document set and use that to build an explicit schema in the SQL database.

4.2.2 Using composition to manipulate data

By representing data operations as messages, you allow them to be componentized. That is, after all, one of the core benefits you're seeking from the microservice architecture. Consider the scenario shown in figure 4.3, using the *article-page* and *article* services from chapter 2. The *article* service exposes article data using the *get/add/remove/list-article* set of messages.[10] These are sent by the *article-page* service. The *article-page* service performs business-logic operations (formatting and displaying articles), and the *article* service exposes article data.

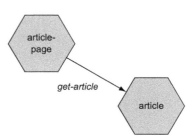

Figure 4.3 Interaction between the *article-page* and *article* services

Chapter 2 briefly discussed the use of componentization to extend this structure. You can introduce new microservices that intercept the data-operation messages. For example, you can introduce a caching microservice that first checks a cache before querying the *article* service (see figure 4.4).

---

[9] In practice, variations in the syntax and semantics of each database's SQL language dialect can trip you up.

[10] These names aren't message types. Strictly, they refer to the messages that match certain patterns. These names are abbreviations of the patterns. The patterns will vary depending on the implementation, and thus the specific patterns aren't relevant to this discussion.

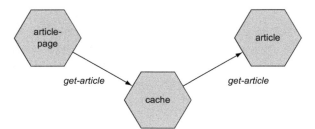

**Figure 4.4 Composing the *article-page*
and *article* services together**

The key principle here is that the *article-page* and *article* services have no knowledge of
this interception and behave as they always have. This message-interception strategy
isn't limited to caching. You can perform validation, access control, throttling, modification, or any other manipulation of that data. The interception strategy is a general
ability that a messages-first approach gives you; by confining data operations to messages, you gain the ability to extend the data operations with a well-defined component model.

This approach also lets you use alternative data-flow models. For example, The
pathway that data takes when written doesn't have to be the same as the pathway it
takes when read. You can make your write operations asynchronous and your read
operations synchronous. This is a common architecture when you need performance,
and eventual consistency is an acceptable strategy to achieve it. As mentioned earlier,
this family of data-flow models is known as Command Query Responsibility Segregation (CQRS); it adds complexity to your system and is considered acceptable only
when you need the performance benefits. In the message-oriented microservice
world, this consideration doesn't apply. Asynchronous writes and synchronous reads
correspond to a message-routing configuration and are a natural capability of the system. There's nothing special about the data-flow model, as shown in figure 4.5. From
the perspective of the business-logic services, the model isn't apparent and has no
effect on implementation. Just as you can change databases more easily mid-project,
you can change data flows if you have unanticipated performance needs.

Exposing data operations as messages also gives you extra abilities. You can easily
adopt a reactive approach: more than one microservice can listen to data-operation
messages. You can also introduce data-modification announcement messages: when
data changes in some way, you announce this to the world, and the world can react as
it needs to.

In the online newspaper case, you'll eventually need to provide a search feature so
readers can search for articles. You can use a specialist search engine solution for this
feature[11] and expose it via a microservice. When an article is saved, you need to make
sure the search engine also indexes it. A simplistic approach is to define an *index-article*
message that the search engine service acts on; the article service sends this message
when it saves an article, as shown in figure 4.6.

---

[11] Elasticsearch is a great choice: www.elastic.co.

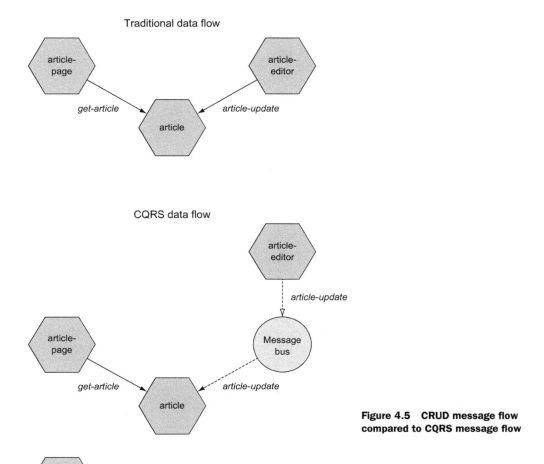

Figure 4.5   CRUD message flow compared to CQRS message flow

Figure 4.6   Direct synchronous interaction with the *search-engine* service

This architecture isn't reactive. It's highly coupled for a microservice architecture, even though it uses patterns to avoid identifying individual services. The *article* service knows that it needs to send messages to the *article-index* microservice and includes these messages in its workflow.

What happens if other services also need to know about changes to articles? Perhaps there's an encoding service that creates download PDFs for each article. A better approach is to announce that the article has changed, and for interested parties to subscribe to changes. Figure 4.7 shows this asynchronous interaction.

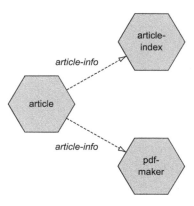

Figure 4.7   Reactive asynchronous interaction with the *search-engine* service

In this approach, the *article* service sends an asynchronous message, *article-info*, which is observed by other microservices. You can easily extend your system to perform other actions when an article changes, without affecting the microservices dealing with article business logic.

Dealing with missing updates

In the reactive data-update scenario, you can reasonably ask what happens if messages get lost. The answer is that your data will slowly become stale. Some articles will never be indexed, and some PDFs will never be generated. How do you deal with this?

You must first accept that your data will be inaccurate. You can't avoid that. The question then becomes one of reconciling conflicts in the data. In some cases, you can generate the correct data on demand. For example, if a PDF is missing when a request comes in for it, you can generate the PDF. You'll have to accept a performance hit for doing so, but this happens in only a small number of cases, because most messages won't be lost.

What about stale PDFs, where the article has changed? In that case, use a versioning strategy to ensure that you serve the correct version. Something as simple as appending the version number to the filename of the PDF will work. Or use a hash of the article contents as part of the filename, if you're paranoid.

In other cases, you'll need to actively correct errors by continuously validating your dataset. In the case of the search engine, you won't detect missing articles just by searching, but you can run a batch process to systematically verify that each article is in the search engine. The exact mechanism will vary with the search engine, although they generally expose some form of key-value view of the data that you can use. A more general solution is to use a distributed event log such as Kafka (https://kafka.apache.org) or DL (http://distributedlog.incubator.apache.org). These maintain a history of all messages, which you can replay against your data stores to ensure that all data-update operations have been effected. Unsurprisingly, you'll need conflict resolution policies to make this work in practice. Making data-update operations idempotent will also greatly simplify things.

In addition, you gain the ability to test microservices easily. Business-logic microservices interact with your data infrastructure only via messages. You don't need to install the data stores and their microservices; you can mock up the data interactions. This allows you to define unit tests without any overhead or dependencies, which makes unit testing extremely fast and easy. You'll see a concrete example of this in chapter 9.

A common technique is to use a microservice that provides a simple in-memory database as your primary data store for local development. Each test then operates against a clean dataset. It also means your development and debug cycle is fast, because you have no dependency on a real database. You perform more-complete integration testing with a real database on your build and staging systems or even, occasionally, on your local machine.[12]

You gain the ability to easily debug and measure data modifications. All data operations are represented as messages and so are subject to the same debugging and measurement tooling as the rest of your microservice system.

The message-oriented approach doesn't apply to all data. It doesn't make sense to embed large binary data in messages; instead, you can provide references to the binary data, which can then be streamed directly from specialist data stores.

4.2.3   *Using the system configuration to control data*

By representing data operations as messages, you gain control over data using only the configuration of the system, in terms of the microservices that handle the messages. This allows you to choose eventual consistency not as an absolute choice, but as something subject to fine-grained tuning. Consider again the user profile data for the newspaper. Users need to be able to view their profile data and update it; you've already seen one configuration for the *profile-load* and *profile-save* messages that serve these purposes. The *user-profile* service responds to these messages, but whether the messages are synchronous or asynchronous depends on your consistency configuration.

The user profile data isn't critical to the basic functioning of the system, so it can be eventually consistent. This lets you, the architect, reduce costs and improve performance by using eventually consistent storage. On the other hand, a business requirement may emerge that requires strict consistency of the user profile data: perhaps the newspaper has a financial focus, and you're adding a "track your share portfolio" feature.

In the eventually consistent case, the system can use an underlying database engine that provides eventual consistency.[13] You front this with multiple instances of the *user-profile* service that connect to one or more database nodes. In this architecture, you deliberately choose inconsistent data in order to improve performance and reduce costs. In practice, this means not every *profile-load* message will return the most recent version of the profile data. Sometimes, a *profile-save* will change a user's profile and a

---

[12] Using a container engine, such as Docker, to run transient instances of databases is convenient for testing.

[13] The individual and separate nodes implementing the database typically communicate between themselves using a gossip protocol to establish consistent data.

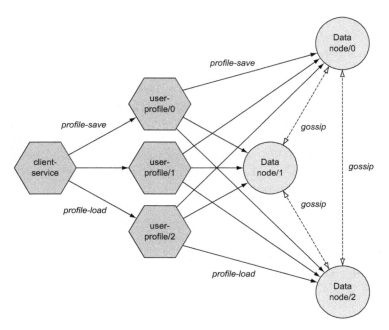

Figure 4.8   Eventually consistent data interactions

subsequent *profile-load*, within a short period of time, will return old data. This interaction is shown in figure 4.8. It's a business decision to accept this system behavior.

Alternatively, for the financial newspaper, you may decide to use a centralized relational database for the user profile data, because it contains share-portfolio details. In this case, the multiple instances of the *user-profile* service connect to the centralized relational database in the same manner as a traditional monolithic system, as shown in figure 4.9. This ensures consistency at the price of introducing the same scaling issues you have with traditional systems. But you isolate technical debt, so this situation is acceptable.

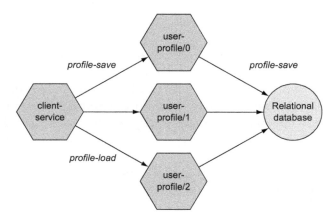

Figure 4.9   Immediately consistent data interactions

How does a message-oriented approach help you here? It allows you to move between these models without committing to them as fundamental architectural decisions. For the financial newspaper, before the portfolio requirement arose, the first version of the site worked fine with the eventually consistent model. But when a business requirement demanded stricter consistency, you could easily move to this model by changing your message-routing configuration. From the perspective of client services, the *profile-load* and *profile-save* messages appear to behave the same way.

You can also use this approach to implement flexible scaling, independent of the underlying database. Let's return to the sharded approach to user profiles. As an architect, you need to decide whether this approach is a good choice for your problem context. It has the advantage of easy scaling. You can increase throughput (the number of requests you can handle per second) linearly; adding a new *user-profile-shard* service always adds the same amount of extra capacity. This happens because shards have no dependencies on each other. In systems that do have dependencies, increasing the number of elements tends to have diminishing marginal returns—each new element gives less capacity.

Although you can increase throughput arbitrarily by adding shards, you can't decrease latency the same way. The path that each message follows is always the same and takes about the same time, so there's a lower limit to latency.[14] Latency is higher than in a non-sharded system, because you have extra message hops. You can prevent increases in latency by adding new services, if the volume of data is causing performance issues in each shard. This architecture deliberately prefers throughput over latency.

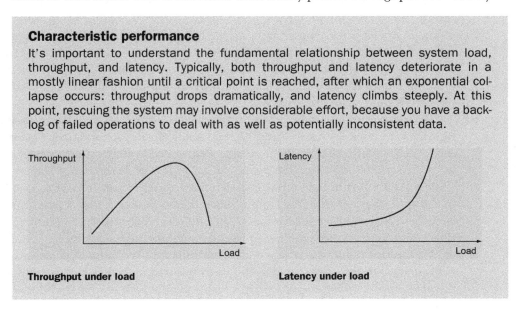

Characteristic performance
It's important to understand the fundamental relationship between system load, throughput, and latency. Typically, both throughput and latency deteriorate in a mostly linear fashion until a critical point is reached, after which an exponential collapse occurs: throughput drops dramatically, and latency climbs steeply. At this point, rescuing the system may involve considerable effort, because you have a backlog of failed operations to deal with as well as potentially inconsistent data.

Throughput under load

Latency under load

---

[14] You can't decrease latency below the speed of light—the speed of light in optical fiber, that is, which is only about 66% of the speed of light in a vacuum.

(continued)

In a production system, you won't be able to detect load-induced failures in a predictable way, because the system may collapse too quickly. The workaround is to build systems that have linear performance characteristics, and measure the failure point of individual elements. This gives you an upper bound to system capacity. To keep your system healthy, make sure that, as a rule of thumb, you preemptively have enough elements deployed to keep system capacity below 50%.

Sharding provides stronger fault tolerance. Shards are independent, and issues in a given shard only affect the data that it owns. Thus, it's essential to ensure that you have an evenly distributed key space for shards (that's why you use hashing to create shard keys). If a shard goes down, you lose access to only a subset of your data. A shard doesn't have to be a single database or instance. Each shard can run in fault-tolerant configurations such as single-writer, multiple-reader. The advantage of sharding here is that when the writer fails, failover is limited to the data on the shard; you don't have to reconcile across your entire dataset, so recovery is faster.

Sharding does have complications. Your data needs to be key-value oriented, because the entity key will be the most efficient retrieval mechanism. General queries must execute across all shards, and then you need to combine the results. You'll have to write the code to do this. You'll also have to run and maintain many databases, and automation will be essential. This has an up-front impact on the project-delivery timeline.

You also have to manage the complexity of shard transitions. Consider the case where you need to deploy each shard onto a larger machine. From a microservice messaging perspective, you want to be able to add a new version of the *user-profile-shard* service for a given shard and then migrate all relevant message traffic (*profile-load/save* messages, and any other profile messages—abbreviate them all with *profile-**) and all existing data to the new shard, while having no downtime. Figure 4.10 shows a possible deployment sequence for doing so.

This deployment sequence demonstrates the standard approach to message reconfiguration in microservice systems. You systematically deploy updated versions of each service, modifying the message flows one step a time. You use multiple staged versions of each service to do this so that you can avoid the need to change service behavior while a service is running (this is known as preserving *immutability*, which we'll discuss in the next chapter). You also follow this staged-version strategy so you can verify, at each step, that the system still works. Zero downtime becomes a (solvable!) message-flow mini puzzle, rather than a sophisticated engineering challenge.

To use this deployment sequence in production, you'll need to automate it and verify it at each step. It's reversible and measurable, and thus safe. More important, it's possible, and it takes less effort and creates far less risk than a traditional database migration.

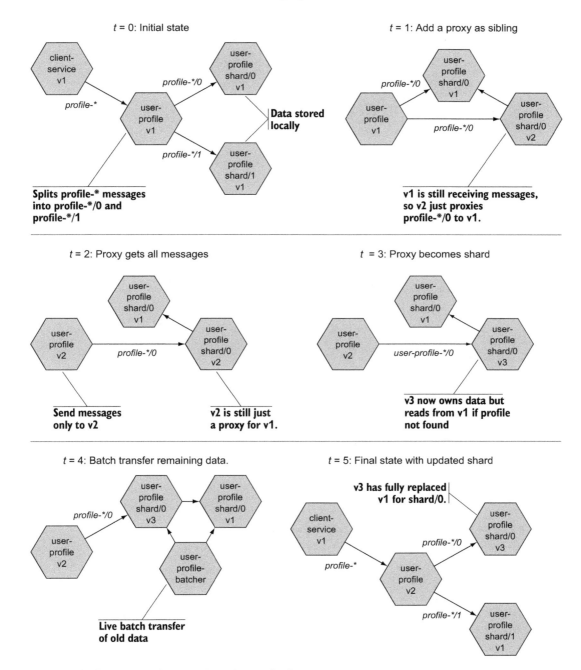

Figure 4.10 Deployment sequence to replace a shard

The other sequences that are important are adding and removing shards. You add a shard to scale up and remove a shard to reduce complexity by using instances with

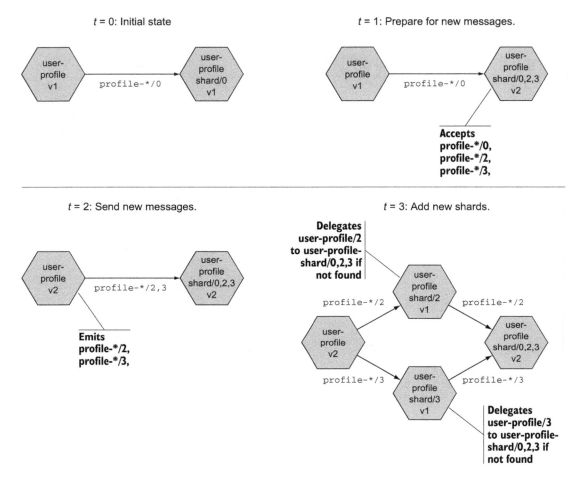

Figure 4.11   Deployment sequence to split a shard

more individual capacity. This change follows the same basic set of steps as a shard upgrade. Figure 4.11 shows the important steps in splitting *shard/0* into *shard/2* and *shard/3*.

The microservice architecture allows you to route messages as desired. You have a flexible tool for controlling the performance and accuracy characteristics of your data, by routing data-access messages to different services. The importance of measurement when doing so can't be stressed enough: you're running a production system, and you need to verify that each transition leaves the system in a good state. There are only two transitions: adding a service instance and removing a service instance. By applying these in a controlled manner, you can keep your data safe under major structural changes, and do so while staying live.

4.2.4   *Using weaker constraints to distribute data*

It's costly to keep distributed data accurate. Often, the cost of accuracy is greater than the benefit. You need to explicitly raise these questions with business decision makers so that you can design an appropriate system. When you make explicit the cost of complete data accuracy—or even high data accuracy—it enables you to have a rational discussion with decision makers.[15] If you can define quantitatively the expected accuracy of the system, you can use weaker constraints on your data to achieve acceptable levels of cost by sacrificing accuracy.

One of the easiest, least damaging, and most widespread forms of constraint weakening is *denormalization*. Traditional best practice in data schema design recommends that you keep data in *normal form*, roughly meaning you shouldn't duplicate data between tables unnecessarily. Instead, use separate tables and foreign keys. The problem with duplicated data is that it risks becoming inconsistent with the authoritative version of the data. This can happen for any number of reasons in a production system, because data is under constant modification.

But denormalization means data is local to where it's needed. By keeping copies of dependent data with primary entities, you significantly improve performance, and you avoid additional database lookups. For example, in the newspaper system, each article has an author. You can store this fact as an author identifier in the article entity and then look up the author's details from the author entity. Or you can duplicate the author's then-current details into the article entity when you first create an article. You then have the author's details available where you need them, saving you a database query because you've denormalized them into the article entity.

The trade-off is that subsequent changes to the author's details will need to be propagated to article entities (if this is a requirement). Such propagation might be implemented as a batch process (with subsequent inaccuracy between batch runs) or as change-announcement messages that the article service can listen for (and some of which might be missed). With this update mechanism, article and author data are unlikely to remain entirely consistent. In the case of the newspaper system, you'd define an acceptable level of accuracy—say, 99%—and occasionally sample your dataset[16] to verify that this is the case (if doing so is deemed necessary—you might take the simpler approach of correcting any author inaccuracies on a case-by-case base as they come to light).

Denormalization is just one example of a more general approach: using conflict resolution *after* the fact (for example, fixing bad data) rather than conflict resolution *before* the fact (for example, strict transactions).[17] If you can define conflict resolution

---

[15] We'll discuss these issues in chapter 8.

[16] Random sampling is a powerful, often-overlooked algorithmic approach. As long as you accept the principle that less than 100% accuracy is acceptable, you can use sampling to measure and solve many data-accuracy issues.

[17] This isn't a book on the theory of distributed data, which is a wide field. As a software architect, you need to be aware that after-the-fact conflict resolution is a workable strategy and that you may need to do some research into the best approaches for your project.

rules, you can weaken many of the constraints on your data processing. The conflict resolution doesn't have to be entirely accurate, just sufficiently so. For example, you can use the last modification date to define a rule that the most recent version of a data entity "wins" when there's a conflict. This makes the assumption that your separate machines have reasonably synchronized clocks; clocks are never entirely synchronized, but you can put in place synchronization protocols that make this a workable assumption. Nonetheless, sometimes old versions will win. How often that's acceptable depends on your acceptable-error rate.

4.3   *Rethinking traditional data patterns*

The traditional structures for data are heavily derived from the relational model. Once you're freed from that model, you can't rely on the standard approaches to data design. In this section we'll look at the alternatives.

4.3.1   *Primary keys*

How do you choose the correct primary keys for your data entities in a microservices context? With traditional enterprise data, in contrast, you can fall back on the established choices for primary key selection. You can use natural keys, such as the user's email address, or you can use synthetic keys, such as an incrementing integer. Relational databases use indexing and data-storage algorithms[18] that are optimized for these kinds of keys. In a microservices context, don't forget the distributed nature of the system: you can't rely on the existence of a centralized database to choose keys for you. You need to generate keys in a decentralized manner. The challenge is to maintain the uniqueness of the keys.

You could rely on the guaranteed uniqueness of a natural key like the user's email address. This might seem like a great shortcut at first, but the key space isn't evenly distributed—the distribution of characters in email addresses isn't uniform. So, you can't use the email address directly to determine the network location of the corresponding data. Other natural keys, such as usernames and phone numbers, tend to have the same issue. To counteract this, you can hash the natural key to get an even distribution over the key space. You then have a mechanism for scaling evenly as your data volume grows.

But there's still a problem. If the natural key changes—a user changes their email address or username—then the hashed key will be different, and you may end up with orphaned data. You'll need to perform a migration to resolve this issue.

As an alternative, you can use synthetic keys for data entities. In this approach, although you can query and search for the data entity via natural keys, the data entity itself has a synthetically generated unique key that isn't dependent on anything, is evenly distributable, and is permanent. GUIDs, both standard and custom, are often used to achieve this goal.

---

[18] The B+ tree structure is often used in database implementations. It has many entries per node, and this reduces the number of I/O operations needed to maintain the tree.

GUIDs have two problems, though. First, they're long strings of random characters, making them difficult for human eyes and brains to recognize quickly. This makes development, debugging, and log analysis more difficult. Second, GUIDs don't index well, particularly in traditional databases. Their strength—their even distribution over the space of possible values—is a weakness for many indexing algorithms. Each new GUID can occur anywhere in the key space, so you lose data locality; every new entry could end up anywhere in the index data structure, necessitating movement of index subtrees. The advantage of an incrementing integer is that inserting new records is relatively efficient, because the key preserves index tree locality.

It's possible to generate a distributed, unique, incrementing integer key, although you'll probably need to build your own solution. This will give you the best of both worlds, but not without trade-offs. For acceptable performance, you can't guarantee that the key increases monotonically: keys won't generate in exactly linear order. Sorting by key only approximates the creation time of the entity, but this is a fact of life in distributed systems.

There's no single correct approach to key generation in a microservice architecture, but you can apply the following decision principles:

- Synthetic keys are preferred, because they can be permanent and avoid the need to modify references.
- GUIDs aren't an automatic choice. Although eminently suited to distributed systems, they have negative effects on performance, especially in relation to traditional database indexes.
- You can use integer keys. They can still be unique, but they're weaker than traditional autoincrementing database keys.

4.3.2   Foreign keys

The JOIN operation is one of the most useful features of the relational model, allowing you to declaratively extract different views of your data based on how that data is related. In a distributed microservice world, the JOIN operation is something you have to learn to mostly live without. There's no guarantee that any given data entities are stored in the same database, and thus no mechanism for joining them. JOIN operations in general, if performed at all, must be performed manually.

Although this may seem to be a crushing blow against the microservice model, it's more of a theoretical problem than a practical one. The following alternatives to JOINs are often better choices:

- *Denormalization*—Embed sub-entities within primary entities. This is particularly easy when you're using a document-oriented data store. The sub-entities can either live entirely within the primaries, which makes life awkward when you need to treat the sub-entities separately; or they can live in a separate data store but be duplicated, which leads to consistency issues. You need to decide based on the trade-offs.

- *Document-oriented design*—Design your data schemas so there are fewer references between entities. Encode small entities using literal values, rather than foreign-key references. Use an internal structure in your entities (for example, store the list of items in the *shopping-cart* entity).

- *Using update events to generate reports*—Publish changes to data so that other parts of the system can act on them appropriately. In particular, reporting systems shouldn't access primary stores, but should be populated by update events. This decouples the structure of the data for reporting purposes from the structure used for production processing.

- *Writing custom views*—Use microservices to provide custom views of your data. The microservice can pull the various entities required from their separate stores and merge the data together. This approach is practical only when used sparingly, but it has the advantage of flexibility. If you're using message-level sharding, you've already done most of the work.

- *Aggressive caching*—With this approach, your entities will still contain references to other entities. These are foreign keys, but you must perform separate lookup operations for each referenced entity. The performance of these lookups can be dramatically improved when you use caching.

- *Using in-memory data structures*—Keep your data in-memory if possible. Many datasets can be stored fully in-memory. With sharding, you can extend this across multiple machines.

- *Adopting a key-value stance*—Think of your data in terms of the key-value model. This gives you maximum flexibility when choosing databases and reduces interrelationships between entities.

4.3.3   *Transactions*

Traditional relational databases generate transactions, so you can be sure your data will remain consistent. When business operations modify multiple data entities, transactions can keep everything consistent according to your business rules. Transactions ensure that your operations are *linearly serializable*: all transactions can be definitively ordered in time, one after the other. This makes your life as a developer much easier, because each operation begins and ends with the database in a consistent state. Let's examine this promise in more detail.

Returning to the digital newspaper, suppose management has decided that micropayments are the wave of the future. Forget about subscriptions—selling articles for a dime each is the new business strategy.

The micropayments feature works like this: The user purchases article credits in bulk—say, 10 articles for $1, with each article costing 10¢. Each time the user reads an article, their balance is reduced, and the count of the articles they've read increases. This feels like something that would require traditional transactions. Figure 4.12 shows the workflow to read an article.

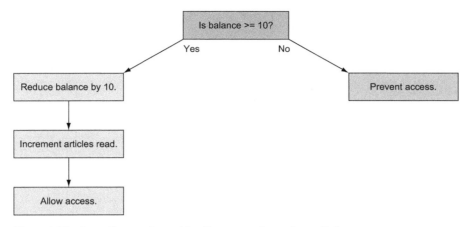

Figure 4.12 Operations performed to allow a user to read an article

To ensure data consistency, you wrap this in a transaction. If there's a failure at any point, the transaction reverts any changes made so far, moving back to a known good state. More important, the database ensures that transactions are isolated. That means the database creates a fictional timeline, where transactions happen one after the other. If the user has only 10¢ left, then they should only be able to read one more article; without a transaction, the user would be able to read extra articles for free.

Table 4.1 shows a possible timeline for how this undesirable situation could happen. In this timeline, the user is reading articles on both their laptop and mobile phone, they have 10¢ remaining, and they've read nine articles. They should be able to read only one more article on one device. The timeline illustrates how data inconsistency can arise if you take a simplistic direct approach to data access.

Table 4.1 Timeline showing data inconsistency

Time	Balance	Articles	Laptop	Mobile
0	10¢	9	Check balance is >= 10¢	
1	10¢	9		Check balance is >= 10¢
2	0¢	9	Reduce balance by 10¢	
3	-10¢	9		Reduce balance by 10¢ (<0!)
4	-10¢	10	Increment articles read	
5	-10¢	11		Increment articles read

If you allow the data operations to interleave, you end up with inconsistent data. At the end of the example timeline, the user's balance is -10¢, and they performed an action they weren't supposed to. At least the article count is correct (11 read).

Database transactions ensure that these sequences of operations occur in isolation from each other; see table 4.2. The entire laptop operation flow completes first. Then the mobile flow starts; it fails because the user's balance is insufficient. Transactions isolate operations from each other by imposing a linear flow of operations through time.[19]

Table 4.2   Timeline with transactions

Time	Balance	Articles	Laptop	Mobile
0	10¢	9	Check balance is >= 10¢	
1	0¢	9	Reduce balance by 10¢	
2	0¢	10	Increment articles read	
3	0¢	10		Check balance is >= 10¢ STOP

But transactions aren't free. You need to keep all relevant data in the same database, which makes you beholden to the way that database wants to work. You're almost certainly using relational schemas and SQL, and you're prioritizing data consistency over user responsiveness. Under heavy load, such as a major breaking news story, these transactions will slow down your article delivery API.[20] You also need to code the transaction contexts correctly. It isn't a trivial thing to define transactions and make sure they don't deadlock.[21]

Let's consider an alternative. You can achieve many of your goals by using *reservations*. Reservations are exactly what they sound like: you reserve a resource for possible future use (just like a restaurant table or an airline ticket), releasing it later if you don't use it.[22] Instead of checking the user's balance, you reserve 10¢. If the user doesn't have sufficient credit, the reservation will fail. You don't need to wait for other transactions; you know immediately not to proceed. You can safely interleave operations, as shown in table 4.3.

Reservations are faster because less coordination is required. But there's a trade-off: you sacrifice data consistency. If you fail to deliver the article, it's probably due to an error in the system, so you're unlikely to be able to restore the user's balance

---

[19] The concept of linear serialization is a powerful simplification of the real world. It's the useful fiction that there's a universal clock and that everything that happens can be synchronized against this clock. This model of the world makes coding business logic much simpler. It's a pity it fails so badly for distributed systems.

[20] If you increase the number of database instances to handle more load, you'll notice that doing so doesn't give you more performance after a certain number of instances. The instances have to communicate with each other to implement distributed transactions, and this communication grows exponentially as the number of instances increases. This is exactly the wrong scaling characteristic.

[21] A *deadlock* between transactions occurs when each transaction waits for the other to complete before proceeding. Because no transaction can complete, the system locks up.

[22] The sample code for chapter 1 contains an example of a reservation system. See https://github.com/senecajs/ramanujan.

Table 4.3   Timeline with reservations

Time	Balance	Articles	Laptop	Mobile
0	10¢	9	Reserve 10¢? YES	
1	0¢	9		Reserve 10¢? NO
2	0¢	10	Increment articles read	
3	0¢	10	Confirm reservation	

correctly.[23] In addition, the read-article counter may miss some articles if there are failures during the operation flow. How much do these inaccuracies matter? That's a question for the business. Your task, as a systems architect, is to determine the acceptable error rates. These dictate the tools you'll use. Transactions may be necessary, but most businesses like to keep the door open even when some shelves are empty.

> **Implementing reservations**
> Reservations aren't difficult to implement, but you need to be careful. A simplistic approach is to use a single service that maintains the reservations in-memory. This isn't particularly fail-safe. A more suitable approach in production is to use atomic operations provided by in-memory stores such as memcached (https://memcached.org) and Redis (http://redis.io). You can even use a relational database: use an UPDATE ... WHERE ... query. In all cases, you'll need a periodic cleanup batch process to review the list of open reservations and cancel those that are too old. For a deeper discussion of the reservation pattern, read the excellent book *SOA Patterns* (Manning, 2012, https://www.manning.com/books/soa-patterns), by Arnon Rotem-Gal-Oz.

The key observation here is that there are degrees of data accuracy, and you can make acceptable trade-offs to meet the demands of the business. A simple mental model for comparing these approaches is to chart performance versus accuracy, as shown in figure 4.13. Moving an approach from its position in this trade-off chart may be logically impossible or expensive.[24]

There's another benefit to the reservations approach that's more important than performance: the flexibility to respond to changing requirements. You can place the reservation logic in a *reservations* microservice and the article-read counts in an *analytics* service. Now, you're free to modify these separately and choose appropriate data stores for the different kinds of data.

---

[23] You'll have to handle orphan reservations; otherwise, all of your resources will end up reserved. Each reservation should have a time limit, and you'll need to periodically review the list of outstanding reservations to see whether any are stale.

[24] For example, if you want faster transactions, then you'll need bigger machines to keep the number of instances low. Figure 4.13 shows the nominal trade-offs, given reasonable resources. The point of engineering isn't that you can build a bridge that won't fall—anyone can do that, given enough money. It's that you can do so in a reasonable time for a reasonable cost.

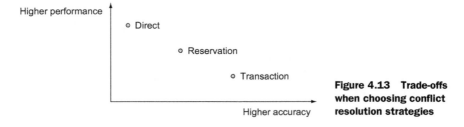

Figure 4.13 Trade-offs when choosing conflict resolution strategies

Reservations are relatively easy to implement, because most data stores provide for atomic updates. The reservations strategy is just one example of an alternative to transactions that's widely applicable in many scenarios.

4.3.4   *Transactions aren't as good as you think they are*

Using database transactions doesn't magically wash away the problem of dirty data. It's a mistake to assume that transactions will give you consistent data without any further thinking required. Transactions come in different strengths, and you need to read the fine print to know what you're getting. The promise that traditional databases make is that their transactions will satisfy the ACID properties:[25]

- *Atomicity*—Transactions either completely succeed or completely fail with no changes to data.
- *Consistency*—Completed transactions leave the data compliant with all constraints, such as uniqueness.
- *Isolation*—Transactions are linearly serializable.
- *Durability*—Committed transactions preserve changes to data, even under failure of the database system.

Although these properties are important, you shouldn't treat them as absolute requirements. By relaxing these properties, you open the floodgates to far more data-persistence strategies and trade-offs.[26] Traditional databases don't deliver the full set of ACID properties unless you ask for them. In particular, the isolation property demands that transactions be linearly serializable. This demand can have severe performance penalties, so databases provide different isolation levels to mitigate the impact of full isolation.

The concept of isolation levels has been standardized.[27] There are four, listed here from strongest to weakest:

- *Serializable*—This is full isolation. All transactions can be ordered linearly in time, and each transaction sees only a frozen snapshot of the data as it was when the transaction began.

---

[25] The material in this section is covered in glorious detail in most undergraduate computer science courses. We'll skim the details for now, just as we did in our original studies!

[26] For example, the Redis database positions itself as an in-memory data-structure server and synchronizes to disk only on a periodic basis.

[27] For more, see the SQL standard: ISO/IEC 9075-1, www.iso.org.

- *Repeatable-read*—Individual data entities (rows) remain fixed when read multiple times within a transaction, but queries within the transaction may return different result sets if other concurrent transactions insert or remove entities.
- *Read-committed*—Individual data entities may change when read multiple times within the transaction, but only changes from committed data modified by other concurrent transactions will be seen.
- *Read-uncommitted*—Uncommitted data from other concurrent transactions may be seen.

In the context of the micropayments example, the direct approach corresponds to the read-uncommitted level. The transaction approach is satisfied by the repeatable-read level. The reservations approach doesn't use transactions but could be considered analogous to the read-committed level, if you're prepared to stretch.

The SQL standard allows database vendors to have different default isolation levels.[28] You might assume the serializable level without getting it. The standard also allows the database to use a higher level when necessary, so you might pay a performance penalty you don't want, or need, to pay.

Traditional databases don't deliver on data consistency when you look closely. As a software architect, you can't avoid your responsibilities by defaulting to using a traditional relational database. The database will make those decisions for you, and the results may not be the ones your business needs. It's acceptable to choose a single-database solution when you're building a monolith, because that approach makes your code less complex and provides a unified data-access layer. This forcing function on your decision making is washed away by the microservice approach. Microservices make it easier to match a data-storage solution to your data-storage needs, as well as to change that solution later.

4.3.5 Schemas draw down technical debt

The worst effect of relational databases is that they encourage the use of canonical data models. This is an open invitation to incur technical debt. The advantages of strict schemas that define a canonical data model are often outweighed by the disadvantages. It's one of the primary positions of this book that this kind of trade-off should be made explicitly and consciously. Too often, the decision to use strict schemas is driven by convention, rather than analysis of the business context and needs of the system.[29]

---

[28] For example, Oracle and Postgres are read-committed by default, whereas MySQL is repeatable-read.

[29] A preference for strict schemas and contracts, versus "anything goes," is predictive of a preference for strong versus weak typing in programming languages. There's much debate about the subject and the relative merits of both positions. Jonathan Swift, author of *Gulliver's Travels*, has the best perspective on this question: "Two mighty Powers have been engaged in a most obstinate War for six and thirty Moons past. It's allowed on all Hands, that the primitive way of breaking Eggs, before we eat them, was upon the larger End: But his present Majesty's Grand-father, while he was a Boy, going to eat an Egg, and breaking it according to the ancient Practice, happened to cut one of his Fingers. Whereupon the Emperor his Father published an Edict, commanding all his Subjects, upon great Penaltys, to break the smaller End of their Eggs. The People so highly resented this Law, that our Histories tell us there have been six Rebellions raised on that account; wherein one Emperor lost his Life, and another his Crown."

A canonical data model, enforced via strict schemas, ensures that all parts of the system have the same understanding of a given data entity and its relationships. This means business rules can be consistently applied. The downside is that changes to the schema necessarily affect all parts of the system. Changes tend to come in big bangs and are hard to roll back. The details of the schema are hardcoded, literally, into the code base.

The model, and the schema describing it, must be determined at the start of the project. Although you can provide some scope for future changes, this is difficult to achieve in all cases. The initial high-level structure of the entities is almost impossible to change later, because too many parts of the system are frozen by implicit assumptions about the schema.[30]

And yet new business requirements must be met. In practice, this means the original schema is extended only where possible so it doesn't break other parts of the system. The schema suffers, because it diverges from an ideal structure for new and emerging requirements. Other parts of the schema become legacy structures that must still be handled in the code base. Current business logic must retain knowledge of the old system; this is how technical debt builds.

To achieve rapid development, it's better to be lenient. New code, delivering new features, shouldn't be constrained by old code. How you deal with forward and backward compatibility shouldn't affect your code. The microservice architecture approaches this problem as a matter of configuration, directing messages that make old assumptions to legacy microservices, and messages that make new assumptions to new microservices. The code in these microservices doesn't need to know about other versions, and thus you avoid building technical debt.

4.4   *A practical decision guide for microservice data*

The principle benefit of microservices is that they enable rapid development without incurring large amounts of technical debt. In that context, data-storage choices are skewed toward flexibility but away from accuracy. The scaling benefits of microservices are important, but they should be a secondary consideration when you're deciding how to proceed. The following decision tree is a rough guide to choosing appropriate data-storage solutions at key points in the lifecycle of your project.

The databases recommended for the different scenarios are broadly classified as follows:

---

[30] Many years ago, I built a system for a stockbroking firm. The system could create historical share-price charts using pricing data from the mainframe. At the start of the project, I was given a list of indicators, price/earning ratios, and so forth. These numerical data fields were given for each stock, and they were all the same. I duly designed and built a relational model with an exact schema matching the indicators. Four weeks before go-live, we finally got access to the full dataset and imported it into the system—but there was a high rate of failure. In particular, the data for financial institutions couldn't be imported. Upon investigation, it appeared that the data from the mainframe was corrupt. It certainly didn't match the schema. I was told, "*Of course* the indicators are different for financial stocks—everybody knows that!" This was a catastrophe—we were close to the deadline, and there was no time for refactoring. I did the only thing I could think of: I shoved the data into incorrectly named columns and added a comment in the code.

- *Memory*—The entire volume of data is stored in memory in convenient data structures. Serialization to disk is optional, is occasional, or may offer strong safety guarantees. This storage solution includes not only specific memory-oriented solutions, such as Redis and memcached, but also custom microservices.
- *Document*—Data is organized as documents. In the simplest case, this reduces to a key-value store, such as LevelDB or Berkeley DB. More-complex storage solutions offer many of the querying features of the relational model, such as MongoDB, CouchDB, and CockroachDB.
- *Relational*—The traditional database model, as offered by Postgres, MySQL, Oracle, and others.
- *Specialist*—The solution is geared toward data with a specific shape, such as time series (for example, InfluxDB) or search (Elasticsearch), or offers significant scaling (Cassandra, DynamoDB).

This classification isn't mutually exclusive, and many solutions can operate in multiple scenarios.

Cutting across this classification is the further decision to make the data local or remote to the service. This selection can't be made freely, because some storage solutions are much easier to run locally. All options are also subject to caching as a mechanism to improve performance and reduce the impact of database choice.

Regardless of the database you choose, it's important to prevent the database from becoming a mechanism for communication. At all times, keep strict boundaries around microservices that can access data, even when multiple microservices are accessing the same database.

Let's look at the data-persistence decision from the perspective of greenfield and legacy scenarios.

4.4.1 Greenfield

You're mostly free to determine the structure, technologies, and deployment of your project, and most code is new.

INITIAL DEVELOPMENT

During this early phase of the project, substantive requirements are discovered. You need to be able to rapidly change design and data structures:

- *Local environment*—Your development machine. You need flexibility and fast unit testing. Data access is performed entirely via messages, so you can use in-memory data storage. This gives you complete flexibility, fast unit tests, and clean data on every run. Local, small installations of document or relational databases are necessary only when you need to use database-specific features. You should always be able to run small subsets of the system and mock data-operation messages.

- *Build and staging*—These are shared environments that typically need some test and validation data to persist, even if the main body of data is wiped on each run. But you need to retain the flexibility to handle schema changes emerging from requirements uncertainty. A document-oriented store is most useful here.

PRODUCTION PHASE

The scope of the system is now well defined. The system has either gone live or is on track to do so, and you must maintain it. Maintenance means not only keeping the system up and within acceptable error rates, but also incorporating new requirements:

- *Rapid development*—The business focus of the system is on rapid development. In this scenario, you gain development speed by retaining the use of document-oriented storage, even when this means lower accuracy. You can also consider keeping certain data local to the service, because it's independent of other services. Specialist databases also have a place in this scenario, because they allow you to take advantage of data-specific features.
- *Data integrity*—If the business focus is on the accuracy of the data, you can fall back on the proven capabilities of relational databases. You represent all data operations as messages, so migrating to a relational model is relatively easy.

4.4.2　Legacy

You must work with an existing system in production, with slow deployment cycles and significant technical debt. The data schema is large and has many internal dependencies.

INITIAL DEVELOPMENT

You must determine what strategies you can adopt to mitigate complexity in the context of the project's business goals, as well as develop an understanding of the legacy system's constraints:

- *Local environment*—If you're lucky, you may be able to run some elements of the legacy system locally. Otherwise, you may be dependent on network access to staging systems or even production. In the worst cases, you have no access—just system documentation. You can still represent the legacy system using messages, and doing so enables you to develop your own microservices against those messages. If you're developing new features, you can create greenfield bubbles within which to make better data-storage choices.
- *Build and staging*—Document-oriented stores offer the most flexibility in these environments. You may also have the opportunity to validate your message layer against a staging version of the production database.

PRODUCTION PHASE

You're running live with both your new code and the legacy system. Your new data-storage elements are also running live. Using messages to wrap the legacy system gives you the benefits of microservices in the new code:

- *Rapid development*—Your data-storage solution uses the legacy system of record as a last resort, and you're rapidly migrating data over to your new database choice. Even if the legacy database remains in production as the SOR, you can make a strategic decision to reduce data accuracy by developing against more-flexible databases. A common architecture is to duplicate legacy relational data into a document store.

- *Data integrity*—The legacy system remains in place as the SOR. Paradoxically, this gives you greater freedom to choose data-storage solutions, because you can always correct the data they contain using the SOR. Nonetheless, you'll pay the price of querying the SOR at a higher volume. A mitigating strategy is to generate data-update events from the SOR, if possible.

4.5 Summary

- The relational model and the use of transactions aren't an automatic fit for every enterprise application. These traditional solutions have hidden costs and may not work as well you expect.

- Data doesn't have to be completely accurate. Accuracy can be delayed, with data being eventually consistent. You can choose error rates explicitly, with the business accepting a given error rate on an ongoing basis. The payoffs are faster development cycles and a better user experience.

- The key principles of microservice messages, pattern matching, and transport independence can be applied to data operations. This frees your business logic from complexity introduced by scaling and performance techniques such as sharding and caching. These are hidden, and you can deploy them at your discretion.

- Traditional techniques such as data normalization and table joins are far less useful in a microservice context. Instead, use data duplication.

Deployment

The organizational decision to adopt the microservice architecture often represents an acceptance that change is necessary and that current work practices aren't delivering. This is an opportunity not only to adopt a more capable software architecture but also to introduce a new set of work practices for that architecture.

You can use microservices to adopt a scientific approach to risk management. Microservices make it easier to measure and control risk, because they give you small units of control. The reliability of your production system then becomes quantifiable, allowing you to move beyond ineffective manual sign-offs as the primary risk-reduction strategy. Because traditional processes regard software as a bag of features that are either broken or fixed, and don't incorporate the concept of failure thresholds and failure rates, they're much weaker protections against failure.[1]

5.1 *Things fall apart*

All things fail catastrophically. There's no gradual decline. There's decline, certainly; but when death comes, it comes quickly. Structures need to maintain a minimum level of integrity before they fall apart. Cross that threshold, and the essence is gone.

This is more than poetic symbolism. Disorder always increases.[2] Systems can tolerate some disorder and can even convert chaos into order in the short term; but in the long run, we're all dead, because disorder inevitably forces the system over the threshold of integrity into failure.

What is *failure*? From the perspective of enterprise software, this question has many answers. Most visible are the technical failures of the system to meet uptime requirements, feature requirements, and acceptable performance and defect levels. Less visible, but more important, are failures to meet business goals.

Organizations obsess about technical failures, often causing business failures as a result. The argument of this chapter is that it's better to accept many small failures in order to prevent large-scale catastrophic failures. It's better for 5% of users to see a broken web page than for the business to go bankrupt because it failed to compete in the marketplace.

The belief that software systems can be free from defects and that this is possible through sheer professionalism is pervasive in the enterprise. There's an implicit assumption that perfect software can be built at a reasonable cost. This belief ignores the basic dynamics of the law of diminishing marginal returns: the cost of fixing the next bug grows ever higher and is unbounded. In practice, all systems go into production with known defects. The danger of catastrophe comes from an institutional consensus that it's best to pretend that this isn't the case.

Can the microservice architecture speak to this problem? Yes, because it makes it easier to reduce the risk of catastrophic failure by allowing you to make small changes that have low impact. The introduction of microservices also provides you, as an architect, with the opportunity to reframe the discussion around acceptable failure rates and risk management. Unfortunately, there's no forcing function, and microservice deployments can easily become mired in the traditional risk management approach of enterprise operations. It's therefore essential to understand the possibilities for risk reduction that the architecture creates.

---

[1] To be bluntly cynical, traditional practices are more about territorial defense and blame avoidance than building effective software.

[2] There are more ways to be disorganized than there are ways to be organized. Any given change is more likely to move you further into disorder.

5.2   *Learning from history*

To understand how software systems fail and how you can improve deployment, you need to understand how other complex systems fail. A large-scale software system is not unlike a large-scale engineering system. There are many components interacting in many ways. With software, you have the additional complication of deployment—you keep changing the system. With something like a nuclear power plant, at least you only build it once. Let's start by examining just such a complex system in production.

5.2.1   *Three Mile Island*

On March 28, 1979, the second unit of the nuclear power plant located on Three Mile Island near Harrisburg, Pennsylvania, suffered a partial meltdown, releasing radioactive material into the atmosphere.[3]

The accident was blamed on operator error. From a complex systems perspective, this conclusion is neither fair nor useful. With complex systems, failure is inevitable. The question isn't, "Is nuclear energy safe?" but rather, "What levels of accidents and contamination can we live with?" This is also the question we should ask of software systems.

To understand what happened at Three Mile Island, you need to know how a reactor works at a high level, and at a low level where necessary. Your skills as a software architect will serve you well in understanding the explanation that follows. The reactor heats water, turning it into steam. The steam drives a turbine that spins to produce electricity. The reactor heats the water using a controlled fission reaction. The nuclear fuel, uranium, emits neutrons that collide with other uranium atoms, releasing even more neutrons. This chain reaction must be controlled through the absorption of excess neutrons; otherwise, bad things happen.

The uranium fuel is stored in a large, sealed, stainless steel containment vessel, about the height of a three-story building. The fuel is stored as vertical rods, about the height of a single story. Interspersed are control rods made of graphite, that absorb neutrons; to control the reaction, you raise and lower the control rods. The reaction can be completely stopped by lowering all the control rods fully; this is known as *scramming*. This is an obvious safety feature: if there's a problem, pretty much any problem, drop the rods![4] Nuclear reactors are designed with many such automatic safety devices (ASDs) that activate without human intervention on the basis of input signals from sensors. I'm sure you can already see the opportunity for unintended cascading behavior in the ASDs.

The heat from the core (all the stuff inside the containment vessel, including the rods) is extracted using water. This coolant water is radioactive, so you can't use it directly to drive the turbine. You have to use a heat exchanger to transfer the heat to a

---

[3] For full details, see John G. Kemeny et al., *Report of the President's Commission on the Accident at Three Mile Island* (U.S. Government Printing Office, 1979), http://mng.bz/hwAm.

[4] The technical term *scram* comes from the early days of research reactors. If anything went wrong, you dropped the rods, shouted "Scram!", and ran. Very fast.

set of completely separate water pipes; that water, which isn't radioactive, drives the turbine. You have a primary coolant system with radioactive water and a secondary coolant system with "normal" water. Everything is under high pressure and at a high temperature, including the turbine, which is cooled by the secondary system. The secondary water must be very pure and contain almost no microscopic particles, to protect the turbine blades, which are precision engineered. Observe how complexity lives in the details: a simple fact—that water drives the turbine—hides the complexity that it must be "special" purified water. Time for a high-level diagram: see figure 5.1.

Now let's go a little deeper. That special purified water for the secondary system doesn't happen by magic: you need something called a *condensate polisher* to purify the water, using filters. Like many parts of the system, the condensate polisher's valves, which allow water to enter and leave, are driven by compressed air. That means the plant, in addition to having water pipes for the primary and secondary cooling systems, also has compressed air pipes for a pneumatic system. Where does the special purified water come from? Feed pumps are used to pump water from a local water source—in this case, the Susquehanna River—into the cooling system. There are also emergency tanks, with emergency feed pumps, in case the main feed pumps fail. The valves for these are also driven by the pneumatic system.

We must also consider the core, which is filled with high-temperature radioactive water under high pressure.[5] High-pressure water is extremely dangerous and can damage the containment vessel, and the associated pipework, leading to a dreaded loss-of-containment accident (LOCA). You don't want holes in the containment vessel. To alleviate water pressure in the core, a *pressurizer* is used. This is a large water tank connected to the core and filled about half and half with water and steam. The pressurizer also has a drain, which allows water to be removed from the core. The steam at the top of the pressurizer tank is compressible and acts as a shock absorber. You can control the core pressure by controlling the volume of the water in the lower half of the pressurizer. But you must never, ever allow the water level to reach 100% (referred to as *going solid*): if you do, you'll have no steam and no shock absorber, and the result

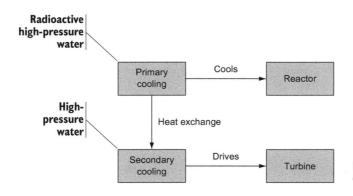

Figure 5.1   High-level components of a nuclear reactor

---

[5]   What fun!

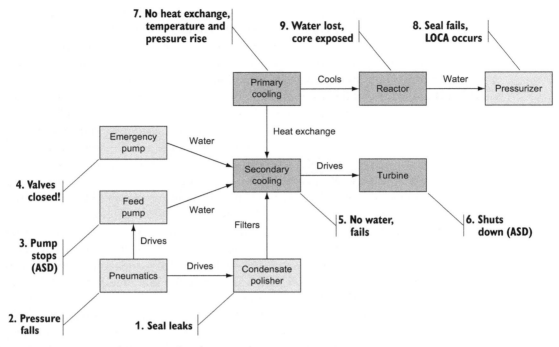

7. No heat exchange, temperature and pressure rise

9. Water lost, core exposed

8. Seal fails, LOCA occurs

Primary cooling → Cools → Reactor → Water → Pressurizer

Heat exchange

Emergency pump → Water → Secondary cooling

4. Valves closed!

Feed pump → Water → Secondary cooling

3. Pump stops (ASD)

Secondary cooling → Drives → Turbine

Filters

5. No water, fails

6. Shuts down (ASD)

Pneumatics → Drives → Feed pump

Pneumatics → Drives → Condensate polisher

2. Pressure falls

1. Seal leaks

Figure 5.2   A small subset of interactions between high and low levels in the reactor

will be a LOCA because pipes will burst. This fact is drilled into operators from day one. Figure 5.2 shows the expanded diagram.

THE TIMELINE OF THE ACCIDENT

At 4:00 a.m., the steam turbine *tripped*: it stopped automatically because the feed pumps for the secondary cooling system that cools the turbine had stopped. With no water entering the turbine, the turbine was in danger of overheating—and it's programmed to stop under these conditions. The feed pumps had stopped because the pneumatic air system that drives the valves for the pumps became contaminated with water from the condensate polisher. A leaky seal in the condensate polisher had allowed some of the water to escape into the pneumatic system. The end result was that a series of ASDs, operating as designed, triggered a series of ever-larger failures. More was to come.

With the turbine down and no water flowing in the secondary coolant system, no heat could be extracted from the primary coolant system. The core couldn't be cooled. Such a situation is extremely dangerous and, if not corrected, will end with a meltdown.

There was an ASD for this scenario: emergency feed pumps take water from an emergency tank. The emergency pumps kick in automatically. Unfortunately, in this case, the pipes to the emergency pumps were blocked, because two valves had been accidentally left closed during maintenance. Thus the emergency pumps supplied no water. The complexity of the system as a whole, and its interdependencies, are apparent here; not just the machinery, but also its management and maintenance, are part of the dependency relationship graph.

The system had now entered a cascading failure mode. The steam turbine boiled dry. The reactor scrammed automatically, dropping all the control rods to stop the fission reaction. This didn't reduce the heat to safe levels, however, because the decay products from the reaction still needed to cool down. Normally this takes several days and requires a functioning cooling system. With no cooling, very high temperatures and pressures built up in the containment vessel, which was in danger of breaching.

Naturally, there are ASDs for this scenario. A relief valve, known as the pilot-operated relief valve (PORV), opens under high pressure and allows the core water to expand into the pressurizer vessel. But the PORV is unreliable: valves for high-pressure radioactive water are, unsurprisingly, unreliable, failing about 1 in 50 times. In this case, the PORV opened in response to the high-pressure conditions but then failed to close fully after the pressure was relieved. It's important for operators to know the status of the PORV, and this one had recently been fitted with a status sensor and indicator. This sensor also failed, though, leading the operators to believe that the PORV was closed. The reactor was now under a LOCA, and ultimately more than one third of the primary cooling water drained away. The actual status of the PORV wasn't noticed until a new shift of operators started.

As water drained away, pressure in the core fell, but by too much. Steam pockets formed. These not only block water flow but also are far less efficient at removing heat. So, the core continued to overheat. At this point, Three Mile Island was only *13 seconds* into the accident, and the operators were completely unaware of the LOCA; they saw only a transient pressure spike in the core. Two minutes into the event, pressure dropped sharply as core coolant turned to steam. At this point, the fuel rods in the core were in danger of becoming exposed, because there was barely sufficient water to cover them. Another ASD kicked in—injection of cold, high-pressure water. This is a last resort to save the core by keeping it covered. The problem is that too much cold water can crack the containment vessel. Also, and far worse, too much water makes the pressurizer go solid. Without a pressure buffer, pipes will crack. So the operators, as they had been trained to do, slowed the cold-water injection rate.[6]

The core became partially exposed as a result, and a partial meltdown occurred. Although the PORV was eventually closed and the water was brought under control, the core was badly damaged. Chemical reactions inside the core led to the release of hydrogen gas, which caused a series of explosions; ultimately, radioactive material was released into the atmosphere.[7]

---

[6] Notice that the operators were using a mental model that had diverged from reality. Much the same happens with the operation of software systems under high load.

[7] An excellent analysis of this accident, and many others, can be found in the book *Normal Accidents* (Princeton University Press, 1999) by Charles Perrow. This book also develops a failure model for complex systems that's relevant to software systems.

LEARNING FROM THE ACCIDENT

Three Mile Island is one of the most-studied complex systems accidents. Some have blamed the operators, who "should" have understood what was happening, "should" have closed the valves after maintenance, and "should" have left the high-pressure cold-water injection running.[8] Have you ever left your home and not been able to remember whether you locked the front door? Imagine having 500 front doors—on any given day, in any given reactor, some small percentage of valves will be in the wrong state.

Others blame the accident on sloppiness in the management culture, saying there "should" have been lock sheets for the valves. But since then, adding more paperwork to track work practices has only *reduced* valve errors in other reactors, not eliminated them. Still others blame the design of the reactor: too much complexity, coupling, and interdependence. A simpler design has fewer failure modes. But it's in the nature of systems engineering that there's always hidden complexity, and the final version of initially simple designs becomes complex as a result.

These judgments aren't useful, because they're all obvious and true to some degree. The real learning is that complex systems are fragile and will fail. No amount of safety devices and procedures will solve this problem, because the safety devices and procedures are *part* of the problem. Three Mile Island made this clear: the interactions of all the components of the system (including the humans) led to failure.

There's a clear analogy to software systems. We build architectures that have a similar degree of complexity and the same kinds of interactions and tight couplings. We try to add redundancy and fail-safes but find that these measures fail anyway, because they haven't been sufficiently tested. We try to control risk with detailed release procedures and strict quality assurance. Supposedly, this gives us predictable and safe deployments; but in practice, we still end up having to do releases on the weekend, because strict procedures aren't that effective. In one way, we're worse than nuclear reactors—with every release, we change fundamental core components!

You can't remove risk by trying to contain complexity. Eventually, you'll have a LOCA.

5.2.2 *A model for failure in software systems*

Let's try to understand the nature of failure in software systems using a simple model. You need to quantify your exposure to risk so that you can understand how different levels of complexity and change affect a system.

A software system can be thought of as a set of components, with dependency relationships between those components. The simplest case is a single component. Under what conditions does the component, and thus the entire system, fail?

To answer that question, we should clarify the term *failure*. In this model, failure isn't an absolute binary condition, but a quantity you can measure. *Success* might be 100%

---

[8] Or should they? Doing so might have cracked the containment vessel, causing a far worse accident. Expert opinion is conflicted on this point.

uptime over a given period, and *failure* might be any uptime less than 100%. But you might be happy with a failure rate of 1%, setting 99% uptime as the threshold of success. You could count the number of requests that have correct responses: out of every 1,000 requests, perhaps 10 fail, yielding a failure rate of 1%. Again, you might be happy with this. Loosely, we can define the *failure rate* as the proportion of some quantity (continuous or discrete) that fails to meet a specific threshold value. Remember that you're building as simple a model as you can, so what the failure rate is a failure *of* is excluded from the model. You only care about the rate and meeting the threshold. *Failure* means failure to meet the threshold, not failure to operate.

For a one-component system, if the component has a failure rate of 1%, then the system as a whole has a failure rate of 1% (see figure 5.3). Is the system failing?

If the acceptable failure threshold is 0.5%, then the system is failing. If the acceptable failure threshold is 2%, then the system is *not* failing: it's succeeding, and your work is finished.

$$C_0$$
$$P_0 = 1\%$$

Figure 5.3 A single-component system, where P_0 is the failure rate of component C_0

 This model reflects an important change of perspective: accepting that software systems are in a constant state of low-level failure. There's always a failure rate. Valves are left closed. The system as a whole fails only when a threshold of pain is crossed. This new perspective is different from the embedded organizational assumption that software can be perfect and operate without defects. The obsession with tallying defective features seems quaint from this viewpoint. Once you gain this perspective, you can begin to understand how the operational costs of the microservice architecture are outweighed by the benefit of superior risk management.

A TWO-COMPONENT SYSTEM

Now, consider a two-component system (see figure 5.4). One component depends on the other, so both must function correctly for the system to succeed. Let's set the failure threshold at 1%. Perhaps this is the proportion of failed purchases, or maybe you're counting many different kinds of errors; this isn't relevant to the

Figure 5.4 A two-component system, where P_i is the failure rate of component C_i

model. Let's also make the simplifying assumption that both components fail independently of each other.[9] The failure of one doesn't make the other more likely to fail. Each component has its own failure rate. In this system, a given function can succeed only if *both* components succeed.

Because the components fail independently, the rules of probability say that you can multiply the probabilities. There are four cases: both fail, both succeed, the first

---

[9] This assumption is important to internalize. Components are like dice: they don't affect each other, and they have no memory. If one component fails, it doesn't make another component more likely to fail. It may *cause* the other component to fail, but that's different, because the failure has an external cause. We're concerned with internal failure, *independent* of other components.

fails and the second succeeds, or the first succeeds and the second fails. You want to know the failure rate of the system; this is the same as asking for the probability that a given transaction will fail. Of the four cases, three are failing, and one is success. This makes the calculation easier: multiply the success probabilities together to get the probability for the case where the entire system succeeds. The failure probability is found by subtracting the success probability from 1.[10] Keeping the numbers simple, assume that each component has the same failure probability of 1%. The gives an overall failure probability of $1 - (99\% \times 99\%) = 1 - 98.01\% = 1.99\%$.

Despite the fact that both components are 99% reliable, the system as a whole is only 98% reliable and fails to meet the success threshold of 99%. You can begin to see that meeting an overall level of system reliability—where that system is composed of components, all of which are essential to operation—is harder than it looks. Each component must be a lot more reliable than the system as a whole.

MULTIPLE COMPONENTS

You can extend this model to any number of components, as long as the components depend on each other in a serial chain. This is a simplification from the real software architectures we know and love, but let's work with this simple model to build some understanding of failure probabilities. Using the assumption of failure independence, where you can multiply the probabilities together, yields the following formula for the overall probability of failure for a system with an arbitrary number of components in series.

$$P_F = 1 - \prod_{i=1}^{n} (1 - P_i)$$

Here, P_F is the probability of system failure, n is the number of components, and P_i is the probability that component i fails.

If you chart this formula against the number of components in the system, as shown in figure 5.5, you can see that the probability of failure grows quickly with the number of components. Even though each component is reliable at 99% (we've given each component the same reliability to keep things simple), the system is unreliable. For example, reading from the chart, a 10-component system has just under a 10% failure rate. That's a long way from the desired 1%.

The model demonstrates that intuitions about reliability can often be incorrect. A convoy of ships is as slow as its slowest ship, but a software architecture isn't as unreliable as its most unreliable component—it's *much more unreliable,* because the other components can fail, too.

The system in the Three Mile Island reactor definitely wasn't linear. It consisted of a complicated set of components with many interdependencies. Real software is much

---

[10] The system can be in only one of two states: success or failure. The probabilities of both must sum to 1. This means you can find one state if you can find the other, so you get to choose the one with the easier formula.

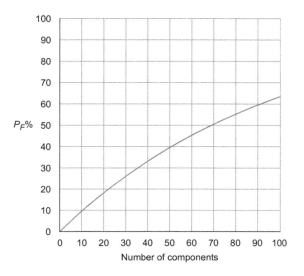

Figure 5.5 **Probability of system failure against the number of components, where all components are 99% reliable**

like Three Mile Island, and software components tend to be even more tightly coupled, with no tolerance for errors. Let's extend the model to see how this affects reliability. Consider a system with four components, one of which is a subcomponent that isn't on the main line (see figure 5.6). Three have a serial dependency, but the middle component also depends on the fourth.

Again, each of the four components has the same 99% reliability. How reliable is the system as a whole? You can solve the serial case with the formula introduced earlier. The reliability of the middle component must take into account its dependency on the fourth component. This is a serial system as well, contained inside the main system. It's a two-component system, and you've seen that this has a reliability of 100% - 1.99% = 98.01%. Thus, the failure probability of the system as a whole is 1 − (99% x 98.01% x 99%) = 1 − 96.06% = 3.94%.

What about an arbitrary system with many dependencies, or systems where multiple components depend on the same subcomponent? You can make another simplifying assumption to handle this case: assume that all components are necessary, and there are no redundancies. Every component must work. This seems unfair, but think of how the

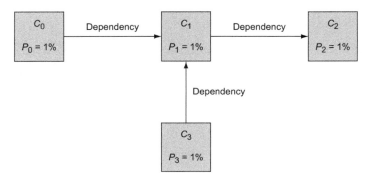

Figure 5.6 **A nonlinear four-component system**

Three Mile Island accident unfolded. Supposedly redundant systems such as the emergency feed pumps turned out to be important as standalone components. Yes, the reactor could work without them, but it was literally an accident waiting to happen.

If all components are necessary, then the dependency graph can be *ignored*. Every component is effectively on the main line. It's easy to overlook subcomponents or assume that they don't affect reliability as much, but that's a mistake. Interconnected systems are much more vulnerable to failure than you may think, because there are many subcomponent relationships. The humans who run and build the system are one such subcomponent relationship—you can only blame "human error" for failures if you consider humans to be part of the system. Ignoring the dependency graph only gives you a first-order approximation of the failure rate, using the earlier formula; but given how quickly independent probabilities compound, that estimate is more than sufficient.

5.2.3   *Redundancy doesn't do what you think it does*

You can make your systems more reliable by adding redundancy. Instead of *one* instance of a component that might fail, have many. Keeping to the simple model where failures are independent, this makes the system much more reliable. To calculate the failure probability of a set of redundant components, you multiply the individual failure probabilities, because all must fail in order for the entire assemblage to fail.[11] Now, you find that probability theory is your friend. In the single-component system, adding a second redundant component gives you a failure rate of 1% x 1% = 0.01%.

It seems that all you need to do is add lots of redundancy, and your problems go away. Unfortunately, this is where the simple model breaks down. There are few failure modes in a software system where failure of one instance of a component is independent of other components of the same kind. Yes, individual host machines can fail,[12] but most failures affect all software components equally. The data center is down. The network is down. The same bug applies to all instances. High load causes instances to fall like dominoes, or to flap.[13] A deployment of a new version fails on production traffic.

Simple models are also useful when they break, because they can reveal hidden assumptions. Load balancing over multiple instances doesn't give you strong redundancy, it gives you capacity. It barely moves the reliability needle, because multiple instances of the same component are *not* independent.[14]

---

[11] The failure probability formula, in this case, is $P_F = \prod_{i=1}^{n} P_i$.

[12] Physical power supplies fail all the time, and so do hard drives; network engineers will keep stepping on cables from now until the end of the universe; and we'll never solve the Halting Problem (it's mathematically impossible to prove that any given program will halt instead of executing forever—you can thank Mr. Alan Turing for that), so there will always be input that triggers infinite loops.

[13] *Flapping* occurs when services keep getting killed and restarted by the monitoring system. Under high load, newly started services are still *cold* (they have empty caches), and their tardiness in responding to requests is interpreted as failure, so they're killed. Then more services are started. Eventually, there are no services that aren't either starting or stopping, and work comes to a halt.

[14] The statement that multiple instances of the same software component don't fail independently is proposed as an empirical fact from the observed behavior of real systems; it isn't proposed as a mathematical fact.

Automatic safety devices are unreliable

Another way to reduce the risk of component failure is to use ASDs. But as you saw in the story of Three Mile Island, these bring their own risks. In the model, they're additional components that can themselves fail.

Many years ago, I worked on a content-driven website. The site added 30 or 40 news stories a day. It wasn't a breaking news site, so a small delay in publishing a story was acceptable. This gave me the brilliant idea to build a 60-second cache. Most pages could be generated once and cached for 60 seconds. Once expired, any news updates appeared on the regenerated pages, and the next 60-second caching period would begin.

This seemed like a cheap way to build what was effectively an ASD for high load. The site would be able to handle things like election day results without needing to increase server capacity much.

The 60-second cache was implemented as an in-memory cache on each web server. It was load tested, and everything appeared to be fine. But in production, servers kept crashing. Of course, there was a memory leak; and, of course, it didn't manifest unless we left the servers running for at least a day, storing more than 1,440 copies of each page, for each article, in memory. The first week we went live was a complete nightmare—we babysat dying machines on a 24/7 rotation.

5.2.4 *Change is scary*

Let's not throw out the model just yet. Software systems aren't static, and they suffer from catastrophic events known as *deployments*. During a deployment, many components are changed simultaneously. In many systems, this can't be done without downtime. Let's model this as a simultaneous change of a random subset of components. What does this do to the reliability of the system?

By definition, the reliability of a component is the measured rate of failure in production. If a given component drops only 1 work item in 100, it has 99% reliability. Once a deployment is completed and has been live for a while, you can measure production to get the reliability rate. But this isn't much help in advance. You want to know the probability of failure of the new system *before* the changes are made.

Our model isn't strong enough to provide a formula for this situation. But you can use another technique: Monte Carlo simulation. You run lots of simulations of the deployment and add up the numbers to see what happens. Let's use a concrete example. Assume you have a four-component system, and the new deployment consists of updates to all four components. In a static state, before deployment, the reliability of the system is given by the standard formula: $0.99^4 = .9605 = 96.1\%$.

To calculate the reliability after deployment, you need to estimate the *actual* reliabilities of each component. Because you don't know what they are, you have to *guess* them. Then you run the formula using the guesses.

If you do this many times, you'll be able to plot the distribution of system reliability. You can say things like, "In 95% of simulations, the system has at least 99% reliability.

Deploy!" Or, "In only 1% of simulations, the system has at least 99% reliability. Unplanned downtime ahead!" Bear in mind that these numbers are just for discussion; you'll need to decide on numbers that reflect your organization's risk tolerance.

How do you guess the reliability of a component? You need to do this in a way that makes the simulation useful. Reliability isn't normally distributed, like a person's height.[15] Reliability is skewed because components are mostly reliable—most components come in around 99% and can't go much higher. There's a lot of space below 99% in which to fail. Your team is doing unit testing, staging, code reviews, and so on. The QA department has to sign off on releases, and the head of QA is pretty strict. There's a high probability that your components are, in fact, reliable; but you can't test for everything, and production is a crueler environment than a developer's laptop or a staging system.

You can use a skewed probability distribution[16] to model "mostly reliable." The chart in figure 5.7 shows how the failure probabilities are distributed. To make a guess, pick a random number between 0 and 1, and plot its corresponding probability. You can see that most guesses will give a low failure probability.

For each of the four components, you get a reliability estimate. Multiply these together in the usual manner. Now, do this many times; over many simulation runs, you can chart the reliability of the system. Figure 5.8 shows the output from a sample exercise.[17] Although the system is often fairly reliable, it has mostly poor reliability compared to a static system. In only 0.15% of simulations does the system have reliability of 95% or more.

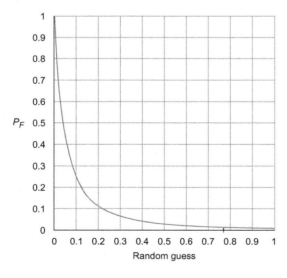

Figure 5.7   A skewed estimator of failure probability

---

[15] The normal distribution assumes that any given instance will be close to the average and has as much chance of being above average as below.

[16] The Pareto distribution is used in this example, because it's a good model for estimating failure events.

[17] In the sample exercise, 1,000 runs were executed and then categorized into 5% intervals.

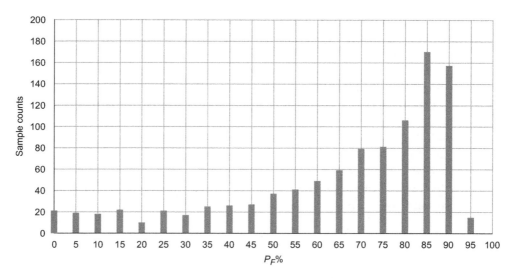

Figure 5.8 Estimated reliability of the system when four components change simultaneously

The model shows that simultaneous deployment of multiple components is inherently risky: it almost always fails the first time. That's why, in practice, you have *scheduled* downtime or end up frantically working on the weekend to complete a deployment. You're really making multiple repeated deployment attempts, trying to resolve production issues that are almost impossible to predict.

The numbers don't work in your favor. You're playing a dangerous game. Your releases may be low frequency, but they have high risk.[18] And it seems as though microservices must introduce even more risk, because you have many more components. Yet, as you'll discover in this chapter, microservices also provide the flexibility for a solution. If you're prepared to accept high-frequency releases of single components, then you'll get much lower risk exposure.

I've labored the mathematics to make a point: no software development methodology can defy the laws of probability at reasonable cost. Engineering, not politics, is the key to risk management.

5.3 *The centre cannot hold*

The collective delusion of enterprise software development is that perfect software can be delivered complete and on time, and deployed to production without errors, by force of management. Any defects are a failure of professionalism on the part of the team. Everybody buys into this delusion. Why?

This book does *not* take the trite and lazy position that it's all management's fault. I don't pull punches when it comes to calling out bad behavior, but you must be careful to see organizational behavior for what it is: rational.

---

[18] The story of the deployment failure suffered by Knight Capital, in chapter 1, is a perfect example of this danger.

We can analyze corporate politics using Game Theory.[19] Why does nobody point out the absurdities of enterprise software development, even when there are mountains of evidence? How many more books must be written on the subject? Fortunately, we live in an age where the scale of the software systems we must build is slowly forcing enterprise software development to face reality.

Traditional software development processes are an unwanted Nash equilibrium in the game of corporate politics. They're a kind of prisoner's dilemma.[20] If all stakeholders acknowledged that failure rates must exist and used that as a starting point, then continuous delivery would be seen as a natural solution. But nobody is willing to do so; it would be a career-limiting move. Failure isn't an option! So we're stuck with a collective delusion because we can't communicate honestly. This book aims to give you some solid principles to start that honest communication.

WARNING It isn't advisable to push for change unless there's a forcing function. Wait until failure is inevitable under the old system, and then be the white knight. Pushing for change when you have no leverage is indeed a career-limiting move.

5.3.1   *The cost of perfect software*

The software that controlled the space shuttle was some of the most perfect software ever written. It's a good example of how expensive such software truly is and calls out the absurdity of the expectations for enterprise software. It's also a good example of how much effort is required to build redundant software components.

The initial cost estimate for the shuttle software system was $20 million. The final bill was $200 million. This is the first clue that defect-free software is an order of magnitude more expensive than even software engineers estimate. The full requirements specification has 40,000 pages—for a mere 420,000 lines of code. By comparison, Google's Chrome web browser has more than 5 million lines of code. How perfect is the shuttle software? On average, there was one bug per release. It wasn't completely perfect!

The shuttle's software development process was incredibly strict. It was a traditional process with detailed specifications, strict testing, and code reviews, and bureaucratic signatures were needed for release. Many stakeholders in the enterprise software development process believe that this level of delivery is what they're going to get.

---

[19] The part of mathematics that deals with multiplayer games and the limitations of strategies to maximize results.

[20] A *Nash equilibrium* is a state in a game where no player can improve their position by changing strategy unilaterally. The prisoner's dilemma is a compact example: two guilty criminals who robbed a bank together are captured by the police and placed in separate cells where they can't communicate. If they both stay silent, then they both get a one-year sentence for possession of stolen cash, but the police can't prove armed robbery. The police offer a deal separately to each criminal: confess and betray your accomplice, and instead of three years for armed robbery, you'll only get two years, because you cooperated. The only rational strategy is for each criminal to betray the other and take the two years, because their partner might betray them. Because they can't communicate, they can't agree to remain silent.

It's the business of business to make return-on-investment decisions. You spend money to make money, but you must have a business case. This system breaks down if you don't understand your cost model. It's the job of the software architect to make these costs clear and to provide alternatives, where the cost of software development is matched to the expected returns of the project.

5.4 Anarchy works

The most important question in software development is, "What is the acceptable error rate?" This is the first question to ask at the start of a project. It drives all other questions and decisions. It also makes clear to all stakeholders that the process of software development is about controlling, not conquering, failure.

The primary consequence is that large-scale releases can never meet the acceptable error rate. Reliability is so compromised by the uncertainty of a large release that large releases must be rejected as an engineering approach. This is just mathematics, and no amount of QA can overcome it.

Small releases are less risky. The smaller, the better. Small releases have small uncertainties, and you can stay beneath the failure threshold. Small releases also mean frequent releases. Enterprise software must constantly change to meet market forces. These small releases must go all the way to production to fully reduce risk; collecting them into large releases takes you back to square one. That's just how the probabilities work.

A system that's under constant failure isn't fragile. Every component expects others to fail and is built to be tolerant of failure. The constant failure of components exercises redundant systems and backups so you know they work. You have an accurate measure of the failure rate of the system: it's a known quantity that can be controlled. The rate of deployment can be adjusted as risks grow and shrink.

How does the simple risk model work under these conditions? You may be changing only one component at a time, but aren't you still subject to large amounts of risk? You know that your software development process won't deliver updated components that are as stable as those that have been baked into production for a while.

Let's say updated components are 80% reliable on first deployment. The systems we've looked at definitely won't meet a reliability threshold of 99%. Redeploying a single component still isn't a small enough deployment. This is an engineering and process problem that we'll address in the remainder of this chapter: how to make changes to a production software system while maintaining the desired risk tolerance.

5.5 Microservices and redundancy

An individual component of a software system should never be run as a single instance. A single instance is vulnerable to failure: the component could crash, the machine it's running on could fail, or the network connection to that machine could be accidentally misconfigured. No component should be a single point of failure.

To avoid a single point of failure, you can run multiple instances of the component. Then, you can handle load, and you're more protected against some kinds of failure. You aren't protected against software defects in the component, which affect all instances, but such defects can usually be mitigated by automatic restarts.[21] Once a component has been running in production for a while, you'll have enough data to get a good measure of its reliability.

How do you deploy a new version of a component? In the traditional model, you try, as quickly as possible, to replace all the old instances with a full set of new ones. The blue-green deployment strategy, as it's known, is an example of this. You have a running version of the system; call this the *blue* version. You spin up a new version of the system; call this the *green* version. Then, you choose a specific moment to redirect all traffic from blue to green. If something goes wrong, you can quickly switch back to blue and assess the damage. At least you're still up.

One way to make this approach this less risky is to initially redirect only a small fraction of traffic to green. If you're satisfied that everything still works, redirect greater volumes of traffic until green has completely taken over.

The microservice architecture makes it easy to adopt this strategy and reduce risk even further. Instead of spinning up a full quota of new instances of the green version of the service, you can spin up one. This new instance gets a small portion of all production traffic while the existing blues look after the main bulk of traffic. You can observe the behavior of the single green instance, and if it's badly behaved, you can decommission it: a small amount of traffic is affected, and there's a small increase in failure, but you're still in control. You can fully control the level of exposure by controlling the amount of traffic you send to that single new instance.

Microservice deployments consist of nothing more than introducing a single new instance. If the deployment fails, rollback means decommissioning a single instance. Microservices give you well-defined primitive operations on your production system: add/remove a service instance.[22] Nothing more is required. These primitive operations can be used to construct any deployment strategy you desire. For example, blue-green deployments break down into a list of add and remove operations on specific instances.

Defining a primitive operation is a powerful mechanism for achieving control. If everything is defined in terms of primitives, and you can control the composition of the primitives, then you can control the system. The microservice instance is the primitive and the unit with which you build your systems. Let's examine the journey of that unit from development to production.

---

[21] Restarts don't protect you against nastier kinds of defects, such as poison messages.

[22] More formally, we might call these primitive operations *activate* and *deactivate*, respectively. How the operations work depends entirely on the underlying deployment platform.

5.6 *Continuous delivery*

The ability to safely deploy a component to production at any time is powerful because it lets you control risk. *Continuous delivery* (CD) in a microservice context means the ability to create a specific version of a microservice and to run one or more instances of that version in production, on demand. The essential elements of a CD pipeline are as follows:

- A *version-controlled local development environment* for each service, supported by unit testing, and the ability to test the service against an appropriate local subset of the other services, using mocking if necessary.
- A *staging environment* to both validate the microservice and build, reproducibly, an artifact for deployment. Validation is automated, but scope is allowed for manual verification if necessary.
- A *management system,* used by the development team to execute combinations of primitives against staging and production, implementing the desired deployment patterns in an automated manner.
- A *production environment* that's constructed from deployment artifacts to the fullest extent possible, with an audit history of the primitive operations applied. The environment is self-correcting and able to take remedial action, such as restarting crashed services. The environment also provides intelligent load balancing, allowing traffic volumes to vary between services.
- A *monitoring and diagnostics system* that verifies the health of the production system after the application of each primitive operation and allows the development team to introspect and trace message behavior. Alerts are generated from this part of the system.

The pipeline assumes that the generation of defective artifacts is a common occurrence. The pipeline attempts to filter them out at each stage. This is done on a per-artifact basis, rather than trying to verify an update to the entire system. As a result, the verification is both more accurate and more credible, because confounding factors have been removed.

Even when a defective artifact makes it to production, this is considered a normal event. The behavior of the artifact is continuously verified in production after deployment, and the artifact is removed if its behavior isn't acceptable. Risk is controlled by progressively increasing the proportion of activity that the new artifact handles.

CD is based on the reality of software construction and management. It delivers the following:

- *Lower risk of failure* by favoring low-impact, high-frequency, single-instance deployments over high-impact, low-frequency, multiple-instance deployments.
- *Faster development* by enabling high-frequency updates to the business logic of the system, giving a faster feedback loop and faster refinement against business goals.

- *Lower cost of development,* because the fast feedback loop reduces the amount of time wasted on features that have no business value.
- *Higher quality,* because less code is written overall, and the code that's written is immediately verified.

The tooling to support CD and the microservice architecture is still in the early stages of development. Although an end-to-end CD pipeline system is necessary to fully gain the benefits of the microservice architecture, it's possible to live with pipeline elements that are less than perfect.

At the time of writing, all teams working with this approach are using multiple tools to implement different aspects of the pipeline, because comprehensive solutions don't exist. The microservice architecture requires more than current platform-as-a-service (PaaS) that vendors offer. Even when comprehensive solutions emerge, they will present trade-offs in implementation focus.[23]

You'll probably continue to need to put together a context-specific toolset for each microservice system you build; as we work through the rest of this chapter, focus on the desirable properties of these tools. You'll almost certainly also need to invest in developing some of your own tooling—at the very least, integration scripts for the third-party tools you select.

5.6.1   *Pipeline*

The purpose of the CD pipeline is to provide feedback to the development team as quickly as possible. In the case of failure, that feedback should indicate the nature of the failure; it must be easy to see the failing tests, the failing performance results, or the failed integrations. You also should be able to see a history of the verifications and failures of each microservice. This isn't the time to roll your own tooling—many capable continuous integration (CI) tools are available.[24] The key requirement is that your chosen tool be able to handle many projects easily, because each microservice is built separately.

The CI tool is just one stage of the pipeline, usually operating before a deployment to the staging systems. You need to be able to trace the generation of microservices throughout the pipeline. The CI server generates an artifact that will be deployed into production. Before that happens, the source code for the artifact needs to be marked and tagged so that artifact generation can be *hermetic*—you must be able to reproduce any build from the history of your microservice. After artifact generation, you must be able to trace the deployment of the artifact over your systems from staging to production. This tracing must be not only at the system level, but also within the system, tracing the number of instances run, and when. Until third-party tooling solves this problem, you'll have to build this part of the pipeline diagnostics yourself; it's an essential and worthwhile investment for investigating failures.

---

[23] The Netflix suite (http://netflix.github.io) is a good example of a comprehensive, but opinionated, toolchain.

[24] Two quick mentions: if you want to run something yourself, try Hudson (http://hudson-ci.org); if you want to outsource, try Travis CI (http://travis-ci.org).

The unit of deployment is a microservice, so the unit of movement through the pipeline is a microservice. The pipeline should prioritize the focus on the generation and validation of artifacts that represent a microservice. A given version of a microservice is instantiated as a fixed artifact that never changes. Artifacts are *immutable*: the same version of a microservice always generates the same artifact, at a binary-encoding level. It's natural to store these artifacts for quick access.[25] Nonetheless, you need to retain the ability to hermetically rebuild any version of a microservice, because the build process is an important element of defect investigation.

The development environment also needs to make the focus on individual microservices fluid and natural. In particular, this affects the structure of your source code repositories. (We'll look at this more deeply in chapter 7.) Local validation is also important, as the first measure of risk. Once a developer is satisfied that a viable version of the microservice is ready, the developer initiates the pipeline to production.

The staging environment reproduces the development-environment validation in a controlled environment so that it isn't subject to variances in local developer machines. Staging also performs scaling and performance tests and can use multiple machines to simulate production, to a limited extent. Staging's core responsibility is to generate an artifact that has an estimated failure risk that's within a defined tolerance.

Production is the live, revenue-generating part of the pipeline. Production is updated by accepting an artifact and a deployment plan and applying that deployment plan under measurement of risk. To manage risk, the deployment plan is a progressive execution of deployment primitives—activating and deactivating microservice instances. Tooling for production microservices is the most mature at present because it's the most critical part of the pipeline. Many orchestration and monitoring tools are available to help.[26]

5.6.2 Process

It's important to distinguish *continuous delivery* from *continuous deployment*. Continuous deployment is a form of CD where commits, even if automatically verified, are pushed directly and immediately to production. CD operates at a coarser grain: sets of commits are packaged into immutable artifacts. In both cases, deployments can effectively take place in real time and occur multiple times per day.

CD is more suited to the wider context of enterprise software development because it lets teams accommodate compliance and process requirements that are difficult to change within the lifetime of the project. CD is also more suited to the microservice architecture, because it allows the focus to be on the microservice rather than code.

If we view "continuous delivery" as meaning continuous delivery of microservice instances, this understanding drives other virtues. Microservices should be kept small

---

[25] Amazon S3 isn't a bad place to store them. There are also more-focused solutions, such as JFrog Artifactory (www.jfrog.com/artifactory).

[26] Common choices are Kubernetes (https://kubernetes.io), Mesos (http://mesos.apache.org), Docker (www.docker.com), and so forth. Although these tools fall into a broad category, they operate at different levels of the stack and aren't mutually exclusive. The case study in chapter 9 uses Docker and Kubernetes.

so that verification—especially human verification, such as code reviews—is possible with the desired time frames of multiple deployments per day.

5.6.3   *Protection*

The pipeline protects you from exceeding failure thresholds by providing measures of risk at each stage of production. It isn't necessary to extract a failure-probability prediction from each measure.[27] You'll know the feel of the measures for your system, and thus you can use a scoring approach just as effectively.

In development, the key risk-measuring tools are code reviews and unit tests. Using modern version control for branch management [28] means you can adopt a development workflow where new code is written on a branch and then merged into the mainline. The merge is performed only if the code passes a review. The review can be performed by a peer, rather than a senior developer: peer developers on a project have more information and are better able to assess the correctness of a merge. This workflow means code review is a normal part of the development process and very low friction. Microservices keep the friction even lower because the units of review are smaller and have less code.

Unit tests are critical to risk measurement. You should take the perspective that unit tests must pass before branches can be merged or code committed on the mainline. This keeps the mainline potentially deployable at all times, because a build on staging has a good chance of passing. Unit tests in the microservice world are concerned with demonstrating the correctness of the code; other benefits of unit testing, such as making refactoring safer, are less relevant.

Unit tests aren't sufficient for accurate risk measurement and are very much subject to diminishing marginal returns: moving from 50% test coverage to 100% reduces deployment risk much less than moving from 0% to 50%. Don't get suckered into the fashion for 100% test coverage—it's a fine badge of honor (literally!) for open source utility components but is superstitious theater for business logic.

On the staging system, you can measure the behavior of a microservice in terms of its adherence to the message flows of the system. Ensuring that the correct messages are sent by the service, and that the correct responses are given, is also a binary pass/fail test, which you can score with a 0 or 1. The service must meet expectations fully. Although these message interactions are tested via unit tests in development, they also need to be tested on the staging system, because this is a closer simulation of production.

Integrations with other parts of the system can also be tested as part of the staging process. Those parts of the system that aren't microservices, such as standalone databases, network services such a mail servers, external web service endpoints, and others, are simulated or run in small scale. You can then measure the microservice's behavior with respect to them. Other aspects of the service, such as performance,

---

[27] You could use statistical techniques such as Bayesian estimation to do this if desired.

[28] Using a distributed version control system such as Git is essential. You need to be able to use pull requests to implement code reviews.

resource consumption, and security, need to be measured statistically: take samples of behavior, and use them to predict the risk of failure.

Finally, even in production, you must continue to measure the risk of failure. Even before going into production, you can establish manual gates—formal code reviews, penetration testing, user acceptance, and so forth. These may be legally unavoidable (due to laws affecting your industry), but they can still be integrated into the continuous delivery mindset.

Running services can be monitored and sampled. You can use key metrics, especially those relating to message flow rates, to determine service and system health. Chapter 6 has a great deal more to say about this aspect of the microservice architecture.

5.7 *Running a microservice system*

The tooling to support microservices is developing quickly, and new tools are emerging at a high rate. It isn't useful to examine in detail something that will soon be out of date, so this chapter focuses on general principles; that way, you can compare and assess tools and select those most suitable for your context. You should expect and prepare to build some tooling yourself. This isn't a book on deployment in general, so it doesn't discuss best practices for deploying system elements, such as database clusters, that aren't microservices. It's still recommended that these be subject to automation and, if possible, controlled by the same tooling. The focus of this chapter is on the deployment of your own microservices. Your own microservices implement the business logic of the system and are thus subject to a higher degree of change compared to other elements.

5.7.1 *Immutability*

It's a core principle of the approach described here that microservice artifacts are immutable. This preserves their ability to act as primitive operations. A microservice artifact can be a container, a virtual machine image, or some other abstraction.[29] The essential characteristics of the artifact are that it can't be changed internally and that it has only two states: active and inactive.

The power of immutability is that it excludes side effects from the system. The behavior of the system and microservice instances is more predictable, because you can be sure they aren't affected by changes you aren't aware of. An immutable artifact contains everything the microservice needs to run, at fixed versions. You can be absolutely sure that your language-platform version, libraries, and other dependencies are exactly as you expect. Nobody can manually log in to the instance and make unaudited changes. This predictability allows you to calibrate risk estimations more accurately.

Running immutable instances also forces you to treat microservices as disposable. An instance that develops a problem or contains a bug can't be "fixed"; it can only be deactivated and replaced by a new instance. Matching capacity to load isn't about building new installations on bigger machines, it's about running more instances of

---

[29] For very large systems, you might even consider an AWS autoscaling group to be your base unit.

the artifact. No individual instance is in any way special. This approach is a basic building block for building reliable systems on unreliable infrastructure.

The following subsections provide a reference overview of microservice deployment patterns. You'll need to compare these patterns against the capabilities of the automation tooling you're using. Unfortunately, you should expect to be disappointed, and you'll need to augment your tooling to fully achieve the desired benefits of the patterns.

Feel free to treat these sections as a recipe book for cooking up your own patterns rather than a prescription. You can skim the deployment patterns without guilt.[30] To kick things off, figure 5.9 is a reminder of the diagramming conventions. In particular, the number of live instances is shown in braces ({1}) above the name of the microservice, and the version is shown below (1.0.0).

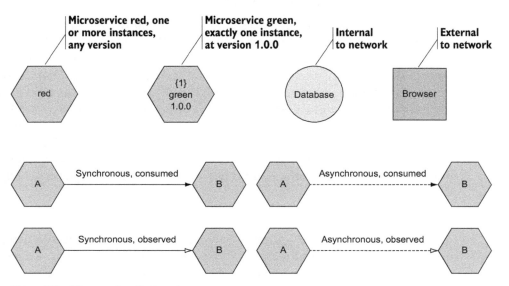

Figure 5.9   Microservice diagram key

ROLLBACK PATTERN

This deployment pattern is used to recover from a deployment that has caused one or more failure metrics to exceed their thresholds. It enables you to deploy new service versions where the estimated probability of failure is higher than your thresholds, while maintaining overall operation within thresholds.

To use the Rollback pattern (figure 5.10), apply to a system the *activate* primitive for a given microservice artifact. Observe failure alerts, and then *deactivate* the same artifact. Deactivation can be manual or automatic; logs should be preserved. Deactivation should return the system to health. Recovery is expected but may not occur in cases where the offending instance has injected defective messages into the system (for this, see the Kill Switch pattern).

---

[30] In production, I'm fondest of the Progressive Canary pattern.

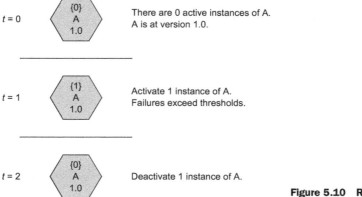

Figure 5.10 Rollback pattern sequence

HOMEOSTASIS PATTERN

This pattern (figure 5.11) lets you maintain desired architectural structure and capacity levels. You implement a declarative definition of your architecture, including rules for increasing capacity under load, by applying activation and deactivation primitives to the system. Simultaneous application of primitives is permitted, although you must take care to implement and record this correctly. Homeostasis can also be implemented by allowing services to issue primitive operations, and defining local rules for doing so (see the Mitosis and Apoptosis patterns).

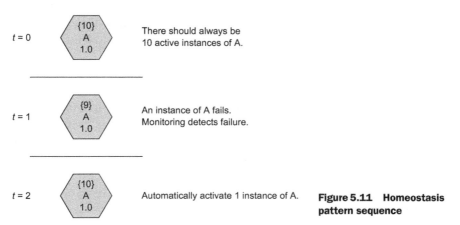

Figure 5.11 Homeostasis pattern sequence

HISTORY PATTERN

The History pattern (figure 5.12) provides diagnostic data to aid your understanding of failing and healthy system behavior. Using this pattern, you maintain an audit trail of the temporal order of primitive operation application—a log of what was activated/ deactivated, and when. A complication is that you may allow simultaneous application of sets of primitives in your system.

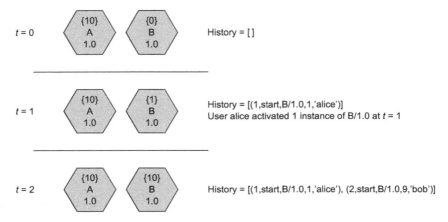

Figure 5.12   History pattern sequence

The audit history lets you diagnose problems by inspecting the behavior of previous versions of the system—these can be resurrected by applying the primitives to simulated systems. You can also deal with defects that are introduced but not detected immediately by moving backward over the history.

5.7.2   *Automation*

Microservice systems in production have too many moving parts to be managed manually. This is part of the trade-off of the architecture. You must commit to using tooling to automate your system—and this is a never-ending task. Automation doesn't cover all activities from day one, nor should it, because you need to allocate most of your development effort to creating business value. Over time, you'll need to automate more and more.

To determine which activity to automate next, divide your operational tasks into two categories. In the first category, Toil,[31] place those tasks where effort grows at least linearly with the size of the system. To put it another way, from a computational complexity perspective, these are tasks where human effort is at least $O(n)$, where n is the number of microservice types (not instances). For example, configuring log capture for a new microservice type might require manual configuration of the log-collection subsystem. In the second category, Win, place tasks that are less than $O(n)$ in the number of microservice types: for example, adding a new database secondary reader instance to handle projected increased data volumes.

The next task to automate is the most annoying task from the Toil pile, where *annoying* means "most negatively impacting the business goals." Don't forget to include failure risk in your calculation of negative impact.

Automation is also necessary to execute the microservice deployment patterns. Most of the patterns require the application of large numbers of primitive operations

---

[31] This usage of the term originates with the Google Site Reliability Engineering team.

over a scheduled period of time, under observation for failure. These are tasks that can't be performed manually at scale.

Automation tooling is relatively mature and dovetails with the requirements of modern, large-scale enterprise applications. A wide range of tooling options are available, and your decision should be driven by your comfort levels with custom modification or scripting; you'll need to do some customization to fully execute the microservice deployment patterns described next.[32]

CANARY PATTERN

New microservices and new versions of existing microservices introduce considerable risk to a production system. It's unwise to deploy the new instances and immediately allow them to take large amounts of load. Instead, run multiple instances of known-good services, and slowly replace these with new ones.

The first step in the Canary pattern (figure 5.13) is to validate that the new microservice both functions correctly and isn't destructive. To do so, you activate a single new instance and direct a small amount of message traffic to this instance. Then, watch your metrics to make sure the system behaves as expected. If it doesn't, apply the Rollback pattern.

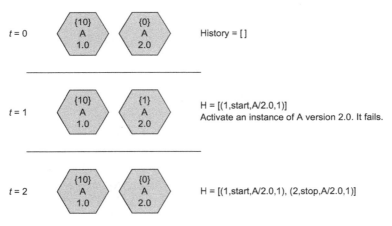

Figure 5.13   Canary pattern sequence

PROGRESSIVE CANARY PATTERN

This pattern (figure 5.14) lets you reduce the risk of a full update by applying changes progressively in larger and larger tranches. Although Canary can validate the safety of a single new instance, it doesn't guarantee good behavior at scale, particularly with respect to unintended destructive behavior. With the Progressive Canary pattern, you deploy a progressively larger number of new instances to take progressively more traffic, continuing to validate during the process. This balances the need for full

---

[32] Plan to evaluate tools such as Puppet (https://puppet.com), Chef (www.chef.io/chef), Ansible (www.ansible .com), Terraform (www.terraform.io), and AWS CodeDeploy (https://aws.amazon.com/codedeploy).

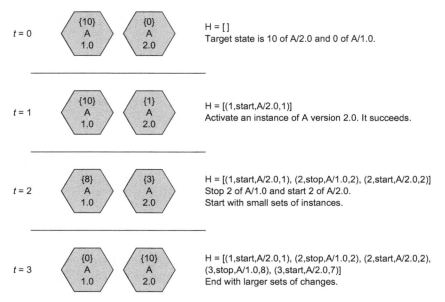

t = 0   {10} A 1.0   {0} A 2.0   H = [ ]
Target state is 10 of A/2.0 and 0 of A/1.0.

t = 1   {10} A 1.0   {1} A 2.0   H = [(1,start,A/2.0,1)]
Activate an instance of A version 2.0. It succeeds.

t = 2   {8} A 1.0   {3} A 2.0   H = [(1,start,A/2.0,1), (2,stop,A/1.0,2), (2,start,A/2.0,2)]
Stop 2 of A/1.0 and start 2 of A/2.0.
Start with small sets of instances.

t = 3   {0} A 1.0   {10} A 2.0   H = [(1,start,A/2.0,1), (2,stop,A/1.0,2), (2,start,A/2.0,2),
(3,stop,A/1.0,8), (3,start,A/2.0,7)]
End with larger sets of changes.

Figure 5.14   Progressive Canary pattern sequence

deployment of new instance versions to occur at reasonable speed with the need to manage the risk of the change.

Primitives are applied concurrently in this pattern. The Rollback pattern can be extended to handle decommissioning of multiple instances if a problem does arise.

BAKE PATTERN

The Bake pattern (figure 5.15) reduces the risk of failures that have severe downsides. It's a variation of Progressive Canary that maintains a full complement of existing instances but also sends a copy of inbound message traffic to the new instances. The output from the new instances is compared with the old to ensure that deviations are below the desired threshold. Output from the new instances is discarded until this criterion is met. The system can continue in this configuration, validating against production traffic, until sufficient time has passed to reach the desired risk level.

This pattern is most useful when the output must meet a strict failure threshold and where failure places the business at risk. Consider using Bake when you're dealing with access to sensitive data, financial operations, and resource-intensive activities that are difficult to reverse.[33] The pattern does require intelligent load balancing and additional monitoring to implement.

---

[33] The canonical description of this technique is given by GitHub's Zach Holman in his talk "Move Fast & Break Nothing," October 2014 (https://zachholman.com/talk/move-fast-break-nothing). It isn't necessary to fully replicate the entire production stack; you only need to duplicate a sample of production traffic to measure correctness within acceptable levels of risk.

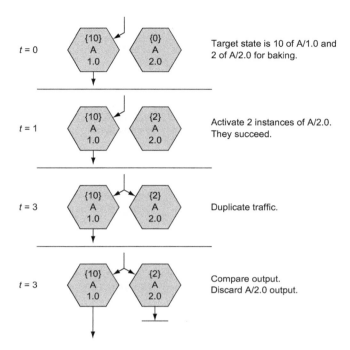

$t = 0$	Target state is 10 of A/1.0 and 2 of A/2.0 for baking.
$t = 1$	Activate 2 instances of A/2.0. They succeed.
$t = 3$	Duplicate traffic.
$t = 3$	Compare output. Discard A/2.0 output.

Figure 5.15 Bake pattern sequence

MERGE PATTERN

Performance is impacted by network latency. As the system grows and load increases, certain message pathways will become bottlenecks. In particular, latency caused by the need to send messages over the network between microservices may become unacceptable. Also, security concerns may arise that require encryption of the message stream, causing further latency.

To counteract this issue, you can trade some of the flexibility of microservices for performance by merging microservices in the critical message path. By using a message abstraction layer and pattern matching, as discussed in earlier chapters, you can do so with minimal code changes. Don't merge microservices wholesale; try to isolate the message patterns you're concerned with into a combined microservice. By executing a message pathway within a single process, you remove the network from the equation.

The Merge pattern (figure 5.16) is a good example of the benefit of the microservices-first approach. In the earlier part of an application's lifecycle, more flexibility is needed, because understanding of the business logic is less solid. Later, you may require optimizations to meet performance goals.

SPLIT PATTERN

Microservices grow over time, as more business logic is added, so you need to add new kinds of services to avoid building technical debt. In the early lifecycle of a system, microservices are small and handle general cases. As time goes by, more special cases are added to the business logic. Rather than handling these cases with more complex

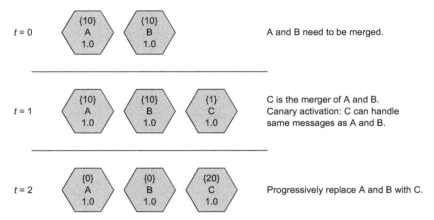

Figure 5.16   Merge pattern sequence

internal code and data structures, it's better to split out special cases into focused microservices. Pattern matching on messages makes this practical and is one of the core benefits of the pattern-matching approach.

The Split pattern (figure 5.17) captures one of the core benefits of the microservice architecture: the ability to handle frequently changing, underspecified requirements. Always look for opportunities to split, and avoid the temptation to use more-familiar language constructs (such as object-oriented design patterns), because they build technical debt over time.

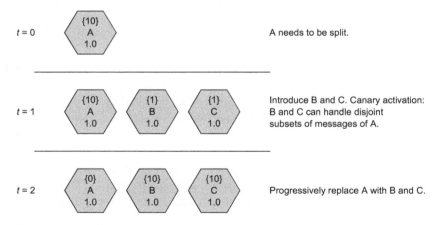

Figure 5.17   Split pattern sequence

5.7.3   *Resilience*

Chapter 3 discussed some of the common failure modes of microservice systems. A production deployment of microservices needs to be resilient to these failure modes. Although the system can never be entirely safe, you should put mitigations in place. As always, the extent and cost of the mitigation should correspond to the desired level of risk.

In monolithic systems, failure is often dealt with by restarting the instances of that fail. This approach is heavy-handed and often not very effective. The microservice architecture offers a finer-grained menu of techniques for handling failure. The abstraction of a messaging layer is helpful, because this layer can be extended to provide automatic safety devices (ASDs). Bear in mind that ASDs aren't silver bullets, and may themselves cause failure, but they're still useful for many modes of failure.

SLOW DOWNSTREAM

In this failure mode, taking the perspective of a given client microservice instance, responses to outbound messages have latency or throughput levels that are outside of acceptable levels. The client microservice can use the following dynamic tactics, roughly in order of increasing sophistication:

- *Timeouts*—Consider messages failed if a response isn't delivered within a fixed timeout period. This prevents resource consumption on the client microservice.
- *Adaptive timeouts*—Use timeouts, but don't set them as fixed configuration parameters. Instead, dynamically adjust the timeouts based on observed behavior. As a simplistic example, time out if the response delay is more than three standard deviations from the observed mean response time. Adaptive timeouts reduce the occurrence of false positives when the overall system is slow and avoid delays in failure detection when the system is fast.
- *Circuit breaker*—Persistently slow downstream services should be considered effectively dead. Implementation requires the messaging layer to maintain metadata about downstream services. This tactic avoids unnecessary resource consumption and unnecessary degradation of overall performance. It does increase the risk of overloading healthy machines by redirecting too much traffic to them, causing a cascading failure similar to the unintended effects of the ASDs at Three Mile Island.
- *Retries*—If failure to execute a task has a cost, and there's tolerance for delay, it may make more sense to retry a failed message by sending it again. This is an ASD that has great potential to go wrong. Large volumes of retries are a self-inflicted *denial of service* (DoS) attack. Use a retry budget to avoid this by retrying only a limited number of times and, if the metadata is available, doing so only for a limited number of times per downstream. Retries should also use a randomized exponential backoff delay before being sent, because this gives the downstream a better chance of recovery by spreading load over time.
- *Intelligent round-robin*—If the messaging layer is using point-to-point transmission to send messages, then it necessarily has sufficient metadata to implement round-robin load balancing among the downstreams. *Simple round-robin* keeps a list of downstreams and cycles through them. This ignores differences in load between

messages and can lead to individual downstreams becoming overloaded. *Random round-robin* is found empirically to be little better, probably because the same clustering of load is possible. If the downstream microservices provide backpressure metadata, then the round-robin algorithm can make more-informed choices: it can choose the least loaded downstream, weight downstreams based on known capacity, and restrict downstreams to a subset of the total to avoid a domino effect from a circuit breaker that trips too aggressively.

UPSTREAM OVERLOAD

This is the other end of the overload scenario: the downstream microservice is getting too many inbound messages. Some of the tactics to apply are as follows:

- *Adaptive throttles*—Don't attempt to complete all work as it comes in. Instead, queue the work to a maximum rate that can be safely handled. This prevents the service from *thrashing*. Services that are severely resource constrained will spend almost all of their time swapping between tasks rather than working on tasks. On thread-based language platforms, this consumes memory; and on event-driven platforms, this manifests as a single task hogging the CPU and stalling all other tasks. As with timeouts, it's worth making throttles adaptive to optimize resource consumption.

- *Backpressure*—Provide client microservices with metadata describing current load levels. This metadata can be embedded in message responses. The downstream service doesn't actively handle load but relies on the kindness of its clients. The metadata makes client tactics for slow downstreams more effective.

- *Load shedding*—Refuse to execute tasks once a dangerous level of load has been reached. This is a deliberate decision to fail a certain percentage of messages. This tactic gives most messages reasonable latency, and some total failure, rather than allowing many messages to have high latency with sporadic failure. Appropriate metadata should be returned to client services so they don't interpret load shedding incorrectly and trigger a circuit breaker. The selection of tasks to drop, add to the queue, or execute immediately can be determined algorithmically and is context dependent. Nonetheless, even a simple load shedder will prevent many kinds of catastrophic collapse.

In addition to these dynamic tactics, upstream overload can be reduced on a longer time frame by applying the Merge deployment pattern.

LOST ACTIONS

To address this failure mode, apply the Progressive Canary deployment pattern, measuring message-flow rates to ensure correctness. Chapter 6 discusses measurement in more detail.

POISON MESSAGES

In this failure mode, a microservice generates a poisonous message that triggers a defect in other microservices, causing some level of failure. If the message is continuously retried against different downstream services, they all suffer failures. You can respond in one of these ways:

- *Drop duplicates*—Downstream microservices should track message-correlation identifiers and keep a short-term record of recently seen inbound messages. Duplicates should be ignored.
- *Validation*—Trade the flexibility of schema-free messages for stricter validation of inbound message data. This has a less detrimental effect later in the project when the pace of requirement change has slowed.

Consider building a *dead-letter service*. Problematic messages are forwarded to this service for storage and later diagnosis. This also allows you to monitor message health across the system.

GUARANTEED DELIVERY

Message delivery may fail in many ways. Messages may not arrive or may arrive multiple times. Dropping duplicates will help within a service. Duplicated messages sent to multiple services are more difficult to mitigate. If the risk associated with such events is too high, allocate extra development effort to implement idempotent message interactions.[34]

EMERGENT BEHAVIOR

A microservice system has many moving parts. Message behavior may have unintended consequences, such as triggering additional workflows. You can use correlation identifiers for after-the-fact diagnosis, but not to actively prevent side effects:

- *Time to live*—Use a decrementing counter that's reduced each time an inbound message triggers the generation of outbound messages. This prevents unbounded side effects from proceeding without any checks. In particular, it stops infinite message loops. It won't fully prevent all side effects but will limit their effects. You'll need to determine the appropriate value of the counter in the context of your own system, but you should prefer low values. Microservice systems should be shallow, not deep.

CATASTROPHIC COLLAPSE

Some emergent behavior can be exceptionally pathological, placing the system into an unrecoverable state, even though the original messages are no longer present. In this failure mode, even with the Homeostasis pattern in place, service restarts can't bring the system back to health.

For example, a defect may crash a large number of services in rapid succession. New services are started as replacements, but they have empty caches and are thus unable to handle current load levels. These new services crash and are themselves

---

[34] Be careful not to overthink your system in the early days of a project. It's often better to accept the risk of data corruption in order to get to market sooner. Be ethical, and make this decision openly with your stakeholders. Chapter 8 has more about making such decisions.

replaced. The system can't establish enough capacity to return to normal. This is known as the *thundering herd* problem. Here are some ways to address it:

- *Static responses*—Use low-resource emergency microservices that return hard-coded responses to temporarily take load.
- *Kill switch*—Establish a mechanism to selectively stop large subsets of services. This gives you the ability to quarantine the problem. You can then restart into a known-good state.

In addition to using these dynamic tactics, you can prepare for disaster by deliberately testing individual services with high load to determine their failure points. Software systems tend to fail quickly rather than gradually, so you need to establish safe limits in advance.

The following sections describe microservice deployment patterns that provide resilience.

APOPTOSIS PATTERN

The Apoptosis[35] pattern removes malfunctioning services quickly, thus reducing capacity organically. Microservices can perform self-diagnosis and shut themselves down if their health is unsatisfactory. For example, all message tasks may be failing because local storage is full; the service can maintain internal statistics to calculate health. This approach also enables a graceful shutdown by responding to messages with metadata indicating a failure during the shutdown, rather than triggering timeouts.

Apoptosis (figure 5.18) is also useful for matching capacity with load. It's costly to maintain active resources far in excess of levels necessary to meet current load. Services can choose to self-terminate, using a probabilistic algorithm to avoid mass shutdowns. Load is redistributed over the remaining services.

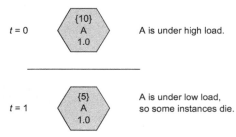

Figure 5.18   Apoptosis pattern sequence

MITOSIS PATTERN

The Mitosis[36] pattern responds to increased load organically, without centralized control. Individual microservices have the most accurate measure of their own load levels. You can trigger the launching of new instances if local load levels are too high; this should be done using a probabilistic approach, to avoid large numbers of simultaneous launches. The newly launched service will take some of the load, bringing levels back to acceptable ranges.

---

[35] Living cells commit suicide if they become too damaged: apoptosis. This prevents cell damage from accumulating and causing cancers.

[36] Living cells replicate by splitting in two. *Mitosis* is the name of this process.

Mitosis (figure 5.19) and Apoptosis should be used with care and with built-in limits. You don't want unbounded growth or a complete shutdown. Launch and shutdown should occur via primitive operations executed by the infrastructure tooling, not by the microservices.

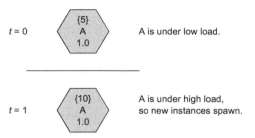

Figure 5.19   Mitosis pattern sequence

KILL SWITCH PATTERN

With this pattern (figure 5.20), you disable large parts of the system to limit damage. Microservices systems are complex, just like the Three Mile Island reactor. Failure events at all scales are to be expected. Empirically, these events follow a power law in terms of occurrence. Eventually, an event with potential for significant damage will occur.

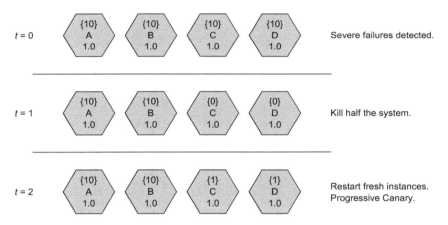

Figure 5.20   Kill Switch pattern sequence

To limit the damage, rapid action is required. It's impossible to understand the event during its occurrence, so the safest course of action is to scram the system. You should be able to shut down large parts of the system using secondary communication links to each microservice. As the event progresses, you may need to progressively shut down more and more of the system in order to eventually contain the damage.

5.7.4   *Validation*

Continuous validation of the production system is the key practice that makes microservices successful. No other activity provides as much risk reduction and value. It's the only way to run a CD pipeline responsibly.

What do you measure in production? CPU load levels? Memory usage? These are useful but not essential. Far more important is validation that the system is behaving as desired. Messages correspond to business activities or parts of business activities, so you should focus on the behavior of messages. Message-flow rates tell you a great deal about the health of the system. On their own, they're less useful than you may think, because they fluctuate with the time of day and with seasonality; it's more useful to compare message-flow rates with each other.

A given business process is encoded by an expanding set of messages generated from an initial triggering message. Thus, message-flow rates are related to each other by ratios. For example, for every message of a certain kind, you expect to see two messages of another kind. These ratios don't change, no matter what the load level of the system or the number of services present. They're *invariant*.

Invariants are the primary indicator of health. When you deploy a new version of a microservice using the Canary pattern, you check that the invariants are within expected bounds. If the new version contains a defect, the message-flow ratios will change, because some messages won't be generated. This is an immediate indicator of failure. Invariants, after all, can't vary. We'll come back to this topic in chapter 6 and examine an example in chapter 9.

The following sections present some applicable microservice deployment patterns.

VERSION UPDATE PATTERN

This pattern (figure 5.21) lets you safely update a set of communicating microservices. Suppose that microservices A and B communicate using messages of kind *x*. New business requirements introduce the need for messages of kind *y* between the services. It's unwise to attempt a simultaneous update of both; it's preferable to use the Progressive Canary deployment pattern to make the change safely.

First, you update listening service B so that it can recognize the new message, *y*. No other services generate this message in production yet, but you can validate that the new version of B doesn't cause damage. Once the new B is in place, you update A, which emits *y* messages.

This multistage update (composed of Progressive Canaries for each stage) can be used for many scenarios where message interactions need to change. You can use it

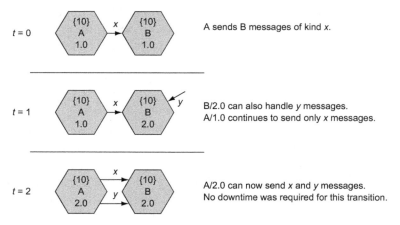

Figure 5.21   Version Update pattern sequence

when the internal data of the messages changes. (B, in this case, must retain the ability to handle old messages until the change is complete.) You can also use it to inject a third service between two existing services, by applying the pattern first to one side of the interaction and then to the other. This is a common way to introduce a cache, such as the one you saw in chapter 1.

CHAOS PATTERN

You can ensure that a system is resistant to failure by constantly failing at a low rate. Services can develop fragile dependencies on other services, despite your best intentions. When dependencies fail, even when that failure is below the acceptable threshold, the cumulative effect can cause threshold failures in client services.

To prevent creeping fragility, deliberately fail your services on a continuous basis, in production. Calibrate the failure to be well below the failure threshold for the business, so it doesn't have a significant impact on business outcomes. This is effectively a form of insurance: you take small, frequent, losses to avoid large, infrequent, losses that are fatal.

The most famous example of the Chaos pattern is the Netflix Chaos Monkey, which randomly shuts down services in the Netflix infrastructure. Another example is Google Game Days, where large-scale production failures are deliberately triggered to test failover capabilities.

5.7.5 *Discovery*

Pattern matching and transport independence give you decoupled services. When microservice A knows that microservice B will receive its messages, then A is *coupled* to B. Unfortunately, message transport requires knowledge of the location of B; otherwise, messages can't be delivered. Transport independence hides the mechanism of transportation from A, and pattern matching hides the identity of B. Identity is coupling.

The messaging abstraction layer needs to know the location of B, even as it hides this information from A. A (or, at least, the message layer in A) needs to discover the location of B (in reality, the set of locations of all the instances of B). This is a primary infrastructural challenge in microservice systems. Let's examine the common solutions:

- *Embedded configuration*—Hardcode service locations as part of the immutable artifact.
- *Intelligent load balancing*—Direct all message traffic through load balancers that know where to find the services.
- *Service registries*—Services register their location with a central registry, and other services look them up in the registry.
- *DNS*—Use the DNS protocol to resolve the location of a service.
- *Message bus*—Use a message bus to separate publishers from subscribers.
- *Gossip*—Use a peer-to-peer membership gossip protocol to share service locations.

No solution is perfect, and they all involve trade-offs, as listed in table 5.1.

Table 5.1   Service-discovery methods

Discovery	Advantages	Disadvantages
Embedded configuration	Easy implementation. Works (mostly) for small static systems.	Doesn't scale, because large systems are under continuous change. Very strong identity concept: raw network location.
Intelligent load balancing	Scalable with proven production-quality tooling. Examples: NGINX and Netflix's Hystrix.	Non-microservice network element that requires separate management. Load balancers force limited transport options and must still discover service locations themselves using one of the other discovery mechanisms. Retains identity concept: request URL.
Registry	Scalable with proven production-quality tooling. Examples: Consul, ZooKeeper, and etcd.	Non-microservice network element. High dependency on the chosen solution, because there are no common standards. Strong identity concept: service name key.
DNS	Unlimited scale and proven production-quality tooling. Well understood. Can be used by other mechanisms to weaken identity by replacing raw network locations.	Non-microservice network element. Management overhead. Weak identity concept: hostname.
Message bus	Scalable with proven production-quality tooling. Examples: RabbitMQ, Kafka, and NServiceBus.	Non-microservice network element. Management overhead. Weak identity concept: topic name.
Gossip	No concept of identity! Doesn't require additional network elements. Early adopter stage, but shown to work at scale.[a]	Message layer must have additional intelligence to handle load balancing. Rapidly evolving implementations.

a The SWIM algorithm has found success at Uber. See "How Ringpop from Uber Engineering Helps Distribute Your Application" by Lucie Lozinski, February 4, 2016, https://eng.uber.com/intro-to-ringpop.

5.7.6   *Configuration*

How do you configure your microservices? Configuration is one of the primary causes of deployment failure. Does configuration live with the service, immutably packaged into the artifact? Or does configuration live on the network, able to adapt dynamically to live conditions, and providing an additional way to control services?

If configuration is packaged with the service, then configuration changes aren't different from code changes and must be pushed through the CD pipeline in the same manner. Although this does provide better risk management, it also means you may suffer unacceptable delays when you need to make changes to configuration. You also add additional entries to the artifact store and audit logs for every configuration change, which can clutter these databases and make them less useful. Finally, some network components, such as intelligent load balancers, still need dynamic configuration if they're to be useful, so you can't place all configuration in artifacts.

On the other hand, network configuration removes your ability to reproduce the system deterministically or to benefit fully from the safety of immutability. The same artifact deployed tomorrow could fail even though it worked today. You need to define separate change-control processes and controls for configuration, because you can't reuse the artifact pipeline for this purpose. You'll need to deploy network services and infrastructure to store and serve configuration. Even if most configuration is dynamic, you still have to bake in at least some configuration—in particular, the network location of the configuration store! When you look closely, you find that many services have large amounts of potential configuration arising from third-party libraries included in them. You need to decide to what extent you'll expose this via the dynamic-configuration store. You're unlikely to find much value in exposing all of it. The most practical option is to embed low-level configuration into your deployment artifacts.

You'll end up with a hybrid solution, because neither approach provides a total solution. The immutable-packaging approach has the advantage of reusing the delivery pipeline as a control mechanism and offering more predictable state. Placing most of your configuration into immutable artifacts is a reasonable trade-off. Nonetheless, you should plan for the provision and management of dynamic configuration.

There are two dangerous anti-patterns to avoid when it comes to configuration. Using microservices doesn't protect you from them, so remain vigilant:

- *Automation workarounds*—Configuration can be used to code around limitations of your automation tooling: for example, using feature flags rather than generating new artifacts. If you do too much of this, you'll create an uncontrolled secondary command structure that damages the properties of the system that make immutability so powerful.
- *Turing's revenge*—Configuration formats tend to be extended with programming constructs over time, mostly as conveniences to avoid repetition.[37] Now, you have a new, unasked-for programming language in your system that has no formal grammar, undefined behavior, and no debugging tools. Good luck!

5.7.7 Security

The microservice architecture doesn't offer any inherent security benefits and can introduce new attack vectors if you aren't careful. In particular, there's a common temptation to share microservice messages with the outside world. This is dangerous, because it exposes every microservice as an attack surface.

There must be an absolute separation: you need a *demilitarized zone* (DMZ) between the internal world of microservice messages and the outside world of third-party clients. The DMZ must translate between the two. In practice, this means a microservice system should expose traditional integration points, such as REST APIs, and then convert requests to these APIs into messages. This allows for strict sanitization of input.

Internally, you can't ignore that fact that microservices communicate over a network, and networks represent an opportunity for attack. Your microservices should live in their own private networks with well-defined ingress and egress routes. The rest

---

[37] Initially declarative domain-specific languages, such as configuration formats, tend to accumulate programmatic features over time. It's surprisingly easy to achieve Turing completeness with a limited set of operations.

of the system uses these routes to interact with the microservice system as a whole. The specific microservices to which messages are routed aren't exposed.

These precautions may still be insufficient, and you need to consider the case where an attacker has some level of access to the microservice network. You can apply the security principle of *defense in depth* to strengthen your security in layers. There's always a trade-off between stronger security and operational impact.

Let's build up a few layers. Microservices can be given a right of refusal, and they can be made more pedantic in the messages they accept. Highly paranoid services will lead to higher error rates but can delay attackers and make attacks more expensive. For example, you can limit the amount of data a service will return for any one request. This approach means custom work for each service.

Communication between services can require shared secrets and, as a further layer, signed messages. This protects against messages injected into the network by an attacker. The distribution and cycling of the secrets introduces operational complexity. The signing of messages requires key distribution and introduces latency.

If your data is sensitive, you can encrypt all communication between microservices. This also introduces latency and management overhead and isn't to be undertaken lightly. Consider using the Merge pattern for extremely sensitive data flows, avoiding the network as much as possible.

You need secure storage and management of secrets and encryption keys in order for these layers to be effective. There's no point in encrypting messages if the keys are easily accessible within the network—but your microservices must be able to access the secrets and keys. To solve this problem, you need to introduce another network element: a key-management service that provides secure storage, access control, and audit capabilities.[38]

5.7.8   *Staging*

The staging system is the control mechanism for the CD pipeline. It encompasses traditional elements, such as a build server for CI. It can also consist of multiple systems that test various aspects of the system, such as performance.

The staging system can also be used to provide manual gates to the delivery pipeline. These are often unavoidable, either politically or legally. Over time, the effectiveness of CD in managing risk and delivering business value quickly can be used to create sufficient organizational confidence to relax overly ceremonial manual sign-offs.

The staging system provides a self-service mechanism for development teams to push updates all the way to production. Empowering teams to do this is a critical component in the success of CD. Chapter 7 discusses this human factor.

Staging should collect statistics to measure the velocity and quality of code delivery over time. It's important to know how long it takes, on average, to take code from concept to production, for a given risk level, because this tells you how efficient your CD pipeline is.

---

[38] Some examples are HashiCorp Vault (www.vaultproject.io), AWS key-value stores (KVS), and, if money is no object, hardware security modules (HSMs).

The staging system has the most variance between projects and organizations. The level of testing, the number of staging steps, and the mechanism of artifact generation are all highly context-specific. As you increase the use of microservices and CD in your organization, avoid being too prescriptive in your definition of the staging function; you must allow teams to adapt to their own circumstances.

5.7.9 Development

The development environment needed for microservices should enable developers to focus on a small set of services at a time—often, a single service. The message-abstraction layer comes into its own here, because it makes it easy to mock the behavior of other services.[39] Instead of having to implement a complex object hierarchy, microservice mocking only requires implementing sample message flows. This makes it possible to unit-test microservices in complete isolation from the rest of the system.

Microservices can be specified as a relation between inbound and outbound messages. This allows you to focus on a small part of the system. It also enables more-efficient parallel work, because messages from other microservices (which may not yet exist) can easily be mocked.

Isolation isn't always possible or appropriate. Developers often need to run small subsets of the system locally, and tooling is needed to make this practical. It isn't advisable for development to become dependent on running a full replica of the production system. As production grows to hundreds of different services and beyond, it becomes extremely resource intensive to run services locally, and, ultimately, doing so becomes impossible.

If you're running only a subset of the system, how do you ensure that appropriate messages are provided for the other parts of the system? One common anti-pattern is to use the build or staging system to do this. You end up working against shared resources that have extremely nondeterministic state. This is the same anti-pattern as having a shared development database.

Each developer should provide a set of mock messages for their service. Where do these mock messages live? At one extreme, you can place all mock-message flows in a common mocking service. All developers commit code to this service, but conflicts are rare because work isn't likely to overlap. At the other extreme, you can provide a mock service along with each service implementation. The mock service is an extremely simple service that returns hardcoded responses.

The practical solution for most teams is somewhere in the middle. Start with a single universal mocking service, and apply the Split pattern whenever it becomes too unwieldy. Sets of services with a common focus will tend to get their own mocking service. The development environment is typically a small set of actual services, along with one or two mocking services. This minimizes the number of service processes needed on a developer machine.

---

[39] For a practical example, see the code in chapter 9.

The mock messages are defined by the developers building a given microservice. This has an unfortunate side effect: Some developers will focus on expected behavior. Others will use their service in unexpected ways, so the mocking will be incomplete. If you allow other developers to add mock messages to services they don't own, then the mocks will quickly diverge from reality. The solution is to add captured messages to the list of sample messages. Capture sample message flows from the production or staging logs, and add them to the mock service. This can be done manually for even medium-sized systems.

Beware the distributed monolith!

How do you know you're building a distributed monolith? If you need to run all, or most, of your services to get any development work done. If you can't write a microservice without needing all the other microservices running, then you have a problem.

It's easy to end up needing to run a large cloud server instance for every developer—in which case development will slow to a crawl. This is why you must invest in a messaging abstraction layer and avoid the mini-web-servers anti-pattern.

You'll need to think carefully about the mocking strategy you'll use in your project. It must allow your developers to build with chosen subsets of the system.

5.8   *Summary*

- Failure is inevitable and must be accepted. Starting from that perspective, you can work to distribute failure more evenly over time and avoid high-impact catastrophes.
- Traditional approaches to software quality are predicated on a false belief in perfectionism. Enterprise software systems aren't desktop calculators and won't give the correct answer 100% of the time. The closer you want to get to 100%, the more expensive the system becomes.
- The risk of failure is much higher than generally believed. Simple mathematical modeling of risk probabilities in component-based systems (such as enterprise software) brings this reality starkly into focus.
- Microservices provide an opportunity to measure risk more accurately. This enables you to define acceptable error rates that your system must meet.
- By packaging microservices into immutable units of deployment, you can define a set of deployment patterns that mitigate risk and can be automated for efficient management of your production systems.
- The accurate measurement of risk enables the construction of a continuous delivery pipeline that enables developers to push changes to microservices to production at high velocity and high frequency, while maintaining acceptable risk levels.

Part 2

Running microservices

For the most part, software is written by people in organizations. People and organizational context greatly impact the success of your project. This part of the book is all about using the engineering advantages of the microservice architecture to overcome some of the challenges that this context brings. Once again, there's no silver bullet, but you can implement a strategy of focusing on delivering features that matter to the business by using the tactics covered here:

- Chapter 6 connects business goals to your code. You need to build a system that's sufficiently reliable but no more so than necessary, and you need to demonstrate that you're meeting business goals. This chapter covers what to measure and how to measure it.

- Chapter 7 walks you through the work of moving from a legacy monolith to a microservice system. This will be the most likely reality for you as a software architect. Practical approaches to isolating and managing the suffocating technical debt of the monolith are the primary topics.

- Chapter 8 addresses your greatest challenge: dealing with the politics of organizational change. Microservices make it easier to deliver results more quickly and to keep pace with the chaos in most companies. That said, you must still choose your political tactics carefully and grow a base of support for your activities.

- Chapter 9 is an end-to-end journey through the development of a new system, using the microservice architecture aggressively from the beginning. This chapter is focused on source code and tooling, allowing you to gauge the practical implications of choosing microservices for software teams doing real work.

Microservices aren't always appropriate, and even when they are, your organization may not be ready to make the changes necessary to fully benefit from them. Your career can suffer if you don't choose your timing and projects wisely. Even then, you'll be politically exposed as the introducer of new things. This part of the book will help you navigate these treacherous waters.

Measurement

Microservice systems need to be monitored. More than that, they need to be *measured*. The traditional approach to monitoring, where you collect time-series metrics such as CPU load and query response times, isn't as useful when you have a system of many small moving parts. There are too many microservices to think about each one individually.

Instead, we must widen the concept of system observation. You want to measure the system, rather than monitor it. A microservice system grows organically as business needs change, and taking a measurement-oriented approach allows you to discover and understand the system as it is, rather than how it was designed. Such measurements aren't limited to the dimension of time. You also want to measure the ever-changing network of relationships within the system.

As always, you need to ask where the value is. What purpose does measurement serve? You want to do three things:

- *Validate the business requirements*—You want a set of measurements that demonstrate progress toward your business goals.
- *Verify and understand the technical functioning of the system*—You want to make sure things are working as they should and will continue to do so.
- *Manage risk so you can move fast*—You want to be able to make rapid changes to the system without breaking it.

We'll use the microblogging system from chapter 1 to demonstrate how to apply and visualize measurements.[1]

6.1 *The limits of traditional monitoring*

The monitoring typically used for monolithic systems is more properly called *telemetry*. It's focused on metrics per server. The metrics are mostly time series, with a few capacity checks thrown in. You measure the CPU and memory loads on your machines (even if virtual), network traffic, and disk space. You also measure response times on web service endpoints, and you log slow queries.

When you're load balancing over a small number of application servers, each using one primary database and a few secondary databases for reading, these metrics are good enough. When you deploy a new version of the monolith, it's pretty obvious when there's a problem, because response times and error rates crash and spike. You can easily connect each chart with the system element responsible for the problem. Diagnosis is simple because there are only a few parts.

It's the database index

When an application that was working fine yesterday suddenly starts to misbehave, it's almost certainly because you need to index a database column. This is the first thing to look for and the first thing to eliminate as a cause.

An application searches many database columns as part of its core logic. Often these are primary keys, which are always indexed, so increasing numbers of records won't cause issues. You also explicitly index columns that you know will be used in queries.

But it's easy to miss some columns that have a critical impact on performance. Often it becomes clear only after you've been running in production for a while, and accumulating data, that there's a dependency on certain columns. The database reaches a tipping point, and performance suddenly declines.

Unfortunately, this isn't a problem microservices can solve. The same forces and issues apply. When the behavior of a microservice with data responsibility declines, check your indexes!

---

[1] It's worth returning to chapter 1 and reviewing the full microservice diagram (figure 1.5) for the microblogging system. Only the relevant subsections of that diagram will be shown in this chapter.

6.1.1   Classical configurations

In the microblogging system from chapter 1, a core feature is the display of the user's timeline. The timeline for a user is all the entries the user should see from all the people they follow. The responsiveness of the timeline is vital to the correct functioning of the system. Any increase in latency due to an issue in the system is something you want to know about.

For a moment, imagine the microblogging system as a monolith. Perhaps you have eight application servers running all the functionality. Then, you collect response times for the timeline query and store them as time series data. For each query, you store the time it occurred and how long it took to return a result. You do this for all eight application servers and use a time series database and an associated monitoring tool[2] to generate charts showing response times over time. You can show the average response times of each server. If a server is having issues, you should be able to pick this up from the charts, because you can see the change over time. In the charts in figure 6.1, you can see that the average response time of server A shows a problem.[3]

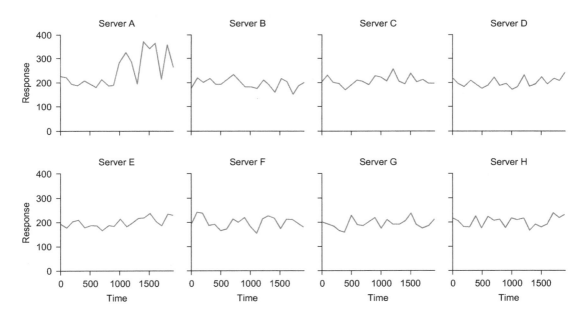

Figure 6.1   Classical response-time charts

---

[2]   Perhaps a commercial solution such as New Relic (https://newrelic.com) or an open source solution such as Graphite (https://graphiteapp.org).

[3]   The charts in this chapter were generated using Python data-science tools, in particular seaborn (http://seaborn .pydata.org). The data is simulated to be clear and to help make pedagogical points. Your real data will be messier.

Time series data

Time series data is shown as the change in a measure over time. The measure might be the number of inbound requests or the response time of those requests. You're presented with a nice line chart that has time on the horizontal axis and the value on the vertical axis.

It's important to understand what you see. Each point on the chart is not a specific event: it's a summary of a set of events over a given time period. To draw the chart on a per-second basis, all the events in each second are averaged, and the average value is used to draw the chart.

This isn't the only way to do it. You can use other summary statistics, such as the median (the halfway point), or a rolling average that averages over the last 30 seconds, say.

The underlying data is a set of values at specific time points. Usually, there's too much data to store or send over the network. So, most analytics solutions aggregate the data before sending it from the client to a time series database. The time series database then summarizes older data to reduce storage needs.

Time series charts are a useful tool, but you should bear in mind that quite a bit of magic is going on behind the scenes.

Now, consider this approach from the perspective of a production microservice system. Many types of microservices are collaborating to produce the timeline, and there are many instances of each microservice type. There can easily be hundreds of response-time charts to review. This isn't feasible. The traditional time series approach to system measurement doesn't give you the same insights when it comes to microservices. You need to adopt a measurement approach that can handle large numbers of independent elements.

Why not just use alerts?

The discussion in this chapter is focused on diagnosing issues and understanding the structure of a microservice system. Once you understand an underlying issue and are happy that the system in production matches your design, you can monitor important measures directly.

You can use these measures to define and generate alerts when thresholds are crossed. You can use these alerts to scale the system up and down and send pages when there are critical failures.

The challenge with alerts is to get the sensitivity right. If there are too many failure alerts that aren't really critical, whoever's on call that week will start ignoring them. Calibrating scale-up and scale-down is often achieved by (expensive!) trial and error.

6.1.2 *The problem with averages*

There are some improvements to be made to the basic time series charts. We won't abandon time series charts entirely, because they're useful when used appropriately, but charting the average response time isn't ideal. An average, also known as the *mean*, is a summary statistic, which by definition hides information. If response times were distributed evenly and tightly around the average, then it would be a good indication of what you care about—the user's experience of performance. The problem is that response times have a *skewed* distribution.[4] They don't keep close to the average. Some response times are much higher, and some users may experience very low performance despite the average response time appearing to be acceptable. If you sort the response times into buckets of 50 ms and then chart the number of responses in each bucket, you end up with the histogram chart shown in figure 6.2.[5]

Suppose that, in an attempt to improve performance, you decide to add a caching mechanism. The average comes down, and you're delighted. But customers still keep complaining about performance. Why? The cache has made about half your requests much faster, but the other requests perform as before, and you still have a small num-

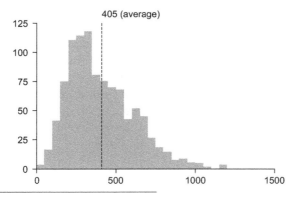

Figure 6.2 Histogram chart showing response times

---

[4] The average, or mean, is a great summary of numbers that come from the *normal* distribution. The normal distribution is a mathematical model of randomness that assumes measured values will be close to, and balanced around, some central "true" value.

[5] A histogram shows how many items occur in each category of interest. You can construct the categories from numeric ranges to organize the response-time data. This lets you see which response times are more prevalent than others.

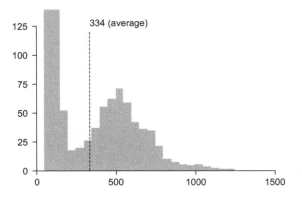

Figure 6.3   Histogram chart showing response times, with caching causing two peaks

ber of requests that are really slow. The average now sits in the middle, as shown in figure 6.3, and doesn't describe the experience of most users: only a small set of users experience "average" performance.

There are other statistics to consider. You want to better characterize the experience of most users so you can know that system performance is acceptable. The *median* is the value that divides the data in half. If you take the median response time, you know that half the users experienced a faster response time and half experienced a slower response time. This is more meaningful than the average, but the median still doesn't tell you that some users see very bad performance. You need to know how many people are having a bad experience. Some always will, but you need to know how many so that you can set an acceptable error rate.[6]

6.1.3   *Using percentiles*

One useful solution to this problem is to start from the perspective of business value. What percentage of users can experience poor performance without impacting the business severely? It's only worth spending money on more servers to improve performance up to this point. This is often a subjective judgment, and an arbitrary answer of 10%, 5%, or 1% is chosen. Regardless of how the figure is determined, you can use it to define your goal in terms of response times. If you decide that responses times should be at most 1 second and that at most 10% of users should experience performance slower than 1 second, then you can invert the percentage to ask the question in a more convenient manner: what was the response time that 90% of users didn't exceed? This response time should be at or below 1 second to meet your performance requirement. It's known as the *90thpercentile*.[7]

---

[6]   It doesn't make sense to build a system that has perfect performance for all users. It's *possible* to build such a system, but the cost doesn't justify the business benefit. There's always an acceptable level of failure that balances cost with business objectives. For more on this principle, see chapter 8.

[7]   To calculate a percentile, take all of your data points, sort them in ascending order, and then take the value that's at index $(n \times p / 100) - 1$, where n is the number of values and p is the percentile. For example, the 90th percentile of {11,22,33,44,55,66,77,88,99,111} is 99 (index is 8 == $(10 \times 90 / 100) - 1$). Intuitively, 90% of values are at or below 99.

Percentiles are useful because they align better with business needs. You want most customers to have a good experience. By charting the percentile, rather than the average, you can directly measure this, and you can do so in a way that's independent of the distribution of the data. This handles the caching scenario (where you had two user experience clusters) and still provides a useful summary statistic.

Figures 6.4 and 6.5 add the 90th percentile to the previous histograms of response times. Although caching improves the average response time, you can see that the 90th percentile doesn't improve: 10% of responses are still greater than about 680 ms.

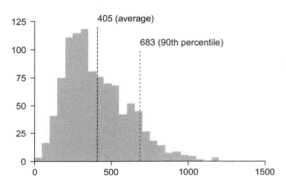

Figure 6.4　Histogram chart (no cache) showing response times, with 90th percentile

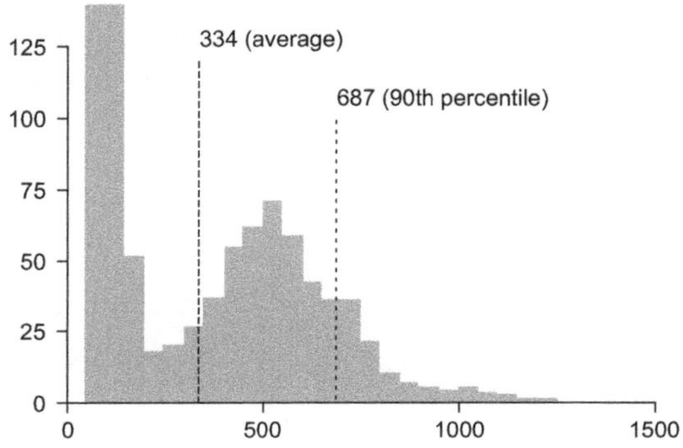

Figure 6.5　Histogram chart (with cache) showing response times, with 90th percentile

Let's consider a failure scenario in the context of a monolith and see how percentiles can help. Suppose you have a system with tens of servers at most. One of these servers is experiencing problems with a specific API endpoint. In your daily review of the system metrics, the response-times chart for this API endpoint for the server in difficulty looks like figure 6.6.

This chart shows response time over time. For each time unit, the chart calculates the average and the 90th percentile. To help you understand how the underlying data is distributed, each individual response time is also shown as a gray dot (this isn't something normally shown by analytics solutions). By comparing historical performance to current performance, you can see that there was a change for the worse. By using percentiles, you avoided missing the problem, because the average doesn't show

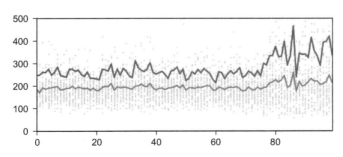

Figure 6.6　Time series chart of average and 90th percentile response times

it unambiguously. This approach will work when you're reviewing a small number of servers, but it clearly won't scale to microservices.

Summary statistics are terrible

A summary statistic creates one number out of many. It's meant to give you a feel for the larger dataset of numbers by condensing them into a single number. This can be misleading, because information is lost. In particular, the shape of the dataset is lost—but the way the data is distributed can be just as important as the average value.

A famous example is *Anscombe's quartet*: four datasets of x and y values that have the same summary statistics, despite being very different. The average of the x values is always 9, and of the y values is always 7.5.

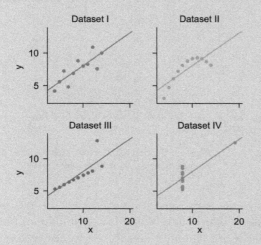

Anscombe's quartet: the averages of x and y are the same in each dataset.

These datasets also have the same values for more-technical summary statistics such as variance. Anscombe's quartet shows the importance of visualizing the measurements from your microservice system, rather than just summarizing them.

Percentiles are better than averages for understanding system performance, but you shouldn't be seduced by them, either. They're still summary statistics, and they hide information. Nor should you be naïve about the cost of calculating them (lots of data points must be sorted). Many analytics solutions give you a percentile estimate, rather than the true value. Read the fine print.

6.1.4   *Microservice configurations*

Microservices create some difficult problems for the traditional approach to metrics. The network includes an order of magnitude more elements. You'll have hundreds of microservice instances in a production system, multiple instances of each kind of service, and several different versions that live in production at the same time. You'll probably use containers on top of virtual machines.

Although you'll always want to have time series metrics such as CPU load at a fine-grained level, for each microservice, it's infeasible to review all of them. When something goes wrong—when the response time of an important web-service endpoint degrades—where do you start looking? You don't want to have to laboriously open each microservice to check its metrics.

Here are the measurement problems you need to solve:

- Observing the health of the system without needing to observe each component
- Understanding the structure of the system as it is in reality
- Diagnosing and isolating faults quickly and easily
- Predicting where problems will arise

Somehow, you must summarize the state of the system into a set of useful measurements. The problem with time series charts is that you must either plot data for all the services, leading to a noisy chart that's impossible to decipher, or statistically summarize the data (using means or percentiles) and lose resolution on the aberrations you're looking for.

The *scatterplot* is an alternative visualization that's better suited to microservice architectures. It's suitable for analyzing the relationships of large numbers of elements—precisely the circumstance you're in.

6.1.5   *The power of scatterplots*

In the case of the monolith, you noticed that something was awry by comparing historical and current response times. You did this visually: you saw the line in the chart curve upward. The chart showed performance over time, and it was easy to adjust to show the historical and current response times. You could compare the current problematic response times to earlier times when performance was healthy. This comparison is the key to identifying the performance problem. You can use scatterplots to perform the same comparison over hundreds of microservices, all on the same chart.

A *scatterplot* is a way to visually compare two quantities. You have a list of things, such as servers, messages, or microservices, and each thing becomes a dot on the chart. Each thing should have two numerical attributes that you want to compare: one for the x-axis and one for the y-axis. A classic scatterplot example compares the weights and heights of a group of people (see figure 6.7): you expect taller people to be heavier, so the dots form a shape that tends upward and to the right. This shows that the two quantities are correlated.[8]

---

[8] This public domain data is sampled from the following report: *Anthropometric Reference Data for Children and Adults: United States, 2007–2010*, National Center for Health Statistics, Centers for Disease Control and Prevention. Scatterplots are often used to show a *correlation* between two variables in a scientific study in order to investigate whether one variable causes changes in the other. Correlation by itself can't do this because it shows only the relationship between the variables. An underlying scientific theory is needed to argue for causality. For our purposes, in the muck and grime of production software systems, we're mostly concerned with the relationship as a diagnostic tool, rather than demonstrating causality.

You need two numerical attributes, and that presents a problem for time series data, because you have only one: the value of the measurement at a given time.[9] How can you define two numbers to describe response times so that you can compare current and historical behavior for each microservice? The answer is in the statement of the question—you use summary statistics for a historical period and for the current period.

Let's use response times over the last 24 hours as the historical data and response times over the last 10 minutes as the current data.[10] You could summarize the data using the average response time, but as you've seen, this isn't a useful statistic when you're interested in the experience of the majority of users. Instead, let's use the 90th percentile. If you have 100 microservices, you can calculate these numbers for each one and then chart the scatterplot, as shown in figure 6.8.

If everything is working as expected, then current performance should resemble historical performance. The response times should be highly correlated and form a nice, obvious upward line in the chart. In the figure, there's one outlier, and you can easily identify the errant server.[11] This scatterplot is a great way to visualize current behavior.

The scatterplot is a historical snapshot of a single point in time, and this is a significant difference from a time series chart. It can be useful to generate a series of scatterplots over time and then animate them together, showing the system changing over time.

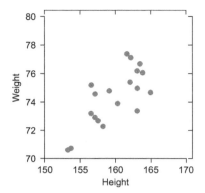

Figure 6.7   Scatterplot of weight (in kilograms) versus height (in centimeters)

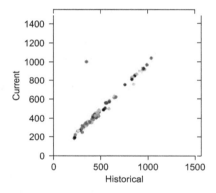

Figure 6.8   Current-behavior scatterplot of microservice response times

6.1.6   *Building a dashboard*

It's strongly recommended that you sign up for a third-party analytics service and use it to collect measurements. A wide range of competent solutions are available on the market.[12] Unfortunately, most of them are focused on the monolithic architecture. This means they don't handle large numbers of network elements well and focus

---

[9] Just plotting over time gives … a time series.

[10] Adjust the historical and current time ranges as needed for your own data and system.

[11] In this context, "easily" means you're using a charting library that can interactively identify data points.

[12] Commercial solutions include New Relic (https://newrelic.com), AppDynamics (www.appdynamics.com), Datadog (www.datadoghq.com), and similar.

primarily on time series analysis. But this is still useful, and these aspects of your microservice system are important.

To fully measure your system, and to make the measurement techniques discussed in this chapter available to your teams, you'll need to consider building a small custom solution. Over time, more and better support for microservices will appear in the analytics services, reducing the amount of custom work you'll need to do. As with deployment, choosing microservices means a commitment to custom tooling in the interim, and it's important to factor this into your decision to use microservices.

Unfortunately, most of the open source analytics and dashboard solutions also focus on traditional use cases. You'll need to choose a set of open source components that let you build custom data processing and custom charting relatively easily.[13] Don't be afraid to build "good-enough" dashboards. You can achieve a great deal by loading raw data (suitably summarized) into the browser and generating charts by hand with a charting library.

You also don't need to build an interactive dashboard. An increasing number of data science tools are available, both commercial and open source, that allow you to analyze data and generate reports[14] using scatterplots. This might be a manual process initially, but it can easily be automated if necessary. The reports won't be real-time and won't help with that class of faults. Many faults aren't real-time, however. They're persistent issues—ongoing problems you're living with. Data science tools are useful for diagnosing and understanding these types of problems.

6.2 Measurements for microservices

You need a structure to define the measurements for a microservice system. You can use the pathway from business requirements to messages to services that we've already defined; this gives you three layers of measurement.

6.2.1 The business layer

Business requirements tend to be both qualitative and quantitative. The qualitative ones describe user experiences in terms of workflows, capabilities, and subjective experiences. The quantitative requirements, which are often fewer in number, tend to focus on easily quantified business goals, performance levels, system capacity, and, if we've made our point, acceptable error rates.

Your dashboard absolutely must capture and display these quantified business metrics, and capturing them shouldn't be an afterthought. (Chapter 7 discusses the importance of these metrics to project success.) From a technical perspective, you can simplify capturing these metrics by using the flow of messages in the system. For example, the conversion rate of an e-commerce application is the ratio of confirmation to

---

[13] Try InfluxDB (www.influxdata.com), Graphite (https://graphiteapp.org), or Prometheus (https://prometheus.io).

[14] Data science tools can be effective and are worth taking a little time to learn. A good place to start is Anaconda (http://continuum.io), which is a curated package of Python, R, and Scala tooling.

checkout messages.[15] Not all metrics can be captured in terms of messages, but you should use message analytics to the fullest extent possible.

What about the qualitative aspects of the business requirements? Aren't these impossible to measure?[16] The answer is an emphatic no! Anything can be measured, in the sense that you can always reduce your uncertainty about something, even with indirect measurements. For example, workflows through the system are represented by message flows through microservices. By tracing the causal flow of messages through the system, you can verify that workflows are being followed as designed. This is a measure of the alignment of the system with the business analysis that produced it. Instead of trying to enforce correctness, you accept that there will be deviations in practice, and you find out what they are. Maybe the workflows that get built in practice are better than the original designs. Maybe they failed to understand a key business driver, and you need to correct them.

How do you measure a goal like "The system should be user-friendly"? Here's one approach: measure goal completion effort.[17] The business requirements define sets of user goals, such as "find a product," "perform a checkout," "sign up for a newsletter," and so on. How much effort does it take the user in terms of time and interactions to achieve these goals? Although these interactions differ from workflows in that they're undirected and the user can achieve the goal state via many paths, you can still use message flows as a proxy for measuring effort. In this case, rather than a causal trail through the messages, you track the flow by another attribute, such as the user identifier.

The perspective to take with the qualitative requirements is that you can often recode them in terms of message interactions and then measure the message interactions as a proxy for the qualitative requirement. For example, a completed order must generate a confirmation email and an instruction for the warehouse. The counts of the messages representing these business activities should correlate. Once again, you use messages as a representation of many aspects of the system. This is an advantage of the microservice architecture that isn't immediately apparent and is easier to achieve once you take a message-oriented, rather than service-oriented, perspective.

6.2.2 *The message layer*

At the message layer, you can use a uniform set of measurements against each message. By reducing most interactions to message flows, you can analyze everything using the same tools. This lets you validate not only the business requirements, but also the correctness and good behavior of the system. Messages have causal relationships with each other by design, and you can verify that the system is adhering to these desired relationships by watching what the messages do in production.

---

[15] This shouldn't be your primary authoritative measure of conversions. Message-flow rates should be used as a first-pass confirmation that you're hitting your targets.

[16] For a pragmatic perspective on system measurement, see *How to Measure Anything* by Douglas Hubbard (Wiley, 2014). It's a highly recommended read.

[17] There are other approaches that you should consider, such as user surveys.

Consider a message from service A to service B. You know that when this message leaves A, it can be synchronous or asynchronous. When it arrives at B, it can be consumed or observed. You can use this model to develop a set of measurements for messages. Let's start at the top and work our way down.

Service instances and types

A *service instance* is a specific operating system process. It may be running in a container on a virtual machine, or it may be running as a bare process on the host system of a developer laptop. There may be hundreds of service instances in a microservice system.

A service *type* is a shorthand expression for a group of service instances. The type can be a common message pattern that the service instances send or receive, or it can be a deployment configuration. Services can be tagged with a name, and the type may be all versions of service instances with the same tag.

It can be useful to define measurements against a set of service types so that you can understand the behavior of groups of services. The definition of the types is determined by your needs and the architecture of your system. The ability of your analytics solution to handle groupings like this is important and should be a consideration in your choice of analytics system.

UNIVERSAL MEASUREMENTS

There are universal measurements that apply to all messages. The number of messages sent per unit of time is a measure that's always applicable. How many login messages per second? How many blog posts per minute? How many records loaded per hour? In general, if you capture the message-flow rate as messages per second, for each message pattern in your system, you have a great starting point for analysis.

Message-flow rates measure load on your system directly, and they do so independently of the number of services, which is a useful advantage as a measurement. Charting them as a time series per message allows you to see characteristic behavior over time, such as usage spikes at lunchtime. You can also trigger alarms if the flow rates go outside expected levels, or use the flow rates to trigger scaling by provisioning more servers. Rather than use indirect metrics, such as response times or CPU levels, you can use message-flow rates as a direct measure of load on the system.

The message-flow rate is by far the most important universal measurement, but there are others you'll want to capture as well. How many messages of each pattern are sent on a historical basis? How many messages have errors, and what's the error rate? What size are the messages? You can use these metrics to develop a historical perspective on your system, allowing you to verify that changes are having the desired effects and to diagnose long-running issues.

Choosing an analytics solution for microservices

It's unlikely that you'll be able to use a single analytics solution for your microservice system. Certainly, you can use commercial services where doing so makes sense. Such things as API endpoint performance, client-side error capture, page-load times, mobile session durations, and so forth remain relevant whatever your underlying architecture.

To capture measurements that tell you about your microservice system, you'll need to do some custom work. As time goes by, analytics vendors and open source projects will provide better support for architecture with large numbers of elements. Unfortunately, it's likely that the emphasis will still be on services, rather than messages.

You can use the message abstraction layer to capture the data you need. Integrate distributed tracing at this point.[18] You can also capture message counts and flow rates. It's unwise to send the raw data to an analytics collection point, because the volumes will be too high. Instead, you'll have to summarize or sample the data. A summary might be the metric "messages seen per minute," sent once a minute. A sample might be to capture the details of 1% of messages.

You'll then store these measures using a time series database and use the data in that database to generate a custom dashboard. You can read this chapter as a high-level description of what you'll need to build.

MEASURING SYNCHRONOUS AND CONSUMED MESSAGES

You can establish well-defined measures for synchronous and consumed messages, some of which you can reuse for other message types. Suppose a message leaves service A at a time local to A, and you want to capture this event using your analytics system. You want to count the number of messages of each pattern that service A emits and calculate the message-flow rates for that service instance and service type and for the entire system. The analytics system should combine all the reports from all services so that you can get the total counts for each message pattern.

> **NOTE** The following sections of this chapter, outlining the basic ways to measure messages, should be considered reference material for building your microservice analytics and as a starting point for your own fine-grained, context-specific metrics. Please feel free, as with the other reference sections in this book (such as the list of message patterns in section 3.5), to skim on first reading.

Your analytics solution should allow you to aggregate message events so that you can calculate message counts and timing means and percentiles over periods of time that are of interest to you. Message-flow rates are most useful on a per-second basis, because you want to react quickly to changes. Message counts and timings can use longer time

---

[18] An important paper to read on distributed tracing is "Dapper, a Large-Scale Distributed Systems Tracing Infrastructure" by Benjamin H. Sigelman et al., Google Research, 2010, https://research.google.com/pubs/pub36356.html. A good open source implementation is Zipkin (http://zipkin.io).

periods, from minutes to hours to days. On this basis, you can define the measures per message instance per pattern, shown in table 6.1.

Table 6.1   Outbound message measures

Case	Measure	Type	Aggregation	Description
outbound-send	*count*	*event*	Count over a time period.	Capture the number of messages sent.
outbound-send	*pass*	*event*	Count over a time period.	Capture the number of messages successfully sent.
outbound-response	*count*	*event*	Count over a time period.	Capture the number of message responses received.
outbound-response	*pass*	*event*	Count over a time period.	Capture the number of successful message responses.
outbound-response	*time*	*duration*	Time taken as mean or percentile over message-response times.	Capture the response time.

You use *outbound-send/count* to see how many messages are being sent. Each message is a data point, and the count is a count of the data points. It's useful to know whether messages are being successfully sent, independent of successful receipt or processing—this is captured by *outbound-send/pass*. This gives you the perspective of the sending service with respect to network health.[19]

Here's an example scenario. You're using intelligent load balancing to route messages based on their pattern. One of the load balancers is intermittently defective, so sending services sometimes can't contact it. In this case, *outbound-send/pass* will be less than 100% of *outbound-send/count*. A useful chart, therefore, is the ratio of these two measures. Because the aggregation is a count function, it's independent of the number of services and the subdivision of patterns, so you don't lose information by aggregating all the behavior in the system into more-general charts.

The *outbound-response/count* measure captures the number of message responses received. If everything is working, then *outbound-send/count* and *outbound-response/count* should be closely correlated, with some jitter due to network traversal time. You can generate a scatterplot to verify this; see figure 6.9.

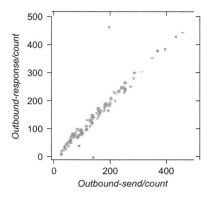

Figure 6.9   Synchronous message outbound send and response counts

---

[19] One useful derivative is *outbound-send/fail*, calculated by subtracting passes from the total count. A useful extension is *outbound-send/wtf*, where the nature of the error response is wholly unexpected. This can indicate potentially catastrophic edge cases in production that you need to handle more deliberately.

In the scatterplot, you can see three message patterns that are behaving oddly. Each message pattern is plotted using a different marker shape so you can tell them apart.[20] The upward-arrow marker shape indicates that the associated message pattern is receiving no responses. Clearly, something is broken. The left-arrow marker shape shows response counts well below send counts, indicating a situation that isn't healthy. Finally, the downward-arrow marker shape shows responses far above sends. This happens when you add capacity to clear a backlog. This scatterplot is sensitive to the time period it represents, so you should plot it over several orders of magnitude.[21]

The responses to synchronous messages can be error responses, meaning the receiving side failed to process the message and is sending back an error response. You can track the success rate of responses with *outbound-response/pass* and derive the error rate from that. Bear in mind that you need to calibrate the time period. It can also be useful to classify the type of error response. Was it a timeout, a system error on the receiving side, a badly formed message, or something else? You can then use these classifications to drill down into the failure events. Charting the error rates over time is a good way to get a quick view of system health; see figure 6.10. Error counts should be low, so you can take the shortcut of charting them all together, because problematic services will stand out.

The *outbound-response/time* measure captures the response time of the message. This is the total response time, including network traversal and processing time on the receiver. You can use this measure to identify messages and services that have degraded performance. This measure must be aggregated over a set of messages. As discussed earlier, the most desirable aggregation is the percentile. Sadly, this can be expensive to compute, because the data points have to be sorted, which is prohibitive for large datasets. Some analytics tools let you estimate the percentile by sampling, and this is still a better measure than the mean. The mean is easier and much faster to calculate, so you may decide to use it for interpretation with appropriate care.

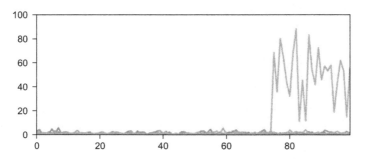

Figure 6.10 Outbound response failure counts over time

---

[20] Shapes are used here because in a book, the chart isn't interactive!

[21] If messages are backlogged in a queue, then even though the send and response counts might be correlated, the responses are for older messages, and latency is probably unacceptably high, even if throughput is OK.

The *outbound-response/time* measure is useful for generating current-behavior scatterplots. You can see whether the current response times are healthy compared to historical behavior. The scatterplot can show response times for each message, or you can aggregate over message types using pattern matching. The scatterplot in figure 6.11 collects all message types into 20 major families (taking the average within each family). The downward arrow indicates a family of messages that might be of concern.

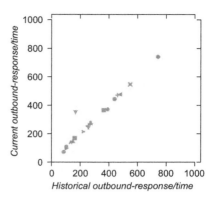

Figure 6.11   Current response-time behavior by message family

The receiving side of the synchronous-consumed interaction also provides some measures that are important, as listed in table 6.2.

Table 6.2   Inbound message measures

Case	Measure	Type	Aggregation	Description
inbound-receive	count	event	Count over a time period.	Capture the number of messages received.
inbound-receive	valid	event	Count over a time period.	Capture the number of received messages that are valid and well-formed.
inbound-receive	pass	event	Count over a time period.	Capture the number of received messages that are successfully processed.
inbound-response	count	event	Count over a time period.	Capture the number of responses sent.
inbound-response	pass	event	Count over a time period.	Capture the number of successful responses.
inbound-response	time	duration	Time taken to process the message, as mean or percentile over message-response times.	Capture the processing time.

The number of inbound messages is captured by *inbound-receive/count*. You can compare this with *outbound-send/count* to verify that messages are getting through. Again, this is independent of the number of services or the rate of messages. The number of responses is captured with *inbound-response/count*; you can compare this with *outbound-response/count*. The success or failure status of the message is captured with *inbound-response/pass*. Again, you should classify failures: Was the sender unreachable? Was there a processing error? Did you send a message to a service you depended on, that failed? Use *inbound-receive/valid* to count separately the number of messages received that aren't invalid or badly formed; this is useful to detect issues with services that send messages to you.

The processing time for messages is captured using the *inbound-response/time* measure. As with *outbound-response/time*, this needs to be aggregated over time using a mean or percentile, and the same issues with interpretation and estimation apply. You can also use scatterplots for this measure to view message health.

There's a useful scatterplot you can generate if you compare *outbound-response/time* and *inbound-response/time*; see figure 6.12. This shows you how much network latency affects your messages, and which messages may be slower due to size or routing issues.

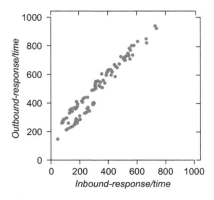

Figure 6.12   Different message transports have different delivery speeds.

In this scatterplot, you can see that most messages incur an additional 200 ms or so of network traversal. This includes not only transmission time, but also routing and parsing time through the message abstraction layer. A group of messages is faster than this, incurring only 100 ms. This is probably a different, faster, message transport. Each message transport will have its own performance characteristics that become evident when shown this way. Such a scatterplot can guide your intuition about what system behavior "should" look like.

MEASURING SYNCHRONOUS AND OBSERVED MESSAGES

This message interaction describes the scenario where you have additional services observing a primary synchronous interaction. For example, you might have an auditing service, you might be capturing event flows for review, or you might have secondary business logic. From the perspective of the sender, the additional services are invisible, so there are no measurements to capture. From the perspective of the additional observers, you can capture the measurements listed in table 6.3.

Table 6.3   Inbound message measures

Case	Measure	Type	Aggregation	Description
inbound-receive	*count*	*event*	Count over a time period.	Capture the number of messages received.
inbound-receive	*pass*	*event*	Count over a time period.	Capture the number of received messages that are successfully processed.

These are used in the same manner as inbound messages to the primary receiver. You can compare the measures to the primary sender, and to the primary receiver to verify that messages are all being delivered and processed properly. Be careful to compare only on a per-observer-type basis, because each observer will receive a copy of the message, and thus the measures aren't independent of the number of observer types.

MEASURING ASYNCHRONOUS AND OBSERVED MESSAGES

This is the classic fire-and-forget pattern. You emit events into the world as messages, and you don't care who receives them or what they do. The measurements are thus all on the sending side; see table 6.4.

Table 6.4 Outbound message measures

Case	Measure	Type	Aggregation	Description
outbound-send	*count*	*event*	Count over a time period.	Capture the number of messages sent.
outbound-send	*pass*	*event*	Count over a time period.	Capture the number of messages successfully sent.

These metrics mirror those for the synchronous case. There's no set of measures for the responses, because there are no responses. Be careful to count *outbound-send/pass* only for each message, not for each receiver. This retains the utility of the measure as something you can use for comparisons, independent of the number of services.

On the inbound side, you can capture measures on a per-service-type basis; see table 6.5.

Table 6.5 Inbound message measures

Case	Measure	Type	Aggregation	Description
inbound-receive	*count*	*event*	Count over a time period.	Capture the number of messages received.
inbound-receive	*pass*	*event*	Count over a time period.	Capture the number received of messages that are successfully processed.

As with observed synchronous messages, observed asynchronous messages need to be aggregated on a per-observer-type basis for comparison purposes.

MEASURING ASYNCHRONOUS AND CONSUMED MESSAGES

This interaction is almost the same as the synchronous-observed interaction, except that only one service consumes the message. Thus, you can compare the measures directly without worrying about multiple receivers.

6.2.3 *The service layer*

In practice, you'll capture the message measurements directly within each service, using the data-collection framework of your analytics system. That means you can also analyze these metrics down to the service, giving you a perspective on individual service instances.

This isn't as useful as it sounds. Individual service instances are ephemeral in a microservice architecture, and you monitor them precisely because you want to quickly eradicate problematic service instances and replace them with healthier ones. So, it's more useful to think in terms of families of service types and perform your analysis at that level. In particular, this allows you to identify problems introduced by new versions of services, ideally during the rollout of a Progressive Canary (discussed in chapter 5) so that you can roll back to a known-good version if it proves problematic.

You should still collect all service-instance telemetry. This is important supplementary data for debugging and understanding production issues. Fortunately, most analytics systems are focused on collecting this data, so you won't need to do much, if any, custom work, even when you're running thousands of microservices. Your message metadata should include service-instance identifiers so that you can match up the data later.

WHERE'S THE PROBLEM?

If a new version of a service is causing problems, you want to know about it. Again, by "problems" I mean poorer-than-expected behavior in terms of performance or correctness, shorter lifetimes, and other issues that aren't immediately fatal. These nonfatal deviations are an inevitable consequence of building software quickly; but if you're unable to resolve them in a timely fashion, they'll remain in the system to accumulate. They're a form of technical debt.

Let's take a service perspective, rather than a message perspective, for a change. Each service type has a set of messages that arrive from upstream services and a set of messages that are sent to downstream services. When there's a problem, it's natural to ask whether the location of the problem is upstream from, local to, or downstream from the service under investigation.

UPSTREAM PROBLEMS

The *inbound-receive/count* will change if upstream services are in trouble. They may be sending too few messages or sending too many. You can generate a current-behavior scatterplot for service types over the *inbound-receive/count* to observe these changes. You should also check *inbound-receive/valid* to make sure you aren't receiving invalid messages.

LOCAL PROBLEMS

The problem could be local to your service. If your service is unable to handle the load, you'll see aberrations in the *inbound-receive/count* and *inbound-response/count* relationship, which you can detect via a scatterplot.

Automated scaling should prevent this from occurring, so you have work to do to figure out why the scaling isn't doing its job. Sometimes the load grows too quickly.

If the *inbound-receive/count* and *inbound-response/count* relationship looks OK, then you need to check for elevated levels of message-processing errors using *inbound-response/pass.* You can use a current-behavior scatterplot to find the errant service types and drill down using the time series for those services.

Perhaps your service is just slow. In that case, you can use a current-behavior scatterplot over *inbound-response/time* to find aberrations, and time series charts to examine individual service types.

Finally, your responses may not be getting through. If you're using separate transport channels for requests and responses,[22] this is entirely possible. Use *inbound-response/pass* to catch this.

DOWNSTREAM PROBLEMS

Your service may be returning errors or running slowly only because something it depends on is behaving badly. If you rely on downstream services, you need to validate the health of those services from your perspective. They may be the cause of the errors or slowness.

Use the *outbound-send* family of measures to diagnose downstream problems. If you can't reach downstream services, then the correlation between *outbound-send/count* and *outbound-send/pass* will degrade, and you can catch this using a current-behavior scatterplot.

If you can reach downstream services but they're having difficulties, then *outbound-response/pass* will deviate. Perhaps a new data field on a message has triggered an unforeseen bug, and the downstream services can only return error responses.

If downstream services are slow, then the *outbound-response/time* measure will deviate. You can use the usual scatterplot followed by time series analysis.

SERVICE-INSTANCE HEALTH

Sometimes it's necessary to review the health of an individual service instance. This review is at the level of service-instance processes or, more typically, containers. You should anticipate having hundreds of service instances, so the current-behavior scatterplot is a good place to start. But sometimes it isn't sufficient, because you need to review behavior over a period of time for many services. You could plot them all on a time series chart, but as you've seen, this is too noisy for large numbers of services.

One solution is to use a categorical scatterplot.[23] This shows all events in a given time period for each member of a category. In this case, this would be per service instance. The advantage of such a plot is that you can compare services over time in a clear way, and it works well up to tens of services. In practice, this limit isn't a problem, because you'll generally want to focus on the instances within service families.

Let's construct a scenario. Suppose you have 20 instances of a service running. This service uses local storage as part of its business logic. Each instance runs on a container in a virtual machine, and the orchestration and deployment system allocates the service containers automatically. First, you chart the current behavior with respect to response time, but it isn't clear where the problem lies, because the services are

---

[22] Some transport configurations use a message bus for outbound messages and then use direct HTTP for the response. This is to avoid churn on the response queues.

[23] There's no second numerical attribute, because categories aren't numbers, so the standard scatterplot won't work.

behaving relatively consistently (see figure 6.13). If any service is slow, it's consistently slow.

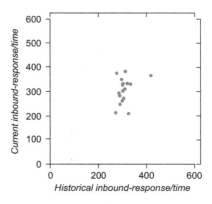

Figure 6.13   Current behavior of service instances of the same type

Now, let's use the categorical scatterplot. For each service, plot the response times for all messages over a given time period (see figure 6.14). Each dot represents a message, and the vertical axis is the response time. The horizontal axis lists the service instances; it's a category, not a number. To make the data easier to see, you add some horizontal jitter to the dots so they don't obscure each other as much.

In this chart, you can see that service *s03* has poor performance. Further investigation shows that the container for this service has been allocated to a virtual machine that's running out of memory and swapping to disk. Now you know where to focus your efforts.

The categorical scatterplot is useful not only for service instances, but also for any categories within the system, such as service types, versions, or message patterns. It provides another way to understand your system.

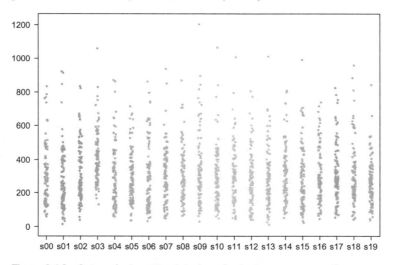

Figure 6.14   Categorical scatterplot of service-instance response times

6.3   *The power of invariants*

Message-flow rates are a useful tool for determining the health of the system, but they have issues that make them difficult to use directly. Consider user logins. Each user login generates a message. You can track these messages and calculate the flow rate. The problem is that the flow rate fluctuates over time: there are more logins during the day than at night.

You can use the raw flow rate for scaling. If lots of people want to log in, then you'll need more user login services. You can determine appropriate levels for the number of services for a given flow rate, trigger new instance deployments when the flow rate goes up, and trigger instance retirements when the flow rate goes down.

The flow rate will also identify extreme conditions. If you deploy a new login service that's fundamentally broken, the user login message-flow rate will decline dramatically. Similarly, if a misbehaving service is stuck in a loop and generating lots of user login messages, you'll catch that as well.

You'd like to catch logic bugs that affect only a subset of data. The flow rate is down a little, but it's hard to tell why. You'd also like to verify deployments of new versions of the user login service while limiting the impact of any new issues.

You need a measurement that's independent of flow rate. The load on the system doesn't matter; you're interested in the correctness of the system. To achieve these goals, you can use the ratios of causally related message-flow rates.

In the user login example, a successful login loads the user's profile to build their welcome page. A successful *user-login* message always causes a *load-user-profile* message. In any given time segment that's not too small, the number of *user-login* messages should be about the same as the number of *load-user-profile* messages. In other words, the ratio of the flow rates should be about 1.

A ratio is a good measure because it's dimensionless. Flow-rate ratios have the property that they're the same no matter what the load is on the system or how many services are sending and receiving messages. All that matters is how many messages per second are flowing through the system.

Calculating message-flow rates and ratios

How do you calculate the message-flow rate? Your message transport, if it's a message bus, may be able to do this for you. If not, you'll need to do it yourself within the message abstraction layer, reporting the numbers back to your analytics solution.

A simple approach is to count the number of messages of each type seen in a given time window. You don't store these numbers; you pass them on to be analyzed.

Calculating the ratio of message-flow rates is more difficult. Some time series databases allow you to do this directly. If not, then you'll have to do it yourself within the message-abstraction layer. This isn't ideal, because you'll need to decide in advance which ratios to calculate, and you'll also need to collect ratios from each service and average them.

None of this is rocket science, but you must factor it into your planning when you decide to use microservices. The development, deployment, and measurement infrastructure is necessarily more complex than it is for monoliths.

Ratios of message-flow rates are system *invariants*. That means that for a given configuration of message patterns, they remain the same despite changes to load, services, and network. You can use this fact to verify the correctness of the system. If you know

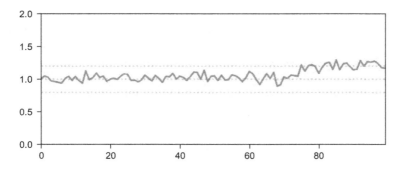

Figure 6.15   Ratio of message-flow rates

there's a causal relationship between two messages, in that the arrival of one causes the other to be sent, then you can capture the ratio of their flow rates over time. Deviations from the expected ratio value represent incorrect behavior. Figure 6.15 shows an example chart for the *user-login* versus *load-user-profile* case; as you can see, there's been a worrying change in the ratio.

You can use this ratio chart as a control chart. If you deploy a new version of the *user-login* service using the Progressive Canary deployment pattern from chapter 5, then you can use the flow-rate ratio as validation that the new version hasn't broken anything. If the new version of the service is completely broken, you'll still see a change in the ratio—this is far more significant that a mere dip in the user login rate. The ratio should *never change*—that's the nature of an invariant.

6.3.1   *Finding invariants from the business logic*

Each business requirement that's encoded by a message flow establishes an invariant. Consider the microblogging system. When posting a new entry, it generates a synchronous message to the entry store and an asynchronous announcement message about the entry (see figure 6.16). Thus the flow-rate ratio between the *post:entry* message and the two messages it causes (*info:entry* and *store:save,kind:entry*) is 2.

Starting from the basic approach to microservice system design—the decomposition of business rules into message flows—you can build this set of invariants to validate the system under continuous change. This allows you to make changes quickly and safely without breaking things. When one or more invariants deviate, you can roll back the last change.

Invariants also let you check the health of the live system. Between deployment changes, many other

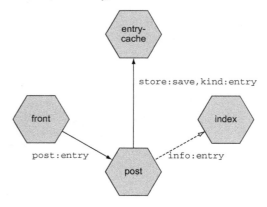

Figure 6.16   Messages caused by posting an entry

things can go wrong: bugs can be triggered, load thresholds can be reached, memory leaks can push systems over the edge, poison messages can cause progressive degradation, and so on. You can use invariants to monitor the system for any failure to operate as designed. A problem, by definition, impacts the correct functionality of the system and breaches the invariants.

You should consider automating the configuration of invariants derived from business rules. Because the business rules are expressed directly as message flows, you can do this for every business rule.

6.3.2 *Finding invariants from the system architecture*

You can also derive invariants from the topology of the system architecture by working at the level of service instances. A synchronous/consumed message represents a classic request/response architecture. But you don't implement this with just one service doing the requesting and just one service doing the responding. Typically, you scale with multiple requesters and responders, and you round-robin the messages over the responders using an appropriate algorithm.

ACTOR-STYLE INVARIANTS

There's an invariant here: the number of outbound events represents the total of each message sent. Every responder should see some fraction of that total, depending on how many responders there are. Given one requester and four responders, as shown in figure 6.17, each responder should see one quarter of the total messages as inbounds. In terms of the measurements defined earlier, *inbound-receive/count* for any given responder should be one quarter of *outbound-send/count*.

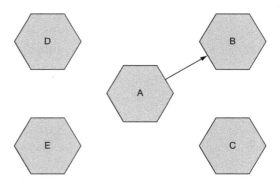

Figure 6.17   Actor/service interaction

PUBLISH/SUBSCRIBE-STYLE INVARIANTS

The asynchronous/observed pattern has a similar analysis, except that each observer should see all the outbound messages (see figure 6.18). Thus, the ratio of *outbound-send/count* to *inbound-receive/count* per service is 1.

CHAIN-STYLE INVARIANTS

You can also construct invariants based on chains of causal messages. A single triggering message causes a chain of

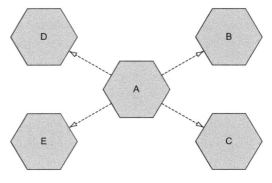

Figure 6.18   Publish/subscribe service interaction

other messages over downstream services (see figure 6.19). Each downstream service represents a link in the chain, and the number of links is the invariant. This invariant is a useful way to capture problems with an entire causal chain that wouldn't be obvious from observing one-on-one service interactions.

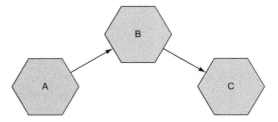

Figure 6.19   Service/chain interaction

TREE-STYLE INVARIANTS

More often than not, the chain is part of a tree of interactions, where a triggering message causes a number of resulting message chains that themselves may cause subsequent chains (see figure 6.20). You can form invariants using each individual chain, and you'll probably want to do this. But doing so doesn't tell you directly whether the entire tree completed successfully. To do that, you can form an invariant using the tree's leaf services.

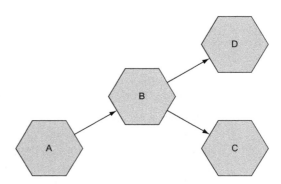

Figure 6.20   Service/tree interaction

Eventually, all message chains must end, and the number of leaves (the final link in each chain) must always be the same.

How do you choose a system invariant to use? This decision isn't as simple as the case with business rules, because you have far more possibilities to choose from. You'll need to examine the system and make an educated guess as to the most useful invariants, building them using the patterns we've discussed. Over time, your choices will improve as you gain familiarity with the system's operational characteristics.

6.3.3   *Visualizing invariants*

Invariants are time series–based data. You calculate the ratio at a point in time (representing some previous time window). You'll have lots of invariants, so you'll again run into the problem of reviewing large numbers of time series charts. As before, you can use a current-behavior scatterplot to solve this problem.

By charting all the invariants in a scatterplot, you can get a full overview of the correctness of the entire system. This is particularly useful for highlighting any unintended consequences of the changes you make. You can use this approach to verify changes to services as well as changes to the network topology.[24]

---

[24] An embellishment to consider is an animated scatterplot that shows the evolution of the system over time by animating the snapshots. It takes a little more work to build this as a custom chart, but it's satisfying to observe in practice.

6.3.4 *System discovery*

If the microservice architecture is doing its job and letting you build functionality quickly, you'll soon have hundreds of services and messages. Even though you designed most of the service interactions, other interactions in the system arise organically as teams respond quickly to business needs. You may not be sure exactly what's going on anymore.

It's important to call out this situation as one of the dangers of the microservice architecture. As complexity moves out of code and into the service interactions, you lose full understanding of the message flows, especially as you deploy ever-more-specialized services to handle new business cases. This is a natural result of the architecture and something to expect. Complexity can't be destroyed, only moved around.

This effect is why it's so important to have a message abstraction layer: it allows you to follow the principles of transport independence and pattern matching for messages. Doing so preserves the description of the messages in homogeneous terms, rather than making messages specific to services. Microservice systems that are built as lots of services interacting directly with each other quickly become a mess exactly because messages are specific to services. They're effectively distributed monoliths that are just as difficult to understand, because there's no easy way to observe all the message flows in a unified way.

DISTRIBUTED TRACING

A common messaging layer lets you introduce a common distributed tracing system. Such a system works by tracking message senders and receivers using correlation identifiers. The messaging layer can again help by providing these and attaching the necessary metadata to messages.

The distributed tracking system works by resolving the flow of messages over the system. It works out the causal structure of message flows by observing messages in the wild. In the microblogging example, a *post:entry* message triggers a *store:save,kind:entry* message and a *post:info* message. The *post:info* message triggers a *timeline:insert* message. If you trace this over time, you can build a progress diagram like that shown in figure 6.21.

The trace chart shows the chain of message interactions; read downward from the first message. Each line represents a new triggered message in the chain. The timings show how long it took to get a response (or for an observed message to be delivered). Using the progress chart, you can analyze the actual message flows in the system, see the services they impact, and understand the message-processing times.

Capturing the data to build such diagrams from a live system is expensive. You don't want to trace every flow, because doing so puts too much load on the system. But you can build up an accurate view by sampling: trace a small percentage of all messages. This doesn't affect performance and gives you the same information.

Finally, message traces allow you to reverse-engineer message interactions. You can build a diagram of the relationships between the services based on the observed messages. This diagram then gives you an understanding of the system as it is. You can

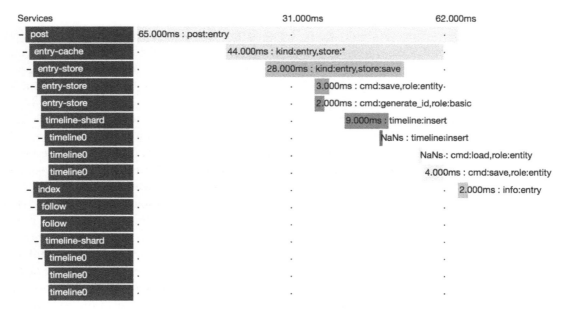

Figure 6.21   Distributed trace of an entry post over microservices

compare it against your desired design to uncover deviations and determine where complexity has arisen. Often, this is business complexity that's unavoidable, but at least you know that it exists and where it lives.

DISTRIBUTED LOGGING

You should capture the microservice logs for each service instance. To do this, you'll need to invest in a distributed logging solution. It isn't feasible to review the logs of individual service instances directly as a general practice—there's too much data. This is another consequence of the microservice architecture and another example of the fact that you'll need more infrastructure to implement it.

The easiest approach to distributed logging, if your business and confidentiality constraints allow it, is to use an online logging service. Such services provide agents for log collection, log storage, and, most important, user-friendly search capabilities. If you're unable to use an online service, open source solutions are available.[25] You'll need one that provides the best search interface.

In a monolithic system, you can get away with grepping[26] log files on the server to debug issues—almost. With a microservice system—and I'm speaking from personal experience—it's almost impossible to trace message-correlation identifiers over numerous log files to debug a production issue. That's why you need strong search capabilities.

---

[25] Elasticsearch (www.elastic.co) is a good option here.
[26] To *grep* is to manually search text files on the command line, using the `grep` command.

Manually reviewing logs should happen toward the end of your investigations. Once you've narrowed the issue to specific patterns, services, instances, or data entities, you can search the logs effectively.

ERROR CAPTURE

Closely related to log capture is error capture. You should capture all errors in the system on both the server and client sides. Again, commercial offerings are available to do this, but you can also find open source solutions.

Although a distributed logging solution can also capture errors and will log them, it's better to move error analysis to a separate system. Errors can occur in a far wider range of domains, such as mobile apps, and attempting to force them into the logging model will prevent effective analysis. It's also important to use the errors for alerting and deployment validation; you don't want them to be constrained by the processing volume of ordinary logs.

6.3.5 Synthetic validation

You don't need to wait for problems to find you—you can find them. As part of your monitoring, you can use synthetic messages to validate the system. A *synthetic message* is a test message that doesn't affect real business processes. It's a fake order or user, executing fake actions.

You can use synthetic messages to measure the correctness of the system on a continuous basis. They aren't limited to API requests, as with a monolith. You can generate any message and inject it into the system. This is another advantage of the homogeneous message layer.

There's no need to limit synthetic test messages to development and staging systems; you can also run them in production to provide a strong measure of the system under the continuous deployment of new services. This mechanism is good at capturing unintended consequences: you can break services far from the one you're working on, and you'll find that the chain of causality between messages can be wide in terms of both space and time.

6.4 Summary

- Measuring microservice systems starts with appreciating their scale in terms of the number of elements. Traditional monitoring that focuses on individual elements won't suffice. Nor can you understand the microservice system by using standard summary statistics. You need to use alternative measurements and visualizations to understand what's going on.
- There are three layers of measurements: the business requirements, the messages that encode them, and the services that send and receive the messages. These layers can be used to structure and organize the monitoring of the system.
- To comprehend a system with large numbers of moving parts, you can use scatterplots as a visualization technique. These allow you to compare the behavior of

a large number of appropriately grouped elements. The current-behavior scatterplot lets you compare behavior over time by plotting against historical norms.

- In the business layer, you can use message flows to validate the correctness of defined workflows and calculate key performance indicators.
- The measures to use in the message layer can be derived from the categorization of messages into synchronous/asynchronous and observed/consumed. For each category, you can count the number of occurrences of important events, such as outbound and inbound messages, and timings of message processing and network traversal.
- In the service layer, you can map the network structure to expected relationships between message counts and timing at both the service type and service instance level. This allows you to verify that your architecture and message-flow design are operating as designed. It also lets you identify problematic network elements.
- You can establish invariants—dimensionless numbers—that should be effectively constant if the system is operating correctly and is healthy. Invariants can be derived from the ratios of message-flow rates, both at the message-pattern level and at the service level.
- Correlation identifiers are a vital tool and serve as input to tracing and logging systems. The tracing system can build a live map of the architecture using the traces, and the logging system, by allowing you to search by correlation identifier, provides an effective mechanism for debugging the live system.

7

This chapter covers

- Migrating from a monolith to microservices
- Exploring an e-commerce website example
- Understanding migration tactics
- Adopting refinement as a core construction philosophy
- Moving from the general to the specific

You'll seldom have the luxury of making the move to microservices without considering the impact of your new architecture on your organization's legacy systems. Even if you're lucky and able to use microservices for a new project, you'll still have to integrate with existing systems and work within the operational constraints imposed by your environment, such as strictly enforced quality assurance policies. The most likely scenario is that you'll need to migrate an existing monolith to the brave new world of microservices. You'll have to do this while at the same time continuing feature development, maintaining a live system, and keeping all the other stakeholders in your organization not only happy but also willing to sign off on your experiment.[1]

---

[1] A reading of Niccolò Machiavelli's *The Prince* is much recommended for those introducing microservices to a large organization, for "… there is nothing more difficult to take in hand, more perilous to conduct, or more uncertain in its success, than to take the lead in the introduction of a new order of things. Because the innovator has for enemies all those who have done well under the old conditions, and lukewarm defenders in those who may do well under the new."

7.1   *A classic e-commerce example*

Let's assume you have official permission to move to the microservice architecture. Many of the tactics described in this chapter will also work in a guerrilla scenario, where you don't have permission, but we'll consider that out of scope. How do you go about making this move? You can't stop the world to refactor your code and your infrastructure. You need to follow an incremental approach. You'll also have to accept that you may never make a complete move and that there will always be some legacy monoliths[2] left in your system.

Let's make the discussion in this chapter more concrete. Suppose your monolith is an e-commerce application (in this scenario, there's only one monolith). The visitor load increases during daylight hours and falls off at night. The business is currently focused on one geography, and part of the reason you're moving to a new architecture is to support a global expansion with multiple websites. There are occasional large load spikes, caused by special offers. You have two versions of your mobile app supporting the two largest mobile platforms. Building the mobile apps forced you to finally create an API, and it mostly follows REST principles.[3]

7.1.1   *The legacy architecture*

The system runs co-located on your own servers (see figure 7.1).[4] The architecture is relatively modern. You have a load balancer, and you have static web servers that proxy dynamic content. The dynamic content and the business logic are delivered by a set of application servers (the *monolith*). You can scale to a certain extent by adding new application servers, although you'll suffer from diminishing marginal returns.[5] You're using a write-through cache, and you're running your relational database in a one-writer/many-readers configuration, where one instance takes all the writes, and multiple replicated database instances take the reads. Your database indexes are well-configured,[6] but your schema has grown complex and hairy. Finally, you have an administration server for running batch processes and other ad hoc tasks.

---

[2] Your system is likely to contain quite a few of these. You'd be unwise to tackle more than one at a time.

[3] The term *representational state transfer (REST)* was coined by Roy Fielding, one of the authors of the HTTP specification and a major contributor to the Apache web server. The practical interpretation of REST is that web services should limit themselves to transferring documents that represent entities, manipulating those entities using only standard HTTP verbs such as GET and POST. As with all software architectures, the meaning of REST is somewhat context dependent, and most RESTful APIs don't strictly follow the prescriptions of the architecture. The value of the REST style is that it keeps communication simple, and it's often used for naïve implementations of microservice messaging.

[4] *Co-located servers* are physical machines that you own or rent, situated in a specific data center. If a power supply fails, it's your problem. Cloud computing, on the other hand, is completely virtual. You never have to worry about power supplies—you just spin up another virtual instance. The trade-off is loss of control, which corporate IT can be slow to accept politically.

[5] Adding new application servers gives you ever-decreasing performance improvements. You're mostly limited by the data persistence layer.

[6] As a general rule, whatever your architecture, tuning your database indexes is the easiest and quickest way to solve performance problems.

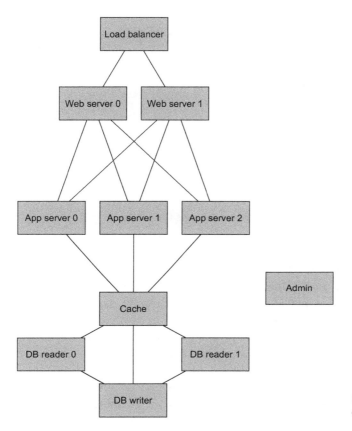

Figure 7.1 The basic legacy e-commerce architecture

The system talks to the outside world, and the many ways in which it does so are shown in table 7.1. Most important, you have a payment-gateway integration. A close second in importance is generating reports for your finance department. You also have integrations with the third-party logistics providers that ship your products to your customers, as well as with online service providers. You need transactional email delivered,[7] website visitor analytics tracked, applications monitored, and reports generated. You also have to integrate with suppliers; this is great fun, because their systems are even older than yours, and you've found that uploading and downloading CSV files from FTP servers is better than parsing and generating schema-compliant XML.[8] Some suppliers even need direct access to your database.

---

[7] *Transactional email* refers to user registrations, password reminders, invoices, and so forth. You don't want these emails to end up in a user's spam folder. It takes a lot of work to achieve reliable mail delivery, from DNS configuration to proper email content, and that process is best left to specialists.

[8] Anything is better than parsing schema-compliant XML! I still love XML, and Tim Bray (http://tbray.org/ongoing) is a personal hero, but WSDL, XML Schema, and similar are a corruption of the original intent.

Table 7.1 **External integrations of the e-commerce system**

External system	Inbound integration	Outbound integration
Payment gateway	Monolith provides a web service (JSON)	Monolith calls a web service (JSON)
Financial reports	Monolith generates Excel for download	None
Logistics	Monolith provides a web service (JSON)	Monolith calls a web service (JSON)
Online service providers	Monolith provides a web service (JSON)	Monolith calls a web service (JSON)
Supplier type A	None	Monolith calls a web service (XML)
Supplier type B	None	Monolith uploads CSV files to an FTP server
Supplier type C	Supplier system has direct access to the database	None

7.1.2 *The software delivery process*

Your software delivery process has the usual pathologies of enterprise risk aversion. You have decent developer machines, but you work in an open-plan office. At least you're using distributed version control that can properly handle branches and merging. This is necessary because you have to bug-fix the live version, work on the development version, and deliver test versions to the quality assurance team.

You use a version of Agile with two-week iterations. Your organization's version of the Agile process has evolved over the last decade, is idiosyncratic, and is *the way things are done around here*.[9] You have a build server that builds once an hour (builds take 25 minutes) and a bug tracker that you actually use.[10] You have unit tests and moderately good coverage.

Your release cycle is the problem. You release only three or four times per year, and never during critical sales periods. November and December are frozen: you can only release emergency fixes. Each release is a big deal, takes a lot of effort, and always involves weekends. The developer group interacts with marketing, business analysts, quality assurance, and operations for each release, trying to push out features that implement new business initiatives dictated by the executive suite many floors above. Each of these groups protects their own interests and acts to minimize risk to themselves. They slow you down (a lot), but you can't blame them for what is rational behavior from the perspective of corporate politics.

---

[9] "Happy families are all alike; every unhappy family is unhappy in its own way." The opening line of Leo Tolstoy's *Anna Karenina* is an astute observation of the power of entropy. There are many ways to fail and only a few ways to succeed. If you read the original edition of *Extreme Programming Explained* by Kent Beck (Addison-Wesley Professional, 1999), you'll notice that he stresses the importance of using all the techniques together; he says that cherry-picking is much less effective. *Agile* is a euphemism for the compromises and damage done to the original vision of extreme programming to make it acceptable to organizations.

[10] If you're a fan of Joel Spolsky (founder of Stack Overflow, http://joelonsoftware.com), your organization is rated at 7–9ish on the Joel Test (an informal measure of an organization's ability to build good software). A point worth repeating is that even a good score doesn't make up for the engineering limitations imposed by the monolith.

The development group is split into functional teams: designers and multiple frontend teams, mobile platform teams, multiple server-side teams, the architecture committee, and quite a few project managers and business analysts. It's difficult to move between teams, and one team almost never touches another team's code.

The big issue, acknowledged by everyone, is that delivery of new features takes far too long. The technical debt built up in the existing system is impossible to overcome, and a new start is needed. An ambitious vice president has backed your call for implementing microservices, and you've been given a shot. She believes you can help her get promoted by delivering a new revenue-generating initiative on time and on budget. This is day zero.

7.2   Changing the goal posts

You're playing a game you can't win. It's not enough to change your software development process or your technology. The problem isn't delivering software faster, it's delivering the *right* software faster. What is the right software? That which delivers business value. The unwritten rule of success for the software architect is finding the real business value in what you're doing.

> **What is business value?**
>
> The concept of business value is broader than the idea that you must generate ever-higher profits. The concept includes all stakeholders in the business and both tangible and intangible value. The business can choose to prioritize the value to different stakeholders as a matter of strategy.
>
> Thus, the business currently may be deferring profits to build market share, or investing heavily in research to build proprietary technology. The business value you should care about as a software architect in a large organization can vary greatly depending on the circumstances and political context. It's your job to find out what value your team needs to build.

Change the rules of the game. Software delivery is traditionally measured by the number and correctness of features delivered and the timeliness of their delivery. But consider for a moment how distant these measures are from the true business purpose of building any given feature. The real game is to meet the business objectives set by the business's leadership. You can deliver every feature you've committed to, on time, and still fail to meet the business objectives driving the project in the first place. Who knows what features are ultimately important? That can only be determined by building them and exposing them to the market.[11]

Insist that your work be evaluated based on real value: not the number of features you build, but how much they push forward the business objectives. Start every project by asking these fundamental questions:

---

[11] The iPhone was launched by Steve Jobs on January 9, 2007. On that day, Jobs spent the first 30 minutes of his presentation talking about Apple TV.

- *What is the definition of success?* Search carefully for the real answer. It can be as simple as improving a given metric or as devious as ensuring the promotion of a vice president. Play the technical fool, and keep asking innocent, but leading, questions. Then, shut up and listen. As technical people, we're far too eager to offer solutions. Don't do that. Listen.

- *What metrics demonstrate success?* Once you have some understanding of the definition of success, quantity this understanding. Define metrics that demonstrate success. These metrics should relate directly to business value. Avoid metrics that measure software output—you're attempting to get away from the game of feature delivery for its own sake. Once you have metrics to work against, don't assume they will always be important. Use your face time with senior executives to revalidate your assumptions about success.

- *What is the acceptable error rate?* To enable you to fully utilize the microservice architecture, you need to be able to deliver features quickly. The key to doing this is to get the business to accept that there will be failure. At first, you'll be told that there are no acceptable errors: the error rate must be 0%. But then, start asking about the situation on the ground. You'll soon discover that there is, in fact, an existing error rate, but the sky isn't falling. When everyone accepts that errors exist, the business can determine an acceptable error rate, which is what gives you the flexibility to deliver fast.

- *What are the hard constraints?* There will always be things you can't change (this year, at least). What are the regulatory constraints? What are the compliance requirements? Where will you have to give ground politically? Be explicit about communicating the constraints back to the stakeholders, and make sure you explain the impact and relate this back to your measures of success. Don't make promises you can't keep.

Once you've established a way to demonstrate success with numbers, you can use it to build trust incrementally. By initially choosing small, safe areas to refactor into microservices, you can demonstrate the effectiveness of the architecture. It's important to build trust this way, with small steps, because you want to move everything to this mode of operation. You want to deliver software in a low-risk environment where everybody accepts that there will be a continuous stream of small, low-risk changes that deliver incremental improvements to metrics.

Reporting is a good place to start

The reporting system is often your greatest opportunity for a big early win. It's common for the reporting system to grow organically without much design effort. Paradoxically, this is because reporting is important. Those who have power demand new reports, so you must scramble to build them as quickly as possible. Each report can be relatively independent of the others, so there's less need for a coordinated approach. You can usually get away with adding a few new database indexes to make performance acceptable. Old reports are never removed, just used less frequently.

(continued)
Moving reporting out of the mainline is a great strategy because you can begin to visibly deliver much higher performance. Build your reports using replicated data: not only will the reports build more quickly, but you'll also reduce impact on the online applications. The reports already exist; you're just "speeding them up," so you aren't on an immediate critical path. You'll get the opportunity to introduce additional data stores into the infrastructure, which helps overcome a major hurdle you'll face with the gatekeepers in operations.

Perhaps most important, you can open a discussion about eventual consistency and frame it in a way that avoids confrontation. Ask this question: "Do you want a preview of the report before all the data is in? It will be slightly inaccurate but will give you a good feel for the top-line numbers." Not many managers will say no to this.

You'll need sponsors and advocates. You're operating within the context of a human organization, and that's the way the world works. Take time to write about your activities for internal newsletters. If you can write external blog posts, do so.[12] Use internal talks to explain how you work, and why. Give the same talk again and again. This is more effective than you may think: you'll reach a wider audience and get better at arguing your case, and the simple act of repeating your message makes it stick. In your audience, you'll find enthusiastic fans at all levels of the organization. Take your talks outside to meetups and conferences once you've refined the message. This will build your internal political capital.

Success breeds more success. Your group will begin to attract better developers, internally and externally. Self-selection is a powerful force and relieves you of the pressure to find good people—they will find themselves and bring their friends. You'll attract the attention of more-senior people internally, as well. Everybody can smell success.

As you gain credibility, you can put your new political capital to work. Remove from your team as much of the fossilized process overhead as you can. Normally, it's difficult to eradicate process, but as you start to deliver faster and more successfully, you'll find that resistance to your new approach becomes weaker. Use a combination of reasoned argument, asking for trust, and simple disobedience to change the rules of the game to suit your needs. The golden rule is this: never fail to deliver business value—keep your eye on those metrics.

7.2.1 The practical application of politics

Let's apply this approach to the e-commerce application. The primary goal is to be able to launch sites targeted at specific geographies. This means each site needs to have its own content, possibly in a different language, and also separate business rules

---

[12] Why is Julius Caesar so famous? How did he manage to usurp the old Roman Republic? He was history's first blogger. No matter how hard the campaign trail in Gaul, he always took time to work on his great book, *The Gallic Wars*, sending new chapters back to Rome. The plebeian masses loved these "blog posts," and they loved Caesar. Propaganda works.

for things like sales-tax regulations. In this release, you're supposed to go live with at least one new site, put in place a system for making new sites easier to develop, and deliver a set of minor features as part of ongoing operations.

Start with the minor features. What's their purpose? What drove the business analysts to select these features? Has the marketing team determined strategic goals that have been interpreted by the analysts? You need to know whether these features are meant to improve conversion rates from inbound advertising and content, or to increase engagement by increasing the amount of time spent on the site—or does marketing just want to improve social media shares? Find out. Then, make sure you build a microservice early in the project that shows these metrics as a dashboard. Now, you can begin to incrementally deliver the features requested and validate the effect of those features using the dashboard. You'll be able to argue effectively for modifications to the feature list, based on real data. You can double down on features that deliver business value and safely drop those that don't, and have political cover for doing so. This technique should become part of your day-to-day work practice.

Deploying a new site is more problematic. It's an all-or-nothing event. The big risk comes on launch day: if things are broken, you'll take heat. Certainly, you'll work late. The ideal, from your perspective, is to build the new site entirely from microservices, in a greenfield context. This means the new site can be delivered incrementally, and you can push to have it go live well before the release date as a soft launch with a restricted set of users. This is how you should build systems using microservices.

Realistically, you'll only be able to use incremental deployments for parts of your system, if at all. Other stakeholders will still have too much power in the first release cycle, before you've demonstrated your effectiveness. If you're forced to provide a full implementation, then you must do something unnatural: copy the entire system, and start modifying. Normally, this would be the worst thing you could do—now you have to maintain two systems! But you're moving to microservices anyway, so you'll be able to avoid paying back most of the technical debt; it will become irrelevant.

What about the other major requirement, the flexible system to handle multiple websites in different languages with different business rules? You can ignore it. The microservice architecture *is* that flexible system.

7.3 *Starting the journey*

Let's survey the current system. You have three source code repositories: two for the mobile apps and one for each platform. You have a main repository for everything else: user interfaces, business logic, batch scripts, database definitions, stored procedures, test data, and so on. You develop on the master branch. Each release gets its own branch, and you merge hotfixes back into the master. You also use branches to submit versions to quality assurance for testing on a biweekly basis.

Making changes to existing features, or adding new features, requires touching multiple parts of the application. In the beginning, there was a component model that used the built-in features of your chosen programming language. Although it hasn't entirely collapsed, there's considerable coupling between components, and the boundaries of components are fuzzy. Adding a new data field to a data entity requires changes over the entire code base, from the database schema up to the UI code. The code has many baked-in assumptions about data entities, and schema changes often have unintended side effects and introduce new bugs. It's difficult to validate that business rules are properly enforced. You're aware of several data fields that have been overloaded, and the data they contain must be interpreted based on other data fields.

A solution you've tried more than once is to declare a refactoring iteration: you stop feature development and try to resurrect the component model and untangle some of the dependencies. Although this has been beneficial, the improvements are never substantive and never yield faster feature delivery for long. The reason is simple: you can't predict the future, so you don't know how business requirements will evolve. Thus, you often spend time refactoring parts of the system that aren't relevant to the real work you have to do later.

You're at the start of a release cycle. You have three months. Your plan is to build the new features as microservices. You'll still have to maintain the monolith, and you'll still need to add features to the monolith code. Some members of your team advocated for a complete rewrite; they suggested forming a separate team and rewriting everything from scratch using microservices. This would take at most six months, they claimed, after which you could drop the monolith and enter paradise.

You rightly rejected this approach. Their estimate was overly optimistic—that's always a truth of software development. They underestimated the amount of business complexity the monolith has captured over the years; this business complexity encodes large amounts of value in the form of institutional knowledge that it's vital to preserve. And then there's the problem of the "big bang": when the new microservice system is complete, it would need to be deployed as a replacement for the monolith in one clean weekend of migration, without hitch or fail. What could possibly go wrong? You again rightly rejected this plan as conduct unbecoming an engineer.[13]

You're going to do this professionally, using an incremental strategy that has low risk. This strategy involves three tactics: strangling the monolith by wrapping it in a proxy that lets you redirect feature subsets to microservices, building a greenfield delivery and deployment environment to host your microservices, and splitting the monolith into *macroservices* to contain the spread of technical debt.

7.4   The strangler tactic

The strangler vine seeds in the branches of a host tree and, over time, slowly strangles the host plant, replacing it. The strangler tactic takes the same approach.[14] Consider the monolith to be the old tree that you'll strangle over time. This is less risky than just chopping it down.

---

[13] Knowingly participating in an engineering project that will almost certainly fail is unethical. Yes, we all do it. That doesn't mean we can't work toward a better place.

[14] This tactic derives directly from an approach and metaphor developed by Martin Fowler: www.martinfowler .com/bliki/StranglerApplication.html.

All systems interact with the outside world. You can model these interactions with the outside world as discrete events. The implementation of the strangler tactic is a proxy that intercepts these events and routes them either to a new microservice or to the legacy monolith. Over time, you increase the proportion of events routing to microservices. This tactic gives you a great measure of control over the pace of migration and lets you avoid high-risk transitions until you're ready.

> ### Modeling the interactions of the monolith as events
>
> The strangler tactic relies on a conceptual model of the monolith as an entity with strong boundaries. Anything outside these boundaries that impacts the monolith is modeled as an information-carrying *event*. The monolith impacts everything outside its boundaries, also using events. The term *event* in this context is very broad; it shouldn't be interpreted as a discrete message, but rather as an information flow.
>
> To define strong boundaries, you may need to expand your understanding of what constitutes the monolith, to include supporting systems. In this sense, you can view the monolith not just as a single code base, but as a monolithic system of secondary parts tightly coupled to a primary core. You need to strangle the monolith system, not just the core.
>
> One of the most important pieces of analysis you'll do on the existing system will be determining the boundary and what information flows through it.

Although the basic proxy approach is a simple model, in reality things are messier. In the ideal case of a standalone monolithic web application, you can use a web proxy to route inbound HTTP requests, thus capturing all external interactions. You install the proxy in front of the application and start reimplementing individual pages as microservices. But this is an ideal case.

Consider something more realistic. What events represent interactions with the outside world? These can be web requests, messages from a message bus, database queries, stored procedure invocations, FTP requests, appending data to flat files, and many more exotic interactions. It may not be possible, technically or cost-wise, to write proxies for all the different types of interaction events. Nonetheless, it's important to map them all so that you understand what you're dealing with.

7.4.1 Partial proxying

Your proxy doesn't have to be complete: full coverage of the monolith isn't required, and it may not need to be particularly performant. It's useful to realize that a great deal can be achieved by partial proxying. By taking an incremental approach even to basic pieces of the migration architecture such as the proxy, you can focus on delivering production features sooner. In an ideal world, you'd complete the proxy before moving on to the migration work. But the world isn't fair, and you'll be blamed for the technical debt of the monolith if you try to do too much at the beginning. Better to start delivering early, rather than have your migration project canceled just as you're about to begin making real progress. Your overall velocity will be slower, because you have to keep extending the proxy, but this will be mitigated by focusing on building only features that are needed.[15]

To make the strangler tactic more effective, you can often migrate interactions to preferred channels. That is, instead of extending the proxy, it may make more sense to move interactions to channels that you're already proxying. Let's say you have a legacy RPC mechanism.[16] You can refactor the RPC client and server code to use a web service interface, instead. Now, you can proxy the web service using your existing proxying infrastructure. Refactoring RPC code is easier than you may think. Consider that you already have an abstraction layer in the code interface to the RPC mechanism. Replace the RPC implementation with your messaging layer.

Let's take the case of database interactions. Databases are often misused as communication channels. Different processes and external systems are given access to a database so they can read and write data. And database triggers update data based on database events—another hidden interaction. You may or may not need to solve this problem. If the database interactions don't impact the areas where you need to add features, or if you can deprecate or drop the functionality, then leave them alone. If you do have to deal with them, then the early period of your migration project will need to include the development of microservices that provide the same data interactions.

Your preferred approach should be to write new microservices that handle these interactions. Unfortunately, these microservices will still talk to the legacy database at first, but you'll at least have given yourself freedom to resolve that issue over time. The new microservices should expose the data via web service interfaces so that you can collect as many external interactions as possible into one interaction channel. The challenge is that the external systems using this data will need to be modified to use the new channels. This isn't as impossible as it first appears: you can set a deprecation and migration timeline, and external systems that find your data valuable will have to find the resources to make the change. This is a good test of how valuable your company is to external partners.

7.4.2 *What to do when you can't migrate*

In other cases, you may be politically or contractually constrained and unable to force a migration. In that case, you can still isolate the interaction. The end goal is to move away from using the database for communication. Despite the political constraints,

---

[15] Conversely, building the microservice infrastructure incrementally, as part of a monolith migration, is *not* an optimal approach. Remember that you're judged against the standards of the old system, and it's political death to deliver something worse. Your nascent microservice infrastructure will be worse in the early days. Although this isn't a problem for new projects, where you can't suffer by comparison, it's a common pitfall for migration projects. I have indeed learned from bitter experience.

[16] *Remote procedure call* (RPC) refers to any network communication layer that attempts to hide the existence of the network and make the transfer of messages look like local invocations. A first principle of the microservice message layer is that all communication should be considered remote.

you still have to provide a database interface for the interactions, and these will consume development time and resources.

Here are some options for implementing this interface:

- *Direct queries*—If the external system is reading and writing to individual tables without complex transactions, you can create a separate integration database for this purpose. Data synchronizations with the monolith are performed by a microservice written for this purpose. This allows you to move the authoritative data elsewhere and eventually rely solely on microservices for the interaction. It's an abuse of the database engine to use it as a communication medium, but that's the medium expected by the external system.

- *Complex transactions*—If the external system is using complex transactions, the situation is more challenging. You can still use a separate integration database, but you must accept some loss of data consistency in the system because the system of record is no longer protected by transactions. You'll need to make your system and microservices tolerant of inconsistent data. Alternatively, you can leave things as they are, with the monolith and external system both using the same database, but move the SOR elsewhere. The monolith must synchronize with the authoritative data. This option, by its nature, tends to be available only at a later stage in migration projects, when the monolith matters less.

- *Stored procedures*—The business logic in stored procedures needs to be moved into microservices—this is the purpose of the change you're making. When a stored procedure isn't directly exposed, doing so is much easier. But let's assume a stored procedure is directly invoked by the external system. Although a separate integration database to support execution of the stored procedure as is may be an option, this often isn't the case due to the complexity of the stored-procedure code. It can be less work to intercept the database's wire protocol[17] and simulate the stored-procedure data flow. This isn't as daunting as it sounds, because you only have to simulate a limited subset of the wire protocol. This type of scaffolding work is easy to underestimate in a migration project, so look carefully for scenarios where all options involve Sisyphean labor, and you have to pick the least-worst option.[18]

The e-commerce system offers examples of all three scenarios. First, the third-party report generator reads directly from the primary database. Second, one of the third-party logistics companies that delivers your goods built its own custom system, which uses CORBA for integration.[19] Many years ago, your company decided that the best way to integrate, given that the company had no CORBA knowledge, was to install on your

---

[17] The *wire protocol* is the binary exchange between the database client and server over the network.

[18] Sisyphus was punished for his belief that he could outwit Zeus. Microservices are great, but they're not *that* great. Be careful to avoid hubris when you explain their benefits, and remember that good engineering can't defeat bad politics.

[19] CORBA is an acronym for Common Object Request Broker Architecture. If you know what that is, no more need be said. If you don't, no more should be.

network a physical machine provided by the logistics company. This machine runs transactions against your database on your side; it communicates over a VPN on the other side, back to the logistics system. Upgrades are essentially no longer possible, because neither you nor the supplier still employs the original developers. Finally, stored procedures generate financial data for your accounting system. These stored procedures encode all sorts of business logic that changes annually as tax rules are modified. The financial data is extracted using ODBC libraries on the client side,[20] because that's the "industry standard."

Carefully identifying all of these interactions with the outside world, and determining those most likely to cause you problems, is the first job you should do on a monolith migration project.

7.4.3 *The greenfield tactic*

To begin building microservices, you need to create a home for them to live in. If you start a greenfield project, with no legacy monolith to migrate from, you spend some time at the start of the project putting in place the correct infrastructure to develop, deploy, and run microservices in production. Migrating from a monolith doesn't relieve you of this requirement—you must still provide the right conditions for your microservices. You may see this as an unavoidable cost of the migration, but you can also view it as an opportunity. By putting in place a complete microservice infrastructure, you give yourself the freedom to treat some aspects of the migration as greenfield developments, considerably reducing the complexity of the task.

You must not treat the development of the microservice environment as part of the migration process. Trying to build the microservice infrastructure at the same time you build the microservices, when everything must run in production and serve business needs immediately, isn't wise. The need to handle established production traffic is the essential difference between migration and true greenfield development—you aren't slowly building a user base.

In a true greenfield project, you have time to build up your microservice infrastructure in parallel with the development of the microservices. During the early days of a greenfield project, you aren't running in production, and you only have to support demonstrations of the system. You don't have to support high load, and production failures have no business consequences. You're free to deliver functionality early and quickly, even if it can't yet run in production.[21] This is a virtue, because you resolve the inherent fuzziness of the requirements as quickly as possible.

But in the migration scenario, the requirements are easier to define. Observe the behavior of the old system, and write down what it does. The migration is expected to be time consuming and painful. But service is also expected to continue. Therefore, as part of your migration planning, you have the political capital to schedule time for

---

[20] *Open Database Connectivity* (ODBC) is a complex client-side API for database access. ODBC drivers translate database interactions into the specific wire protocol of a given database.

[21] The is the approach taken in the case study in chapter 9.

building a production-grade microservice infrastructure, using the migration work as cover. You'll need to build the entire software-delivery pipeline—from the developers' machines, through the continuous delivery system, all the way to production—before you start any serious migration to microservices.

Control and management of the new microservice infrastructure must be handled in a new way. This is the time to introduce real collaboration between developers and systems engineers. Developer teams need to be responsible for the microservices they build, all the way to production. Operations needs to let the developers take responsibility by enabling access to the production system. This type of collaboration is difficult to introduce into existing systems, but you should use the opportunity provided by the greenfield development to make it happen.

THE E-COMMERCE GREENFIELD SCENARIO

In terms of the e-commerce example, you can build the microservice infrastructure early in the project when you're also setting up the initial strangler proxies. You should aim for a second phase when you have a running microservice infrastructure ready to accept new functionality. The goal will be to start strangling the monolith by moving over integration events. You may be tempted to begin with user-facing aspects of the system; but that's usually too much complexity to take on initially, because user experience flows tend to have many touch points. There's one exception, which you should grab with both hands: brand-new user experience flows. Successful delivery of these provides considerable early political capital and lets you demonstrate the development speed that microservices make possible.

Which subsets of existing integration events should you target for initial migration? Try to choose those that are as orthogonal to the main system as possible. For example, in the e-commerce example, the product catalog contains product images. Each product has multiple images, and each image needs to be resized for various formats: thumbnails, mobile, magnified, and so on. The images are uploaded by staff using the legacy administration console. The original image data is stored as binary using the database's binary large object (BLOB) data type.[22] The monolith then executes scripts to resize the images, save the files to the file system used for content delivery, and upload the image files to a content delivery network (CDN).

This workflow provides an excellent opportunity for migration. You can proxy the image-upload page to a new microservice. You can introduce a new strategy for storing the original image files—perhaps a document store is a better solution. And you can write microservices to handle the image resizing and CDN uploads. This work is orthogonal, because it doesn't impact any other parts of the monolith: the only change you have to make to the monolith is to modify the image-processing scripts so

---

[22] Enterprise databases provide special data-storage facilities for binary data, with varying degrees of success. There's a natural friction between the concept of a data column, with reasonably sized content, and a large BLOB of opaque data. No matter how the database tries to hide it, you'll always have to handle the binary data separately, and performance demands that you stream this data. Treating binary data as different from textual and numeric data seems like a more sensible approach, but enterprise databases attempt to solve every problem.

they no longer do any work. Even if technical debt has intermingled business logic with the image-processing code on the monolith, you can execute that code, because it doesn't affect the image-resizing work directly.

Once again, it's important to stress that you need to choose your microservices carefully. Just because image resizing is easy to extract doesn't mean it makes sense to do so. Does the new functionality that you need to deliver depend on the features you're extracting? If not, then it doesn't make sense to do the extraction in the short term. Always be driven by business needs.

The most difficult decisions are those that would require you to change the behavior of a subsystem in the monolith, when you estimate that the cost of rebuilding the subsystem in microservices would be slightly higher than the cost of patching up the monolith. But isn't the purpose of the migration to move to microservices so that you can proceed more quickly down the road? Yes, but don't be seduced by the logic of that thinking. You'll lose credibility if you spend too much time rebuilding. You must invest in rebuilding at least some of the subsystems, or you'll never be able to deliver significant business value by moving faster; but you must be careful to balance this with the inevitable need to keep working on the old monolith. In the migration's early days, expect to spend more than half of your development time on the monolith, to maintain your credibility as someone who can deliver software.

Finally, as part of the greenfield infrastructure rollout, make sure to invest time in building the measurement infrastructure. Doing so is critical, because you'll use this ability to begin measuring the monolith's business performance. This is how you can move the goal posts: you'll compare the KPIs of the monolith against the KPIs of the new microservices, and you'll use your measurements to demonstrate business value. It's critical to avoid defining success merely by the number of features you've delivered or adherence to an arbitrary schedule.

7.4.4 *The macroservice tactic*

What about the monolith—that tangled mess of millions of lines of code? A monolithic code base suffers from many disadvantages: it must all be deployed at once, making changes riskier; it allows technical debt to grow by enabling complex data structures; and it hides dependencies and coupling in code, making the monolith hard to reason about. You can reduce the impact of these issues by reducing the size of the monolith. One way to do this is to break the monolith into separate large pieces. Although these aren't microservices, they can be treated almost as such, and you can reap many of the same benefits. Most usefully, you can often subsume the pieces of the monolith into your microservice deployment pipeline.[23] These chunks of the former monolith can reasonably be called *macroservices.*

---

[23] For example, a payment-provider integration may already be reasonably isolated in the monolith's class structure, because the original developers wanted to make it possible to change providers. Pull this out into a separate process, and deploy it as if it were just another microservice.

To break down the monolith into macroservices, begin by analyzing the monolith's structure to identify the coarse-grained boundaries within the system. These boundaries are of two kinds: the vestiges of the original design, and naturally occurring boundaries that reflect organizational politics. The boundaries won't be clean, and identifying them will be more difficult than you think. Code-structure-analysis tools can help.[24] Draw boundaries around code structures that have many dependencies between them and fewer with other, similar, clusters of code structures.

Once you've identified some of the boundaries, what you do with them depends on where you are in the migration project. You shouldn't feel the need to fully decompose the monolith. If you aren't going to touch some areas of functionality, leave them alone. Before the greenfield microservice infrastructure is ready, there's little point in extracting any macroservices—wait until you can use your new deployment and management system. You won't gain much from adding deployment complexity to the old infrastructure.

In the early stages of the project, you can start the process of strengthening boundaries. As part of any work to implement features on the monolith, invest some effort in refactoring to decouple code structures. This work should be ongoing even after you begin to pull out macroservices. The reason for refactoring on a continuous basis is that your team is best placed to do it when you're in front of the relevant code from the monolith. Macroservice extraction is tedious and difficult and causes lots of breakage, by its nature, so reduce this cost by using the transient knowledge you have of the arcane workings of the monolith.

MACROSERVICE EXTRACTION

Once your microservice infrastructure is up and running, you're ready to perform extractions. Attempt each extraction by itself to keep the complexity of the work under control. Even if you have a large team, don't be tempted to extract more than one macroservice at a time—too many things will break. Retain respect for the monolith. It's taken many years to build, and it embodies a great deal of business knowledge. Don't break things you don't have to.

Extracting a macroservice will often depend heavily on the strangler proxy to route inbound interaction events to the right macroservice. This is another reason to delay macroservice extraction until you have a robust infrastructure in place. It's important to realize that extraction doesn't necessarily mean removal: leaving the old code in place may be the best option. The first step is always to copy out the relevant code and see if you can get it up and running in a standalone system. This is the hard part, because you have to establish how many dependencies the extracted code has on the monolith. Some work is always required, to remove or replace dependencies that are too big to bring along. Don't forget, you always have the option of dropping features—politics is an efficient way to reduce your workload! Also, don't forget that it

---

[24] I recommend Structure101 (http://structure101.com), but I must disclose that I know the founder.

isn't a sin to cut and paste library code into the macroservice[25]—that's a legal move in the game of monolith migration.

Choose your macroservices on the basis of business need. Where will you have to make the most changes to deliver the features needed to hit your success metrics? Balance that with the level of coupling potential macroservices have with the monolith. You can almost always pull out things like reporting and batch processing more easily than user-interaction flows.

Stay true to the fundamental principles of transport independence and pattern matching for this dependency. You should introduce your message-abstraction layer into the macroservices and use it as the communication layer between them. Avoid creating a separate communication mechanism between macroservices or trying to "keep it simple" by using direct calls between macroservices. You need to homogenize your communication layer as much as possible to get the full benefits of the microservice architecture.

The message-abstraction layer
You need a message-abstraction layer. It isn't sufficient to choose a well-known message-transport mechanism, such as REST, or to choose a specific messaging implementation. The problem with that approach is that you lose transport independence. This has the obvious disadvantage of making it more difficult to change your transport layer if you need to; it also locks you into certain messaging styles, such as favoring synchronous over asynchronous.

The more significant problem is that hardcoding a messaging implementation prevents you from hiding the identity of other services. Using pattern matching as your message-routing algorithm is the solution, as we've discussed. To give yourself the freedom to do this, you need to fully abstract the sending and receiving of messages. To do that, you need a message-abstraction layer.

This layer is so important that it's one of the few shared libraries it makes sense to use across your entire body of microservices. Even then, you can get away with not using the same version everywhere, if you're careful to maintain backward and forward compatibility in your message structure by adhering to Postel's law: be strict in what you emit and lenient in what you accept.

Responsibility for the messaging layer should be restricted to a small set of your best developers. These developers are probably spread over multiple teams, and maintaining the messaging layer will be an additional responsibility for them. Although this breaks from the ideal and reduces the distribution of knowledge, it's necessary in this case. You need to maintain the quality and coherency of the messaging layer. This is an unavoidable complexity of microservice project management.

What do you do with the macroservices, once they're established? It's valid to leave them in place. Update and modify them as necessary, viewing them as aberrant microservices

---

[25] *Non est bibliotheca sanctorum.*

that are too large. This is an effective tactic to maintain the speed of feature delivery. One modification you'll make to the macroservices is to move them away from a dependency on other macroservices, to a dependency on your new microservices. The macroservices will remain under continuous change throughout the project. You won't get away from the legacy of the monolith that quickly.

7.5   The strategy of refinement

One of the most important things the microservice architecture brings to the table is the ability to refine your application quickly and easily—most directly by adding new microservices. Refinement is your most powerful weapon to deal with the vagaries of corporate software development and to maintain development speed.

The strategy of refinement is this: build the general case first, and then refine it by handling special cases separately. This is different from traditional software development, where you're supposed to collect all the requirements first and then design the system fully—algorithms and data structures—before starting development. The core idea of Agile software development is to enable refinement by making it easy to refactor code. Sadly, methodology alone has proven unable to achieve this. Without a component model that enables refinement, you'll still build technical debt.

Nor can you ignore the need to think carefully about the algorithms and data your system must deal with. But you can think about these from the perspective of expected scaling, rather than trying to model a complex business domain from scratch. The case study in chapter 9 provides a practical example of working through this process.

7.6   Moving from the general to the specific

Let's look at three examples of the development strategy of building the general case first, getting that into production, and then adding more features (in descending order of business value) by building more-specific cases.

7.6.1   Adding features to the product page

The e-commerce website has a page for each product. There's a generic product page, but you also have special versions for certain product types: some products need more images, some have videos, and others include testimonials. In the legacy code base, these multiple versions have been implemented by extending the data structure that's used to build the product page and using lots of conditional expressions on the product-page template. As the complexity of this approach became unmanageable over the years, two product types were given separate data structures and templates. You now have the worst of many worlds: increasing technical debt in the data structures and template logic, multiple versions to maintain, and shared code that needs to work with those multiple versions and that keeps breaking one or more of them when it changes.

You can use the strangler proxy to move product-page delivery to a new microservice (as shown in figure 7.2). At first, you'll build only the generic case—and even then, only a simplified version. This microservice is vertical, in the sense that it handles the

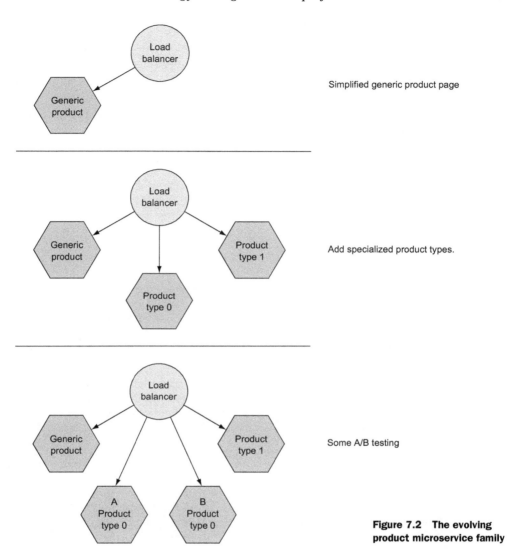

Simplified generic product page

Add specialized product types.

Some A/B testing

Figure 7.2 The evolving product microservice family

frontend and backend work needed to deliver a product page. Now is the time to reassess some of the features on the product page that have been added over the years and ask whether they're truly necessary. If you're lucky, you'll find a set of products that can be presented with your simplified page, and you can go live quickly. Prerequisites to building this generic product-page microservice are production deployment of the strangler proxy, with sufficient routing logic in the proxy, and a messaging layer that provides product data the microservice can use.

Now, you can begin to add complexity. You can build the product page back up toward the full feature set of the monolith, but you have the opportunity to measure the impact of each feature. To add a feature, you add a new product-page microservice that extends the previous version with the new feature.[26] It's critical that you also add capabilities to measure the effectiveness of that feature against the overall business goals. For example, if the goal is to increase conversions (purchases from the product page), then you can demonstrate whether the feature does that. Using the established principles of microservice deployment, such as Progressive Canary (discussed in chapter 5), allows you to simultaneously conduct A/B testing. You can compare the business-metric performance of the old version of the product page with your new version. Do this again and again, for each feature. You'll build trust and support from marketing and product-management stakeholders as you do this, because you're moving the needle for them. Once you start to demonstrate effective delivery of business value, it will become easier to have conversations about reducing the number and complexity of features, avoiding vanity features, and staying focused on the user. The numbers don't lie.

Using microservices for A/B testing

A/B testing is widely used, especially in e-commerce, to optimize user-interaction flows with the purpose of driving desired user behaviors. It works by presenting the user with different variants of the same page at random, and statistically analyzing the results to determine which variant is more effective. You aren't limited to web page designs; A/B testing can be considerably more complex.

The microservice architecture is amenable to the implementation of A/B testing. On a conceptual level, A/B testing is nothing more than a type of message routing. The logistics of A/B testing are provided naturally by the message-based nature of microservices. This also means that testing different business rules is no different than testing different designs, so you have deeper and wider scope to optimize user interactions.

In the e-commerce example, you can use A/B testing to optimize not only product-page layouts, but also the types of special offers presented or the algorithms that determine the special offers. You can use A/B testing on the checkout process, the handling of return visitors, or pretty much any user interaction. You'll still need to analyze the results, but A/B testing services make it easy to feed in the raw interaction data, which you can derive by recording message flows.

As you continue to expand the product-page microservice, its complexity will increase, and you'll need to split the service. Ideally, you want to be able to rewrite a microservice in one iteration, which gives you a rule of thumb to trigger splitting. Stick to the rule of refinement: identify the general types of product pages, and build microservices for those. Rinse and repeat as you continue to build complexity and have to deal with more product types. You'll end up with a distribution of microservices that tends to follow a power law: a core set of microservices that handles the

---

[26] Some features may require additional microservices—that's OK.

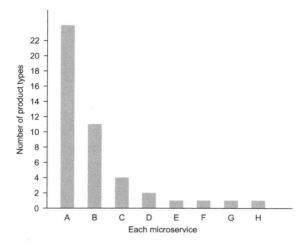

Figure 7.3 Number of product types that each microservice handles

main product types, followed by a long tail of special cases.[27] If you chart the number of product types that each microservice handles, you'll end up with a chart that looks something like figure 7.3.

This distribution of work is the typical result of using a refinement strategy. You'll notice that special cases have little impact on the main body of work. This reduces your risk considerably: you won't end up breaking your site by trying to customize the product page of one special product.

The product-page example shows the case where microservices are independent specializations. None of the product-page microservices depend on each other. This is the best case, and you should look for opportunities to implement this approach. Remember that you invoke each microservice based on the pattern of the inbound message. In this case, the strangler proxy performs the pattern matching on HTTP requests, but you can use the same procedure deeper in the system.[28]

7.6.2 Adding features to the shopping cart

Let's move on to another example, where the microservices aren't independent. The e-commerce site has a shopping cart, and you're reimplementing it as a microservice. You begin by writing a microservice that provides only the basic functionality: a list of items and a total. When the user adds an item to their cart, you emit a message indicating this; the *shopping cart* microservice accepts the message and updates the persistent representation of the cart, which it owns. The *cart* microservice is also responsible for providing the cart details for display on the checkout page.

---

[27] This is an example of Zipf's law in action. The proportion of product types a given microservice handles, compared to the microservice that handles the most, is approximately $1/rank$, where *rank* is the position of that microservice in an ordered list from most product types handled to least. For example, the second-placed microservice handles half as many product types $(1/2)$ as the first.

[28] Other examples in this book include the user login and sales tax cases from earlier chapters.

This simple first version of the cart isn't suitable for production, but you can use it for iteration demonstrations to maintain a healthy feedback loop with stakeholders. The cart will need additional features, such as the ability to support coupons, before it can go live. In the monolith, the shopping cart code is a classic example of procedural spaghetti, where an extremely lengthy function with all sorts of interdependencies and shared variables applies all the business rules sequentially. It's the source of many bugs.

To apply refinement to this situation, consider the case of coupons. Coupons have multiple aspects, including a coupon lookup and a set of business rules around validity, such as expiry dates and product validity. Then the coupon needs to be applied to the shopping cart total, so the cart microservice will need to handle it in some way.

Let's start from first principles. The set of microservices that handle the shopping cart business rules needs to be able to manage activities such as adding an item to the cart, removing an item, validating a coupon, and so forth. These activities are encoded as messages emitted by the UI microservices. Following the approach that this book advocates, the next step is to assign these messages to microservices. You could make the cart more complex and send all the messages to one microservice, but that doesn't feel right. Let's have a coupon service that knows how to look up coupons, validate them, apply their business rules, and so forth.

You then need to modify the cart service. It doesn't know about coupons, but you need to handle a coupon's effect, such as applying a 10% discount. Let's expand the concept of a cart item a little. There are products, as before, but there are also invisible entries that can modify the total. Calculating the shopping cart total consists of "executing" each item in turn to generate an amount to add to the total. That amount will be negative for coupons. Now you need to expand the *add-item* and *remove-item* messages so that you can add and remove invisible entries. You've built the general case; coupons are one example of a dynamic item. The *shopping-cart* service doesn't know about coupons, only that it supports dynamic entries.

Now, you can pull everything together. When the user adds a coupon to their cart, this triggers an *add-coupon* message.[29] The coupon service handles this message. Then the coupon service generates an *add-item* message for the cart service, detailing a dynamic item to add. The dynamic item specifies the rule for the coupon: subtract 10% from the total. Let's look at examples of these messages.

The following message adds a normal product to the shopping cart. The message is routed to the cart service directly:

```
{
  "role": "cart",
  "cmd": "add",
  "item": {
    "name": "Product A",
    "price": 100
  }
}
```

---

[29] The term *add-coupon* stands not for a message type, but for a set of patterns. It's a conceptual abbreviation, nothing more.

The next message creates a coupon:

```
{
  "role": "cart",
  "cmd": "add",
  "type": "coupon",
  "item": {
    "code": "xyz123"
    "discount": 10
  }
}
```

This message is routed to the coupon service, pattern matching on `type:coupon`. The sender of the message doesn't need to know that; the sender is sending a message to the cart service and doesn't care that the cart service has been decomposed into other microservices.

The coupon service sends out the following *add-item* message, and this message is routed to the cart service.

Listing 7.1 Add coupon item message

```
{
  "role": "cart",
  "cmd": "add",
  "item": {
    "type": "dynamic"
    "name": "Discount",
    "reduce": 10
  }
}
```

The cart adds a dynamic item to implement the discount.

This example shows you how to use refinement when there's a dependency. Introduce the minimum amount of additional functionality to an existing service—in this case, add dynamic items to the cart—and use a new microservice for the bulk of the new work—in this case, coupon lookup and validation.

It's also useful to consider this approach from the perspective of deployment and the production system. You can use the deployment techniques discussed in chapter 5 to safely make these changes without downtime.

7.6.3 Handling cross-cutting concerns

The final example of refinement is the introduction of cross-cutting concerns, such as caching, tracking, auditing, permission, and so forth. You've seen this in earlier chapters, but we'll now explicitly bring it under the umbrella of the refinement strategy. Instead of adding these capabilities to the code base directly or spending time and effort creating code abstractions to hide them, you can intercept, translate, and generate messages to provide these features.

Consider the lookup of product details for a product page. A simple system has a microservice that fronts the data persistence layer. A more production-ready system will have a caching service that first intercepts the *product-detail-lookup* messages so that it can check the cache. An even more realistic system will use a *cache-and-notify* interceptor service. This service does the cache lookup and also emits an asynchronous observed message to let other interested microservices know that a user has looked at a product page. Tracking microservices can then collect viewing statistics for analysis.

The refinement strategy is the primary reason to use pattern matching as your message-routing approach. It means you can write generic microservices and then leave them alone and avoid adding complexity to them. Each new feature can be delivered as a new, special-case microservice.[30] This is your biggest weapon against unwanted coupling between components and unwanted growth in technical debt.

Reducing technical debt is the primary reason to use refinement. It lets each software component avoid knowing too much about the world. In particular, it keeps the complexity of your data structures in check, preventing them from accumulating complexity from special cases.

The reduced need for coordination between people is the primary reason to keep technical debt in check. Low technical debt means you can work independently without breaking things for your coworkers; you know your changes won't affect them. Reduced coordination overhead frees you from expending time in meetings and on process ceremony and keeps your development velocity high.

A closing note from history

Migrating a monolith is thankless drudgery. A great deal of it is political work, and we'll talk about that in the next chapter. For now, here are some comforting words:

Begin each day by telling yourself: Today I shall be meeting with interference, ingratitude, insolence, disloyalty, ill-will, and selfishness—all of them due to the offenders' ignorance of what is good or evil. But for my part, I have long perceived the nature of good and its nobility, the nature of evil and its meanness, and also the nature of the culprit himself, who is my brother (not in the physical sense, but as a fellow creature similarly endowed with reason and a share of the divine); therefore none of those things can injure me, for nobody can implicate me in what is degrading. Neither can I be angry with my brother or fall foul of him; for he and I were born to work together, like a man's two hands, feet or eyelids, or the upper and lower rows of his teeth. To obstruct each other is against Nature's law—and what is irritation or aversion but a form of obstruction.

—Marcus Aurelius, AD 121–180, Roman emperor and Stoic philosopher

---

[30] Yes, you'll end up with hundreds of microservices. Complexity doesn't go away, but it can be made friendlier to human brains. Would you rather multiply and divide in Roman numerals or decimal notation? Representation matters. Better to represent complexity with a single language—message patterns—than a hodgepodge of hairy interfaces and arbitrary programming language constructs.

7.7   *Summary*

- If, by the time you read this book, most new projects are being built using microservices, it won't help you much, because *you* will be working on a monolith migration. There are too many old monoliths, and there's lots of money to be made fixing them.

- You should prepare to migrate a monolith. This is by far the most common experience of those adopting microservices. Use the strangler proxy, greenfield, and macroservice strategies to effect the migration.

- You'll need to keep working on the monolith and delivering features on the old code base, to maintain your credibility as someone who can deliver. Accept this from day one.

- Build out your microservice infrastructure fully before using it for production. This is a political necessity. It's easy for your foes to portray an accidental failure to be portrayed as a fundamental flaw.

- Move as much communication as possible over to your new messaging layer so you can start applying transport independence and pattern matching to the monolith.

- Your guiding philosophy should be the principle of refinement. Solve the general case first, leaving out all the messy details. Then specialize, building only the details that matter.

People

8

Software development is a human activity, and that fact has a massive impact on the outcomes of software development projects. This book communicates a strong message: that the engineering problems of software development have for too long been neglected in favor of meandering arguments about process. Microservices are effective because they address the engineering problems. However, this book doesn't claim that microservices by themselves deliver great projects. They must be implemented by people, and you can't ignore the human factor. Nor can you ignore the organizations where those people work. The behaviors of organizations are emergent properties of human nature and will definitely be your concern as an architect.

8.1 Dealing with institutional politics

Software development and institutional politics are both detail-oriented activities. As a software architect, you're probably better at politics than you think.

This book doesn't give you grand strategies for the victorious delivery of successful software projects; rather, you must prepare for an unending war of attrition, using many tactics on a daily basis to slowly change the organization and create an environment in which you can succeed. Your secret weapon is the technical efficiency of the microservice approach, compared to the current state of the art for software architectures. But that by itself isn't enough. You must be prepared to work the system, build trust, develop alliances and support, win over skeptics, neutralize foes, and apply many disparate minor weapons. Accepting this fact is the first step on the road to success. Every organization is unhappy in its own way, so you must also contextualize the tactics discussed in the following sections.

8.1.1 Accepting hard constraints

Every organization contains entrenched power centers that impose constraints on your working practices. Sometimes, you'll have enough political capital to change these constraints, but often, you won't. The ambitious vice president who allocated the budget for your project may not be prepared to go all in and may hedge on contentious interactions with other parts of the organization. Don't be surprised by this. Even if you have the political capital to break a hard constraint, consider spending it elsewhere, because you'll have many important battles to fight.

To handle hard constraints, you first need to enumerate them. Take time at the start of the project to understand what you can and can't do. It's a serious error to make assumptions or to take assurances at face value. Even if you're told that you'll be able to do something, push deeper, and verify. Ask for policy documents, and talk to lower-level staff in the relevant department. Make sure of the facts. Then, put your understanding in writing, and copy all relevant parties.

When you've identified the hard constraints, bring them into the light. Document them, make them part of the project, and indicate how you'll work with and around them, and the impact they'll have on the project. Use them to redefine the interpretation of success.

If you're lucky, something wonderful will happen: constraints that are hard at the beginning of the project can soften when you build trust and confidence. Identifying constraints early gives you the ability to keep highlighting them and discussing their impact with stakeholders, which creates opportunities to defeat them. This is ugly work, but it's necessary.

8.1.2 Finding sponsors

Who is the primary sponsor of your project? Is it that ambitious vice president or a mid-level manager? Do they understand and buy into the microservice approach, or is their sponsorship based on personal affinity for you? Are *you* the sponsor?

Just because you have project approval doesn't mean you'll get the resources you need to be successful. Nor does it mean other parts of the organization will get out of your way. Finding and working with sponsors is another ugly piece of work, but you're introducing a new approach to your organization, so you need to do it—because you're vulnerable. Minor issues can be magnified by your foes. And sometimes, projects fail because the benign indifference of the universe works that way. To help avoid these issues, you'll need sponsorship.

Nurturing sponsors is an ongoing task for you as the architect of the system. You need to constantly strengthen existing sponsors and find new ones. How? Existing sponsors need care and feeding—that means giving them information. Ask them what format they prefer: a weekly meeting, a status-update email, a dashboard, and so on. Make sure you keep your sponsors up to date, and never let them be caught by surprise because you didn't provide them with the information they needed.

This is easy advice to give, but it's difficult to do in practice. When you're busy on a project, it's probably in your nature as a software developer to focus on the code and put in long hours solving technical problems. You prioritize effort, and things like weekly update emails get pushed to the side. Don't do this. Prioritizing your sponsors is one of the best ways to ensure project success.

How do you find new sponsors? Take every opportunity to network internally. The sponsors you need are those with real power in the organization—and these people aren't necessarily the ones with titles. Identify people who are early employees, who've been in the organization for years, who have external credibility, or who are charming and influential. Go where they are, and meet them. Attend business events, such as internal talks given by guest speakers. You'll find the right kinds of sponsors at these events, because influential people invest time in building their networks. You should, too.

Again, you may find it difficult to invest time in this activity when you get busy. This is a mistake. Networking always pays off; many a project has been saved by a chance encounter with the right person.

How to decide what to do next

There are many detailed, complex ways to decide what to work on next, and you can spend a lot of time building prioritization matrixes for this purpose. But you probably already have a reasonably rough idea of what's important. Here's a quick way to communicate your thinking to your team and thereby validate your analysis.

Start by listing your known deliverables and their deadlines. Then, estimate the full effort to deliver each one, using a comfortable metric for estimation, such as developer days. These are rough estimates, and it's more important that they be accurate relative to each other than accurate in an absolute sense. Now, chart this data, as shown here.

(continued)

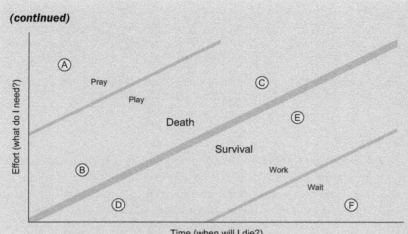

Survival chart

The bold line upward from the origin (Death/Survival) is the maximum amount of effort you can exert in a given time: the line of the possible. Things above the line are impossible; you'll definitely fail to meet those deadlines, because you don't have enough resources in the given time frame. This is the Death zone. Below the line, you have enough resources and time. This is the Survival zone.[1]

The Death zone has two subdivisions: Pray and Play. The Pray zone contains problems so bad you might as well ignore them (A) or else start praying, depending on your world view. The descent phase of a thermonuclear warhead aimed at your location would be a good example. The Play zone contains problems that can only be solved by playing politics (B). Reducing the feature set sufficiently will move the problem vertically down below the line of the possible, so that you have enough resources to deliver it. Extend the deadline, and the problem moves to the right, hopefully crossing the line at some point.

Deliverables in the left half of the Play zone are your immediate political priority. In terms of the chart, spend political capital on B, not C (deliverables that can wait awhile).

The Survival zone also has two subdivisions: Work and Wait. The Work zone is where you achieve feasible results. Deliverables in the left half of the Work zone are your immediate development priority; work on D before E. The Wait zone contains deliverables that require few resources and are far in the future (F). Don't spend time on these yet.

---

[1] The deadlines are charted independently of each other. You deliberately don't take into account cumulative resource expenditure. To do that, remove the highest-priority item, and rechart. But really, this is about identifying the single most important thing to do next.

(continued)

It's a useful exercise to rebuild the chart at the start of each iteration. Engineers are prone to work on items in the Pray and Wait zones, because they're the most, and least, challenging. This is a mistake, because it's the least optimal use of resources.

There's an obvious mapping of microservices to deliverables, so this analysis can help your team decide which microservices need to be built next.[2]

8.1.3 Building alliances

In every job I've ever had, there are two key people I like to get friendly with as soon as I can: the system and office administrators. They're often busy and underappreciated, yet hard-working and competent. They also have deep knowledge of the organization. Align yourself with these key individuals, and your life will be much easier.

It's enough to show them that you understand the challenges of their world. Recognition is a powerful and ethical political act, and people appreciate it. It's obvious that you'll need to spend time building alliances with senior people, and everybody will be aware that you're doing that. But alliances with people on the ground are valuable too and can help you solve different sorts of problems. Every time you solve a problem using a senior ally's authority, you burn political capital in a public way and create enemies. It's much better to receive voluntary help from others. Project success can also depend on gatekeepers looking the other way when you need them to.

You'll need to build traditional alliances as well, but you knew that already. When you're building a microservice architecture for the first time, you need to find a way to work with the operations and IT groups in your company. Of all the groups that can stymie your efforts, these are the most dangerous. You're the representative of many bad things: DevOps culture, the move to the cloud, heterogeneous environments,[3] pager calls at 4:00 a.m., compliance breaches, security headaches, and so on. Operations and IT have every reason to be wary. You won't solve this one overnight, but you must open a dialogue and try to create personal connections that can help overcome the inevitable conflicts.

It may be tempting to use senior allies to override the sysadmins. This must be a last resort. You'll pay dearly if you go to war with them.

8.1.4 Value-focused delivery

I'm repeating this tactic because it's that important. You must get away from the drudgery of feature delivery and arguing over bugs versus enhancements—you'll lose that battle every time. Business value isn't an abstract concept; it's shorthand for identifying the measurements that most closely track the business goals your leadership

---

[2] This style of thinking is very much inspired by Andy Weir's *The Martian* (Crown, 2014) and Neal Stephenson's *Seveneves* (William Morrow, 2015). Consider both essential reading for the aspiring software architect.

[3] No developer should ever need administrator access to their own machine. The very thought!

cares about. Get all those involved to agree to measure, get agreement about the measurements, and then track them aggressively. Doing so will keep everyone honest.

In every situation, ask, "Does this improve the numbers?" This will give you objective criteria for making and evaluating decisions. It will also protect you from higher-ranking colleagues who are defending their territories. This tactic is the one to fight for and on which you should expend political capital. Delightfully, it aligns perfectly with the philosophy of microservices.

8.1.5 Acceptable error rates

This is a difficult point to win. It will be easier if you first win the point about measurement, because measuring the error rate is predicated on the acceptability of measurement as an activity.

The best approach is to not reveal your hand at first. Ask lots of questions about current problems: the level of customer dissatisfaction, the frequency of customer complaints, and so on. Ask for data on performance, uptime, and failed transactions. If it doesn't exist, ask to track it.

Once you've established a credible current error rate, you can use it as a baseline to judge your team. If the business is surviving with a given error rate, then errors per se can be seen as nonfatal. Reduce the power of errors to terrify, and you're halfway there.

Now, you can argue that anything that improves the error rate is good, and that's what your team intends to do. Measure the error rate from the first day of the project, and use the microservice deployment pipeline to manage your risk and stay below that error rate, on average.

The ability to deploy code into production on a continuous basis relies on the company accepting that this will cause transient errors. Getting the business to understand and accept that this trade-off is not only acceptable but also one of the key productivity improvements delivered by the microservice architecture should be a primary goal of your transition project.

8.1.6 Dropping features

Don't be afraid to drop features. Software systems accumulate features over time, because there's little business incentive to remove them. This happens despite the significant cost these legacy features impose through technical debt. The value of individual features varies over time; if you chart the value, you'll end up with a power-law distribution.[4] Now, chart those features against the complexity they introduce. The measure of complexity can be crude (lines of code, anyone?)—it doesn't matter for the purposes of this analysis. Figure 8.1 shows the stereotypical 2 × 2 matrix beloved of consultants everywhere.

---

[4] Admittedly, this is *anecdata* from observation, experience, and reading, rather than repeated experiments. I'm not aware of any studies on this topic.

The lower-right box is the problem: these features deliver low value but have high complexity. It's valid to question their continued existence. Removing a feature without cause is asking for trouble—you have to expend effort, and you might annoy a vocal minority. But if reimplementing, refactoring, or providing supporting logic for a feature has a negative impact on your development velocity, you can legitimately question the need for the feature. Propose that it be removed. You won't always win, but if you don't ask, you won't get.

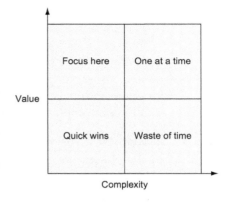

Figure 8.1   **Value versus complexity matrix**

8.1.7   *Stop abstracting*

Developers are trained to abstract the world. Abstractions are the things they *develop* and then express in code. The trouble with abstractions is that they have unbounded growth and eventually collapse under their own weight. Your challenge is to get your team—many of whom may not be familiar with the core ideas of the microservice architecture or may not completely buy into it—to stop abstracting.

This is a difficult people-management challenge. Developers love abstracting and get into a positive mental feedback loop when doing so. This is the dreaded sin of overengineering. It's much easier to control if you keep your microservices small and default to implementing new features using new microservices. But your team will push back, because they've been taught to solve problems by extending data models. They need to learn to use pattern matching.

You need to get your team to stop using the tactic of going from the specific to the general, which is the common experience of programming, and instead go from the general to the specific. This is a message you'll need to broadcast and defend on a daily basis. New team members will have to be brought on board. If you don't keep an eye on this, you'll end up with a distributed monolith.

8.1.8   *Deprogramming*

Software projects are difficult to investigate using the scientific method. It's hard to distinguish between mere correlations and actual causation. Strong experiments with proper protocols are expensive, and there are few examples of such experiments in the literature.

When humans try to comprehend things we don't understand, we use our powerful pattern-matching brains to invent superstitions. Perhaps we can't prove that superstitious rituals work,[5] but we perform them anyway, just in case. One ritual might not

---

[5] For example, it's bad luck to wish an actor "Good luck!" before they go on-stage. "Break a leg!" is the preferred send-off.

be too expensive, but accumulate a few together, and you can get a big drain on productivity and resources.

Software development methodologies, processes, and best practices are all suspect. Everybody in development suffers from unsubstantiated beliefs, and developers are the worst. There's a reason for the cliché that developers are "religious."[6]

I guarantee that you and your team suffer from preconceptions. Some are beneficial to microservices (decent unit testing), some are neutral (agile methodology du jour), and some are harmful (Don't Repeat Yourself). You'll need to be honest and explicit with your team about the fact that you're going to break some established conventions. You'll have to ask for their trust. If you aren't up front about this, your efforts will be negatively affected by both conscious and subconscious performance of the cargo-cult[7] rituals of modern enterprise software development.

8.1.9 *External validation*

Many organizations actively promote themselves in the developer community, as a recruitment tactic. If your organization already does this, you're well placed to talk about what you're doing with your new, innovative microservice approach. If your organization doesn't do this, start talking to those who care about recruitment, and show them how effective developer engagement can be.

The benefit to you is that external validation builds internal political capital. You're making your organization and your boss look good, you're solving a problem—recruitment—for both yourself and others, and you're generating enthusiasm for your efforts. These effects combine to make organizational roadblocks easier to overcome.

What if you aren't naturally inclined to present your work in public? This is a skill you need to develop, because it's become essential for any significant architect role. Start small: go to meetups, and get a feel for the territory and the types of talks they look for. Trust me, all meetup organizers are desperate to fill their speaking calendars; it's a monthly headache. Many meetups encourage and support new speakers. They want new people to present. Cut your teeth at meetups, and before you know it, you'll be speaking at conferences. You can give the same talk again and again—that's what everyone does. It's how you end up with a professional, polished presentation.

8.1.10 *Team solidarity*

The microservice architecture is an engineering tactic that's a partial solution to the larger problem of effective software delivery. But it doesn't free you from the problems of managing a team—you still have to get all the humans in the room to work together.

---

[6] Watch the "tabs versus spaces" scene from season 3, episode 6 of *Silicon Valley*. It's worth it.
[7] *Cargo culting* is the performing of rituals that have no effect or mechanism and can't affect the thing you care about. The term arises from the observed behaviors of indigenous islanders in the South Pacific, who copied the appearance of airfields in the early twentieth century in the hope that planes filled with cargo would appear and land. The term is pejorative.

There are time-honored practices for making a team work—far too many to enumerate or discuss here. It's your duty and responsibility to study, learn, and apply excellent professional practices for managing people, and to keep studying, learning, and applying them.

Your biggest weakness as a coder comes from your greatest strength: you can solve problems with code, so you try to solve *all* problems with code. Trying to solve people problems with code is a mistake, but we've all done it: instead of dealing with mismatched delivery expectations, we work all weekend to get it done the way "they" want it, so we don't have to deal with conflict. Try to swing the pendulum far in the other direction. How many code problems can you solve by engaging with people? That's why you ask if you can drop features. Many other problem-resolution opportunities are purely people based. Go look for them.

You should also measure your team as a whole. Do this collaboratively; don't impose the process on them. The purpose is not to measure performance, but to expose systematic issues. A weekly survey, which may or may not be anonymous, can help to raise issues that are hidden or that everybody is collectively ignoring. It's hard to ignore bad numbers, and they're a good way to start a discussion. You can score these measures on a scale of 1 of 10, or use 5 stars or whatever works for you, as long as you can quantify them. Here are some examples of things you can measure:

- *Overall happiness*—An emerging low score can tell you that organizational issues you may not be aware of are affecting your team.
- *Level of recommendation*—Would team members recommend to a friend that they join this team? This is a good way to get honest feedback about your performance as a manager, because the question is indirect.
- *Technical assessments*—Is performance OK? Do team members expect catastrophic failures? Are they happy with code quality? These questions can help you catch deviations from the team's desired technical outcomes. Code rots when you don't pay attention to it.

8.1.11 *Respect the organization*

Microservices are sometimes portrayed as a way to escape from Conway's Law. This is the observation, made in 1967 by Melvin Conway, that "Any organization that designs a system will produce a design whose structure is a copy of the organization's communication structure."[8] In my first job, for a web consultancy in the 1990s, our version of this was, "You need a menu tab for each department in the client company."

There's no reason the organizational design of a group of political humans should determine a good design for a system's software architecture. Software developers rail against Conway's Law as an example of the polluting influence of corporate politics: if only they were free to design the system properly without keeping the department heads happy, then they could deliver on time.

---

[8] For details of the original paper, see www.melconway.com/Home/Conways_Law.html.

Conway's Law deserves a more subtle reading. It should be taken as an observation of a natural force that creates movement in a certain direction, not as an immutable law or something inherently bad. It's a social observation. You can choose to fight it, or you can choose to use it. Either response may be appropriate, depending on your circumstances.

How you handle Conway's Law shouldn't be determined by your choice of the microservice architecture. Microservices don't compel you to reverse Conway's Law; they just make it easier, if that's what you want to do.

8.2 The politics of microservices

The microservice architecture creates its own political dynamics. The way these dynamics will play out in the long term, and the best approaches to dealing with them, will take years to understand fully. Therefore, if you're leading a microservices project, you'll need to pay close attention to the forces that drive team behavior. Be prepared to adjust course.

The most important principle to preserve is the decision-making pathway that decides what microservices to build. Begin with business requirements, express them as message flows, and then assign the messages to services. Developers who are writing services can undermine this principle by making individual services more important than they should be. This is a form of technical debt that will slow you down. Services must remain the least important thing in a microservices architecture.

8.2.1 Who owns what?

How do you distribute microservices among teams? Consider these scenarios:

- *1–1*—One team per service.[9] These are probably macroservices.
- *1–n*—One team owns many services. These are probably microservices.
- *n–1*—Many teams own one service. This is a monolith.
- *n–n*—Everybody works on all services. These are microservices, without a hierarchical ownership protocol.

As you migrate away from a monolith (n–1), you'll end up with a configuration of 1–1 and 1–n teams. Ideally, you'll end up with all teams in a 1–n configuration when the last macroservice is retired, but this rarely happens in practice.

The n–n configuration at the interteam level isn't practical, because it essentially negates the concept of a team; at the time of writing, no organization has demonstrated defensible evidence that this degree of flatness can work.[10] Even open source development has loose hierarchies.

---

9 t–s, where t is number of teams and s is the number of services. Cardinalities are denoted by 1 for one and n for many.

10 *Holacracy* is an organizational design that can be seen as a recent attempt to make this work. The results have been mixed and inconclusive. Holacracy seems to require a great many rules in order to work, which tends to defeat the purpose.

The *n–n* configuration *within* a team is a different story. This works and is the best configuration. Every team member can work on every service owned by the team, and no service is owned by any individual team member. This isn't a natural state for a team: team members will gravitate toward their specialties, assert implicit ownership over code they wrote and architectural structures they proposed, and avoid code they don't understand. In other words, individuals tend toward the 1–*n* configuration. You have to encourage *n–n* instead.

Why is *n–n* best for teams? Because it removes privileged code. No code or microservice is special. Everything is disposable and reconfigurable.

Microservices give you the technical ability to reconfigure your system cost effectively, but they don't automatically give you that on the human side. Be explicit with your teams: *teams*, not individuals, own microservices.

The tyranny of shared libraries

The term *shared library* refers to code components that are used by more than one microservice. They introduce complexity because you need to know which versions of which library should run on which microservices, what the current distribution of versions is, and what the incompatibilities are. To update a version of a shared library, you need to engage in complex planning that affects many microservices simultaneously. This is pretty much the opposite of what you're looking for from the microservice architecture.

There are two types of shared library: utility and business logic. Business logic in a shared library is the real killer and is almost impossible to justify. It's dangerous because it necessarily describes behaviors of the system that affect users. Breakage is highly noticeable—and breakage is what you'll get when you try to keep that business logic consistent over many teams and microservices. Instead, shared business logic should go in a separate microservice and be accessed via message flows. This is a fundamental tenet of the architecture.

Utility code is different, but not *that* different. Low-level utility code is safe enough—especially open source libraries. Updates tend to be the local decision of a single developer working on one microservice, so you should be able to catch breakage via the deployment pipeline. You're not trying to update the entire system at once.

Writing your own utility libraries can also be justified, but be conservative. These libraries have to be maintained, and the maintainers will be a small group, so you're exposed if they aren't available for some reason. Because the utility code is specific to your project, it can introduce system-wide compatibility issues and require system-wide updates. Nonetheless, you'll probably end up with shared libraries for logging, data access, and the like.

There's one shared library you can't avoid: the message abstraction layer. Fortunately, if you build it to be lenient when accepting messages, you won't suffer much from compatibility issues, even if you run multiple version of the layer in production.

8.2.2 Who's on call?

The *DevOps* movement is independent of the microservice movement but has heavily influenced the thinking about microservices. You can do DevOps without doing microservices, but it's difficult to do microservices without having a DevOps mentality. Microservices move complexity into the network, and that complexity is most fully understood by the developers writing the microservices.

Does the term *DevOps* means developers get to touch live production machines? Or does it mean developers and sysadmins should get better at collaborating? This is a wide-ranging discussion, so let's narrow our scope to the question of DevOps for microservices.

In the microservices world, nobody touches production machines. You have to automate. This makes it much safer for amateurs, such as developers, to modify the production system. But you still require expertise to run and maintain that system. This expertise is necessarily specialist, especially for large systems.[11]

The structure you end up using for the microservice architecture means the term *DevOps* in a microservice context refers to the operation of the upper layer of the automation system, rather than the more traditional system administration duties that full DevOps includes. This is where the developers affect the live system, through a well-defined set of operations that enable microservice deployment patterns. The lower layer is operated by systems engineers as a service for the developers.

There are many variants of this architecture; the distinction between the upper and lower layers isn't a hard boundary, merely a limit that you naturally approach when building very large systems. In the early days, when the greenfield microservice system is small, members of the development team often work on the full stack, crossing the boundary without restriction. The existing operations team runs the monolith and slowly moves into roles supporting the lower layer as the system grows.

Once the greenfield infrastructure is up and running, you have to address the question of how a development team maintains a deployment pipeline and a production system on an ongoing basis. Yes, the operations group is there to help and maintain the upper layer, but who operates it?

The solution that works best is to rotate each developer on the team through an on-call iteration (one week is best). For that week, the developer

- *Doesn't code.* This is the most important rule. The on-call team member needs to be in an interrupt-driven frame of mind. They can't do good, focused work in this state.[12]
- *Does pager duty.* Nobody likes this, but it's the trade-off for flexible and faster deployment to production. You need to be clear and up front with your team about the need to commit to pager duty.

---

[11] The Google role of Site Reliability Engineer is perhaps the best example of the need for systems specialists at scale.

[12] This guideline derives from the observation that human minds can enter a state of high productivity and focus, known as *flow*. Interruptions break flow, so you can't write great code when you're on call. For more, see the writings of Mihály Csíkszentmihályi.

- *Becomes the team concierge.* During each person's on-call week, they clean the toilets (figuratively—although, in a startup, it could be literally). Their job is to remove technical roadblocks for the team. That means they're on point for bugs, issues, support, meetings, and moving furniture. They keep the deployment pipeline healthy, liaise with operations, and talk to other teams. But they don't do politics; that's the job of the project leader and architect.
- *Performs deployments.* Only one person does deployments. Yes, technically you have a deployment pipeline that can support free deployments by anyone, because you've measured and contained the risk. But you don't have an organization that can handle it. Somebody needs to be directly responsible and act as the contact point with people outside the team.

Everyone on the team rotates through being on call—even you, the project leader.

8.2.3   *Who decides what to code?*

Distributed intelligence is a powerful way to solve problems. Let those who know the most make the detailed decisions. Provide a set of common goals, and then sit back and watch the magic happen.

That's the theory. In practice, it can go horribly wrong if you don't put supporting structures in place.

If you allow teams and team members to pluck work items from a backlog, even if you prioritize the backlog using some definition of business value, you'll quickly lose many of the benefits of the microservice architecture. It's worth stressing again: microservices make it *possible* to go faster, but they don't make it inevitable. Teams and individual developers tend to Balkanize into antagonistic, isolated domains. This is a natural social phenomenon: the formation of tribes. The effect is self-supporting. Small initial variations will build until you're back to the situation of ossified frontend and backend developers, and frontend and backend teams. The benefits you were hoping for, such as being able to quickly redeploy people and distribute knowledge to create redundancy, will erode and disappear. Let's look at some tactics you can use to prevent this from happening.

AUTONOMY AND VALUES

The question of who decides what to code is really a question of how choices are resolved. All decisions are reified in code,[13] so you need to find a balance between full autonomy and strict hierarchy. The former leads to Balkanization, the latter to low-grade problem solving.

This is one of the first discussions you need to have with your team. Openly discuss the level of autonomy the team can expect. Acknowledge that the issue is difficult and probably unsolvable. Collectively come up with a set of operating principles that

---

[13] The lawyer and digital-rights advocate Lawrence Lessig has made the argument that, because code controls much of the modern world, code is what determines what's allowed, not people. Laws may say one thing, but it's their (perhaps inaccurate) translation into code that's enforced.

produce the balance you and the team are looking for. Recognize that not only can you change the principles over time to better reach the balance you seek, but you can also change the balance point. You'll need to change the balance point as the project progresses and less freedom is required, given that many problems have been "solved."

This approach is an explicit rejection of the idea that there's an optimal software development methodology, that you should be a cult follower of one or another school or author, and that the methodology, once in place, can never be changed. The remaining tactics discussed in this section should all be considered in this light; they've been found useful by many teams, but they aren't religions.

EVERYBODY CODES

Everybody should write at least some code. To refine this idea, everybody should contribute construction effort, not just coordination. Some code full time; others, especially at the higher levels, may be distracted by management duties, depending on your organizational context.

To make it possible for everybody to write a little code, consider some practical approaches. Coding requires extended periods of concentration. Senior people will have trouble achieving this unless you create formal time periods that are safe from interruptions. This can be done, but it's difficult to enforce. A better approach is for senior people to restrict themselves to longer-term work, such as utility code or better algorithm implementations, that can be worked on over a period of weeks without affecting delivery. Senior people will also, of course, suffer the on-call rotation periodically, and will be able to flex their coding muscles on bug fixes.

For those who aren't able to write code, every project requires grunt work: manually verifying the user interface, replicating user-reported issues, doing usability testing, performing detailed business analysis, and so on. There's always something to do.

If everybody codes, then everybody gets some exposure to the problems on the ground. At a management level, it's easy to solve problems with the blunt force of labor. You command, and it's done, usually by people working late. This means your team ends up working hard when you need them to be working smart. You can't understand, evaluate, or direct solutions that reduce Toil[14] when you don't understand its dynamics.

If everybody codes, then knowledge of the system is deeper and more widely distributed. Group problem solving is more efficient because you can spend less time on communication. Politics is fed by lack of shared understanding and lack of agreement about shared facts: increase both of these, and you reduce the amount of energy you have to expend on politics to get decisions made.

THE TOWER OF BABEL

Before you build your first production microservice system, you may view a polyglot services architecture—one where any developer can build any service in whatever language they like—as either a massive advantage or a terrible disadvantage. Here's what

---

[14] See section 5.7.2.

happens in practice, regardless of your initial decision. Let's say you decide to stick to a single language. You'll encounter situations where you need to use other languages—sometimes for performance, sometimes for specialist features, sometimes because it's the quickest way to turn existing code into a service. A small percentage of services will be implemented in other languages.

Conversely, let's say you allow complete choice. One language will start off with a small advantage. Perhaps it's the new language everyone wants to learn, maybe it's the old language everyone already knows, or perhaps your most productive developer is just cranking out code in their language of choice. Soon, everyone will have to work with this language on a regular basis, and it will become the default choice for new services because it has low friction. Over time, although other languages will be present, one language will dominate.

Whichever starting point you use, the result is the same: our old favorite, a power-law distribution. Most services are written in the dominant language, and then there's a long tail of oddities. How do you deal with this situation from a maintenance perspective? Who looks after the oddities? If you lose a key person who understands the language R, say, what happens when you need to make changes?

This situation can't be avoided. You *will* end up with nonstandard services. Use it as an opportunity for team members to expand their knowledge of the programming universe. Use the rotation already in place to make sure everybody is exposed to everything over time. Make a team decision that if you introduce a language, you need to mentor those who want to work with it.

This won't provide full backup, and losing key people will still hurt, but the remaining people will include understudies who can keep things going. Also, remember that you can always replace services by rewriting them; this may be the best option, even if you have to compromise on performance or capacity cost.

Starter kits

The strategy of refinement means you'll build a lot of new services on an ongoing basis. You should make it easy to build new services in your primary language. Doing so will also reduce the enthusiasm for polyglot services, because building them will be more difficult, with more manual labor: the capabilities of the non-primary language will have to provide a significant advantage to overcome the ease of creating a service using the primary language.

Create a set of templates so developers can quickly get started coding a new service. At first, build a core template. Later, it may make sense to have different templates for such things as data exposure, user interface elements, business rules, and so forth. Who builds and maintains the templates? The same group that looks after the messaging library.

BIG-PICTURE THINKING

Despite the fact that the monolith is one large codebase in one large repository, developers can mentally isolate themselves from most of the system. To understand other parts of the system, you have to read the code for those parts to see how everything fits together—and that's hard work. Monoliths are opaque, because it's difficult to comprehend large-scale structures.

The microservice architecture is different because it offers another level above the code: message flows. Although this level will grow in time to be on the order of many hundreds or thousands of message flows, it's possible for a single human mind to understand the bigger picture in a usefully detailed way. With the monolith, all developers may understand the top-level architecture, but they'll find it difficult to get information about anything below that (apart from the local code they're working on).

Everybody can move from business requirements to messages. As the system grows, you can create conceptual groupings to organize messages. This aids global understanding: all team members can participate in and understand big-picture architectural discussions, because a large element of those discussions is the message flows they engender or the effect of the message flows on infrastructure decisions.

DISPOSABLE CODE

The idea that code can be disposable isn't something that requires microservices, but is something they enable. This book has argued that by following the basic principles of the architecture, you'll end up with microservices that can mostly be rewritten from scratch in one iteration. You can dispose of any given microservice by writing a replacement. As I've said multiple times, "replaceable within one iteration" is an excellent standard for determining the right size for a microservice.

What does this mean from a political perspective? First, you should openly discuss and acknowledge this principle with your team. Anyone's code can be replaced. Write something better, deploy it side by side with the existing code in production, measure the results, and may the best microservice win. Of course, you probably wouldn't want your team to be aggressively competitive in this manner—it's more that everybody is aware that their code is ephemeral and transient. This has the following effects:

- Mistakes are easier to unwind because you can focus on the technical decision, rather than the emotional impact. Nobody has too much skin in the game; even if a change stings a little, it's only one microservice among many.
- Technical debt is kept in check because there's no point in investing in complexity within one microservice, and little time to do so.
- Utility code and shared libraries are better quality. They aren't ephemeral and will be used by many generations of microservices. The effort to write quality code, which is a long-term effort involving many revisions, goes into core code, rather than business logic, which can be swept away in an instant if business strategy changes.

From a business perspective, disposability makes it easier to perform business experiments. The technical team won't actively push back. When working on a traditional monolith, you push back forcefully, because you can't afford the time for experiments—and you'll be blamed for the breakage they cause elsewhere.

In the e-commerce example in this chapter, you can perform complex A/B testing of new user-interaction flows and expect to dispose of most of them. It's worth it to find the user interactions that work well. Or consider a feature such as special offers. You can use the scatter/gather pattern to implement an ongoing evolution of many different kinds of special offers; then, you can measure which ones are more effective and allow those to dominate over time.[15]

VALUABLE MISTAKES

There will be mistakes. There will be downtime.[16] How you deal with this will directly affect your development speed and your ability to succeed in the long term. If your team is afraid of making mistakes, then they'll slow down to reduce risk, and you'll lose most of the benefits you're looking for. Monolithic development is slow in part because people are so afraid of breaking things.

Allow mistakes. Let people learn from them. When a mistake happens, let the person who made the mistake run the post mortem and explain it to others. Hold this meeting on a blame-free basis. You'll need to work hard to make this possible: remind everybody that complex systems fail because they *are* complex, and sometimes there's no root cause.

You also need to make sure information about mistakes isn't presented or leaked in the wrong way higher up the chain of command. Aim to establish a feedback loop that prevents you from making the same mistake twice.

Just because mistakes are allowed doesn't mean you should invite them. You need to maintain trust with the rest of the organization. You've agreed to an acceptable error rate—stick to it! Stay safe by using your deployment process to manage risk, as described in chapter 5.

8.3   *Summary*

- Microservices create a new environment for software development, one that's conducive to getting things done. But this is an engineering advance, not a political one. You must turn it into a political tool. Be aware that you're a disruptive influence in an established political scene, and prepare to face the consequences.

- Focus on visibly and quantifiably delivering business value. Doing so builds trust, and thus political capital, allowing you to remove even more roadblocks and accelerate even faster.

---

[15] Consider using *multi-armed bandit* algorithms.

[16] Section 3.6 reminds you of all the ways microservices can fail.

- When you move fast, you break things. To create enough safe space to do this, get the organization to accept that there's an existing error rate and that you can operate below it. Make errors acceptable, to reduce their impact. This is one of the more difficult political battles you'll face, but it's essential to win.
- There are many other tactics and considerations you'll need to pay attention to. Large human organizations are complex things; you must embrace the work of politics and accept that it's as important as getting the technical details right.
- The microservices architecture isn't a promised land that removes politics from the creation of software. It brings its own pitfalls and forces. Design your rules of ownership carefully, and recognize the difference between the way teams interact and the way developers on a team interact.

Case study: Nodezoo.com

This chapter covers

- Designing a full microservice system
- Building core services
- Creating a flexible development environment
- Developing a risk-reducing, continuous delivery pipeline
- Growing, adapting, and scaling the system

Working code is the best way to demonstrate any software engineering principle. You deserve to see what microservice code looks like in a real system, so that you can make a genuine assessment of the consequences of using this architecture. This chapter walks you through a small but complete system that covers all the topics discussed in this book.

This is a learning system, and there are many obvious omissions and flaws that would be fatal in production. This is deliberate, for two reasons: limited space in this book and, of far more consequence, because this is exactly the way you should develop a production system in its early days! The microservice architecture is supposed to make it easier to go from a toy demonstration to a high-scale production system, in a finite number of iterations. Early in any project, the biggest win comes from showing working code, even if it's just on your laptop. If this case study were a commercial project for a client, I'd build it following a path similar to that described here.[1]

The case study is nodezoo.com, a little search engine for Node.js modules. (The Node.js ecosystem has a perfectly serviceable search engine already, provided by the Node.js module registry, npm [http://npmjs.com]. You won't offend anyone by building a pale imitation.) The purpose of the system is to provide free text search over the full list of Node.js modules (of which there are at least half a million at the time of writing). You should be able to view details about any given module, such as its author and description. The system should also collect information from other sources, such as GitHub, and combine it all into an information summary page for each module.

All the code for this case study is available online at www.manning.com/ books/the-tao-of-microservices and also at http://github.com/nodezoo/tao. The system is written in JavaScript using Node.js. Even if your skin has begun to crawl, you should be able to read and understand the code—everybody can read JavaScript! There isn't much code, because I've kept things as simple as possible. The text shows short code extracts, rather than full listings, so it's worth visiting the project to see the full context of the examples. The system necessarily uses specific development, testing, monitoring, deployment, and orchestration tools, and the repositories contain the relevant installation and configuration instructions. These tools will be discussed from a general point of view. I won't attempt to tutor you in the use of such tools, because there are much better resources for doing so. Nor should you assume that the tools chosen for this case study are preferred. I chose them for their simplicity, and the configurations used are most certainly not appropriate for production.

9.1 Design

Let's follow the analysis process that this book advocates. You'll define a set of informal business requirements, represent them with messages, and use the message interactions to decide which services to build. At the start of a project, this task is a distinct piece of work. Later in the project, it becomes a natural part of enhancing and extending the system.

9.1.1 What are the business requirements?

The purpose of the system is to make it easier to find information about Node.js modules. For every conceivable programming problem, the Node.js registry contains several modules solving that exact problem: one module uses streams, another uses promises, yet another is written in CoffeeScript, and so on. It's important to select the right module, and the only safe way to do so is to choose the most popular one, based on GitHub stars.[2]

---

[1] I beg forgiveness for the considerable poetic license in the timeline of the iterations, but they also serve as headings in this chapter!

[2] Pretty much. Also, try to pick modules that have been updated in the last six months. There's a good chance the maintainer still cares.

Suppose you talk to a few Node.js developers and find that they want quick results from a free text search, rather than criteria-based search.[3] They also want to view all the details about a given module so they can decide whether to use it.

You also ask about accuracy and acceptable failure rates. You're told that people often search for modules they half-remember and recognize when they see them. Using the latest module isn't a priority, so the results can be a little out of date. The information for each module should have the most important details and also be quick to load; but complete, up-to-date details aren't essential. Developers can always go to the original GitHub project for that, which they will do anyway before making a final decision. This is the most important outcome of your requirements analysis, whatever the project: determining the acceptable failure modes and error rates.

So much for the user survey. Back at your desk, you realize that you'll need to use an open source search engine, and you'll need to collect data for each module from a variety of sources. You'll need to track changes to modules and use a message queue to push updates. But you realize that you're jumping ahead to implementation, in typical programmer fashion. This is difficult to avoid; it takes deliberate intention to stay focused on writing the business requirements in an implementation-neutral way.

Starting again from the user's perspective, you draft a list of business requirements, validate them in discussion with your potential users, and end up with the following small, simple list of business requirements (BRs):

- *BR1*—The result list for a search should return in at most 1 second, as should the information page.
- *BR2*—The module search should be free text, and the results should be ordered in terms of relevance.
- *BR3*—An information page will show information about a specific module, collected from various sources.
  - *BR3.1*—The initial sources will be http://npmjs.com and http://github.com. More sources will be added later.
- *BR4*—The system should stay up to date as module updates are published to http://npmjs.com, but it doesn't need to be real-time and can be delayed up to an hour.

In the real world, you'll have a much longer list and schedules of business data, such as product categories. It isn't unusual to spend a week discovering the requirements and another week drafting and validating them.[4] There are diminishing returns if you have to spend longer than this, and it might be an indication that the system or the political context of the project isn't suitable for the microservice approach.

An implicit requirement is that the project owner has bought into continuous delivery (CD) as an approach and also into the microservice architecture that makes CD easy to accomplish. That's how the project owner will get the rest of their requirements.

---

[3] This is the era of AI, and machines should do our thinking for us!

[4] These are the requirements for going live, not for the full version of the system.

Although you may struggle to communicate the technical aspects of this assumption, you should be clear with the stakeholders that delivery will be incremental and that the first few iterations will be far below production standard. The benefit to them is that they will continue to have an active, consequential voice in the refinement of the system, and they aren't bound by the initial requirements.

You should also agree with the stakeholders at this point about the quantifiable definition of success. For the example search engine, success is defined by the response times and update frequencies outlined in the BRs. You must accept that the stakeholders almost certainly mean these numbers to be taken on a percentile basis, rather than an average basis. It's a lot easier to hit a 1-second average response time than a 1-second, 90th percentile response time, but 1 second is the requirement.[5]

9.1.2 *What are the messages?*

Some potential services are probably already suggesting themselves to your programming subconscious. Resist this temptation, and stay focused on the messages. You need to think in terms of activities, not entities. This is in direct contradiction to most classical training in computer science.[6] Attempting to carve a messy, ever-changing world into neat categories is a futile task. All you'll get is an inflexible database schema riddled with technical debt.

The BRs describe what *happens*, not what *is*.[7] Look at them from the perspective of the actions defined. The entities affected by those actions can have many representations, of which systems of record (SORs) are just one. The action that a BR represents is more essential and is independent of the attributes of the entities. Taking the principles of pattern matching and transport independence introduced in chapter 2, you can safely define messages without overthinking the problem. By avoiding strict schemas for your messages, you retain the flexibility to adapt to new actions as they emerge from ongoing business change.

What about performance?

BR1 and BR4 contain specific performance goals, and you've committed to these goals as success criteria. This commitment is in direct opposition to the need to remain flexible, which is delivered by loose schemas and *inefficient* message transports. Wouldn't it be better to commit up front to efficient message encodings and protocols (which tend to require hard serialization schemas), making the messaging layer superfluous?

---

[5] Even if your stakeholders insist on averages, you should design for percentiles; then you'll have the luxury of explaining your overdelivery.

[6] If you have a degree in Computer Science, you know how to draw entity-relationship diagrams, and you instinctively turn nouns into a class diagram. This approach puts the emphasis on things rather than actions.

[7] Follow Heraclitus of Ephesus (c. 535–475 BC): "Everything changes and nothing remains still … you cannot step twice into the same stream."

(continued)

Before you start to panic, remember the Pareto Principle: 80% of the effects come from 20% of the causes. It's most likely that the performance constraints will apply to a small subset of messages. You won't face production traffic until later in the project. At that stage, you'll have converged on a schema that needs fewer changes over time, having gone through a process of refinement. You can then make the decision to trade flexibility for speed, and harden the schema. Transport independence means you can choose a faster, less flexible, transport mechanism. Perhaps you'll need to hardcode network locations and be more careful with deployments, rather than enjoying the frictionless CD of peer-based service discovery. So be it, if the business goals make this trade-off worthwhile. The trick is to make these trade-offs only after they've shown that they can pay their own way.[8]

Before you begin to represent business activities as messages, it's worth settling on a few conventions. What patterns will you use? Here are some suggestions. Actions often have an *actor*, the thing that performs the action. It's too limiting to think of this as an entity in the domain of the business problem you're solving or as a microservice in the system you're building. Different things will perform different actions at different times. It's useful to think of *roles* as performing the actions. Then you can assign the roles as needed later, and you retain flexibility. Using a `role` property in your messages gives you a useful namespace for pattern matching.[9]

Certain actions are clearly commands from one actor to another or, at least, from one role to another. Not all messages are commands, but they're often a sizable plurality if not a modest majority.[10] It's natural to name the commands and use a message property such as `cmd` to specify the name. This is useful for pattern matching. Don't fall into the trap of equating commands with remote procedure calls; you can pattern-match on much more than the value of the `cmd` property.

BR1: PERFORMANCE

You'll meet this requirement by making sure you set up your system infrastructure early in the project. Monitoring and measurement are part of that infrastructure, so you should always know whether you're meeting this requirement. The way to stay fast is to *never go slowly*. Even if a microservice deployment is functionally correct, roll it back if performance doesn't meet the goal. The example code for this chapter includes a performance measure to ensure that you meet the 1-second goal.

---

[8] "The real problem is that programmers have spent far too much time worrying about efficiency in the wrong places and at the wrong times; premature optimization is the root of all evil (or at least most of it) in programming." Donald E. Knuth, "Computer Program-ming as an Art" (1974 Turing Award Lecture), *Communications of the ACM* 17, no. 12 (December 1974): 667–673, http://mng.bz/Ob91.

[9] Not all messages will need a `role`. Don't start a new religion!

[10] This is an empirical observation acquired from building microservice systems, not something to measure yourself against—trust your own design instincts on your own system!

It's a universal law of enterprise software development that performance, when you go live, will be abysmal. There will be crying and gnashing of teeth, as well as lost weekends and evenings. Despite microservices introducing more latency, they still help you avoid this problem by facing it up front, and they also help you isolate the problem to specific message and services.[11]

BR2: MESSAGES RELATING TO SEARCH

Let's use the *search* role to describe these messages. You need messages to perform a search and index a module for searching. You'll use concrete examples of messages because they're easier to think about and extract the message patterns from. The messages use JSON format. The following message performs a search for Node.js modules:

```
{
  role: 'search',
  cmd: 'search',        Assume the search
  query: 'foo'      ◁⎯  term is "foo".
}
```

This message suggests the pattern `role:search, cmd:search`. You add this to your list of patterns for the system. The `query` property isn't part of the pattern. Services accepting the `role:search, cmd:search` pattern should look for the `query` property; if it isn't present or isn't a string, they should ignore it and respond with an empty result list.[12]

A command message usually expects a reply and fits most naturally into the request/response message interaction. You can define a response to a search:[13]

```
{
  items: [ {...}, ... ]
}
```

The `items` property is an array of response objects. You don't define anything about the response objects yet but assume you'll add fields as needed. No schemas!

This message has the pattern `role:search, cmd:insert` and is used to add a Node.js module to the search index:

```
{
  role: 'search',
  cmd: 'insert',        Data for a module;
  data: { ... }     ◁⎯  undefined at this point
}
```

The service that accepts this message should probably be idempotent. You can insert the same module as many times as you like, and the last insert wins. This lets you update modules without worrying about creating them first. The data for each module should be open; you'll probably want to add more data fields down the road.

---

[11] "Slow is smooth, smooth is fast," as any Navy SEAL will tell you.

[12] Remember Postel's Law: "Be liberal in what you accept, strict in what you emit."

[13] Responses aren't considered first-class messages—see chapter 2.

Does this message have a response? Perhaps. It could happily be synchronous or asynchronous. To making testing easier, it may make sense to respond with a summary of the output of the search engine.

The list of messages in the system thus far is as follows:

- `role:search,cmd:search`
- `role:search,cmd:insert`

BR3: MESSAGES RELATING TO MODULE INFORMATION

Let's use the *info* role for these messages. You'll need messages to get all the information about a module, and messages to request module information from each source. You don't control the sources, so an asynchronous scatter/gather approach (as described in chapter 3) is probably best:

```
{
  role: 'info',
  cmd: 'get',            The module's name
  name: 'express'   <──┘ is "express".
}
```

The message pattern is `role:info,cmd:get`, and the response should be all the information you have about a module, keyed by the source:

```
{
  npm: { ... },
  github: { ... },
  ...
}
```

You don't dictate the data fields of each information source.

To get the information from each source, you scatter an asynchronous message and wait to gather an asynchronous reply at a later time:

```
{
  role: 'info',          Announces that you need
  need: 'part',          part of the information
  name: 'express'   <──┘ for a module
}
```

Later, the information is gathered:

```
{
  role: 'info',
  collect: 'part',        Collects part of the
  name: 'express',   <──┘ information for a module
  data: { ... }
}
```

Although you haven't yet assigned any services to handle these messages, it should be clear that multiple services (at least one for each source) will collaborate to implement the *info* role. Roles are a pattern convention, not a mapping to services!

The list of messages is now as follows:

- `role:search,cmd:search`
- `role:search,cmd:insert`
- `role:info,cmd:get`
- `role:info,need:part`
- `role:info,collect:part`

BR3.1: MESSAGES RELATING TO SOURCES

These messages will be mostly consistent over the set of sources, so let's focus on http://npmjs.com and duplicate the messages for http://github.com. Each source should get its own role, because you may need multiple services to fully integrate with a source, and you may need custom messages for a given source.

These custom messages can be used to provide source-specific extension points (to allow for custom parsing, say) and to allow you to drive the system manually for testing and administration.

> ### The power of the REPL
>
> It's a good idea to provide a *read-evaluate-print loop* (REPL) for any system you build, microservice or monolith. A REPL is a dynamic, interpreted, textual interface to the system. You should be able to the connect to the REPL remotely (using the `telnet` command, say) and execute commands and expressions against the live system.
>
> A REPL is particularly useful for the messy work of integrating with third-party data sources. In the microservice case, the REPL should let you manually inject messages directly into the system. This is an incredibly valuable development, testing, and management tool, and it can *save your life*. The example code for this chapter includes a REPL service.

The following message gets information about a Node.js module from npm:

```
{
  role: 'npm',
  cmd: 'get',
  name: 'express'
}
```

This message has the pattern `role:npm,cmd:get` and responds with a message containing the data fields provided by npm. Which data fields? These will change over time, both from your perspective in terms of the data fields you want, and from the npm perspective in terms of the fields it provides. This feels like a necessary extension

point, so let's create a message to specifically interact with and query the
http://npmjs.com service:

```
{
  role: 'npm',
  cmd: 'query',
  name: 'express'
}
```

The pattern is `role:npm,cmd:query`, and the response is a set of parsed data fields.

Duplicating these patterns for http://github.com, the system becomes as follows:

- `role:search,cmd:search`
- `role:search,cmd:insert`
- `role:info,cmd:get`
- `role:info,need:part`
- `role:info,collect:part`
- `role:npm,cmd:get`
- `role:npm,cmd:query`
- `role:github,cmd:get`
- `role:github,cmd:query`

You can see that this list of messages by itself is a succinct yet descriptive specification of the system. You can even organize this list into a hierarchy, using the `role` property at first and other properties later. This becomes essential when you have hundreds of messages.

BR4: MESSAGES RELATING TO MODULE CHANGES

Finally, you need to handle module updates. These occur when a new version of a module is published to npm, so one way to detect changes is to listen to the event stream that npm provides. But other sources may not play as nicely and will need to be polled. Regardless of how you implement this, you need an asynchronous message announcing that a change has occurred. Interested services can then decide to update their data. Here's the event message announcing that a module has changed in some way:

```
{
  role: 'info',
  event: 'change',
  name: 'express'
}
```

`role:info,event:change` is your final pattern. This completes the initial message analysis of the system. As you implement the system, and as BRs change, expect to see changes to the pattern list.

9.1.3 What are the services?

You determine the services by analyzing the message interactions. Who's sending, and who's receiving? Is there a receiver? Let's take each message interaction in turn.

MESSAGE PATTERN: ROLE:SEARCH,CMD:SEARCH

This message is triggered by a user entering a search query, so it comes from the UI. You need a *web* service to display the search page and send the message. The receiving service should respond with a list of search results: this is the *search* service (see figure 9.1).

In more-complex production systems, you'll have many services implementing parts of the UI. A common approach is to have one service per page. In this little system, one service will

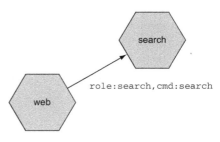

Figure 9.1 The role:search, cmd:search interaction

look after the UI. The *web* service will deliver not only the search results but also the module information page. You'll give the *web* service a proper JSON API as well so that you can validate it using tools like curl.[14]

The *search* service has to perform free text searches. This is a specialist function that you should delegate to a third party. In this example, you'll use Elasticsearch.[15] Nonetheless, you don't interact with Elasticsearch directly. Instead, you write the *search* service to handle search messages and encapsulate all the interactions with Elasticsearch, insulating the system from your chosen search engine.

MESSAGE PATTERN: ROLE:SEARCH,CMD:INSERT

With this message, you insert into, or update a module in, your search engine. This message is clearly received by the *search* service. But who sends it? The data to be indexed is the result of the role:npm, cmd:query message, so it seems natural to send the insert message from the service that handles the integration with npm: call this the *npm* service (see figure 9.2).

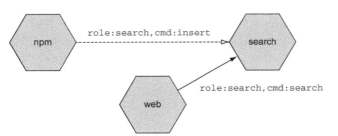

Figure 9.2 The role:search, cmd:insert interaction

---

[14] Once the system is up, you should be able to run curl http://localhost:8000/api/query?q=foo_ to search for modules. See https://curl.haxx.se for more information about the curl command-line utility.

[15] Elasticsearch is a reliable, scalable, full-text search engine. See www.elastic.co.

This decision is somewhat arbitrary, but you're not locked into it. Other services can send the insert message if you decide to change things later. Also, you don't need a response, so this message can be asynchronous.

MESSAGE PATTERN: ROLE:INFO,CMD:GET

The UI displays a web page showing information for a module, so the *web* service is the sender in this case. You need a service to collect all the information in one place and to orchestrate integrations with the information sources. To do so, you create an *info* service as the receiver of `role:info,cmd:get` that mediates between the *web* service and each source-integration service (see figure 9.3).

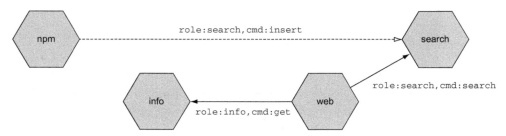

Figure 9.3 The `role:info,cmd:get` interaction

The *info* service will handle a large volume of these messages; because you only need to be up to date within an hour, you should cache the responses in the *info* service. In production, you'll have multiple *info* services, each with its own internal cache, all slightly inconsistent with the most up-to-date version of the data.[16]

These caches are in memory inside the service. Are they large enough? You'll need to measure your cache-hit ratio[17] in production to answer that question. If they aren't large enough, consider using an external shared cache with sufficient capacity. But there's no need to plan ahead for that now; changing the *info* service to use an external cache is a small change that affects only that service, so you can safely not think about this problem. This is what microservices deliver—things you don't have to think about.

What about cache invalidation?[18] The module data will get stale. Well, you could develop a cache-invalidation algorithm, but that's hard work. Why not recycle the *info* services on an hourly basis (meeting that BR)? Killing old *info* services removes their invalid caches and allows new *info* services to build up new caches that are more up to date. Microservices allow you to use your investment in infrastructure automation to solve problems without writing more code.

---

[16] This is compliant with the acceptable error levels you negotiated with the project stakeholders.

[17] The number of times something was in the cache when sought (a *hit*) versus not (a *miss*). This should be fairly high, to justify using a cache.

[18] Using a cache will *always* introduce stale-data bugs. "There are two hard things in computer science: cache invalidation, naming things, and off-by-one errors." (Jeff Atwood, Tim Bray, and Phil Karlton)

MESSAGE PATTERNS: ROLE:INFO,NEED:PART AND ROLE:INFO,COLLECT:PART

Let's decide which services implement this scatter/gather interaction. You've already identified one of the source-integration services, *npm*, and if you get information from GitHub, you'll need a *github* service as well. The *info* service will emit the role:info,need:part message asynchronously, and it will be observed by these source-integration services. These will then subsequently emit role:info,collect:part messages containing their contribution to the module information page (see figure 9.4).

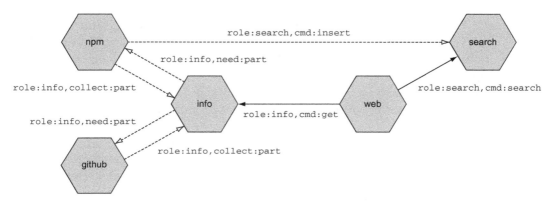

Figure 9.4 The role:info,need/collect:part interactions

The *info* service should allow a small interval of time for the source-integration services (*npm*, *github*, and others that you implement later) to send back messages with module information. Any messages that arrive after this interval are ignored, and that data won't be displayed. That's OK, because it's acceptable under the terms of your acceptable error behavior.

MESSAGE PATTERNS: ROLE:NPM,CMD:GET AND ROLE:NPM,CMD:QUERY

Let's focus on the npm integration, because similar messages are implemented by the other source-integration services. Who sends the role:npm,cmd:get message? In the current design, nobody! It's triggered by the role:info,need:part message. The *npm* service listens for role:info,need:part messages; when it receives one, it calls role:npm,cmd:get on itself and sends back the result using role:info,collect:part.

Why doesn't the *info* service call role:npm,cmd:get directly? It could, and perhaps you'd do it that way in a very early implementation or if you were implementing a tracer bullet.[19] But consider the consequences. Now the *info* service has to know about every source integration; whenever you add a new source, you also have to update the *info* service. This isn't what you want, and the scatter/gather interaction avoids this coupling.

So why does the *npm* service need its own messages? Why not just implement the role:info message handler directly? Because that would hardcode the scatter/gather

---

[19] A *tracer bullet* is a vertical feature implementation that covers the entire system stack from top to bottom but ignores almost everything else. It's a quick way to tell whether a feature is possible.

interaction on the other side, make testing more difficult, and prevent you from creating other interactions with the *npm* service.

The general strategy here is to define naturalistic messages for each activity and define focused services to handle them. With more-complex interactions, such as scatter/gather, use specific messages for that purpose, and translate them into the naturalistic messages. Interaction-specific messages keep everything flexible and decoupled. If performance concerns emerge later, you can always hardcode the relevant message flows.

The `role:npm,cmd:query` message is also an internal message (for now—perhaps you'll split the *npm* service later, as complexity increases). It represents an extension point for customization and is a place where you anticipate changes over time (as npm updates and changes its API). In this case, you piggy-back on the messaging infrastructure to make your component architecture more pluggable (see figure 9.5).

You also need to consider the question of data persistence for the *npm* service. It can't query http://npmjs.com every time you want information about a module; that would be too slow and wasteful. You need to store the module information in a database. You also need to worry about updating the data when modules change.

You can insulate yourself from making the wrong decision here by representing data operations as messages.[20] If you decide to use a shared database, you'll write a data service to handle these messages and mediate between the *npm* service and the database. Or, you might merge the data service into the *npm* service to avoid the network overhead.

In this case, let's take an aggressively microservice-style approach so you can see how that would work. Each *npm* service will store all of its data locally, using an embedded

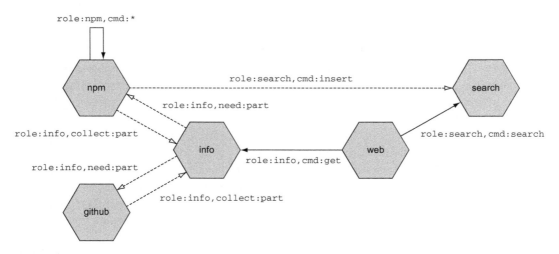

Figure 9.5   The role:npm,cmd:* interactions

---

[20] As discussed in section 4.2.2. In the example code, these messages will use the pattern `role:entity`.

database engine.[21] That means each *npm* service instance needs a persistent volume. You'll need to use your deployment infrastructure to manage the association of service instances to volumes to avoid losing data.

That said, maybe data loss isn't so bad. Consider that the data stored by a given instance may become slightly out of date if the occasional role:info,event:change message is lost. If the *npm* services query http://npmjs.com on demand, then they'll always be able to retrieve the data for any module, even if they don't yet have it locally. Given the acceptable error behavior, this still works even if http://npmjs.com is occasionally unreachable. If you put all of this together, your production system consists of a set of *npm* service instances, each with its own expanding copy of the module data, all slightly inconsistent, but not so much that it matters. You recycle the *npm* instances, perhaps on a weekly basis, rebuilding the database for each new instance. The advantage of this approach is that you now have no database server to manage, because the services look after their own data.[22]

MESSAGE PATTERNS: ROLE:GITHUB,CMD:GET AND ROLE:GITHUB,CMD:QUERY

The internal message patterns for the *github* service follow the same operational model as the *npm* service. We again use naturalistic internal messages (with namespace pattern role:github), but keep them decoupled from other services by responding to the role:info messages.

MESSAGE PATTERNS: ROLE:INFO,EVENT:CHANGE

This message means a module's data has changed and needs to be queried again. The *npm* service should listen for this message and trigger an internal role:npm,cmd:query to get the most recent data for a given module. Who sends the message? You need an *updater* service to listen for updates from http://npmjs.com (see figure 9.6).

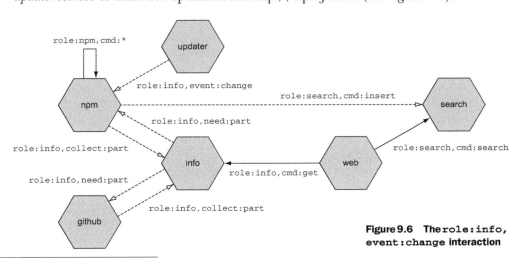

Figure 9.6 The role:info, event:change **interaction**

---

[21] In the example code, for local development, the database is JSON files on disk. For staging and production, LevelDB is used (see http://leveldb.org).

[22] Refer to chapter 4 for a more detailed discussion of data strategies for microservices.

The *updater* service is also a good place to put some code to populate the system at the start. It can download a list of all known modules and work through them all. You'll probably want to rate-limit this batch process to ensure that you don't annoy the external sources. The process is inherently idempotent, so you don't need to spend too much energy worrying about consistency. And you can have a separate *updater* instance in parallel making sure you don't miss any updates that occur while you're processing the initial batch.

9.2   *Deliver*

We'll follow development, rollout, and maintenance of the system using a series of idealized iterations. Iterations are a convenient and common way to organize software development projects. We won't assume any strict process, however, because the microservice architecture frees you from the necessity of such ceremonial trappings.

9.2.1   *Iteration 1: Local development*

To get the project off to a good start and build stakeholder trust, it's always advisable to build and present a working system, however small, at the end of the first week. In practical terms, this means you should focus on getting a local development environment up and running, and on keeping your team small so that you do as little integration work as possible. Aim to run the demonstration from a developer machine, and don't worry about build, staging, or production environments. Nor should you worry too much about correctly configuring and installing third-party systems such as database servers. Mock them up using messages, if necessary.

You need decide how to organize your code. Should you use separate source code repositories for each microservice, or put everything into a so-called *monorepo*?[23] Ultimately, you need to make a decision based on contextual factors such as the personalities on your team and your degree of organizational flexibility. When you're maintaining a large production microservice system with many services, it's ultimately easier to place each service in its own repository. This lets you build and deploy services individually and gives you the freedom to move services between teams easily. Using one repository per service does impose a cost in that you need to maintain multiple repositories on your development machine and ensure that they're in the correct state.[24] This case study uses one repository per service and a system repository containing shared tooling and scripts.

You also need to think about how to run multiple services at the same time on your development machine. This case study is so small that you can open multiple terminal windows and run everything manually. Even then, it's pretty tedious. Local development is much easier if you use a process manager to stop and start the services, and use

---

[23] Google is famous for its enormous monorepo, containing over a billion files. The ramanujan example system from chapter 1 also uses a monorepo.

[24] This is another microservice trade-off. You have to write your own tooling to manage multiple repositories, or find community solutions such as Lerna (https://lernajs.io).

a configuration file to describe your development configuration. You can also use a container manager such as Docker as a convenient way to run third-party servers (such as Elasticsearch); this obviates installing and configuring them. The ephemeral nature of the containers is an advantage, because you always start with a clean state. You could also use the container manager to run your own microservices, although you'll have a faster build/run/test cycle if you run your services directly as normal processes.

SERVICE: WEB

Let's build the first service! The *web* service displays web pages for the UI, provides a small API, and sends microservice messages into the internal network to get results to show the user. All the code for the *web* service is available at www.manning.com/books/the-tao-of-microservices and also at http://github.com/nodezoo/nodezoo-web.[25]

The user interface code looks after text input to the query field and dynamic display of the query results. This code isn't a concern here; you can assume it "just works."[26]

The web-server code uses hapi as the web framework,[27] which provides URL route mapping. Most of this code is scaffolding, so I omit it here. One example will suffice: the code that sets up the URL route for the home page.

Listing 9.1 nodezoo-web/web.js: home page route

The URL route is /, which you'd expect for the home page!

The view component loads a file called index.html, passing a title parameter.

```
server.route({
  method: 'GET',
  path: '/',
  handler: function (request, reply) {
    reply.view('index', {title: 'nodezoo'})
  }})
```

The HTTP method for this route is GET.

The handler function passes in request and reply objects, and is called when there's an HTTP request against the path.

For the microservice messaging layer, you'll use the Seneca framework,[28] which happens to provide transport independence and pattern matching. The messaging layer has two primary methods: add, which adds a message pattern and implementation, and act, which sends a message. Seneca integrates with hapi, so you can access a Seneca instance using server.seneca. Here's what happens when you search for a module:

---

[25] All the repositories for the example code are under the http://github.com/nodezoo organization. Start with http://github.com/nodezoo/tao for setup instructions. The discussion assumes all repositories are checked out to the same root folder.

[26] The UI code is written in jQuery. We'll have none of that new-fangled React nonsense in this book! I use jQuery for the same reason I use Node.js: everybody can read the code.

[27] See http://hapijs.com for more information. This framework was developed at Walmart and is designed for enterprise workloads.

[28] I'm the maintainer of Seneca, so you'll have to forgive me some bias in my choice of microservice framework. For more, see http://senecajs.org.

1 The frontend code makes a request to the /api/query API endpoint with a query parameter. Example: `http://nodezoo.com/api/query?q=foo`, where "foo" is the search term.

2 The *web* service accepts the request, creates a `role:search,cmd:search` message, and sends it to the *search* service.

3 The *search* service queries Elasticsearch and responds with a list of results.

The following listing shows the *web* service code to handle the search query.

Listing 9.2   nodezoo-web/web.js: api/query route

```
server.route({
    method: 'GET',
    path: '/api/query',
    handler: function (request, reply) {
        server.seneca.act(
            {
                role: 'search',
                cmd: 'search',
                query: request.query.q
            },
            function (err, out) {
                if (err) {
                    out = {items: []}
                }

                reply(out)
}) } })
```

- **Sends a message using seneca.act** → `server.seneca.act(`
- **Constructs the contents of the message, using the role:search,cmd:search pattern** ← `role: 'search', cmd: 'search',`
- **Adds the query term to the message using the query property** ← `query: request.query.q`
- **Waits for a response, which will be in the out parameter** → `function (err, out) {`
- **If there was a problem, displays an empty list** → `out = {items: []}`
- **Sends the result back to the web browser** ← `reply(out)`

The *web* service also needs to display an information page for a given module. Use the URL route /info/<module-name> for this page. Thus, nodezoo.com/info/foo displays information about the foo module. The construction of this page works pretty much the same as the call to the query endpoint. You construct a `role:info,cmd:get` message and insert the results into a page template.[29]

To test this service, both manually and using a unit-test framework, you need to be able to run it. How can you do this when it depends on the *search* and *info* services, which haven't yet been written? And even when they're written, how can you test the *web* service independently?

Being able to run a service *without* its dependencies is more important that you might think. Once you have lots of services, even if they're lightweight, it will be impossible to run the entire system on a developer machine: there will be too many services. You could solve this problem by having a shared set of servers, but that's like the bad old days of shared development databases. You can give everybody their own private system—one for each developer—maybe running on a large virtual server,

---

[29] We'll omit this frontend code for brevity, but you can see it all at www.manning.com/books/the-tao-of-micro-services and http://github.com/nodezoo/nodezoo-web.

if you have the money. You can even—and I've seen this done by a well-known consumer-facing site—proxy into production.

The most practical solution is to mock up the dependencies. All you need to do is provide reasonable responses to the outbound messages. When you run a microservice locally, run some mock services as well that provide hardcoded responses to messages.

In this project, each service is composed of at least two types of source-code files. Core business logic source-code files provide the message-handling implementation. Service-execution scripts define how the service communicates with the rest of the world, depending on the environment. You'll have multiple service-execution files, at least one each for development, staging, and production.

Because this is iteration 1, you'll focus on the development-service execution script. You'll assign each service to a local port, counting in tens up from 9000. This is completely unworkable if you have a large number of services—in which case you might use a local DNS server or other service-discovery mechanism—but works fine in the first few iterations.

Listing 9.3   nodezoo-web/srv/web-dev.js: development-service execution

```
var Seneca = require('seneca')
var app = require('../web.js')

var seneca = Seneca({tag: 'web'})          ◁── Creates a Seneca
                                               instance tagged
                                               as a web service
seneca
  .client({pin:'role:search', port:9020})
  .client({pin:'role:info', port:9030})    ◁── Sends ("pin") all messages
  .ready(function () {                          matching role:info to local
    app({seneca: this}) })                      port 9030

var mock = Seneca({tag:'mock'})            ◁── Creates a Seneca instance
                                               to mock messages

if (process.env.MOCK_SEARCH) {             ◁── Only mocks if the relevant
  mock                                         environment variables are set
    .listen(9020)
    .add('role:search', function (msg, reply) {        ◁──
      reply({items: msg.query.split(/\s+/).map(function (term) {
              return {name:term, version:'1.0.0', desc:term+'!'}})
    }) }) }

if (process.env.MOCK_INFO) {
  mock
    .listen(9030)
    .add('role:info', function (msg, reply) {
      reply({npm:{name:msg.name, version:'1.0.0'}})
    }) }
```

Annotations:
- Sends ("pin") all messages matching role:search to local port 9020
- Starts the hapi web server
- The mock search service listens on local port 9020.
- The mock search service responds with fake search results to any message.

In this service-execution script, you use environment variables as flags to turn on message mocking. To run the *web* service completely standalone, use this command:

```
$ MOCK_SEARCH=true MOCK_INFO=true node srv/web-dev.js
```

Open http://localhost:8000 and enter a search term, and you'll get back faked results.

You've already begun to assign ports to services. So far, you have the following:

- 9010: *web* (not used)
- 9020: *search*
- 9030: *info*

In the staging and production systems, all services would listen for messages on the same port, say 9000, and you'd run them in different containers or machines.

SERVICE: SEARCH

The *search* service wraps interactions with the Elasticsearch server.[30] You'll start with the business logic. The Seneca convention is to list all message patterns together near the top of the file, so that you can see the message interface of the service at a glance.

Listing 9.4 nodezoo-search/search.js: message list

```
seneca.add( 'role:search,cmd:insert', cmd_insert )
  seneca.add( 'role:search,cmd:search', cmd_search )
```

The role:search,cmd:insert message is handled by the cmd_insert function.

To perform a search, you need to make an HTTP call to the Elasticsearch web service. Take an inbound role:search,cmd:search message, and translate it into a call to Elasticsearch. The query property of the message should contain the search terms.

Listing 9.5 nodezoo-search/search.js: handler for role:search,cmd:search

Constructs the Elasticsearch URL using configuration options

```
function cmd_search (msg, reply) {
  var url = 'http://' + options.host + ':' + options.port +
          '/' + options.base + '/_search?q=' + encodeURIComponent(msg.query)

  Wreck.get(url, {json: true}, function (err, res, payload) {
    if( err ) return reply(err)

    var items = []
    var hits = result.hits.hits

    if (hits) {
      for (var i = 0; i < hits.length; i++) {
        items.push(hits[i]._source)
      }
    }

    reply({items: items})
  })
}
```

Uses the wreck library (http://github.com/hapijs/wreck) to make an HTTP request

Extracts the result from the Elasticsearch response JSON

Appends each result item to a result list

---

[30] This might be a cluster of Elasticsearch instances in production.

Inserting an entry into the search engine has a similar implementation, except that you send a POST request to Elasticsearch. The data property of the role:search, cmd:insert message should contain the Node.js module details, as shown next.

Listing 9.6 nodezoo-search/search.js: handler for `role:search,cmd:insert`

```
function cmd_insert (msg, reply) {
  var url = 'http://' + options.host + ':' + options.port +
            '/' + options.base + '/mod/' + msg.data.name

  Wreck.post(url, {json: true, payload: msg.data},
    function (err, res, payload) { reply(err, payload) })
}
```

For this service to work, you'll need to run an Elasticsearch server. On a development machine, the easiest way to do this is to use Docker:[31]

```
$ docker run -d -p 9200:9200 \
  docker.elastic.co/elasticsearch/elasticsearch:<VERSION>
```

The development execution file for the *search* service doesn't need to mock anything, because you assume Elasticsearch is running locally. When you first develop the service, it would be nice to be able to test the integration manually in an ad hoc manner. For this purpose, and because it remains useful even in production, you add a network REPL to the service.[32] This allows you to telnet into the service and send it messages by hand.

Listing 9.7 nodezoo-search/srv/search-dev.js: development service execution

```
var Seneca = require('seneca')

Seneca({tag: 'search'})               Loads the search business
  .use('../search.js')       ◁──────┐ logic that defines the
                                       role:search messages

  .use('seneca-repl', {port:10020})   ◁──── Opens a REPL on local port 10020

  .listen(9020)   ◁──── Listens for messages on local port 9020
```

Run this file as follows:

```
$ node srv/search-dev.js
```

To exercise the service, telnet into the REPL, and enter a message:[33]

```
$ telnet localhost 10020
.../search > role:search,cmd:query,query:foo
```

---

[31] You could also install and run Elasticsearch directly.

[32] Seneca provides a REPL plugin for this purpose, and in early development, it's quickest to include a REPL with each service.

[33] Seneca expects JSON messages, but we'll use a terse form that omits quotes. See http://github.com/rjrodger/jsonic.

The *search* service listens for messages on port 9020. It will accept any messages but will ignore those it doesn't recognize.

SERVICE: INFO

The *info* service handles the `role:info,cmd:get` message by orchestrating the scattering of `role:info,need:part` and gathering of `role:info,collect:part` messages. The scatter/gather interaction is asynchronous and observed and corresponds to a publish/subscribe transport model. In production, you might use something like Redis (http://redis.io) to provide this model. For your purposes in development, to get something working in this iteration, you'll use message translation to simulate publish/subscribe. The message abstraction layer is an essential element of any microservice system because it makes these types of decisions safe. You can introduce a real publish/subscribe model later without affecting any business logic code.

The messages handled by *info* are shown next.

Listing 9.8   nodezoo-info/info.js: message list

```
seneca.add( 'role:info,cmd:get', cmd_get )
  seneca.add( 'role:info,collect:part', collect_part )
```

The `role:info,cmd:get` handler sends out a `role:info,need:part` message, waits 200 milliseconds, and then responds with whatever is in the local cache. Hopefully, the cache has been updated by `role:info,collect:part` messages in the meantime.

Listing 9.9   nodezoo-info/info.js: handler for `role:info,cmd:get`

Waits 200 milliseconds (you could make this configurable) →

Emits a role:info,need:part message, adding a name property for the Node.js module name →

```
function cmd_get (msg, reply) {
  this.act('role:info,need:part', {name: msg.name})

  setTimeout(function () {
    reply(info_cache.get(name) || {})
  }, 200)
}
```

Replies with data in the cache for the module, or an empty object if there's nothing

The `role:info,collect:part` handler accepts part data for Node.js modules. The *npm* and *github* services emit this message asynchronously, and the *info* service listens for it.

Listing 9.10   nodezoo-info/info.js: handler for `role:info,collect:part`

The reply is empty because this message handler is asynchronous.

Updates the data store with the data for this part (either npm or github)

Gets the data store object for the Node.js module with the name msg.name

```
function collect_part (msg, reply) {
  var data = info_cache.get(msg.name) || {}
  data[msg.part] = msg.data
  info_cache.set(name, data)         ← Stores the update

  reply()
}
```

The *info* service is a good example of an orchestration service that coordinates the activities of other services. There's no need for complex external orchestration capabilities when you can define exactly what you need in a new service.

The development execution script needs to provide mock implementations of the *npm* and *github* services, as well as the simulation of the publish/subscribe model. To do this, you inject a new `part` property into the translated `role:info` messages and use it for pattern matching to ensure that messages are routed to the right place.

Listing 9.11   nodezoo-info/srv/info-dev.js: development service execution

```
var Seneca = require('seneca')

Seneca({tag: 'info'})
  .use('../info.js')

  .add('role:info,need:part', function (msg, reply) {
    reply()

      this
        .act(msg, {part:'npm'})
        .act(msg, {part:'github'})
    })

  .use('seneca-repl', {port:10030})

  .listen(9030)

  .client({pin:'role:info,need:part,part:npm', port:9040})
  .client({pin:'role:info,need:part,part:github', port:9050})

var mock = Seneca({tag:'mock'}).client(9030)

if (process.env.MOCK_NPM) {
  mock
    .listen(9040)
    .add('role:info,need:part,part:npm', function (msg, reply) {
      this.act('role:info,collect:part',{
        name: msg.name,
        part: 'npm',
        data: {name: msg.name, version:'1.0.0'}
      })

      reply() }) }
```

Annotations:
- **Replies immediately with no response, because this message is asynchronous** → `reply()`
- **Loads the business logic for the info service** → `.use('../info.js')`
- **Intercepts and translates role:info, need:part messages** → `.add('role:info,need:part', ...`
- **Duplicates the message and sends copies to npm and github, using the part property as a pattern marker**
- **Creates a Seneca instance for service mocking, sending all messages back to info** → `var mock = Seneca({tag:'mock'}).client(9030)`
- **Sends role:info,need:part messages outbound to the right places**
- **Mocks up the role:info,need:part messages for npm, sending a role:info,collect:part in response. The github mock works the same way.**

Here's the current list of port assignments:

- 9010: *web* (not used)
- 9020: *search*
- 9030: *info*
- 9040: *npm*
- 9050: *github*

SERVICE: NPM

This is the last service you need to build for iteration 1. You don't need http://github.com data to build a working Node.js search engine with information pages for each module. The data from npm will be sufficient.

On reflection, you decide that another message is needed. (This often happens when you begin writing the code for a microservice.) Not only do you need flexibility for the query integration with npmjs.com, but you also need to have flexibility in how you extract data from the JSON given back by npm.

Here are the messages for the *npm* service.

Listing 9.12   nodezoo-npm/npm.js: message list

```
seneca.add( 'role:npm,cmd:get', cmd_get )
  seneca.add( 'role:npm,cmd:query', cmd_query )
  seneca.add( 'role:npm,cmd:extract', cmd_extract )
```

You'll store the data locally so you don't have to query http://npmjs.com all the time. The Seneca framework provides an ActiveRecord wrapper for data-persistence messages that makes writing code against them easier.[34] When a role:npm,cmd:get comes in, you have to handle these cases (see listing 9.18):

- You already have the data for the module, so return it.
- You already have the data, but the sender wants the latest data, so you should query again.
- You don't have the data, so you should query and store before returning it.

Listing 9.13   nodezoo-npm/npm.js: handler for `role:npm,cmd:get`

```
                        Creates an ActiveRecord object       Loads the npm entity, using the
                                  for entity npm             Node.js module name as a primary key
function cmd_get (msg, reply) {
  this
    .make$('npm')
    .load$(msg.name, function (err, out) {          If there's no data, or the
      if (err) return reply(err)                    update property is true,
                                                    queries http://npmjs.com
      if (!out || msg.update) {
        return this.act('role:npm,cmd:query', {name: msg.name}, reply)
      }

      return reply(out)
    })                      Sends a role:npm,cmd:query message, and passes the
}                           response onward. Note that Seneca merges all the
                            properties into one message; the syntax is a convenience.
```

The query message handler shown in the next listing needs to send an HTTP request to npm, extract data from the response, and then save the data. We won't look at the implementation of role:npm,cmd:extract, because that's data munging.

---

[34] The *ActiveRecord* pattern provides a data object whose fields are the data fields of your data entity, and whose methods let you perform data operations such as saving, loading, and querying.

Listing 9.14   nodezoo-npm/npm.js: handler for `role:npm,cmd:query`

```
function cmd_query (msg, reply) {
  var seneca  = this
                                              Makes the HTTP call to npm
  Wreck.get( options.registry + msg.name, function (err, res, payload) {  ◄───┐
    if(err) return reply(err)
    var data = JSON.parse(payload.toString())    Calls the role:npm,cmd:extract message

    seneca.act('role:npm,cmd:extract', {data: data}, function (err, data) {  ◄──┘
      if(err) return reply(err)

      this
        .make$('npm')
        .load$(msg.name, function (err, npm) {
          if (err) return reply(err)

          if (!npm) {                    ◄─────┐   If the module isn't in the local
            data.id$ = msg.name                    database, creates a new record
            npm = this.make$('npm')                using the name as identifier
          }
          npm
            .data$(data)
            .save$(reply)
        })
    })
  })
}
```

Updates the module data and saves, returning the data entity → `npm` `.data$(data)` `.save$(reply)`

There's something missing. How does the module data get indexed by Elasticsearch? Where's the `role:search,cmd:insert` message? You need to add some more code to make this happen. You can use pattern matching to keep the primary business logic simple—microservices are supposed to be a component model, after all.[35]

You intercept the data-entity message that saves data. The ActiveRecord method `.save$` generates a message with pattern `role:entity,cmd:save,name:npm`, so that's what you need to override.

Listing 9.15   nodezoo-npm/npm.js: intercept for `role:entity,cmd:save,name:npm`

Replies immediately so you're insulated from the search-index insertion

Uses the prior definition of the message—this saves the data

Redefines the role:entity,cmd:save,name:npm message

```
seneca.add('role:entity,cmd:save,name:npm', function (msg, reply) {  ◄───
  this.prior(msg, function (err, npm) {
    reply(err, npm)
    this.act('role:search,cmd:insert', {data: npm.data$()})    ◄───────┐
  })
}
```

Sends an asynchronous message to the search service to index the module data. This is a Sidewinder interaction.

---

[35] Your message abstraction layer should make it possible to intercept and translate messages locally.

To run the *npm* service in development, you'll need to mock the dependencies on *search* and *info,* and you'll need to translate and respond to `role:info` messages.

Listing 9.16   nodezoo-info/srv/npm-dev.js: development service execution

```
Seneca({tag: 'npm'})
  .use('entity')
  .use('jsonfile-store', {folder: __dirname+'/data'})

  .use('../npm.js')

  .add('role:info,need:part',function (msg, reply) {
    reply()

    this.act( 'role:npm,cmd:get', {name: msg.name}, function (err, mod) {
      if( err ) return reply(err)

      this.act('role:info,collect:part,part:npm',
               {name:msg.name, data:mod.data$()})
    })
  })

  .use('seneca-repl', {port:10040})
  .listen(9040)
  .client({pin:'role:search', port:9020})
  .client({pin:'role:info', port:9030})

var mock = Seneca({tag:'mock'})
...
```

Annotations:
- **Uses the Seneca entity plugin to get the ActiveRecord functionality**
- **Stores the data locally using JSON files. This is sufficient for development and makes debugging easier.**
- **Handles role:info,need:part messages**
- **Translates them into a local role:npm,cmd:get message**
- **Listens for inbound messages on local port 9040**
- **Asynchronously provides information to the info service**
- **A REPL is useful for manual testing of this service.**
- **Sends outbound messages to the right places using pattern matching**

PRACTICALITIES

You now have enough services to run a successful demo at the end of iteration 1. Everything is still on your developer machine, and all the data is ephemeral, but you have a working system. It's worth updating the system diagram to see where you are: see figure 9.7.

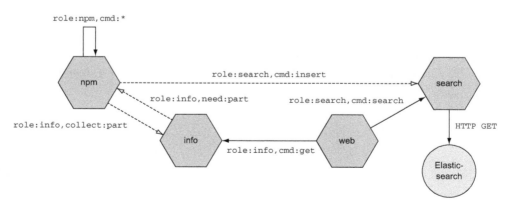

Figure 9.7   The system after iteration 1

Running all the services in separate terminal windows gets old fast. A quick and dirty solution is to write a shell script that launches all the services in the background. You can then stop and start the individual services you want to modify, while the rest of the "system" is running.

You can also use a process manager. The nodezoo system uses a process manager called *fuge*, which is specifically designed for local microservice development.[36] To use fuge, you list all your services in a .yml format configuration file, and then you start an interactive fuge session. You can stop and services, tail log files, restart services when files change, and run multiple instances of services. By keeping all of your development configuration in one place, you don't have to remember the individual configurations needed for each service. The services are executed as ordinary child processes, so you don't need to worry about any complications related to containers or networking.

The system configuration for the various deployments of the nodezoo system is available at www.manning.com/books/the-tao-of-microservices and in the http://github .com/nodezoo/nodezoo-system repository. Here's the fuge configuration file in the fuge folder.

Listing 9.17 nodezoo-system/fuge/fuge.yml: fuge configuration

```
fuge_global:
  tail: true              Each service has its
web:                      own top-level entry.
  type: node
  path: ../../nodezoo-web/srv
  run: node web-dev.js
search:
  type: node
  path: ../../nodezoo-search/srv
  run: node search-dev.js
info:
  type: node
  path: ../../nodezoo-info/srv
  run: node info-dev.js
npm:
  type: node
  path: ../../nodezoo-npm/srv
  run: node npm-dev.js
```

Start fuge by running `fuge shell fuge/fuge.yml` at the command line. Here's an annotated interaction session:

```
$ fuge shell fuge/fuge.yml        Uses the ps command to
> ps                              see the status of services
name            type          status        watch         tail
web             node          stopped       yes           yes
```

---

[36] The fuge tool is maintained by a colleague of mine, Peter Elger, and was written for microservice development. See http://github.com/apparatus/fuge.

Starts all the services (brings up the system)

name	type	status	watch	tail
search	node	stopped	yes	yes
info	node	stopped	yes	yes
npm	node	stopped	yes	yes

```
> start all
... log output ...
> stop search
> ps
```

Stops the search service so you can work on it or test fault tolerance

Starts a new, possibly updated, instance of search

name	type	status	watch	tail
web	node	running	yes	yes
search	node	stopped	yes	yes
info	node	running	yes	yes
npm	node	running	yes	yes

```
> start search
```

9.2.2 Iteration 2: Testing, staging, and risk measurement

You're going to use a three-stage deployment process for nodezoo: development, staging, and production. The workflow for deployment is as follows:

1 Create or update a service.
2 Verify message behavior with unit tests.
3 Build and deploy an artifact to the staging environment.
4 Verify that the staging system still works, using integration and performance tests.
5 Build and deploy an artifact to production, but only if the risk of breakage is sufficiently low (you'll measure this using scoring).
6 Verify that production remains healthy, using a Progressive Canary deployment.
7 Repeat multiple times each day.

The staging system is shared so that you can demonstrate the ability to handle continuous deployments from multiple teams.[37] The on-call developer for this iteration performs the build and deployment to staging.

The purpose of the staging system is to measure the risk of failure in production. You need to generate a score for each service version so that you can make a go/no-go decision on deployment. But staging isn't production—that would be too expensive. Here are the criteria staging has to meet:

- Message transportation should assume multiple hosts and services.
- Multiple instances of services should be running.
- The environment should be lightweight for ease of maintenance and to keep costs down.
- The staging system should validate the correct behavior of services.

For the nodezoo example, a small, single-node Docker swarm is used to keep everything as simple as possible. The Docker swarm functionality makes it easy to deploy and update services. Using Docker also makes it easy to deploy third-party servers like

---

[37] At a larger scale, you might use per-team prestaging environments.

Elasticsearch without worrying too much about configuration. The staging system is assumed to be ephemeral, and data isn't considered persistent beyond the lifetime of a Docker container.

In the development environment, you wired together the services using hard-coded port numbers. This won't scale and is only suitable for prototype systems. A common service-discovery technique is to use a local DNS server and give all of your services hostnames. Each service finds the other services by using predefined host-names. You'll use this approach for staging.[38]

In the development system, you cheated by simulating some of the message-interaction patterns, such as scatter/gather. This was to keep the local development environment simple. On the staging system, you can afford a little more complexity. Let's use Redis (http://redis.io) as a publish/subscribe message bus for the `role:info` interactions. This change also demonstrates the flexibility that maintaining transport independence gives you: you won't need to make any changes to the business-logic code.

You *will* make changes to the execution scripts. For development, you used development scripts. For staging, you'll use separate new scripts. You don't have to worry about mocking or simulating message interactions, so the staging scripts will be simpler.

DOCKER CONFIGURATION

Each service repository has a docker/stage folder. In this folder are a makefile that specifies build instructions for the Docker container that runs the service, and a Dockerfile specifying the contents of the container. The details of these files aren't important; Dockerfiles are mostly about rearranging source files into a consistent folder structure.

The Docker swarm uses an overlay network[39] to allow containers running services to talk to each other. Each service is represented by its own hostname, and Docker makes sure DNS lookups of services by name work properly. Most of the ports exposed by the services aren't exposed outside the overlay network, because they're used for inter-service communication. Some of the services, such as *web*, do need external exposure, and the Docker configuration reflects this. Third-party containers are used to provide certain facilities to the services. You've already used Docker to run Elastic-search, and you'll continue to do so, modifying the configuration slightly to fit into the swarm model. You'll also run a Redis container. Finally, you'll run a custom container to capture risk-measurement statistics. This container uses the open source tools StatsD (http://github.com/etsy/statsd) and Graphite (http://graphiteapp.org) to keep a running score of the risk of deployment. The nodezoo system uses some custom code to capture and submit risk measurements to this container. A nice chart of

---

[38] I'm overloading the demonstration of service-discovery strategies with deployment stages. My preference in the real world, at the time of writing, is to use peer-to-peer for all environments, because it has low maintenance costs.

[39] An *overlay network* is a virtual private network with its own IP address space, overlaid on the network of the host system.

the overall risk score (you'll see how to build this soon) tells you whether it's safe to deploy a service to production.

To start the system, enter the nodezoo-system folder and run this command:[40]

```
$ docker stack deploy -c stage/nodezoo.yml nodezoo
```

STAGED SERVICES

Let's review the execution scripts for staged services and compare them to the development execution scripts. The *web* service can remove mocking code and the REPL, as shown in the following listing.

Listing 9.18 nodezoo-web/srv/web-stage.js: staged service execution

Application business logic remains the same.

All services now listen on port 9000 in their own container, but you allow for variations.

```
var PORT = process.env.PORT || 9000
var Seneca = require('seneca')
var app = require('../web.js')

Seneca({tag: 'web'})
  .listen(PORT)

  .client({pin:'role:search', host:'search', port:PORT})
  .client({pin:'role:info', host:'info', port:PORT})
  .client({pin:'role:suggest', host:'suggest', port:PORT})

  .ready(function(){
    var server = app({seneca: this})
    this.log.info(server.info)
  })
```

Service listens for inbound messages on port 9000, ignoring those it doesn't recognize.

Location of other services is defined by a hostname, not a port. This is more scalable.

The *search* service is almost exactly the same as before, except you remove the REPL. The *info* service is more interesting. The mocks and message simulation are gone, and the message transport is Redis.

Listing 9.19 nodezoo-info/srv/info-stage.js: staged service execution

Loads the Redis message transport plugin.

```
var PORT = process.env.PORT || 9000
var Seneca = require('seneca')

Seneca({tag: 'info'})
  .listen(PORT)

  .use('redis-transport')
  .use('../info.js')

  .client({pin:'role:info,need:part', type:'redis', host:'redis'})
  .listen({pin:'role:info,collect:part', type:'redis', host:'redis'})
```

Transports messages via the Redis server, running on the Redis host container. You no longer need to know the location of the npm service.

---

[40] Docker Swarm, which orchestrates multiple containers over multiple machines, lets you specify an entire system using a .yml format configuration file. See http://docs.docker.com.

The *npm* service is modified in the same manner, as shown next.

Listing 9.20   nodezoo-npm/srv/npm-stage.js: staged service execution

```
var PORT = process.env.PORT || 9000
var Seneca = require('seneca')

Seneca({tag: 'npm'})
  .listen(PORT)
  .use('redis-transport')                                   ← Uses the Redis
  .use('entity')                                              message transport
  .use('jsonfile-store', {folder: __dirname+'/../data'})

  .use('../npm.js')                                         ─┐ You still need to translate
  .add('role:info,need:part',function(msg,reply){         ← │ role:info messages.
    reply()

    this.act(
      'role:npm,cmd:get',
      {name:msg.name},
      function(err,mod){                                       Uses Redis for
        if( err ) return reply(err)                            role:info messages

        this.act('role:info,collect:part,part:npm',
                 {name:msg.name, data:this.util.clean(mod.data$())})
    })
  })
  .listen({pin:'role:info,need:part', type:'redis', host:'redis'})   ←──┘
  .client({pin:'role:info,collect:part', type:'redis', host:'redis'})

  .client({pin:'role:search', host:'search', port:PORT})  ←─┐ You still need an explicit
                                                            │ route to the search
                                                            │ service for indexing.
```

VALIDATION SERVICES

You seem to have lost the useful ability to REPL into the system. Let's fix that by writing a specific REPL service. Seneca makes this easy: you just need to route messages correctly by pattern. You'll often find it useful to have a REPL service in staging and production, because it gives you the ability to manually inject messages for diagnosis and testing. The Docker configuration exposes the REPL port outside the overlay network, allowing you access.

Listing 9.21   nodezoo-repl/srv/repl-stage.js: staged service execution

```
var PORT = process.env.PORT || 9000
var REPL_PORT = process.env.REPL_PORT || 10000
var REPL_HOST = process.env.REPL_HOST || '0.0.0.0'

var Seneca = require('seneca')

Seneca({tag: 'repl'})
  .listen(PORT)
                                                            ─┐ REPL service has
  .use('seneca-repl', {port:REPL_PORT, host:REPL_HOST})   ← │ no business logic
```

```
.client({pin:'role:search', host:'search', port:PORT})
.client({pin:'role:info', host:'info', port:PORT})
.client({pin:'role:npm', host:'npm', port:PORT})
```

Forwards messages
to the appropriate
service

When the system is running, you can submit a standard set of messages to validate behavior. Correct responses to these messages indicate that the system is healthy. The easiest way to set this up is to create a validation service that you can trigger with a message; this lets you execute the validation when you want to measure the deployment risk of a new service. You can also run the validation service on a regular rotation, to pick up emerging problems in production.

Where do you store the results of this health measurement? In your own system, you'll need to make choices about how much of this measurement system to build yourself to meet your needs exactly, and how much to co-opt from existing solutions for this new purpose. For the nodezoo example, you'll reuse the StatsD and Graphite monitoring tools. You'll define a set of gauges to measure the health of various parts of the system. A *gauge* is a numeric level that moves up and down; if a service is behaving correctly, you give the gauge a value of 1, and it's behaving incorrectly, the gauge gets a value of 0. We're keeping things simple here, but you can expand this approach to suit your needs.

The validation service is mostly journeyman code to test each service by sending standard messages to it. Here's a small sample of code that validates the *npm* service:

```
seneca
  .act('role:npm,cmd:get,name:nid', function (err, out) {
    if (err) {
      validation.errors.push(err)
      validation.services.npm = false
      return done()
    }

    validation.services.npm = ( 'nid' === out.id )

    done()
  })
```

Simple Boolean flag
to indicate pass/fail

Extremely simple
test to validate the
message response

The validation service must be able to send any message in the system. The simplest way to do that is to use the REPL service, which can already do that.

You need to measure a few more things before you have a good handle on deployment risk. You want to know whether unit tests are passing, and you want to know whether performance is acceptable. For the unit tests, you can write a script to run them and then update the gauges for each test. As with the messages, each gauge value is 0 (failing) or 1 (passing). For performance, you write a script using a performance-measuring tool,[41] using the 90th percentile response time for each endpoint you want to measure as the value of the gauge.

---

[41] The example code uses the venerable Apache ab load tester (httpd.apache.org/docs/current/programs/ab.html).

To calculate a deployment-risk score, combine all of these gauges by normalizing and weighting them. You're trying to come up with a number between 0 and 100 as the score. Let's arbitrarily decide that you need a score of 95 or above to deploy; you can change this later as you learn more about the risk profile of the system or the risk appetite of the business changes. It's more sensible, mathematically, to generate a score between 0 and 1 and multiply by 100, so let's do that. You have three categories: unit tests, service tests, and performance tests. Assign decimal weights that add up to 1:

- Unit tests—0.3
- Service tests—0.4
- Performance—0.3

Convert each gauge to a number between 0 and 1, and then multiply by the weighting divided by the number of gauges in each category. Add these up to get the score. The unit tests and service tests can only have values 0 and 1, so they're already in the correct range. For the performance results, subtract the millisecond value from the maximum response time you find acceptable. You've agreed with the business stakeholders that any time over 1,000 ms is a fail for nodezoo. If the 90th percentile response time is 400 ms, that's pretty good and should get a better score than, say, 800 ms. Subtracting from 1,000 and normalizing gives this calculation: $(1,000 - 400)/1,000 = 0.6$.[42] You do this so that higher scores mean lower deployment risk, because you're trying to get over that 95 mark.

Next, generate a Graphite chart to show the score. The team decided previously that you need a score of 95 to deploy, as shown by the target line. In the chart shown in figure 9.8, the deployment-risk score (the moving line) falls below 95 when you

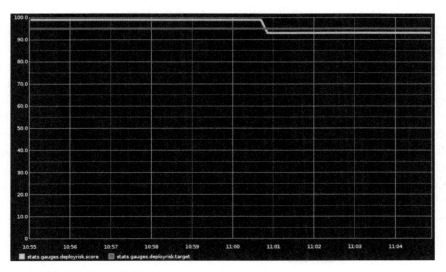

Figure 9.8 Deployment-risk score

---

[42] See the source code file deployrisk.js in the nodezoo-system repository for the full calculation of the score. 800 ms gives $(1000 - 800)/1000 = 0.2$, a lower score, which means higher deployment risk, which is what you want from the risk calculation.

measure a new version of the *search* service, because you've introduced a bug that makes it much slower; thus, this deployment is rejected.

9.2.3   *Iteration 3: The path to production*

To run your system in production, you'll need to automate the delivery of validated artifacts from the staging system to the production system. You'll need automation to implement deployment patterns such as Canary, Progressive Canary, and Bake. Your production automation should adhere to a few key principles:

- *Immutable units of deployment*—Whatever you deploy, whether containers, virtual machine images, or some other abstraction, it shouldn't be possible to modify running deployment instances. You change the system by deploying or scaling, not by modifying.

- *Ephemeral units of deployment*—You must work under the assumption that you'll have high turnover of the units of deployment, and that this constant killing and launching won't be under your control.

- *Scriptable via a well-defined API*—You need this to meet the automation requirements for microservices.

- *Declarative system definition*—The entire system architecture, from networking to storage, from load balancing to monitoring, must be something you can describe in code.

You can build a production-quality deployment system for microservices using many tools, both old and new.[43] For the nodezoo example, you'll use Kubernetes.[44] This lets you reuse the Docker container definitions from the staging system. A full description of Kubernetes, or any production-management system, is beyond the scope of this book; the nodezoo example should be taken merely as a starting point.

For the production system, you'll also use another message transport. The seneca-mesh plugin (http://github.com/senecajs/seneca-mesh) provides a peer-to-peer service-discovery mechanism that makes production scaling and modification easy, because the system self-organizes. As each service joins the network, it advertises the message patterns it can respond to and whether it's a consumer or an observer. This information is disseminated throughout the entire network via an infection-style protocol.[45] The message abstraction layer on each service maintains a routing table for all patterns and provides a local load balancer that can send messages using round-robin or broadcast mode, depending on the consumer or observer status of the message-destination service.

---

[43] See chapter 5.

[44] An open source version of Google's orchestration approach: see https://kubernetes.io.

[45] Seneca-mesh uses the SWIM algorithm. See Abhinandan Das, Indranil Gupta, and Ashish Motivala, "SWIM: Scalable Weakly-consistent Infection-style Process Group Membership Protocol," Proceedings of the 2002 International Conference on Dependable Systems and Networks (2002), http://mng.bz/SOAW.

Kubernetes provides a *pod* abstraction to run containers. Each pod gets its own IP address, and each pod is reachable from any other pod.[46] This is perfect for a peer-to-peer network. To access the system, you expose the nodezoo website and the REPL as external service ports.

THE SERVICE-EXECUTION SCRIPTS

To join the seneca-mesh network, each service needs to connect to at least one other member of the network on startup. Although any member will do, it makes sense to designate some members as well-known base nodes, to simplify configuration. In the example code, the REPL service is used as a base node. In the execution script, it's *no longer necessary to specify the locations of the other services*, because these will be resolved at runtime by the peer-to-peer network (which is the principle advantage you're seeking).

Listing 9.22 nodezoo-repl/srv/repl-prod.js: production execution script

```
Seneca({tag: 'repl'})

  .use('mesh', {          ← Uses a peer-to-peer
    base: true,              service-discovery mesh
    host: '@eth0',
    port: 39000,          ← Uses the Kubernetes pod IP
  })                         address, on network interface
                             eth0, as the location of the service
  .use('seneca-repl', {   ← Exposes a REPL on port 10000, to be
    host: '0.0.0.0',         configured as a Kubernetes service
    port: 10000
  })
```

A base node → `.use('mesh', {`

Uses port 39000 as the base-node port → `port: 39000,`

True to our principles, the system definition is fully defined in a Kubernetes system configuration file. The following listing shows the relevant sections for the *repl* service.

Listing 9.23 nodezoo-system/prod/nodezoo.yml: repl service configuration

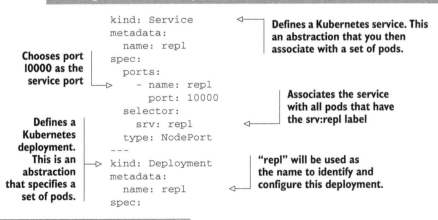

```
kind: Service          ← Defines a Kubernetes service. This
metadata:                 an abstraction that you then
  name: repl              associate with a set of pods.
spec:
  ports:
    - name: repl
      port: 10000
  selector:            ← Associates the service
    srv: repl             with all pods that have
  type: NodePort          the srv:repl label
---
kind: Deployment       ← "repl" will be used as
metadata:                 the name to identify and
  name: repl              configure this deployment.
spec:
```

Chooses port 10000 as the service port

Defines a Kubernetes deployment. This is an abstraction that specifies a set of pods.

---

[46] See the Kubernetes documentation for more about networking.

```
replicas: 1
template:
  metadata:
    labels:
        srv: repl
spec:
  containers:
  - name: repl
      image: nodezoo-repl-prod:1
```

⤙ **This is a base node, so you want only one instance. In a full production system, you'd have multiple base-node deployments for redundancy.**

Name and version of the production container for the repl service

The Kubernetes configuration for the remaining services mostly follows this deployment configuration, changing only the service name in each case.

The *web* service production execution script no longer needs a port number as configuration; rather, it needs the list of base nodes. These are provided as an environment variable. You can get the Kubernetes network IPs for all your pods as follows:

```
$ kubectl get pods -o wide
```

The *web* service uses the base node list to connect to the mesh.

Listing 9.24   nodezoo-web/srv/web-prod.js: production execution script

Again, uses the IP address of network interface eth0 as the service location

```
Seneca({tag: 'web'})
  .use('mesh', {
    bases: process.env.BASES,
    host: '@eth0'
  })
```

Gets the list of base nodes from the environment

The Kubernetes deployment includes the base-node IP list.

Listing 9.25   nodezoo-system/prod/nodezoo.yml: Kubernetes configuration

```
kind: Deployment
metadata:
  name: web
spec:
  replicas: 1
  template:
    metadata:
      labels:
          srv: web
    spec:
      containers:
      - name: web
          image: nodezoo-web-prod:1
          env:
          - name: BASES
            value: "<REPL-POD-IP>:39000"
```

Base-node list

The *web* service also needs a Kubernetes service so that it can be accessed from outside the Kubernetes network. In the example code, a port is exposed directly. In a full production system, you instead expose the service via an external load balancer.

Listing 9.26   nodezoo-system/prod/nodezoo.yml: repl service configuration

```
kind: Service
metadata:
  name: web
spec:
  ports:
    - name: web
      port: 8000
  selector:
    srv: web
  type: NodePort
```

The production execution script for the *search* service must advertise that it can handle `role:search` messages.

Listing 9.27   nodezoo-repl/srv/search-prod.js: production execution script

```
Seneca({tag: 'search'})
  .use('../search.js', {
    elastic: {
      host:  process.env.ELASTIC_SERVICE_HOST
    }
  })

  .use('mesh', {
    pin: 'role:search',
    bases: process.env.BASES,
    host: '@eth0'
  })
```

The location of Elasticsearch is provided via a Kubernetes service definition.

The search service expects to consume all role:search messages.

When the *search* service joins the network, all other services will update their message-pattern matchers to route messages with `role:search` to the location of the *search* service, given by the assigned Kubernetes pod IP.[47]

The *info* and *npm* services work together using a scatter/gather interaction. To make this work in the mesh network, the *info* service still publishes `role:info,need:part` messages, but it needs to advertise that it will observe `role:info,collect:part` messages.

Listing 9.28   nodezoo-info/srv/info-prod.js: production execution script

```
Seneca({tag: 'info'})
  .use('../info.js')

  .use('mesh', {
```

[47] Seneca-mesh randomly chooses a port on the pod IP.

```
   listen: [
     {pin: 'role:info,cmd:get'},
     {pin: 'role:info,collect:part', model:'observe'}
   ],
   bases: process.env.BASES,
   host: '@eth0',
})
```

Consumes role:info,cmd:get messages synchronously, sent by the web service as usual

Observes role:info, collect:part messages asynchronously

Conversely, the *npm* service observes role:info,need:part but publishes role:info, collect:part.

Listing 9.29   nodezoo-npm/srv/npm-prod.js: production execution script

```
Seneca({tag: 'npm'})
  ...
  .use('../npm.js')

  .add('role:info,need:part',function(msg,reply){
    ...
  })

  .use('mesh', {
    listen: [
      {pin: 'role:npm'},
      {pin: 'role:info,need:part', model:'observe'}
    ],
    bases: BASES,
    host: '@eth0',
  })
```

Message translation remains unchanged

Consumes role:npm messages synchronously, as usual

Observes role:info, need:part messages asynchronously

You now have a three-stage workflow for deploying microservices. The business logic for each microservice remains the same, but you connect the microservices differently in each environment, depending on scale and resources. The use of a message-abstraction layer makes this not only possible, but also a matter of configuration.

9.2.4   *Iteration 4: Enhancing and adapting*

With your deployment workflow in place, you can get down to the main work of the project: iterating on the BRs to deliver value. Just pulling data from npm doesn't realize the full vision of the search engine; you also need to pull data from other sources. Most Node.js modules are hosted as open source on GitHub, so that's an obvious place to start.

ADDING A DATA SOURCE

You designed the role:info message interaction to be extensible, because adding new data sources was a definite early requirement. Let's see how that plays out. The *github* service will integrate with http://github.com and have its own set of role:github messages, analogous to the role:npm messages. The *github* service will also participate in the role:info interaction in the same way as the *npm* service.

There's one way in which the *github* and *npm* services differ; it's an implicit design assumption that now bares its teeth. You're using the *npm* service as a system of record— a source of truth. Where will the *github* service get the http://github.com repository URL for any given module? From the *npm* service, which stores that data field. Should you then consider a more abstract service that both the *npm* and *github* services use, and remove this coupling between them? Consider that, in the future, you may introduce services that have a dependency on the http://github.com data. Things could get messy.

On the other hand, this feels like overdesign. You have to make a trade-off between the immediate simplicity of using the *npm* service directly and the more flexible approach of introducing a core data service. Bear in mind that this system is young, and you're not yet sure what the core data is. The pattern-matching approach to messages can help here. You know that you can pattern-match your way out of trouble. If you decide to add a core data service, you can translate the old messages into messages bound for the core data service. With this insurance in mind, the decision becomes easier: you'll talk to the *npm* service directly for now.

Listing 9.30   nodezoo-github/github.js: business logic code

```
seneca.add( 'role:github,cmd:get', cmd_get )
  seneca.add( 'role:github,cmd:query', cmd_query )

  function cmd_get( msg, reply ) {
    this
      .make$('github')
      .load$( msg.name, function (err, mod) {
        if( err ) return reply(err)

        if( mod ) {                         ◁──┐  If the http://github.com data
          return reply(mod)                      already exists, respond with it.
        }

        var m = /[\/:]([^\/:]+?)[\/:]([^\/]+?)(\.git)*$/.exec(msg.giturl)  ◁──┐
        if (!m) return reply()
                                                        Uses a regular expression
        this.act(                                       to extract the owner and
          {                                           repository name from the
            role: 'github',                                          GitHub URL
            cmd: 'query',
            name: msg.name,
            owner: m[1],
            repo: m[2]
          },
          reply)
      })
  }


  function cmd_query( msg, reply ) {
    var seneca      = this
```

Queries the GitHub API to get data for the module repository

```
gitapi.repos.get(                              ◄─┐  Queries the GitHub API to get
    { owner: msg.owner, repo: msg.repo },        │  data for the module repository
    function (err, out) {
      if (err) return reply(err)
```

Stores the → `var data = {`
data you   `owner:    msg.owner,`
care about   `repo:     msg.repo,`
                `stars:    out.data.stargazers_count,`
                `watches:  out.data.subscribers_count,`
                `forks:    out.data.forks_count,`
                `last:     out.data.pushed_at`
              `}`

```
      seneca
        .make$('github')
        .load$(msg.name, function (err, mod) {
          if (err) return reply(err)

          if (mod) {                    ◄──┐  If the module exists,
            return mod                     │  updates the data
              .data$(data)
              .save$(reply)
```

Otherwise, `          }`
creates a `          else {`
new record `            data.id$ = msg.name`
             `            seneca`
             `              .make$('github')`
             `              .data$(data)`
             `              .save$(reply)`
         `} }) }) } }`

To run the *github* service, you need to translate the `role:info,need:part` message as with the *npm* service. There's a complication: you'll need to get the http://github.com URL from the *npm* service if you don't have it already. You're building up a worrying volume of code in the *github* service execution script, but you can deal with this down the road by moving the business logic into a separate Seneca plugin. The reason you tolerate this is to avoid hardcoding the `role:info` interaction into the *github* service; you want to retain flexibility in how you wire services together.

Listing 9.31   nodezoo-github/srv/github-prod.js: execution script

```
Seneca({tag: 'github'})
  ...
  .use('../github.js')                                   The role:info,
                                                         need:part message
  .add('role:info,need:part', function (msg, reply) {    is asynchronous, so
    reply()                                  ◄──┘        return immediately.

    this.act(
      'role:github,cmd:get', {name:msg.name},
      function (err, mod) {
```

```
    if (err) return
    if (mod) {
      return this.act('role:info,collect:part,part:github',
                      {name:msg.name,data:mod.data$()})
    }
    this.act(
      'role:npm,cmd:get', {name:msg.name},
      function (err, mod) {
        if (err) return

        if (mod) {
          this.act(
            'role:github,cmd:get', {name:msg.name, giturl:mod.giturl},
            function( err, mod ){
              if (err) return

              if (mod) {
                this.act('role:info,collect:part,part:github',
                         {name:msg.name,data:mod.data$()})
              }
          })
        }
      })
    })
  })
  .use('mesh', {
    listen: [
      {pin: 'role:github'},
      {pin: 'role:info,need:part', model:'observe'}
    ],
    bases: process.env.BASES,
    host: '@eth0',
  })
```

Annotations in the code:
- **If you have the data, sends it back via role:info,collect:part** — pointing to the `return this.act('role:info,collect:part,part:github'...` line
- **Uses the npm service to get the http://github.com URL** — pointing to the `this.act('role:npm,cmd:get', ...)` line
- **Joins the production mesh as normal, with the same pattern exposure as npm** — pointing to the `.use('mesh', {` line

To deploy this service to production, run through the deployment workflow. Develop locally, and validate with unit tests and manual integration testing. Next, deploy to staging, and measure deployment risk by running the validation service. Then, deploy to production using the Progressive Canary pattern.

The `role:info` interaction makes it easy to add more external data sources that describe Node.js modules. This is one of the benefits of the scatter/gather interaction.

ADDING A FEATURE

Let's look at the introduction of a feature you haven't accounted for in the message patterns. Suppose you want to provide autocompletion on the search field. That is, when you start typing, a list of previous searches will come up so that you can choose one as a shortcut. To implement this, think about the messages first. You need a suggestion when there's a search term, and you need to store suggestions:

- `role:suggest,cmd:suggest`—Responds with a list of suggestions
- `role:suggest,cmd:add`—Adds a search term

The frontend code should present an interactive context menu for the suggestions. We won't focus on that code, but it's at www.manning.com/books/the-tao-of-microservices and http://github.com/nodezoo/nodezoo-web, if you're interested.

What are the message interactions? Clearly, the *web* service needs to send `role:suggest,cmd:suggest` to get suggestions. Who sends `role:suggest,cmd:add`? It's probably best sent by the *search* service, because that's where you know you have a full search term.

You'll implement a *suggest* service that can handle these messages. How do you generate suggestions from previously seen searches? You use a trie data structure,[48] which allows you to look up all the searches with a given prefix (what the user has typed so far). To keep things simple, you'll store the suggestions in memory on a per-service instance basis, without persistence. You can always add this later in an improved version of the *suggest* service. For now, you just want to get things working for your next demo; this will still work in production. The *suggest* instances will live for a few days each and build up enough searches to be useful. If you have multiple instances, many will build up a decent number of search terms most of the time. Good enough is good enough. Perhaps later you'll find that this feature isn't that valuable and will remove it, without having wasted development time making it better than necessary.

The *web* service needs to be updated first. You'll modify it so that it sends `role:suggest` messages but can handle the complete lack of responses. There are never suggestions for any search. You deploy this new version of the *web* service to production first and verify that nothing breaks. This approach is a good example of the general strategy to take when you have to introduce or change dependencies between microservices: create production mocks. Your message abstraction layer should make this easy, because it's essential for one-service-at-a-time production changes.[49]

Listing 9.32 nodezoo-web/web.js: API code

```
server.route({
  method: 'GET', path: '/api/suggest',         ◁——  Exposes an API for suggestions
  handler: function( request, reply ){               on URL path /api/suggest
    server.seneca.act(
      'role:suggest,cmd:suggest',{query:request.query.q,default$:[]},   ◁——
      function(err,out){
        reply(out||[])                          Looks for suggestions, but assumes
      })                                            there may not be an answer
  }})
```

The *search* service needs to be updated next and should be similarly fault tolerant. Do you need to change the business logic of the *search* service? No, because all you need to know is that a `role:search,cmd:search` message has been received. You extract

---

[48] The *trie* data structure stores data keyed by prefix string, so it's highly appropriate for this use case. See http://wikipedia.org/wiki/Trie.

[49] Seneca provides the `default$` message directive to support this case.

the search term and send it to the *suggest* service. This can be done as part of the message pattern configuration in the execution script.

Listing 9.33   nodezoo-search/search.js: API code

**Overrides the role:search,cmd:search pattern,
passing on the message to the original action**

```
seneca
  .add('role:search,cmd:search', function (msg, reply) {
    this.prior(msg, reply)

    this.act('role:suggest,cmd:add',{query:msg.query,default$:{}})
})
```

**Asynchronously sends the search terms to the
suggest service, allowing for the service not to exist**

Deploy this updated version of the *search* service to production, and validate that everything is healthy. Now, you can finally introduce the *suggest* service and allow the mesh (and thus *web* and *search*) to discover that it can handle role:suggest messages. First, here's the business logic.

Listing 9.34   nodezoo-suggest/suggest.js: business logic

```
seneca.add( 'role:suggest,cmd:add', cmd_add )
  seneca.add( 'role:suggest,cmd:suggest', cmd_suggest )

  var trie = Trie([])

  function cmd_add (msg, reply) {
    trie.addWord(''+msg.query)
    reply()
  }

  function cmd_suggest( msg, reply ) {
    var q = ''+msg.query
    reply('' === q ? [] : (trie.getPrefix(q) || []))
  }
```

**In-memory trie
data structure**

And here's the execution script.

Listing 9.35   nodezoo-suggest/ssrv/suggest-prod.js: production execution script

```
Seneca({tag: 'suggest'})
  .use('../suggest.js')

  .use('mesh', {
    pin: 'role:suggest',
    bases: BASES,
    host: '@eth0',
  })
```

**Advertises that
role:suggest messages
are welcome here**

EXTENDING THE SYSTEM

One major piece of functionality is missing from your system: you still have to trigger indexing of Node.js modules manually by deliberately loading them via the information page. This causes the *npm*, *github*, and *search* services to do their thing, and the Node.js module ends up in the system. This was sufficient for demonstration purposes, but not for going live in production.

You need to listen for ongoing updates to modules and populate the system with an initial set of data. The npm API lets you do both: you can download a list of all modules at any time, and you can listen to a stream of module updates. With a list of modules, you can feed the modules into your system one at a time. This is equivalent to handling module updates, because both approaches provide a stream of modules to index. All you need to implement is a service that can handle a stream of module-update events. For each event, you'll emit a `role:info,event:change` message and let the other services do the hard work. The *npm* service, for one, will generate an internal `role:npm,cmd:get`.

The logistics for downloading the current list of modules and listening to the npm feed are mostly mechanical and of little interest; details are in the downloadable source code. The only lines you care about in the *updater* service are shown next.

Listing 9.36   nodezoo-updater/updater.js: production execution script

```
feed.on('change',function(change) {
  seneca.act('role:info,event:change',{name:change.name})    ←┐
})
                                      Sends this message asynchronously,
                                      because you don't use the response
```

The *updater* service can be deployed without changes to the other services. It may seem strange that you can gloss over such a fundamental element of the system, but because the microservice architecture has isolated everything so nicely, you don't have to do so much thinking!

9.2.5   *Iteration 5: Monitoring and debugging*

Once you have a basic system and workflow in place, you can add monitoring. To take a message-oriented perspective, you need to monitor message-flow rates. You also need to monitor your invariants: the ratios of specific message-flow rates that shouldn't change, whatever the load on the system.

The nodezoo system uses StatsD and Graphite to monitor message flows and invariants. The seneca-statsd plugin counts the number of message patterns seen using StatsD, and the Graphite time series system converts these counts to flow rates per second.

Consider the search interaction. A `role:search,cmd:search` message is generated for each search. You can track the flow rate of this message to see the number of searches per second, independent of the number of *web* or *search* service instances. Each time a user searches, you also generate a `role:suggest,cmd:add` message to store the search term for autocompletion suggestions. Because there's one `role:suggest,cmd:add` for each search, the ratio of these flow rates should be around 1.[50] If something is broken in this interaction, the invariant will diverge from the value 1. Whenever you deploy a new version of the *web*, *search*, or *suggest* services, you can use this invariant to verify that the system is healthy.

Figure 9.9 shows the flow rates for the individual messages, as well as the invariants. Notice that the number of searches per second is 1 initially and increases to 5 about halfway through the timeline. The invariant remains at 1 throughout, as it should.[51]

You also want to generate a scatterplot of current versus historical response times for a selection of messages. To build the scatterplot, you'll need to write some custom scripts.[52] In a production system, you'll run these scripts periodically and after deployments, to

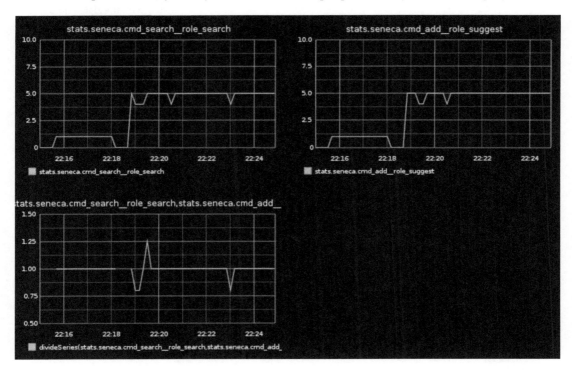

Figure 9.9   Message-flow rates and invariants

---

[50] Remember that ratios are dimensionless.
[51] This sample usage data is generated by a script that's included with the downloadable files.
[52] Again, included with the downloadable files.

verify that performance hasn't been affected by recent changes. Figure 9.10 shows a current behavior scatterplot of nodezoo messages over a 200-second period.

This system looks pretty healthy. There are no obvious outlier messages.

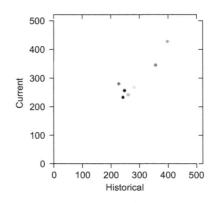

Figure 9.10   Current behavior for message response times

TRACING

The nodezoo example system uses the Zipkin (http://zipkin.io) distributed tracer to follow message causality through the system. The downloadable files include a container configuration for Zipkin. To trace messages, add the seneca-zipkin-tracer plugin to your execution scripts:

```
seneca.use('zipkin-tracer', {host: "zip.kin"})
```
◁——— **Assumes there's a Zipkin instance on the zipkin host**

Using Zipkin to trace the nodezoo system generates the service dependency diagram shown in figure 9.11, which correlates to the original microservice design diagrams but is built dynamically from actual message flows.

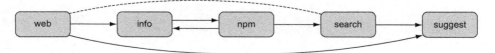

Figure 9.11   Dynamic service relationships

Zipkin generates this diagram by sampling message flows through the system. Figure 9.12 shows a sample message flow for a search.

LOGGING

In the first iteration, you examined individual service logs directly. The demo system was small enough to make this practical. When you build out the staging and production systems, you'll need a scalable logging solution. Sending logs from every service

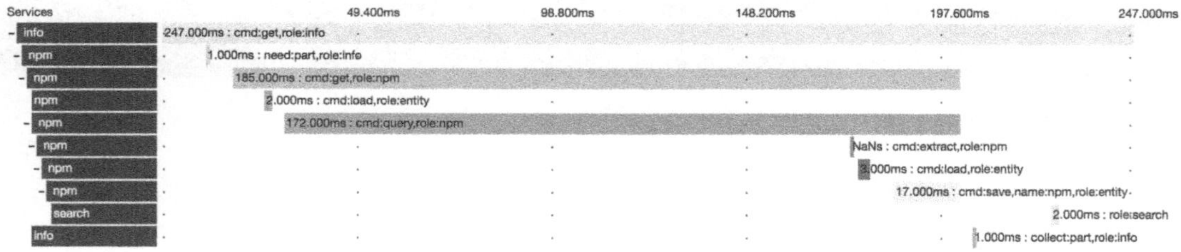

Figure 9.12   Trace of the search message flow over services

to a central location for indexing will enable you to search and review logs from the entire system easily. This is particularly useful when you want to trace a message flow using a correlation identifier.

For log indexing and searching, you can use a commercial service,[53] or you can run your own log indexer. The nodezoo example system uses a local ELK stack.[54] This reuses the existing Elasticsearch server, although in production you'll need to use a separate Elasticsearch cluster for logs.

The Docker containers are configured to log to a remote *syslog* driver, where *Logstash* is waiting to receive the logs. This is just one of many possible configurations; you'll need to determine the best approach for your system. Figure 9.13 shows some log entries for a search interaction.

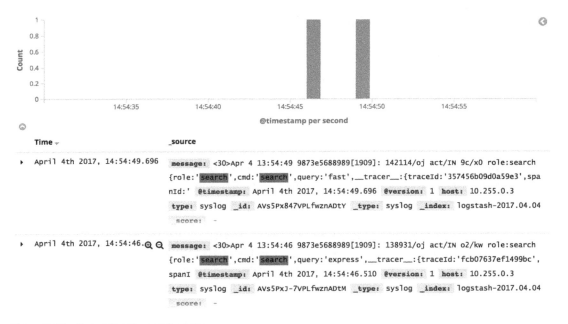

Figure 9.13   Searching the service logs

DEBUGGING

To debug a production microservice system, you need to be able to submit messages manually and review the results. For this purpose, you should always write and deploy a REPL service. Extra care is needed here to secure this service, but it's worth the effort. The nodezoo system exposes a REPL on port 10000. Here's a search interaction:

[53] Such as New Relic (http://newrelic.com) or Logentries (http://logentries.com).

[54] ELK—Elasticsearch, Logstash, and Kibana—is an open source log-capture and -visualization suite provided by Elastic (http://elastic.co).

```
seneca 3.3.0 d5.../14.../1/3.3.0/repl> role:search,cmd:search,query:nid
IN  000000: { role: 'search', cmd: 'search', query: 'nid' }
OUT 000000: { items:
   [ { name: 'nid',
       version: '0.3.2',
       giturl: 'git://github.com/rjrodger/nid.git',
       desc: 'Nice clean-
    mouthed random id generation, without any swearing!',
       readme: '# nid\n\n### Nice clean-mouthed random id generation...',
       id: 'nid' } ] }
```

By submitting messages into the system at various points in the message flows and reviewing log output, you can verify and debug production behavior. The REPL is also useful as a management tool for the production system.

9.2.6   *Iteration 6: Scaling and performance*

As you build out and refine your production system, your user base will grow, and you'll need to make sure your architecture can meet its performance and scale goals. These were part of the original business requirements, after all. The performance goals are easily met at first, but as the load on the system grows, you need to consider how your message interactions and services will scale.

THE WEB SERVICE

This service is stateless. In the nodezoo system, it has multiple jobs: serving static and dynamic content, and providing an API. You can break these functions into separate services to scale each separately. Even within each function, you can write separate services for individual pages or API endpoints; this becomes necessary over time, as complexity grows.

It's important to maintain the stateless nature of the service. This gives you horizontal scalability: you can handle higher loads by adding more service instances. The *web* service isn't problematic from a load-scaling perspective.

It does require a little more work from a development-scaling perspective. Once you have multiple teams, you'll have to coordinate the use of presentation resources for the frontend and manage the development of the frontend code. This is no small challenge, which this book has deliberately ignored. You'll certainly need more automation to ensure consistency of look and feel. It may be worth considering keeping all frontend microservices in the same monorepo, because the frontend developers have to do more coordination work anyway.

THE SEARCH SERVICE

This service is also stateless; it's a wrapper for Elasticsearch. Its message interactions are request/response and fire-and-forget, so it doesn't matter which service instance you talk to. This service can be scaled horizontally without any changes.

What about search performance? Assuming that you've fine-tuned your Elasticsearch cluster, you still pay a penalty for the extra network hop from the *web* service to the *search* service. By the time this becomes an issue, you'll have extracted the search

API into its own service. If you haven't, now is a good time to do so. The search API service and the *search* service can be merged to reduce latency: merging services once performance-sensitive message flows have become apparent is a valid, intentional strategy option.

Don't remove the old search service. There's no reason to do so, and you'll probably need to have it available for feature extension and general use by other services. Cutting and pasting service code to form new services, or merging the code into existing services, is allowed and encouraged. This isn't a monolith, and you aren't building technical debt. You won't have to extend and adapt your data structures or object models to handle new functionality.

THE INFO SERVICE

This service isn't stateless. It maintains an internal cache of Node.js module information and is continuously running a scatter/gather interaction. It seems as though everybody has to talk to the same instance, because otherwise data would end up at the wrong *info* service instance most of the time. An easy way to scale this service is to do so vertically. Hardware is always cheaper than development effort—run it alone on a big machine with lots of memory. This approach will take you far.

You're vulnerable to crashes, but the impact is limited. Some visitors won't get complete module information on the information page, but that will be transient once the service has rebooted. This is within your acceptable error rate.

But the day will come when vertical scaling no longer makes sense cost-wise, or when your error rate must be tightened.[55] How can you scale *info* horizontally? By using message-pattern-matching. Add a unique per-instance marker property to the scatter/gather messages. The data-source services, such as *npm*, can then include this property as part of their `role:info,collect:part` response messages. The message-abstraction layer ensures that messages make their way back to the correct *info* service instance. This approach works particularly well with peer-to-peer message routing, because the responses are sent back directly to the originating service.

Marker properties are a good general solution when you need to scale stateful services that participate in transaction-like interactions that span multiple messages over time. They're also a good example of the power of pattern matching and transport independence as underlying system principles that give you the ability to adapt your system by changing configuration rather than implementation.

THE NPM AND GITHUB SERVICES

The data-source services are stateless but have ephemeral data by design. Here, you use ephemeral data for ease of maintenance and for performance, because the data is stored locally. You'll be able to scale these services horizontally by adding new instances, as long as your data volumes remain reasonably sized. Each instance has to be able to store all the data.

---

[55] A 1% error rate isn't so bad when you have 100 users. When you have 1 million, that's 10,000 annoyed customers.

If your data volume grows, in terms of either the number of records or record size, you'll need to think about other strategies for storing this non-authoritative data. In the nodezoo case, as you add functionality, the individual records are likely to grow large.

You can trade latency for storage size by using a shared external database for the data. This is a big step, because it changes your maintenance costs, and you'll need to make sure the database can scale. Nonetheless, this is a well-understood problem and a perfectly acceptable solution. Good performance from data often requires a schema—something we like to avoid. But by the time you need to use a traditional database, your data will be stable enough to make schemas less dangerous. Schemas are most expensive at the start of a project, because they lock in assumptions, but later they can be built on empirical evidence.

If you want to avoid a shared database, the alternative is to use sharding. You can safely follow the approach described in chapter 1. You can use a shard-orchestrating service,[56] as in chapter 1, or you can use pattern matching to *preshard* the data-entity messages. This is a variant of the marker-property approach used to scale the *info* service.

THE SUGGEST SERVICE

This service is designed to run entirely in memory and to be stateless. The business decision was to provide "good enough" suggestions. Thus, you can scale the service horizontally without changes.

Suppose that after some time in production, user feedback gives the strong message that the autocompletion suggestions are a valuable feature, and users want nearly instantaneous intelligent suggestions. There's no way to meet this goal with the message flows as they're currently designed.

User testing shows that a response time of 50 ms or less delivers an almost-magical experience, and your marketing department is getting excited about the social media implications. Marketing demands action, and you demand a large development budget!

You get the money. Now, you have to delivery sub-50 ms latency. You decide to deliver the suggestion API directly from a custom web server written in C, using a high-performance, embedded key-value store. It will have to run on large machines, and they'll have to share suggestions, probably using a fancy conflict-free replicated data structure. And you'll need to deploy them all over the world to be near users. That should do it.

Your microservice architecture makes this possible. You can build this high-performance specialist solution without impacting other parts of the system; and you can integrate it easily because it's just another microservice, as far as the other components are concerned.

EVERYTHING ELSE

The system consists of more than the microservices. There are load balancers, database engines, search engines, deployment and orchestration systems, log-aggregation

---

[56] The timeline service in iteration 3 of chapter 1 is a good example of such a service.

and -analysis tools, monitoring and alerting, and more. You can choose to use external systems or install third-party software to provide these services, so that you can accelerate development and outsource scaling problems. Choose wisely, and make sure your dependencies also scale.

9.3 *Brave new world*

This book is the result of my five years of working on microservice systems. When I started building applications in JavaScript using Node.js, I quickly realized that the language was at best inadequate, and at worst actively hostile, to the construction of large software systems with many components. I was drawn to the microservices approach by necessity, because it kept my JavaScript programs understandable.

As my experience grew, it became clear that microservices are really a software component model. The most important question becomes how they communicate: not the technical details of the message protocols, but the way messages are represented to the services. How do components come together to form something that's more than the sum of its parts?

I found designing microservice systems to be difficult. I always chose the wrong services. Yes, they were small and easy to throw away, but still, something was conceptually wrong. I moved to messages and put them first, and things became much easier. Messages represent the real world more closely than data abstractions do. The movement from BRs to messages to services flows naturally.

To build components, you need to fit them together. You need the ability to generate arbitrary structures from simple parts. The trick is to have a limited number of basic principles. These principles emerged in the field from many failures. The principle of transport independence makes messages first-class citizens by freeing them from the constraints of any given protocol, and the principle of pattern matching allows you to fit components together in arbitrary ways. Pattern matching is barely sufficient to describe component interfaces, but it's just powerful enough to make them work.

Put all this together, and you get a wonderfully flexible—and fun—way to think about software engineering. Yes, microservices suffer from hype, but don't get bogged down in the technical details, trade-offs, and internecine warfare of a new engineering style. Charles Babbage never finished his computer, but that didn't stop Ada Lovelace from programming. Don't blame broken tools.

Microservices let you move from the general to the specific. As programmers, we're taught to go the other way around. You've written the same code three times? Put it in a function! And so we do. We move from the specific to the general. We add complexity, extensibility, and technical debt, and it crushes us. We invent ceremonial solutions and rigid project and development practices that pacify, but don't vanquish, the gods of complexity. We sacrifice our weekends and lives to these gods.

When you adopt a strategy of moving from the general to the specific, you tame complexity. Complexity never goes away, but you can put it in a box and shut the lid. Start with the simple case and get that right, and it becomes your default. The microservices you write in the early days tend to be the simplest and longest lived. The ones you write later are all about special cases, unanticipated business needs, and performance issues.

The general case is simple. The data structures are simple. The messages are simple. When complexity appears, use pattern matching to route it away safely. Write bad code for the complex cases, and put it in a separate microservice—you'll throw it away soon enough.

Your list of messages will grow, and your understanding of the system will grow, too. Message patterns naturally organize into hierarchies, and message interactions are a small set of design choices. Messages are synchronous or asynchronous, observed or consumed. You can keep it all in your head, and so can the most junior developer on your team.

I know you'll enjoy building microservices. I know you'll enjoy putting the science and engineering of software first, instead of the politics of organizations, and getting real results. Go code!

> *For a successful technology, reality must take precedence over public relations, for nature cannot be fooled.*

—Richard Feynman, 1918–88, Nobel physicist

index

RELATED MANNING TITLES

Microservice Patterns

by Chris Richardson

> ISBN: 9781617294549
> 375 pages,
> April 2018

Spring Microservices in Action

by John Carnell

> ISBN: 9781617293986
> 384 pages,
> June 2017

Reactive Design Patterns

by Roland Kuhn
> with Brian Hanafee and Jamie Allen

> ISBN: 9781617291807
> 392 pages,
> February 2017

Microservices in .NET Core
with examples in Nancy

by Christian Horsdal Gammelgaard

> ISBN: 9781617293375
> 344 pages,
> January 2017

For ordering information go to www.manning.com